The Evolution of Economies

It is clear even to casual observation that economies evolve from year to year and over centuries. Yet mainstream economic theory assumes that economies always move towards equilibrium. One consequence of this is that mainstream theory is unable to deal with economic history. *The Evolution of Economies* provides a clear account of how economies evolve under a process of support-bargaining and money-bargaining. Both support-bargaining and money-bargaining are situation-related – people determine their interests and actions by reference to their present circumstances. This gives the bargaining system a natural evolutionary dynamic. Societies evolve from situation to situation. Historical change follows this evolutionary course.

A central chapter of the book applies the new theory in a re-evaluation of the industrial revolution in Britain, showing how specialist money-bargaining agencies, in the form of companies, evolved profitable formats and displaced landowners as the leading sources of employment and economic necessities. Companies took advantage of the evolution of technology to establish effective formats. The book also seeks to establish how it came about that a 'mainstream' theory was developed that is so wildly at odds with the observable features of economic history and economic exchange. Theory-making is described as a process of 'intellectual support-bargaining' in which theory is shaped to the interests of its makers. The work of major classical and neoclassical economists is contested as incompatible with the idea of an evolving money-bargaining system. The book reviews attempts to derive an evolutionary economic theory from Darwin's theory of evolution by natural selection.

Neoclassical economic theory has had enormous influence on the governance of societies, principally through its theoretical endorsement of the benefits of 'free markets'. An evolutionary account of economic processes should change the basis of debate. The theory presented here will be of interest immediately to all economists, whether evolutionary, heterodox or neoclassical. It will facilitate the work of economic historians, who complain that current theory gives no guidance for their historical investigations. Beyond the confines of professional theory-making, many will find it a revelatory response to questions that have hitherto gone unanswered.

Patrick Spread spent his early years in the Bedfordshire and Hertfordshire villages where his father was vicar. In his teens he was at Wellington College, going on to Oxford University. After a few years in London he went to work overseas, first in the Solomon Islands and then in other countries, including Fiji, Indonesia, Georgia and Ethiopia. In time out from these assignments he worked on theory consistent with the experience. He received a doctorate at the London Business School in 1982. In recent years he has been able to give full attention to theoretical issues.

Routledge Frontiers of Political Economy

For a complete list of titles in this series, please visit: http://www.routledge.com/books/series/SE0345/

161 **Economic Models for Policy Making**
Principles and designs revisited
S. I. Cohen

162 **Reconstructing Keynesian Macroeconomics, Volume 2**
Integrated approaches
Carl Chiarella, Peter Flaschel and Willi Semmler

163 **Architectures of Economic Subjectivity**
The philosophical foundations of the subject in the history of economic thought
Sonya Marie Scott

164 **Support-Bargaining, Economics and Society**
A social species
Patrick Spread

165 **Inherited Wealth, Justice and Equality**
Edited by Guido Erreygers and John Cunliffe

166 **The Charismatic Principle in Social Life**
Edited by Luigino Bruni and Barbara Sena

167 **Ownership Economics**
On the foundations of interest, money, markets, business cycles and economic development
Gunnar Heinsohn and Otto Steiger; translated and edited with comments and additions by Frank Decker

168 **Urban and Regional Development Trajectories in Contemporary Capitalism**
Edited by Flavia Martinelli, Frank Moulaert and Andreas Novy

169 **Social Fairness and Economics**
Economic essays in the spirit of Duncan Foley
Edited by Lance Taylor, Armon Rezai and Thomas Michl

170 **Financial Crisis, Labour Markets and Institutions**
Edited by Sebastiano Fadda and Pasquale Tridico

171 **Marx and Living Labour**
Laurent Baronian

172 **A Political Economy of Contemporary Capitalism and its Crisis**
Demystifying finance
Dimitris P. Sotiropoulos, John G. Milios and Spyros Lapatsioras

173 **Against Utility-Based Economics**
On a life-based approach
Anastasios Korkotsides

174 **Economic Indeterminacy**
The dance of the meta-axioms
Yanis Varoufakis

175 **Freedom, Responsibility and Economics of the Person**
Jérôme Ballet, Damien Bazin, Jean-Luc Dubois and François-Régis Mahieu

176 **Reality and Accounting**
Ontological explorations in the economic and social sciences
Richard Mattessich

177 **Profitability and the Great Recession**
The role of accumulation trends in the financial crisis
Ascension Mejorado and Manuel Roman

178 **Institutions and Development After the Financial Crisis**
Edited by Sebastiano Fadda and Pasquale Tridico

179 **The Political Economy of Gunnar Myrdal**
A reassessment in the post-2008 world
Örjan Appelqvist

180 **Gender Perspectives and Gender Impacts of the Global Economic Crisis**
Edited by Rania Antonopoulos

181 **Hegel, Institutions, and Economics**
Performing the social
Carsten Herrmann-Pillath and Ivan A. Boldyrev

182 **Producer Cooperatives as a New Mode of Production**
Bruno Jossa

183 **Economic Policy and the Financial Crisis**
Edited by Łukasz Mamica and Pasquale Tridico

184 **Information Technology and Socialist Construction**
The end of capital and the transition to socialism
Daniel E. Saros

185 **Beyond Mainstream Explanations of the Financial Crisis**
Parasitic finance capital
Ismael Hossein-zadeh

186 **Greek Capitalism in Crisis**
Marxist analyses
Stavros Mavroudeas

187 **Of Synthetic Finance**
Three essays of speculative materialism
Benjamin Lozano

188 **The Political Economy and Media Coverage of the European Economic Crisis**
The case of Ireland
Julien Mercille

189 Financial Cultures and Crisis Dynamics
Edited by Bon Jessop, Brigitte Young and Christoph Scherrer

190 Capitalism and the Political Economy of Work Time
Christoph Hermann

191 The Responsible Economy
Jefferson Frank

192 Globalization and the Critique of Political Economy
New insights from Marx's writings
Lucia Pradella

193 Exit from Globalization
Richard Westra

194 Reconstructing Keynesian Macroeconomics Volume III
Financial markets and banking
Carl Chiarella, Peter Flaschel and Willi Semmler

195 The European Union and Supranational Political Economy
Edited by Riccardo Fiorentini and Guido Montani

196 The Future of Capitalism After the Financial Crisis
The varieties of Capitalism debate in the age of austerity
Edited by Richard Westra, Dennis Badeen and Robert Albritton

197 Liberal Learning and the Art of Self-Governance
Edited by Emily Chamlee-Wright

198 The Systemic Nature of the Economic Crisis
The perspectives of heterodox economics and psychoanalysis
Arturo Hermann

199 Economies of Death
Economic logics of killable life and grievable death
Edited by Patricia J. Lopez and Kathryn A. Gillespie

200 Civil Society, the Third Sector and Social Enterprise
Governance and democracy
Edited by Jean-Louis Laville, Dennis Young and Philippe Eynaud

201 Economics, Culture and Development
Eiman O. Zein-Elabdin

202 Paradigms in Political Economy
Kavous Ardalan

203 The Economics of Voting
Studies of self-interest, bargaining, duty and rights
Dan Usher

204 The Political Economy of Food and Finance
Ted P. Schmidt

205 The Evolution of Economies
Money-bargaining, economic change and industrial revolution
Patrick Spread

The Evolution of Economies

Money-bargaining, economic change and industrial revolution

Patrick Spread

LONDON AND NEW YORK

First published 2016
by Routledge
2 Park Square, Milton Park, Abingdon, Oxon OX14 4RN

and by Routledge
711 Third Avenue, New York, NY 10017

Routledge is an imprint of the Taylor & Francis Group, an informa business

© 2016 Patrick Spread

The right of Patrick Spread to be identified as author of this work has been asserted in accordance with the Copyright, Designs and Patent Act 1988.

All rights reserved. No part of this book may be reprinted or reproduced or utilised in any form or by any electronic, mechanical, or other means, now known or hereafter invented, including photocopying and recording, or in any information storage or retrieval system, without permission in writing from the publishers.

Trademark notice: Product or corporate names may be trademarks or registered trademarks, and are used only for identification and explanation without intent to infringe.

British Library Cataloguing in Publication Data
A catalogue record for this book is available from the British Library

Library of Congress Cataloging in Publication Data
Spread, Patrick, 1944-
The evolution of economies : Money-bargaining, economic change and industrial revolution / Patrick Spread.
New York : Routledge, 2016. | Includes bibliographical references.
LCCN 2015030224| ISBN 9781138122918 (hardback) | ISBN 9781315649207 (ebook)
LCSH: Evolutionary economics. | Mutualism. | International trade.
LCC HB97.3 .S67 2016 | DDC 330.1–dc23
LC record available at http://lccn.loc.gov/2015030224

ISBN: 978-1-138-12291-8 (hbk)
ISBN: 978-1-315-64920-7 (ebk)

Typeset in Times New Roman
by Cenveo Publisher Services

Contents

List of tables		viii
Introduction		ix
1	Support-bargaining and the evolution of human societies	1
2	Money and money-bargaining	13
3	Macroeconomics and money-bargaining	35
4	Evolutionary economics	67
5	The evolution of money-bargaining	108
6	The state and money-bargaining	175
7	Support-bargaining, credit and confidence	201
8	The evolution of foreign trade	248
9	Information and the evolution of communications	283
Conclusion		313
Bibliography		320
Index		328

List of tables

5.1	Occupations and incomes in England and Wales, 1688, based on the compilations of Gregory King	115
5.2	Value of output of major industries	134
5.3	Gross value of cotton output and cotton exports as proportion of gross output	136
5.4	Relative prices of industry output	137
6.1	Central government revenue from taxation and services, 1700–1950	191
6.2	Central government current expenditure, 1700–1950	192
8.1	Value of shipping tonnage built in Britain and net shipping services	252
8.2	Summary balance of payments, 1816–1913	256
8.3	Comparative advantage and unit cost advantage	267

Introduction

Two hundred years ago most people in Britain lived in abject poverty, working the land for meagre returns or cleaning and cooking in the homes of the affluent. Many children died before their fifth birthday, and the survivors were lucky to reach 50. Malnutrition was common. Most people remained in the locality of their birth, confined by access to land and the uncertain welcome elsewhere. Few people were properly literate and information about anything was scarce. Simple faith in a deity and redeemer helped people to endure their condition.

Now, most people live in or near large cities, working in offices, factories or shops for companies, some of which employ thousands of people around the world. They travel to work by car, bus or train. They are well nourished – many are over-nourished – and well sheltered in comfortably furnished homes. Many take holidays in southern sunshine. They are unlucky if they do not reach 70 years of age. They are all educated, many of them to very high standards. At the flick of a switch or the click of a button they have access to immense amounts of information and entertainment. Most find they can largely dispense with the reassurance of a guardian deity. Clearly, society has evolved over those 200 years.

So, if theory is to explain society, it has to have some component that covers the evolutionary character of society. More than that, evolution has to be a central part of any realistic theory of society. Yet the 'neoclassical' theory of economic activity, the dominant theory taught across the Western world, presents a system that always moves towards equilibrium. A model based on rational choice is held to explain the behaviour of all humans at all times.

The aim of this book is to provide a theory that explains the evolution of human societies, particularly those parts of societies usually understood as 'economic'. These are mostly activities undertaken in return for money or involving the acquisition of goods and services in exchange for money. The book is about the evolution of 'money-bargaining'.

It aims to explain also how neoclassical theory came to be accepted as the mainstream theory of the workings of an economy. Roger Backhouse has pondered the problem before in a slightly different form. The main theme of his analysis of the development of economic theory in *Economists and the Economy: The Evolution of Economic Ideas* is the question of: 'how a body of thought that was so closely concerned with practical, real-world problems developed into something akin to a branch of mathematics'.[1]

The concern over the state of economic theory is widespread in the economics profession. A recent article in the *Cambridge Journal of Economics* noted that. 'Nowadays it is almost beyond dispute that economics has failed both itself and its public in a systematic manner that goes beyond what is reasonable by the standards of either public service and accountability or scientific accuracy and scholarship.'[2] These are strong words from scholars on scholarship. A new start is needed, and there is no better starting point than the major anomaly that is the evolution of economies.

This is the fifth book on the subject of support-bargaining and money-bargaining. It can be read without familiarity with the earlier books. Chapter 1 gives some essentials of the 'story so far'. References are made throughout the present text to sections of the earlier books which expand on aspects of the theory. Since few people are familiar with the earlier works, and because the theory itself has evolved through the books, their content is summarised below.

A Theory of Support and Money Bargaining (1984):[3] This presents the theory of support-bargaining and money-bargaining in the early stages of its development. It covers extensively academic work that has a bearing on the theory. It introduces many of the main components of support-bargaining and money-bargaining, such as the formation of groups through support-bargaining, the significance of bargaining sets and bargaining position, and the bargaining strength of organisations in both political and economic spheres. It links social support-bargaining to the formation of ideas and a process of 'fact-formation'.

Getting It Right: Economics and the Security of Support (2004):[4] This presents the objections to the neoclassical model and seeks to establish money-bargaining as a more realistic theory of economic exchange. It identifies situation as the basis of consumer choice. People buy what fits their situation. It identifies companies as the specialist money-bargaining agencies of money-bargaining systems. It also develops the idea of support-bargaining in its political context and extends it to intellectual support-bargaining. The role of information in support-bargaining and money-bargaining systems is described, including propensities to manipulate information.

Support-Bargaining: The Mechanics of Democracy Revealed (2008):[5] This elaborates on and refines ideas introduced in *Getting It Right*. It spells out in detail how informal and formal support-bargaining functions, and how a support convention is established. It also goes into detail on the formation of theories through intellectual support-bargaining, and how frameworks of theory are developed and used. Theory formation is conceived as an essential part of the support-bargaining process, and hence an essential part of the mechanics of democracy. Theory-making assembles support that can be deployed for political purposes. Economic theory is understood as a creation of intellectual support-bargaining, playing its role in the advancement of interests in support-bargaining societies. There is extensive coverage of the function of companies as agents of money-bargaining systems, their locational formats and their role in foreign trade. The book includes also an account of the historic emergence of a support-bargaining society in Britain, linking it with the present study of the evolution of money-bargaining.

Support-Bargaining, Economics and Society: A Social Species (2013):[6] This book establishes a 'backward' link of support-bargaining to Darwin's theory of natural selection. It is suggested that Darwin underestimated the importance of the human instinct for self-preservation, with an excessive emphasis on human aggression. Concern for self-preservation gives rise to a sense of insecurity and a search for reassuring support. Darwin's account of natural selection has divided social scientists into those who recognise in society the Darwinian traits of aggression and competition and those who reject the Darwinian understanding, seeing rather the cooperative and sociable instincts of humans. 'Social Darwinism' is analysed in terms of intellectual support-bargaining. The book traces the implications of the modified understanding of natural selection for the understanding of social and economic processes. Cultural evolution is a process of support-bargaining. Money and money-bargaining are outcomes of cultural evolution. It is suggested that money-bargaining derives from support-bargaining, sharing the same instinctive dynamic. It is suggested also that our sense of symmetry, regarded as important to natural selection, is important also in economic choice and the behaviour of businessmen.

Preparation of *Support-Bargaining, Economics and Society* involved research into evolutionary economic theory. Economists have sought to adapt Darwinian natural selection to explain the evolution of economic activity. Evolutionary economists make the same point as made above: realistic economic theory *must* be able to explain the observable evolution of economies. The result is, however, generally acknowledged to be unsatisfactory. Biological natural selection does not adapt convincingly to the evolution of economies.[7] However, when it is recognised that natural selection involves support-bargaining, it becomes apparent that societies evolve through a modified form of natural selection. The capacity for support-bargaining that enabled humans to form groups and survive also enabled humans to evolve their societies. What follows takes up the rather sketchy account of economic evolution provided in *Support-Bargaining, Economics and Society* to show in greater detail how economies evolve.

Notes

1 Backhouse, Roger E., 1993, *Economists and the Economy: The Evolution of Economic Ideas*, New Brunswick, NJ, and London: Transaction, p. 196.
2 Freeman, Alan, Chick, Victoria and Kayatekin, Serap, 2014, 'Samuelson's ghosts: Whig history and the reinterpretation of economic theory', *Cambridge Journal of Economics*, Vol. 38, No. 3, pp. 519–29, p. 524.
3 Spread, Patrick, 1984, *A Theory of Support and Money Bargaining*, London: Macmillan.
4 Spread, Patrick, 2004, *Getting It Right: Economics and the Security of Support*, Sussex: Book Guild.
5 Spread, Patrick, 2008, *Support-Bargaining: The Mechanics of Democracy Revealed*, Sussex: Book Guild.
6 Spread, Patrick, 2013, *Support-Bargaining, Economics and Society: A Social Species*, Abingdon and New York: Routledge.
7 See, for example, Witt, Ulrich, 2004, 'On the proper interpretation of "evolution" in economics and its implications for production theory', *Journal of Economic Methodology*, Vol. 11, No. 2, pp. 125–46, p. 127.

1 Support-bargaining and the evolution of human societies

Essentials of support-bargaining

The evolution of economies is part of a broad evolution of societies. The changes mentioned in the Introduction came about as a consequence of political, social and economic forces. In the present account of the evolution of economies, the strictly 'economic' element is understood in terms of 'money-bargaining', while the political and social elements are understood in terms of 'support-bargaining'. Support-bargaining and money-bargaining are so systemically related as to constitute a single process. Neither can be understood in isolation from the other. But at the same time the different nature of the bargaining counters, 'support' and 'money', gives them distinction. The main concern of this book is the evolution of the money-bargaining side of social evolution, but support-bargaining is necessarily involved. This chapter provides a quick 'catch-up' on the idea of support-bargaining, as set out in previous books. There are three essential elements:

- support-bargaining as part of natural selection;
- situation as the basis of interests;
- social and cultural evolution.

Support-bargaining and natural selection

It was suggested in *Support-Bargaining, Economics and Society: A Social Species* that Darwin's theory of natural selection did not provide a complete theory of how humans have evolved.[1] It presents scientific evidence for the survival of species that possessed biological variations suited to the environment in which they found themselves. Those that did not possess such variations died out. The *Origin of Species* suggests a predominantly combative process, a 'struggle for survival', suggesting the importance of variations giving capacity for physical combat. The survival of animal species was attributed to their aggressive instincts, with readers left to deduce for themselves that humans had survived through exercise of similar instincts.

The missing part of the theory is the part played by humans themselves in their survival through exercise of their social capacities. There is no doubt that humans can be individually very aggressive. But aggression at its strongest and most costly in terms of the lives of other humans and animals is commonly displayed in groups. In common with many animal species, humans have a propensity to form groups to engage in violence. Darwin recognised the importance of group formation, but was unable to present strong evidence for any mechanism by which humans form groups. In *The Descent of Man* he argued cogently that humans have traits that make them sociable, but he was unable to establish, even to his own satisfaction, the psychological causation that would explain how men form the strong communal bonds that make them so effective in violence. Hence these traits were not satisfactorily incorporated into his biological theory of natural selection. It remained a theory of individual selection.

It was argued further in *Support-Bargaining, Economics and Society: A Social Species* that Darwin missed the crucial importance of the human instinct for self-preservation. Such was his preoccupation, following the work of Thomas Malthus, with the idea of a 'struggle for existence' that he underestimated the importance of those traits that make humans try to avoid struggle, or any sort of confrontation. His own social status, a wealthy, middle-class Victorian in the heyday of empire, may also have made it easier for him to understand humans as at least assertive, rather than timid and reluctant combatants. Humans individually are commonly anxious and fearful, and in reaction to their fear they seek the support of others. The need for friendly and supportive associates causes them to form groups. In violent times, the formation of groups in this way would be necessary to the retention of territory against rival groups. With the confidence generated in the group, it would be possible also for the group to launch its own assaults on the territory and property of neighbouring groups.

Harmony will not necessarily reign within the group. Each individual in the group needs the support of other members, yet, at the same time, many will want their own way. Individuals will seek to dominate their group, or to impose their own interests on the group. Assertive individuals will make demands on the group, probing how much the group is prepared to concede to retain their membership. Support-bargaining is the often fractious, occasionally harmonious process by which individuals come to terms with their associates to form groups. It is also the process by which individuals are ejected from groups, and find themselves obliged to search elsewhere for the support they require. Some individuals will successfully negotiate their way to positions of ascendancy in their groups. In groups threatened by violence or intending violence, high violent capacity is likely to be seen as the characteristic necessary to the claim of a particular individual to ascendancy in the group. But certain skills in the assembly of support are likely to be necessary also to secure an acknowledged position as head of the group.

Darwin's lack of success in defining a social process by which humans form groups has subsequently been the basis of a great divide among social scientists. Some readily understand society in 'Darwinian' terms as a matter of individualistic struggle for survival and ascendancy. Others see society as, and demand that society should be, more accommodating and communal in its ways. The latter have condemned the former as 'Social Darwinists'.[2] The polarisation of theorists has affected the way Darwin is understood – the aggressive aspects of the theory of natural selection have possibly been given greater prominence than Darwin would have wished. 'Survival of the fittest', the phrase Darwin adopted from Herbert Spencer, has been used as pejorative characterisation of natural selection in general, with an inference that the fittest are the toughest, the most ruthless and the most unpleasant. The phrase has also been used to characterise 'capitalist' economic systems, with similar inference. Individualism and competition are important elements in economic processes. Given that Darwin derived much from the economist Thomas Malthus, it is not surprising that his theories have some of the character of economic theory, and economic theory has some of the character of Darwinian theory.

This division of theorists has centred on Darwin's theory of natural selection, but it would probably have arisen even without his theory, for the process of support-bargaining implies a never-ending tussle between individuals and their associates. It is a struggle for ascendancy in the group, or in society. For the most part it is a verbal and psychological struggle. Concessions are made on the basis of relative levels of support because support is recognised as implying violent capacity. A 'support convention' is operative, whereby support substitutes for actual violence. Support-bargaining is a kind of shadow violence. It is not generally difficult to discern whether people are inclined to the right wing, where the individual is king, or to the left wing, where the communal approach is favoured. The twentieth century saw major international violence between fascists, communists and those who favoured support-bargaining systems that would provide a process for adjusting the balance between individuals and the group.

Situation as the basis of interests

The second essential element in support-bargaining is that humans identify their interests by reference to their situation. This idea is apparent in the way we go about our ordinary business. Before undertaking any action people 'assess the situation' or 'take stock of the situation' in order to identify what is wrong with it that needs putting right. We debate incessantly the current circumstances of family, village, employment, nation and everything else, and give our prescriptions for improvements. By some oversight, however, this situation reference has not been incorporated in formal social scientific theory.

Perhaps most remarkably, the idea of situation-related selection has not been incorporated in economic theory. Neoclassical economics, the mainstream of economic theory, assumes merely that people have 'preferences' and spend their money working through their preferences.[3] Yet clearly we buy clothes with reference to our size, furniture by reference to our home, houses by reference to the location of our employment. Before going shopping we check what is already in the fridge. Neither institutional economics nor evolutionary economics, as will be seen, identify situation as the basis for understanding interests and desirable actions.

It is easy enough to understand that a car with a broken wheel needs a new wheel. But in the more abstract context of political and social support-bargaining the situation reference becomes more complicated. Concepts of situation are themselves developed through support-bargaining. Since the accepted concept of situation will determine interests and actions, the formation of the situation concept will be contested. People may, for example, debate at length whether traffic congestion in a village is causing accidents, or whether the chief problem is excessive noise. Records of accidents and measures of noise will be used to define the situation. If the congestion is causing accidents, the by-pass can run close to the village, on land owned by Mr Brown. If the congestion is noisy, the by-pass has to run farther from the village, on land owned by Mr Black. The definition of situation is crucial to the identification of what is to be done, and the definition of the situation will be arrived at through support-bargaining within the group. Mr Brown and Mr Black will be competing to gain the support of their fellow villagers. It would, furthermore, be surprising if Mr Brown were arguing that the congestion was causing accidents, so that the by-pass should run over his land, and Mr Black were insisting that noise was the problem, and consequently the by-pass should run over his land. People would immediately suspect that compensation for loss of land consequent on construction of the by-pass was generous. The situation becomes more complicated than the incidence of accidents and the levels of noise. Support-bargaining within the village will determine which understanding of the situation prevails and forms the basis for construction of a by-pass.

This situation reference must be an integral part of the process of natural selection. An accurate assessment of situation is necessary to survival. A human group must be able to discern what is relevant to its survival in any circumstances. In hunting, the group must be able to understand 'the lie of the land' and approach its quarry with stealth. In combat with other human groups, it must be able to discern the advantages of high ground and the protection afforded by rivers and marshes. Individuals seeking to lead their group must offer a sense of situation that answers to the interests of the group. At its most fundamental, it means defining a situation in a way that promises survival of the group. The capacity to assess situation with a view to survival may be utilised also to assess situation with a view to construction of a by-pass, or any of the many other enterprises of humanity. It is a capacity essential to the survival of humanity but also a capacity that can bring about social evolution. Societies judge their interests and actions by reference to their situations, and the actions taken change their situations, and give rise to further assessment of interests and appropriate action. The situation reference is the essential grounding of the mechanism of social evolution.

Darwin's process remains fundamental. Biological variations, or in modern forms of the theory, genetic variations, give traits to a species that determine whether the species can survive in whatever environmental conditions it encounters. But one crucial variation is that which gives humans their concern for self-preservation, and with it their sense of insecurity, and with that their desire for the support of those around them. A second crucial variation is that which gives them the capacity to assess situation and judge what needs to be done in order to improve their situation – in the context of natural selection, to ensure their survival.

These traits are so important to human survival that they must be regarded as an integral part of the process of natural selection. They contrast very sharply with the conventional view of natural selection as a matter of individualistic aggression.

It may appear that through engagement in support-bargaining humans are active promoters of their own survival, rather than passive objects of an impersonal process of natural selection. But the instinct for self-preservation, and consequent sensitivity to support – giving humans the capacity for support-bargaining, and the human capacity for formation of concepts of situation originate in biological variation. Consequently, the courses adopted by humans are outcomes of their biological state and not outcomes of any supra-corporeal decision-making capacity or laudable exercise of 'free will'.[4] We do what our minds tell us to do, and our minds react to expressions of support and disapproval from our associates.

Such traits are matters of human intellectual capacity. While many animals display instincts for group formation, and have the capacity to perform tasks in groups, such as hunting, none has these capacities in the advanced forms in which they are found in humans. No animals have the linguistic capacities of humans that are necessary to the conduct of complex support-bargaining. This capacity in humans has made it seem to some observers that Darwinian natural selection does not apply to humans. Even Alfred Russell Wallace, who set out a theory of natural selection at about the same time as Darwin, concluded later that Darwinian natural selection did not apply to humans. Humans, he argued, had been set apart by a higher intelligence with minds that were not subject to the process of natural selection.[5]

Many social theorists have taken up something like Wallace's view, though Wallace's spiritual foundations are too far from their thinking to permit an acknowledgement of the association.[6] They detach social and cultural evolution from biological natural selection. Edward Wilson argued in his book *On Human Nature*, elaborating on theories first set out in his 1975 book, *Sociobiology: The New Synthesis*, that there is a separate process of cultural evolution that has predominated for something like the last 40,000 years, distinguishing that period from the long period of natural selection that preceded it.[7] Samuel Bowles and Herbert Gintis note that, as far as the conditions of the 'evolutionary' period, the Palaeolithic period, can be understood, they were conducive to the operation of a 'group selection' process alongside the Darwinian process of natural selection.[8] Many other writers have argued that social evolution takes place outside and largely independently of Darwinian natural selection.

The approach can be seen as deriving from a sense that something is missing from Darwinian natural selection, and that social theory has to be pursued despite the natural science that apparently identified individualistic aggression as the essential behavioural characteristic of humans. The theory of support-bargaining makes it clear that the capacity for group formation through support-bargaining is an integral part of natural selection. It is the means by which humans cooperate with each another. From the earliest times, support-bargaining would have enabled a group to defend itself and provided a mechanism for its social and cultural evolution. With the idea of support-bargaining, there is no need for independent theories of social evolution; natural selection itself incorporates the mechanism of social evolution.

Because situation determines interests it also determines bargaining positions. A tightly defined situation limits the options of the definer. A loosely defined situation, accepted as malleable, makes for a wide range of acceptable acquisitions, and consequently a strong bargaining position. If a person has to be in a certain place at a certain specific time, then the range of transport options is limited. On train services, for example, commuters commonly pay the 'peak time' fares because their situation is inflexible with regard to getting to work on time. Where the situation is not so tightly defined, people can choose when they go and what form of transport they use. They pay a lower fare. People in modern societies, particularly in towns, know they have numerous options with regard to groups they might join to gain the support they need, and will look for those that best accommodate their own inclinations. But in earlier times, in isolated villages, the options were much more limited, and people found themselves obliged to go along with whatever the village community offered. We have an instinctive sense of bargaining position, synchronous with the instinct for self-preservation that causes us to seek support. It is probably honed through early experience of support-bargaining as we establish a position for ourselves among those close to us.[9]

The pursuit of bargaining position involves also the formation of organisations. Groups in society are generally ill-defined, with similarly ill-defined understanding of situation and purpose. For a strong bargaining position, it is necessary to define purposes more precisely and establish clearly what a group offers to potential supporters. To achieve this, organisation is required. Groups metamorphose into organisations to strengthen their bargaining positions.[10] Organisations assemble different skills and coordinate their activities to a single purpose. They also invariably establish budgets so that money can be used in assembling the necessary skills to define and make known their interests, define and make known the benefits they offer and supervise their membership. The bargaining strength of organisations gives them an important influence on the way situations are defined in societies and the interests that are advanced. Political parties predominate as the strongest bargaining agencies in support-bargaining systems. In money-bargaining companies are established as specialist money-bargaining agencies.

The systemic linkages of support-bargaining and money-bargaining lie in these common elements of bargaining. Both systems depend on situation-related identification of interests and both involve the pursuit of bargaining position. It was suggested in *Support-Bargaining, Economics and Society: A Social Species* that money-bargaining derives from support-bargaining. We use money in a bargaining system that has the essential dynamics of support-bargaining.[11]

Social and cultural evolution

The third essential element in support-bargaining has been touched on above: the support-bargaining that permits humans to act together in groups for their survival also permits them to undertake a great variety of other activities that involve group agreement, cooperation and action. It gives rise to social and cultural evolution. Through the support-bargaining of groups and individuals situations are defined and actions are taken to improve them. A noisy road gives rise to a by-pass over Mr Black's land. The new situation will give rise to further change. Mr Black may buy land elsewhere with his compensation and, after successful negotiations with the local authority, build houses on it. The houses will attract residents; a new village may develop. Alliances formed in the decision over the by-pass may be employed in the promotion of other initiatives or changes in village affairs. Humans have remarkable resilience in adapting to situations, which is part of their success as a species. When a family has the roof of its house blown off, it is upset, but in a short space of time it is asking, 'How do we proceed now?' Similarly, but on a grander scale, people were devastated by the destruction of their cities in the Second World War, but were soon thinking how they should set about recovery. Evolution is a constant process of assessing the current situation and putting right what is agreed to be wrong.

The support-bargaining process also leads to the formation of group purposes or goals. Support-bargaining is based on pursuit of interest, and 'interest' is close to 'purpose'. The 'original' purpose, when humans found themselves on the edge, would be survival. But subsequently a host of purposes have been defined within human groups and pursued with collective vigour, including salvation by one or more deities, material prosperity, intellectual enlightenment, athletic excellence, excellence in drama or music, conquest of other groups and even 'happiness'. The lack of human purpose in Darwin's theory of natural selection was particularly disturbing to his contemporary readers, raised on faith in a merciful and benign deity. The popularity of Herbert Spencer in his time has been attributed in part to his idea of the progression of man to an ideal state.[12] Subsequent writers on social theory have expressed concern that natural selection seems to preclude purpose, when human societies are so manifestly imbued with purpose. Geoffrey Hodgson, one of the leading evolutionary economists, asks,

> The main dilemma can be stated thus: if economic development is determined by some process of natural selection, with something analogous to genetic replication and to random variation and mutation, then what role remains for intentionality, purposefulness or choice, which have been central to economic discourse for well over a hundred years?[13]

With support-bargaining incorporated as an essential part of natural selection, the formation of purpose, including survival and much else, becomes an integral part of the human biological condition. Groups define purpose by reference to their situation, and in pursuing their purposes they generate social and cultural evolution.

Social, political and intellectual support-bargaining

Support-bargaining is ubiquitous. It gives rise to rigid groups and flexible groups, large groups and small groups, well-defined and ill-defined groups, interlocking

8 *The Evolution of Economies*

and overarching groups, ephemeral groups and durable groups. Material, social, spiritual, ethical and intellectual interests will all be mixed up together. To reduce the confusion, even at the expense of some misrepresentation, it is useful to identify three main spheres of support-bargaining in modern societies.

First, there is the sphere of social support-bargaining, conceived as the ordinary, everyday discussion and debate among people as they encounter each other at home, in the streets and in their places of work. Second, there is the sphere of political support-bargaining, concerned with the governance of society and involving formal procedures by which people can express support for political parties in a contest to determine who will govern. Competition for ascendancy in this sphere has generally, in the past, been violent, and violence remains a common means of determining who will govern. But in many societies a support convention, whereby formal expressions of support substitute for violence, is sufficiently well recognised as to eliminate violence almost entirely from the political sphere. The operation of a support convention in a formal support-bargaining system depends on the reduction or refinement of 'support' into quantifiable form. Each citizen under a support convention is entitled to express support as a 'vote'. Contestants in the political sphere draw on the pools of support that develop in a society through social support-bargaining.

They draw also on the pools of support that develop in the third sphere of support-bargaining, that of intellectual support-bargaining. This is concerned with the development and evaluation of ideas about the state of society and the appropriate remedies for its shortcomings. Support-bargaining over ideas is, in many ways, the essence of a bargaining society. Without ideas, political support-bargaining becomes largely a matter of group loyalty and patronage. People give support to those among whom they are born, or those who 'look after them'. Commitments of a tribal nature are predominant. Tribal groups tend to be rigid. Birth determines membership and there is no moving to another tribe. Loyalty to the tribe is the great virtue. Such rigid groups tend to be rigid in their attitudes and find it difficult to change in response to changing situations. Intellectual ideas provide a more flexible basis for group formation. Support can move from one set of ideas to another, as situations change. Different groups gain ascendancy and peace is sustained. Bargaining societies renew themselves from within because of their capacity to react to changing situations through support-bargaining over ideas.[14]

Ideas about situation are shaped by information. Consequently, it is also necessary to a support-bargaining system that there be free flows of information. The evolution of societies depends on availability of information. Information about the world in general is so copious as to be unmanageable, so there has to be means of organising information into comprehensible patterns. Ordinary people have formed a 'common theory' for use in the ordering of information about the world as they experience it, incorporating ideas regarding the existence of material objects and causation. Deriving from that common theory, or in response to questions arising from it, more specialised theories have been formed about the world and human society. Institutions have evolved in which specialists devote themselves to the formation of theory. The institutions, like other organisations, focus the work of many on a specific purpose, giving them bargaining positions in society. The support assembled around the theories developed in these institutions can be utilised in the political support-bargaining sphere that plays the major role in determining the evolution of societies.

While the social, political and intellectual spheres of support-bargaining are identified essentially for purposes of exposition, they are nevertheless given sharper definition by the presence of certain distinctive organisations and institutions. Political parties, legislatures and governments give definition to the political sphere, while universities and other educational institutions give definition to the sphere of intellectual support-bargaining.

Neoclassical theory and bargaining theory

Among the formal theories developed through intellectual support-bargaining is neoclassical economic theory. It constitutes the 'mainstream' of economic thought and teaching, with a large volume of support in academia and among those who have been taught it. Its high levels of support in the best educated sectors of society, including many of those occupying important positions in the civil service and media organisations, mean that it has major influence on decisions taken through political support-bargaining.

Part of the appeal of neoclassical economics lies in its concern with the optimal allocation of scarce resources. It sounds rational, virtuous and disinterested, and consequently something that no one can reasonably object to. Its inception had the highest aspirations. It was developed in its mathematical form from about 1870 on, when physicists in particular among natural scientists were astonishing the world with their revelations about the natural world. It seemed possible that a mathematical approach might give social theory status comparable to that of the natural sciences.

The introduction of neoclassical theory was thus very specifically conceived as giving economics an 'absolute' status. It would reveal and describe the working of an economy in the way that physicists revealed the working of the natural world. Mathematics was seen as providing an objective and precise tool for a depiction of economic processes that could not be challenged without challenging science.

Roger Backhouse notes in his study of *Economists and the Economy* that there are 'absolutists' and 'relativists' among economic historians.[15] The absolutists take as their standards of judgement regarding past theory the standards of present-day economic theory. Mark Blaug, in his book *Economic Theory in Retrospect*, takes an absolutist position. Similarly, Joseph Schumpeter, in his *History of Economic Analysis*, takes Leon Walras's general equilibrium system as the standard by which other theories are to be judged. Relativists, in contrast, 'see economic ideas as dependent for their validity on the historical circumstances in which they are developed'.[16]

The idea of intellectual support-bargaining implies the relativist view of theory formation. Theories are formed through their generation of support in a theory group, and the group will support the sort of theory that advances its interests. The idea that theory is developed in this way constitutes sufficient reason in itself for starting a book on economics with an account of support-bargaining. The neoclassical theory group developed a theory that could be pursued in the isolation of academic intellectual support-bargaining institutions. It emphasised mathematical analysis. It had also the effect of enhancing support for Adam Smith's thesis that the pursuit of individual self-interest would bring social benefit. This gave it support among a wider public with right-wing political interests. The rational approach appeared disinterested, but had the effect of advancing interests in individual primacy, as opposed to the interests of the group. Neoclassical theory was an outcome of intellectual support-bargaining and owed its establishment partly to its usefulness in political support-bargaining. The confidence of neoclassical economists has been built on the accumulation of support in the theory group and the ascendancy it has given them in academic institutions concerned with the propagation of economic ideas.

While physics is the inspiration, the empirical observations of physicists have been largely replaced in neoclassical theory by assumptions about the nature of man and the environment in which he conducts his business. These include the assumption that people choose rationally; that products are uniform, given and highly divisible; that information is perfect; that there are no spatial or temporal complications; and so on.[17] In effect, the assumptions are dictated by the requirements of the mathematics. They are implicit in the mathematics. The theory group accepts that its assumptions are wide of any realistic mark, but protects its inclination to mathematics with the plea that the theory is 'near enough' to the reality to justify its use. Neoclassical economics is full of evasions, 'as ifs' and 'near enoughs' that are accepted by the theory group, because without them the theory is lost, and with it the theory group.[18]

Backhouse sees calculus as a potent factor in the move of economists away from their early focus on practical issues: 'The calculus of maximising behaviour provided a wealth of opportunities for abstract speculation, with theoretical puzzles playing an increasing role in setting the agenda for research.'[19] Calculus is admirably adapted to the central question of neoclassical economists regarding the allocation of resources, or the maximisation of output from a given set of inputs. Calculus is so well adapted to the problem that it seems the question was posed as it was because calculus could answer it.

There is increasing disquiet within the neoclassical theory group regarding the nature of its theory. It is apparent in Backhouse's reassessment of neoclassical theory between the first edition of his book in 1988 and the second edition in 1993. He writes in the 1993 edition:

> Chapter 6, on the other hand, is very different. In the first edition it told the story of ideas about how a market economy worked as one of progress, each generation developing and refining the ideas of the previous generation ... The revised version of the chapter, however, is very different ... Rather, it argues that the dominant branch of present-day economics may have gone astray.[20]

Backhouse's book seeks to relate developments in economic theory to developments in society, so 'going astray' means the theory has diverged from the reality and established its own evolutionary train distinct from the processes which it is claimed to portray.

Various attempts have been made to adapt neoclassical theory so that it bears a closer relationship to reality. Robert Coase suggested in 1937 that companies do not function as portrayed mathematically in neoclassical theory, but owe their existence to the need to minimise transaction costs. Coase's ideas are considered in Chapter 4. John Maynard Keynes made adjustments to the theory to accommodate the very apparent unemployment of the 1930s, a phenomenon that could not be explained in the basic model. Keynesian theory is considered further in Chapter 7. More recently, Joseph Stiglitz has argued that the neoclassical assumption of perfect information is not only untenable but sufficient in itself to discredit the whole model. The idea of 'asymmetric information' is discussed in Chapter 9.

It is increasingly recognised, especially following the global financial crisis that emerged in 2007, that the basic model is beyond adaptation. Because such theories are created and sustained by theory groups it is difficult to replace them from within. The group owes its ascendancy to the theory; associations and experience are tied in to the theory; careers and promotions are dependent on the theory. There has to be some alternative theory in which a new theory group places its confidence before an existing theory group will move away from its position. Even then, the transition may be a matter of generational change, such are the loyalties and fixed ideas generated in theory groups.

Money-bargaining, in association with support-bargaining, is conceived as such an alternative. It is concerned with money and monetary exchange rather than the allocation of resources. It provides an entirely different account of markets and the relationship between consumers and companies, described in the following chapter.[21]

Most importantly, money-bargaining meets the requirement that a theory of economic activity must accommodate the observable evolution of economies. Money-bargaining and support-bargaining are inherently evolutionary, moving from situation to situation. Because of this evolutionary character, they offer insight into historical processes. Chapter 5 provides an account in terms of money-bargaining of the historical evolution of economies, concentrating in particular on the evolution of the British economy up to and through the industrial revolution in which the modern age was born.

Notes

1 Spread, Patrick, 2013, *Support-Bargaining, Economics and Society: A Social Species*, Abingdon and New York: Routledge, Chapter 1, The Problem with Natural Selection.
2 For discussion of Social Darwinism see Spread, 2013, Chapter 7, Theory Making and Social Darwinism.
3 For a contrast between neoclassical economic analysis and situation-related analysis, see Spread, Patrick, 2011, 'Situation as Determinant of Selection and Valuation', *Cambridge Journal of Economics*, Vol. 35, No. 2, pp. 335–56. Reprinted in Spread, Patrick, 2015b, *Aspects of Support-Bargaining and Money-Bargaining*, E-Book, World Economics Association.

4 On determinism and free will, see Spread, 2013, pp. 47–51, 261–4.
5 Crook, Paul, 1994, *Darwinism, War and History*, Cambridge: Cambridge University Press, p. 55.
6 Hodgson, Geoffrey, 2004, *The Evolution of Institutional Economics: Agency, Structure and Darwinism in American Institutionalism*, London and New York: Routledge, pp. 76–7.
7 Wilson, Edward O., 2004/1978, *On Human Nature*, Cambridge MA: Harvard University Press. Wilson, Edward O., 2000/1975, *Sociobiology: The New Synthesis*, Cambridge MA: Belknap Press.
8 Bowles, Samuel and Gintis, Herbert, 2011, *A Cooperative Species: Human Reciprocity and its Evolution*, Princeton, NJ: Princeton University Press.
9 A fuller account of bargaining position is in Spread, Patrick, 2008, *Support-Bargaining: The Mechanics of Democracy Revealed*, Sussex: Book Guild, pp. 93–9, etc.; see also Spread, 2013, pp. 205–6.
10 For further explanation of the bargaining strength of organisations, see Spread, 2008, pp. 39–41, Chapter 4, Organisations: Function and Format; see also Spread, Patrick, 1984, *A Theory of Support and Money Bargaining*, London: Macmillan, Chapter 5, Organisations.
11 See Spread, 2013, p. 205.
12 Hofstadter, Richard, 1983, *Social Darwinism in American Thought*, Boston, MA: Beacon Books, pp. 31, 40.
13 Hodgson, Geoffrey M., 1996, *Economics and Evolution: Bringing Life Back into Economics*, Michigan: University of Michigan Press, p. 26.
14 On rigid groups, see Spread, 2008, pp. 27–31, 377–84, 439–52, etc. See also Spread, Patrick, 2015d, 'The Political Significance of Certain Types of Group', in Spread, 2015b.
15 Backhouse, Roger, 1993, *Economists and the Economy: The Evolution of Economic Ideas*, New Brunswick, NJ, and London: Transaction, pp. 2–4.
16 Backhouse, 1993, pp. 2–4. Backhouse's references: Blaug, Mark, 1985, *Economic Theory in Retrospect*, Cambridge: Cambridge University Press; Schumpeter, J. A., 1954, *History of Economic Analysis*, New York: Oxford University Press, Chapter 6.
17 For a summary comparison of neoclassical assumptions with the concept of money-bargaining, see Spread, 2008, pp. 260–1.
18 On the 'as if' approach to economic theory, see Spread, 2013, pp. 192–5, 232–3. See also Spread, 2012, p. 51.
19 Backhouse, 1993, p. 222.
20 Backhouse, 1993, p. 7.
21 See also Spread, 2008, Chapter 3, Money-Bargaining: Situation and Sets, and Chapter 4, Organisations: Function and Format; see also, Spread, Patrick, 2015a, 'Companies and Markets: Economic Theories of the Firm and a Concept of Companies as Bargaining Agencies', *Cambridge Journal of Economics*, Advance Access published 2 June 2015, doi:10.1093/cje/bev029. Reprinted in Spread, 2015b, *Aspects of Support-Bargaining and Money-Bargaining*, E-Book, World Economics Association.

2 Money and money-bargaining

Early human societies are generally conceived as facing more or less constant threats of violence from neighbouring groups or tribes. The social order is consequently that necessary to military readiness. Those most capable in combat lead the tribe in its offence and defence, and assume a directive role in the social affairs of the tribe. The role of the leader includes overseeing the distribution of land and other necessities to individuals or families of the tribe. Members of the tribal group share whatever food they produce and provide labour for house-building and communal tasks, reckoning that their contributions will by tribal convention be reciprocated in the course of time. The sharing or giving of 'gifts' generates a sense of membership and cohesion in the tribe. The dependence of each on others for purposes of defence means that the tribal group is of paramount importance, with individuals subordinate to the group. Failure of an individual to conform to the customary ways of the tribe is likely to result in the offender being driven out or killed. In violent times, traitors cannot be tolerated. Even the chief will act in accordance with conventions established in the tribe. In terms of support-bargaining, the tribe is held together by bonds of support. An individual giving to others in the tribe, and to the chief, receives the approval, or support, of others for his 'proper' behaviour. Fulfilling customary obligations entitles a member of the tribe to the support of other members. The chief receives support from the tribe for fulfilment of what his people expect of him. The day-to-day accumulation of support establishes an ongoing sense of psychological security in all members of the tribe. The support can be given violent expression when occasion arises in defence of the tribe or advance of its interests against other tribes.

Material requirements, including food and house-building, are met through this dynamic of support-bargaining. Individuals will plant vegetables and distribute them as 'gifts' when they are ready as food. Others may later provide 'gifts' of fruit when they come into season. Failure to maintain the expected level of gift giving is likely to mean withdrawal of communal support from the defaulter. A gift economy involves the use of support-bargaining for exchange of material goods. There are obvious risks with a gift economy, especially when used outside a tight community whose members value the support it generates.

Because of the risk that proper reciprocation of gifts will not be made by people outside the tribe and beyond its conventions, 'foreign' trade is better conducted through the immediate barter of goods. For this to occur, the people of one tribe must be producing something different from those of another tribe, each must want the produce of the other and the different goods must be available at the same time. People living on a coast may have fish, molluscs and salt. People living inland may have grain, vegetables and meat. Individuals or families of an inland tribe can advantageously exchange their produce for that of a coastal tribe. Immediate exchange obviates any necessity for the trust that pertains in a group made cohesive through support-bargaining, except the trust that the process of exchange will remain peaceful.

Such arrangements seem admirable: a stable tribal society of contributions and receipts in accordance with accepted custom is established. The process binds members of the tribe close together in mutual support. It is a political as much as an economic process. Peter Kropotkin describes societies something like this in his study of *Mutual Aid*.[1] Mutual aid is seen as a more potent form of relationship between individuals than mutual struggle. But the potential for disruption is apparent. Support-bargaining implies perpetual competition between individuals and the group. Some individuals will contribute and feel they are not getting their rightful return. So many people may fail to meet their customary obligations that reciprocation becomes uncertain and the system goes into decline. The chief may fail his people, amassing land and property for himself, his family and his henchmen, with no concern for the impoverishment of his people.

Some means of measuring more precisely the contributions and receipts of each member of a tribe, and identifying surpluses and deficits, potentially reduces the risk that obligations will not be acknowledged or met. Barter with 'foreigners' will break down if each of two parties does not have goods of interest to the other, available at the same time, that permit mutually beneficial exchange. An item of universal value that could constitute one component of every exchange offers facilitation of all exchange. As Karl Menger pointed out in an article 'On the Origin of Money' in 1892, people from the earliest times identified certain commodities that were recognised by virtually everyone as valuable, and which could consequently be used as common counters in exchange transactions.[2] Menger identified cattle, skins, cubes of tea, slabs of salt and cowrie-shells as among the commodities that have been used as money.

Menger argues that it was the ready 'saleability' of these commodities that marked them as suitable for use as bargaining counters in a process of exchange. Cattle, skins, tea and salt are potentially useful to many people and hence likely to be accepted in exchange over a wide area, even between people with no communal connections. Menger's list of commodities is short. Glyn Davies provides a list of 25 items that have been used as money, and still remarks that his list is 'but a minute proportion of the enormous variety of primitive moneys'.[3]

Menger's list includes cowrie-shells. This immediately suggests something more than 'valuable commodities' as bargaining counters. Cowrie-shells look nice. The resemblance of their underside to female genitalia may have given them special significance. But they are not useful in the utilitarian sense. Gold and silver have also been seen as having certain special qualities that mark them as desirable beyond the desirability of more utilitarian commodities. Gold is commonly associated with the sun. Both gold and silver have long been prized as adornment for both males and females. Aesthetic qualities have given these items wide acceptance, but without the same utilitarian 'saleability' as tea and salt. Their value is more subjective and consequently more uncertain. Their 'saleability' is less secure, though they have generally supplanted the more distinctly utilitarian commodities as money. Practicality is no doubt part of the reason for favouring them. Cattle are large; they die; they need feeding. But perhaps most importantly the 'saleability' criterion is inadequate since it implies that whatever is used as money is valued as an end in itself, valued for its own inherent qualities, whereas it is an essential characteristic of money that it functions as a means to an end.

With a theory of support-bargaining, it becomes clear how societies invest things with value, over and above any value pertaining to their physical qualities. Communities often attach special characteristics to certain locations, such as rivers, forest clearings, or dells. Gods and spirits are commonly assigned residence in such places. The beauty of such places means they lend themselves to imputation of special qualities to them, but still the qualities imputed to them are a result of communal assertion. Societies can vest squiggles of ink, such as 'gratuitous' or '免费' with complex meaning. There is then little difficulty in assigning special value to materials such as gold and silver or items such as cowrie-shells. These could be used as money because certain communities recognised their function as common counters in an exchange process. As long as their function was accorded communal support, it could be fulfilled. Confidence in their function would grow as their effectiveness was confirmed.

On this understanding, money evolved in response to communal experience of unsatisfactory situations in the processes of gift giving and barter exchange. Uncertainties and imprecision experienced with intra-communal sharing and incompatibilities in barter ambitions and capabilities led to communal support for the use of certain commodities as tokens of universal value for purposes of exchange. Materials and things lend themselves to the role of 'money' when they have 'sex appeal' in the broad colloquial sense of having some instinctive attraction for people. Aesthetic appeal, hints of actual sexuality, spiritual associations and symmetry can all give this 'sex appeal'.[4] Such qualities make easier the assembly of communal support around the notion that the materials or things in question are dependable as the common component of an exchange process. Gold has been notably powerful in its appeal, both in ancient and modern times.

The introduction of money implies a shift from communal support enforcing an informal process of gift giving and reciprocation to communal support for a bargaining counter that represents the value of goods involved in an exchange. The emergence of money is a stage in the cultural evolution of human societies driven by support-bargaining. It constitutes a communal response engineered through support-bargaining to a situation that failed to meet interests of the community.

The emergence of coins as more formal tokens of value constitutes a further stage in the evolution of money. It depends more specifically on the existence of a fairly tight community with communal institutions to undertake the minting and distribution of coins. The dependence of the value of coins on the support of the community is more apparent when the issue of coinage is subject to communal control and the coinage bears marks identifying the community in which it is recognised.

The precise time of the emergence of coins is confused by their similarity to badges worn to indicate membership of a group, or to denote achievement. But coins were definitely made in Lydia in the seventh century BC. These coins were initially made of electrum, a natural alloy of gold and silver, though the Lydians later separated the metals and made gold and silver coins.[5] Coins are credited with the transformation of the economies of Athens and other ancient Greek city states from about 500 BC. The stamping of coins with the likeness of the ruler of the community to which they belonged and in which they had value can be seen as a means of identifying them with the community, invoking support for them and stimulating confidence in their value. The use of gold and silver for coins means that they evoke the aesthetic sentiments associated with the precious metals. The circular shape adopted for most coins reflects the importance humans attach to symmetrical form. Coins exploit certain human sensibilities to attract communal support and bolster confidence in them.

Money does not simply replace the exchange of gifts or barter. It adds new opportunities. Inland people may barter vegetables for salt with a coastal people, but the completion of one set of transactions is not connected with another. With money, the opportunity arises for a merchant to buy a substantial quantity of salt, paying the salt producers in money, and carry the salt up to the inland people. When he gets there, he can sell the salt, buy a large quantity of vegetables from the inland people and carry them down to the coastal people. He instigates a chain of monetary exchanges. He can extend his trade anywhere the money he uses is acceptable, or where he finds the proffered coinage acceptable. If people know a coinage can be used extensively to buy what they want, they will accept it in exchange for their own produce. The merchant does not want either the vegetables or the salt in his immediate trading; he wants money. Money becomes not an end in itself, but an important intermediate end. The introduction of money opens up opportunities for the establishment of specialist money-bargaining agencies engaged in chains of transactions.

Nor do the new opportunities lie only in the chains. The merchant can commission with his money the construction of wharves and jetties to facilitate his trade. He can buy wagons. Money makes possible capital investment on a scale and with diversity that is not feasible through support-bargaining.

One chief function of money is to bridge periods between transactions. It acts as a store of value. The popular choice of gold and silver for money can be attributed partly to the durability of those metals. It is possible to store them, bury them, hoard them for long periods and recover them virtually as they were. This durability creates opportunities for all agents of money-bargaining systems. Instead of the psychological, and consequently ambiguous, store of support that each individual sustains in a support-bargaining community, every agent can budget monetary expenditures at times well removed from the time of monetary receipts.

Money and money-bargaining 17

While coins of gold and silver may be recovered physically unchanged after a period of storage, the usefulness of that physical durability depends on the durability of their value. Durability in their value depends on the stability of prices. If coins are to be worth much the same as when they were stored, prices have to be stable, or near stable, over the period of storage. If the value of money in a savings account is to be worth the same when it comes out as when it went in, prices in the intervening period must be stable. One of the crucial considerations relating to the supply of money is its effects on prices within the community using the money.

A parallel was drawn above between communal creation and acceptance of ideas about gods and spirits inhabiting various natural locations, and the acceptance of the idea of money in a material form. While this analogy demonstrates the force of communal creation, a closer analogy to the use of money, in that it involves physical representation, lies in the use of tokens in games. A money token fulfils a function similar to that of a counter or piece in a game. A draughts counter marks a physical location on a board and certain potential movements. Draughts players could, if they had the mental capacity, hold in their minds all the places occupied by them and their opponents as a result of play. But the counters form convenient markers, relieving the players of the burden of retaining abstract information in their minds, and eliminating disputes over who occupies which space. Money performs a similar function in marking the exchanges of what was formerly support-bargaining or gift giving. It holds certain information agreed or supported by its users. If all those engaged in exchange recognise and support the same significance of the tokens used, money-bargaining can proceed. The analogy suggests that the counter itself needs little significance other than that attributed to it by communal recognition. Money tokens in the past needed the recognition accorded to gold and silver to sustain communal recognition of their significance as money. But money tokens today depend for recognition more on the confidence of the community in the institutional arrangements for sustaining their purchasing power.

It is this recognition of the significance of money tokens that makes them feasible as the means by which exchanges can be made. They do not need to be 'saleable' in the sense that a commodity is saleable because of its usefulness. Draughts counters do not have to have any other function to be effective as counters in the games in which they are used. They are the concrete expressions of shared ideas. It is enough that the relevant community understands and supports their function. It is enough that a society understands the function of its money and acts in accordance with that understanding.

Money-bargaining as derivative of support-bargaining

The adoption of some form of money is clearly advantageous in general, given the difficulties likely in situations without money. Within a community, however, there are likely to be winners and losers. *Support-Bargaining, Economics and Society* describes how a chief might see his ascendancy eroded with the introduction of money.[6] Support-bargaining is necessarily a matter for group engagement. The ascendancy or power gained by an individual in a group through support-bargaining is sustained by group support-bargaining. The gifting conventions within a tribe outlined above generate support within a group and support for the social order within the group. They will normally help to sustain an existing ascendancy. Money, by contrast, is discrete and precise. It is used in transactions in which the items concerned have similar discrete qualities. They tend to be of a material and quantifiable type. Because of that character, support-bargaining and money-bargaining can predominate in different spheres. Support-bargaining involves the creation of policies and political programmes that are broadly defined to gain support from a group, while money-bargaining deals with precisely defined benefits that answer mostly to the interests of specific individuals. Money is well suited to bargaining between individuals for precise material benefits.

This quality means, however, that money can be used to subvert support-bargaining, or divert those involved in support-bargaining from their commitments in support-bargaining. Payments to prominent individuals can subvert political programmes. Individuals getting rich are a potential danger to an ascendancy established by support-bargaining. Rulers will endeavour to ensure that their immediate followers are well enough recompensed in material terms to guarantee that they have little to gain by responding to offers of money from those with ambitions to take over. Rulers may also take steps to ensure that no individuals outside their immediate circle have enough money to deploy for the subversion of their rule. Businessmen known to be antagonistic towards a regime will find their businesses undermined, and may themselves be imprisoned or murdered. Before they can be successful, businessmen may find it necessary to come to terms with the ruling group. Developments in Russia under Vladimir Putin are a modern manifestation of this conflict between a government and private money. Rulers naturally and necessarily try to suppress the appearance of such conflicts, but they are not too difficult to observe in other parts of the modern world.

While most of those who are used to money see it as a major benefit in social intercourse, its implications for support-bargaining mean that it has not been universally welcomed. Many societies, including those described by Kropotkin, shunned the use of money for internal exchange. The hypothetical merchant described above, who trades with money between inland and coastal people, may become alien to both groups – the abominable 'middleman'. Many people in Western Europe today regard their societies as excessively concerned with money and the individualism that goes with it. They advocate a return to more cooperative behaviour – which can only mean a society dependent more on social and political support-bargaining. In some developing countries people still find it difficult to come to terms with the use of money. The evolution of money out of the exchange situations within and between tribes envisaged above would have been slow and tentative, since while some advantages would have been apparent, there would have been apparent also a real risk of loss of communal cohesion and with it the irretrievable breakdown of the society. Support-bargaining and money-bargaining are interwoven across societies. The extensive involvement of governments in modern money-bargaining systems is considered in Chapter 6.

Money is a creation of support-bargaining and a partial substitute for support in bargaining processes. The dynamic of money-bargaining is consequently in some ways close to the dynamic of support-bargaining. We know that if many people want to acquire a certain product with their money, and the product is in such short supply that not everyone can have it, then the money asked for the product by its suppliers will increase. We know it because we know that if, as an individual, we are trying to be part of a group that is very popular with its members, we will have to accept the terms offered by the group. We will have to accept the conditions imposed by the group on its members. If, by contrast, we know that a product is in heavy supply relative to those wanting to buy it, we will try to haggle down the price. We do it because we know that if a group is in need of members to raise its numbers and its significance in a support-bargaining process, it will do what it can to accommodate the particular interests of prospective members. We understand exchange and bargaining positions because we are accustomed to bargaining for our personal security with our associates. We have the idea of bargaining with money because we acquire very early familiarity with the support-bargaining process.

Engagement in money-bargaining distinguishes humans from all other species. It can be inferred that many species engage in some form of support-bargaining, in view of their capacities for hunting and living in groups. But the use of money is unique to humans. It is possible to conceive human society without money and money-bargaining – humans seem to have lived in such circumstances for most of the time they have existed as a distinct species. But modern humans and modern human societies are distinctively concerned with money-bargaining. It would probably be little contested that the present numbers of humans and their overwhelming ascendancy over other species owe much to their engagement in money-bargaining. But then, money-bargaining is a creation of support-bargaining, so money-bargaining is just one of the ways in which the special capacity of humans for support-bargaining has created a dynamic evolutionary culture.

Support-bargaining and the 'impossibility theorem'

The idea that political and economic activities are systemically similar is the basis of public choice theory. While the theory of support-bargaining and money-bargaining connects them through the dynamic of bargaining and distinguishes them through the differences between 'support' and 'money' as bargaining counters, public choice theory connects them on grounds of similarities between 'votes' and 'money'. It models political behaviour in accordance with the neoclassical economic model. 'Votes' are conceived as analogous to money and 'consumers' 'buy' political goods with their votes. The foregoing account of support-bargaining and money-bargaining implies that the public choice formulation is fundamentally misconceived. Politics involves the formation of groups through support-bargaining, while money makes economic activity individualistic. 'Votes' in public choice theory make support individualistic, but votes are only a particular expression of support introduced to make possible the engagement of all individuals in the formal support-bargaining process that is used to determine government under a support convention. Votes are themselves outcomes of support-bargaining. Individuals have a primary requirement for support which fuses them into their societies.

In public choice theory, as in the economic model, the individual is the sole operative agent; 'society' is nothing more than a collection of individuals. The suggestion that individuals are dependent for their well-being, and have always been dependent for their survival, on the support of their associates, is incompatible with public choice theory. It means that individuals will always be engaged in bargaining with their associates to gain the support they need, and will adjust their opinions and behaviour to the requirements of the group in a perpetual contest for ascendancy. There will be no purely individual opinion. Group opinion, social opinion, will be the opinion of no one individual, but an outcome of support-bargaining between many individuals. The potential for violence implicit in support means that people are inclined to defer to expressions of support from well-supported groups. Support-bargaining is generally dominant.

Kenneth Arrow's 'impossibility theorem' depends on the idea that group preferences can only be derived from summation of independent individual preferences. It shows that no voting system can produce a social welfare function, an ordering of social preferences, that is consistent with the aggregated preferences of individuals. It calls into question the democratic ideal of harmonious social order derived from individual voting. Those seeking a rational theory of democracy have stumbled over the impossibility theorem ever since it was first propounded in 1950 as 'A Difficulty in the Concept of Social Welfare'.[7]

Arrow argued that a rational system of collective choice had to have the same properties as a system of individual rational choice – that is, the properties of the neoclassical economic model. In particular, preferences have to be transitive – if an individual prefers outcome A to B, and B to C, then the individual must prefer A to C. In the same way, rational collective choice requires that if a group prefers A to B and B to C, it must also prefer A to C. Arrow showed that under reasonable assumptions about democratic order a collective ordering of preferences conforming to the transitivity requirement cannot be derived from individual orderings where there are two or more preferences. Thus, if an individual X prefers A to B and B to C; an individual Y prefers B to C and C to A; and an individual Z prefers C to A and A to B, a majority prefers B to C, a majority prefers C to A and a majority also prefers A to B. Adding the individual preferences produces no determinate ordering of group preferences. A dictator is required to settle what course is taken by a society.[8]

In terms of support-bargaining, the individualism is a false representation of human behaviour. X, Y and Z will not be independent choosers. Each will be inclined to seek the support of the others. Their opinions will not be independent opinions of isolated agents, but will be tied up with their group membership and their relationships with each other. Politics is substantially concerned with the assembly of support for the passage of measures that will advance the interests of the assembled group. Groups assemble on the basis of support for interests that can be supported across the group. Alliances will be formed to accumulate sufficient support to carry interests agreed in the formation of the alliance. Individuals will accept that they cannot realise their full preferences, but will get as much as possible in the circumstances.

The process involves compromise of the outcomes A, B and C. The identification of distinct 'preferences' is analogous to the identification of homogeneous 'products' in the neoclassical economic model. In support-bargaining the interests of the group are moulded by the support-bargaining that forms the group. Its preferred outcomes will be redefined to assemble the support necessary to gain passage of measures that meet them. The interests, or preferences, and the group are formed in the same process.

Even in its economic context the idea of fixed preferences, or fixed products, is mistaken. In money-bargaining companies shape products to meet the situation-related requirements of potential customers. Customers do not just want a standard 'car'. In a certain situation, a customer may want a car with low-ratio gear box, heavy-duty tyres and a winch. Certain collections of features in vehicles will suit them to the requirements of buyers in different situations. When the critical interest is in the accommodation of situation through features it is no longer obvious that a consumer preferring the selection of features A over the selection of features B, and the selection B over selection C, can be expected to prefer the selection A over selection C. Each selection will be accommodating different elements of situation, so that an element of 'weighting' of the importance of different situation components is implied. In comparing a car A with a car B and the car B with car C, a buyer might put great emphasis on the requirement of comfort, and conclude that car A was more comfortable than car B and car B was more comfortable than car C, and form his preferences accordingly. But if required to compare car A with car C, the buyer might decide that, in that comparison, comfort was of little relevance. Car C might not be very comfortable, but perhaps it is very fast. And that characteristic of the car might prompt a reassessment of the weighting in favour of speed. Instead of settling for middle-aged comfort, the buyer might decide that his or her youthful self should dictate requirements. With an increased weighting for speed the preference might be for car C over car A. The change of weighting for the comparison between car A and car C may be idiosyncratic but it is not irrational. Transitivity is lost, and with it the logic of consumer choice in the economic model.[9] No Pareto optimal distribution of resources is feasible without transitive preferences. In a political context, transitivity is even less likely. Policy and provision outcomes are generally malleable. People are open to persuasion. The assumptions of the economic model are misconceived with regard to economic activity. When transferred to a political context they seem even more out of place.[10]

The supply and value of money

It was seen above that durability in the value of money depends substantially on stability of prices. This in turn depends on the supply of money. If a 'money' is to gain communal acceptance, it must be possible to control its supply so that prices do not fluctuate significantly. Stable prices require that the supply of money is kept in steady proportion to the buying and selling of goods. Supply above the appropriate level can be expected to raise prices; supply below the appropriate level is likely to bring about a fall in prices. In both cases, in the extreme, the money may be rejected by the community that adopted it, though the difficulties of finding an alternative mean that communities tend to tolerate high levels of inflation or falling prices before abandoning a chosen currency. Barter is too cumbersome to be an easy alternative for those accustomed to the use of money. A very marked deficiency in money supply, such as is difficult to accommodate through falling prices, is likely to result in contraction of trade.

It matters also who controls the supply of money. Whoever owns the gold mine is well supplied with money and can buy what he wants, provided the cost of mining does not exceed the cost of the goods that can be bought with the gold. The owner of the mine is likely to control the supply of money to suit his own interests. The supply of money has to be adapted to its communal usage, rather than the advantage of any particular agent.

Gold, silver and the money supply

What is adopted as money in a society is then conditional on satisfactory arrangements for control of its supply, both with regard to the controller and how it is controlled. The allure of precious metals has made them prime candidates for the role of money. Their adoption means also that there is the prospect of automatic provision for control of the supply of money. The overall supply of a metallic money like silver or gold depends on the output of mines. In a national economy without its own mines, the supply of metallic money depends on the level of accumulated bullion and the inflows and outflows resulting from foreign trade. Foreign earnings in excess of expenditures augment bullion reserves and expand the money supply, while overseas earnings below expenditures deplete bullion reserves and reduce the money supply. An expansion of the money supply can be expected to raise prices, reduce overseas sales and attract imports, potentially bringing about an outflow of bullion. A reduction in money supply can be expected to bring about lower prices, making it easier to sell overseas, reducing imports and potentially bringing about an inflow of bullion. Money supply should adjust automatically in accordance with the performance of the economy. David Hume describes a mechanism of this kind.[11] In principle, the mechanism regulates money supply to give stable prices, without any agency having to make decisions.

Given the limited confidence of people in many countries in the capacity of their governments, past and present, to act in the public interest, such automatic control of money supply is a major attraction. It tends to enhance confidence in the stability of a currency. The problem is the mechanism does not work in practice with the same smooth efficiency as it works on paper. The automatic adjustment of prices may be too slow to accommodate the immediate trading requirements of an economy, or may even scarcely work at all. In some circumstances it may be desirable to increase the money supply when the automatic mechanism is restricting it.

The cost of adherence to a metallic standard has been substantial trade dislocation. In Britain in the sixteenth and seventeenth centuries the main symptom of economic crisis was a shortage of coins.[12] Money flowed out for purchase of food when the harvest failed, or in consequence of some other disruption, and stayed out. Prices did not adjust, or did not adjust sufficiently, to bring about an inflow of metal. Without coin, the level of domestic trade contracted.

Nor did the metallic standard obviate entirely the necessity for some agent to control the supply of money. Coins still had to be produced. The task fell naturally on the monarch, especially as it was profitable. Costs of production, including metal content, were lower than the value of the coin, so the more coin the monarch put into circulation, the more revenue he received.

Henry VIII, whose ambitions always stretched his purse, instituted what is known as the 'Great Debasement', running from 1542 to 1551. The silver content of coins was reduced from around three-quarters of their face value to about one third. The debasement is estimated to have doubled the money supply. While cause and effect are not so clear, the debasement coincided with the period of fastest growth in prices, 1540–60, of the whole period 1450 to 1650.[13] The Great Debasement seems to have fuelled inflation, but an increase in money supply by devaluation of the currency through reduction in metal content might have been beneficial to trade in the crises involving shortages of coin.

Debasement meant deception with regard to the amount of precious metal in a currency and potentially a loss of confidence in the currency. Given that people regarded gold and silver as having intrinsic value, any reduction in the amount of these metals in a coin meant a reduction in its value, whatever the face value of the coin. Given the repute of governments in financial matters generally, and coinage in particular, there was the possibility that society might withdraw its support for the currency.

Private people could also profit from this 'debasing' of the currency, though they risked their lives in doing so. Coins were 'clipped' by shaving or cutting precious metal from them. The inflation of the sixteenth century seems to have been caused partly by the flow of gold and silver into Europe from South America, but debasement of coins may have contributed to it.[14]

Malynes, Misselden and Mun

The alternative to a metallic standard is the valuation of a currency in accordance with the requirements of trade. While a metallic standard offers in principle an automatic supply and stabilising mechanism, a currency based on the requirements of trade requires some agency that can assess the requirements and issue the right amount of currency. A central authority is required to judge the volume of money that is required to maintain trade without raising or lowering prices.

Adam Smith advocated that notes should only be issued against 'real bills' – that is bills of exchange pertaining to actual transactions.[15] This would provide the necessary foundation for the issue of currency in accordance with trading requirements, without affecting price levels. Smith was concerned with the issue of a paper currency backed by gold, but the 'real bills' idea suggests a reference for the issue of a stable currency not backed by gold.

One of the most severe trade depressions of the seventeenth century was that of 1620–1. Once again, a shortage of coin was a major feature of the depression, brought about by outflows of coin. Domestic prices did not adjust to reverse the flows of specie out of the country. A theoretical debate arose regarding the causes of the outflow and the appropriate remedies, pitting the proponents of a metallic standard against those who favoured a currency regime tuned to the accommodation of trade.

On the metallic side, Gerard de Malynes argued that the loss of wealth was the result of 'an overbalancing of foreign commodities'. It was a result of selling domestically produced goods too cheaply, while buying foreign goods at too high a price. The imbalance was a consequence of mispricing – quantities and quality of exports and imports were not significant. Malynes's remedy was 'the elimination of fluctuations of exchange rates by pegging the rates at mint parity, combined with a comprehensive system of exchange control'.[16] In other words, exchange rates should be set by reference to metal content, with limits on the availability of currency for foreign trade, so that there was no unmanageable outflow of coin. Where no automatic adjustment took place through changes in prices, currency control would be used to check trade imbalances and maintain domestic money supply.

Rival theorists, led by Edward Misselden and Thomas Mun, argued that an adverse balance of trade had brought about the outflow of coins.[17] Imports were greater than exports. Both Misselden and Mun held what came to be known as the mercantilist view that national prosperity depended on earning more overseas than was spent overseas, in the same way as the prosperity of a business depended on gaining revenues that were greater than the costs incurred. Mun wrote, 'The ordinary means to increase our wealth and treasure is by foreign trade, wherein we must ever observe this rule: to sell more to strangers yearly than we consume of theirs in value.'[18] The solution to the outflow of coinage was to export more than was imported. Misselden recommended devaluation of the currency, so that prices of exports could be reduced, resulting in an increase in exports and an increase in export earnings, while import prices would increase, with a fall in imports and a fall in the cost of imports – now the normal 'trader' solution. Mun rejected devaluation, on the grounds that it would be confusing, would benefit Spain and would be nullified by retaliation by other countries. He nevertheless recognised that movements in exchange rates had to be linked to movements in trade.

Malynes attributes the loss of coin to deviation of exchange rates from their 'proper' parity, while for Misselden and Mun the problem arose from imbalance of trade.[19] For some, stability and prosperity require that people have the confidence in their currency that comes from fixing its value in terms of a precious metal. For others, the expansion of trade is the prime consideration, and exchange rates have to be adjusted to maintain overseas competitiveness.

In this case, the theories are inseparable from the circumstances of their leading advocates. Malynes initially styled himself a merchant, but landed in a debtors' prison. This perhaps gave him the strong aversion to bankers that colours his theories. Bankers were to blame for the export of specie.[20] With a currency value fixed in terms of precious metal, the role of bankers would be confined to that of administering currency controls – that is, preventing any outflow of specie. With an exchange rate fixed by reference to trade balances, the role of bankers was potentially more influential. Malynes was later an advisor to government on issues concerning exchange rates and the minting of coins. Both Misselden and Mun had interests in the primacy of trade or, perhaps more pertinently, in the freedom to export silver. Misselden was Deputy Governor of the Merchant Adventurers Group when he argued against the export of specie by the East India Company. When he obtained employment with the East India Company, where Mun was a director, he was able to agree with Mun on the advantages of the export of specie. Silver was the one commodity that was wanted in Asia, and its export was essential to the development of the trade of the East India Company. Mun argued that many good things came to England in exchange for the silver.[21] For a start, the company carried on a remunerative re-export trade in Asian goods to Europe, by which much coin came back to England. But, clearly, not enough came back to offset an adverse balance of trade and net outflow of specie.

John Locke and recoinage

The depression of 1620–1 was characterised by shortage of coin as a consequence of outflow overseas. Later in the century a serious economic crisis developed as a consequence of clipping. The diarist John Evelyn records, on 1 July 1694: 'Many executed at London for clipping money, now done to that intolerable extent, that there was hardly any money that was worth above half the nominal value.' People were losing confidence in the coinage. Such was the detriment to trade that some remedy had to be found. The question was whether a new coinage should contain silver in accordance with its face value, or whether it should have the same silver content as the clipped coins currently in circulation.[22] One way or the other, confidence in the coinage had to be restored if trade was to be restored to its former level.

John Locke was appointed to study the situation and make recommendations. Locke saw gold and silver as intrinsically valuable, and consequently debasement of coinage was tantamount to fraud. In accordance with this judgement, his recommendation was that the silver content of the coinage should be restored to its original level. The communal understanding of value – including Evelyn's understanding – was weight of silver in the coinage. So this silver content had to accord with the face value put on the coin.

According to Backhouse, this view was out of date. People had come to accept the coins in trade at face value. So when the silver content in the coins was increased in accordance with Locke's recommendation in 1696, people did not accord the new coins any higher value in trade. The coins still bought what they had bought before. The silver content of the coins became worth more than the face value of the coins.[23] Instead of reducing prices in view of the higher metal content of the coins, giving more goods for the same face value, traders sold the same volume of goods for the same face value of coin as they had sold before.

It is perhaps understandable that traders would be reluctant to re-format at lower prices, involving the renegotiation of wages and the prices of inputs, as well as the repricing of their sales. It is, however, difficult to understand why they did not do so when the consequences were so severe. Since the silver in the coins was worth more than the purchasing power of the coins, they were melted down for their silver, or hoarded. Money supply fell dramatically and a severe depression followed.

It seems that the use of silver for coins was frustrated by the commodity value of the silver. In Asia, as has been seen, there was a strong demand for silver.[24] Asians had little taste for European goods, but would give good value for silver. The East India Company needed copious amounts of silver, much more than in the time of Misselden and Mun, to pursue its import trade in spices and other exotic goods from Asia. The company was developing a sophisticated system for acquisition of silver through specialist dealers in London and Antwerp, or sometimes Cadiz or Hamburg.[25] The high returns from silver in trade with Asia must have diverted silver coins from English markets.

Asian demand might have provided motivation for the original clipping of silver coins and for the subsequent withdrawal of full-metal coins from circulation. The outflow of silver left the economy short of silver coinage for its domestic trading. Malynes would have advocated tighter administrative controls on the outflow of bullion and coin. Misselden would have favoured increasing the money supply by using less silver in the coins – that is, accepting something like the de facto devaluation of the currency that was the result of clipping. The other solution is to use an alternative money. Gold coins were in circulation and had not been tampered with, at least not to the same extent as the silver coins. Gold was not in the same great demand in Asia as silver. The continued availability and use of gold coins tends to confirm the importance of the Asian commodity trade in silver in the recoinage crisis. One important consequence of the withdrawal of silver coin was increased reliance on gold coins and paper money, and the de facto adoption of a gold standard.[26] Many years later, in 1774, a formal gold standard was adopted.

Gold and trade in the Napoleonic Wars

The theoretical debate over the management of money was resumed with great intensity during the Napoleonic Wars. By that time, questions of money supply were focused more on the issue of paper currency and the metallic 'backing' of the issue rather than on the metal content of coins. There had emerged also a 'Bank of England', a joint-stock company that financed government and had a 'back-up' role in relation to London banks, and through them to provincial banks.

Financial systems, as will be seen in more detail in Chapter 7, depend on confidence. Currencies depend on the confidence in them of the people who use them. Wars shake confidence like nothing else. In such circumstances, the universal recognition of the value of precious metals can sustain confidence in a currency whose value is tied to a precious metal. So there are clear advantages in maintenance of a gold standard. But any disruption to trade can call into question the successful outcome of war, so there are clear advantages in ensuring that a currency is valued in accordance with requirements for the maintenance of trade. The Napoleonic Wars required that Britain look to its financial arrangements as a crucial factor in its defence.

The outbreak of war in 1793 brought a crisis of confidence over the note issues of the country banks, with a resulting high demand for coins from London banks, and through them from the Bank of England. Following standard banking practice, the Bank of England, acting in the interests of its shareholders, would have reduced its issue of notes to reduce its vulnerability to demands on its metallic reserves. However, it was recognised that such a course would be likely to exacerbate the shortage of money already apparent, and further depress economic activity. After much debate, the Bank of England increased its note issue. The Bank had already established such a reputation in the financial and business community that its notes were accepted, and the crisis was successfully resolved.

This marked the commissioning of an institution other than government, a nominally private institution, as responsible for the administration of a national money supply in the interests of a trading community. Confidence came to rest not just on the currency and its supply, but on an institution given discretionary control of the supply.

The debate over whether the Bank of England should regulate the supply of sterling to maintain a metallic standard or by reference to trade requirements emerged in urgent form around 1810. The British government had been forced to suspend convertibility of sterling in 1797 in the face of an outflow of gold triggered by rumours of a French invasion. In 1802 Henry Thornton published *An Enquiry into the Nature and Effects of the Paper Credit of Great Britain*,[27] described by Backhouse as 'what is arguably the period's, if not the century's, greatest contribution to monetary economics'.[28] Apart from a dip in 1802, sterling remained close to its old gold value up to 1809. But renewed depreciation in that year led to fears of a deeper loss of confidence in sterling. A House of Commons Bullion Committee was established to determine a response to questions regarding the valuation of sterling.

Thornton and his fellow members of the Bullion Committee concluded in their report of 1810 that the over-issue of notes, unconstrained by any obligation to limit their issue in accordance with bullion reserves, threatened the balance of payments and the exchange rate of sterling. It recommended that Parliament should require the Bank of England to restore convertibility within two years. The anti-bullionists, represented by the Bank of England, argued that the note issue was the result of demand for notes. They cited Adam Smith in confirmation of the idea that provided notes were issued only against 'real bills' there would be no ill-effects on prices, bullion reserves or the balance of payments. The note issue would meet only the genuine requirements of business. The bullionists held that confidence in sterling would only be reliably maintained if the value of sterling were fixed in gold, with the automatic control of the money supply that went with it. The anti-bullionists argued that a currency could be issued with confidence by reference to the level of trade.

The government accepted the arguments of the Bank of England and the anti-bullionists.[29] The decision, however, was strictly related to the circumstances of the time. The French embargo on trade with Britain constituted a serious threat to British trade and the determination of the British people to defeat Napoleon. The government was also obliged to spend large sums of money on British and allied armies overseas. Return to a gold standard could mean constraints on trade and payments that would undermine the war effort. For the time being, it was decided to maintain the suspension of sterling convertibility. But with the defeat of Napoleon the costs of military operations came to an end and trade resumed. The arguments of the Bullion Committee were accepted and convertibility was restored in 1821.

The resumption of a gold standard set the scene for the rapid development of London in the nineteenth century as the financial and trading centre of the world. The attractions of London as a financial centre made it a centre also for high volumes of capital for short-term investment in discount markets. Large and volatile capital flows, much in excess of the bullion reserves of the Bank of England, added a new dimension to the management of the currency. Sterling remained anchored to a gold standard, but confidence in its value was sustained also by the strength of the British economy. Sterling became an international currency. Mathias remarks that the international system was based more on a 'sterling standard' than a 'gold standard'.[30] The economic evolution that sustained this international confidence in sterling is described in Chapters 5 to 8.

The allure of gold

The allure of precious metals and gold in particular has been remarkably potent in sustaining support for a currency made of precious metal or backed by precious metal. Confidence has been periodically shaken in Britain by debasement of the currency by government or by private citizens. It has also been shaken by disruptions to trade arising from failures of the 'automatic' mechanism of adjustment of money supply associated with precious metals. Instead of smooth adjustment, acute shortages of coins have brought contractions in trading. In periods of crisis, and particularly in times of war, it has been found necessary to relinquish the link to gold in favour of a currency better attuned to the immediate requirements of trade. The major expansion of global trade in the nineteenth century, using London as its financial centre, occurred when sterling was pegged to gold, but the gold parity itself was protected by the strength of the British economy. Britain's production and trade gave assurance that demand for sterling would be maintained and there would be no reason for people to seek conversion of their sterling into its equivalent value in gold. The expansion of international trade must, to some extent, have strengthened the commitment to gold. Its allure was shared in many different communities and the common attachment was conducive to confidence. The emergence of the Bank of England, with a reputation for probity and good judgement, gave institutional backing for the use of a gold standard. People could be assured that their currency was controlled in accordance with communal interest. But still, in spite of all these props to sustain it, the underlying commitment to a gold-based currency, right up to the latter half of the twentieth century, has been remarkable. It seems a very primitive attachment; one that might have been expected to loosen much earlier, given the evolution that has taken place in economies, international trade and international finance. Even now, though the value of currencies is not specifically linked to gold, central banks around the world keep large holdings of gold 'in reserve'. The experience is consistent with an idea of money as an outcome of communal support-bargaining, dependent for its continued use on effective means of controlling its supply, so that it commands the continued support of the communities using it.

Companies as specialist money-bargaining agencies

The merchant buying vegetables from inland people and selling them to coastal people, and buying seafood and salt from coastal people and selling them to inland people, was referred to above as a specialist money-bargaining agent. This is a distinctive role in money-bargaining systems and the foundation of much of their dynamism. The evolution of economies is, to a considerable extent, the evolution of companies. The role of companies in the evolution of the British economy is described in Chapter 5.

Companies use organisation to establish bargaining position. It was seen in the previous chapter that groups metamorphose into organisations to establish bargaining position. Organisations coordinate various inputs to a single purpose, commonly using hierarchical systems that give different bargaining positions to different groups of people. The different bargaining positions, established as conditions of membership of the organisation, make possible the transmission of instructions to coordinate the activities of the organisation.[31] Organisation also involves the establishment of money budgets, so that money can be used in assembling the necessary skills to operate the organisation. In the case of companies, the budget is a central concern, not merely an adjunct of other organisational purpose, since companies are established to make money for their owners or founders. The bargaining positions established by companies have made them the leading organisations of money-bargaining systems.

Companies pursue their purpose by accommodating the interests of other agents. Buyers, including consumers, have situation-related interests, and by producing goods and services which fit the requirements of buyers companies gain revenues. They produce coats and hats of the right size and fashion, made available in convenient locations and at convenient times. By dint of careful selection of materials and production technologies, the prices of the coats and hats will be such as fit the budgets of potential buyers. Changing situations perpetually throw up new requirements, which constitute new opportunities for company revenues. Companies adapt their own situations to meet the evolving requirements of buyers, thus becoming part themselves of the evolutionary process. A large component of a company's 'situation' is what is more commonly referred to as its 'capacity' for output of goods or services. Whereas 'situation' is generally taken as implying certain requirements, 'capacity' implies the ability to provide. The situations of all agents of bargaining systems give rise to interests and requirements; they incorporate also the capacities of agents to offer goods or services in exchange for accommodation of their requirements. The 'situation' that gives rise to interests and requirements is more strictly the 'non-capacity situation'. In the case of companies, 'capacity' is often used with very specific reference to the output of machinery.

The capacities of companies are generally associated with the technologies they use. Technology is central to the effectiveness of companies in meeting the requirements of customers. Technologies make possible the production of certain products by certain methods. Virtually all businesses are based on technology of some kind. In many cases, particularly with regard to science-based 'high technology', companies are largely defined by their technologies. Electronics companies such as Samsung, Vodaphone, Apple, Microsoft, Panasonic and Sony are all identified in terms of the technologies they develop and the products based on those technologies. Technology dictates not just products and production methods, but also the unit cost of output, and hence the price at which output can be viably sold. Certain technologies permit large production runs of a standardised product at low unit cost. As will be discussed further in Chapter 5, the evolution of companies is bound up with the evolution of technology.

This account of the role and functioning of companies contrasts sharply with the understanding of companies in neoclassical economic theory. Neoclassical theory moulds its understanding of companies to the requirements of the neoclassical model. The outputs of companies are a mathematical function of the inputs. The company itself is not a centre of decision-making. Companies have merely to expand their use of resources in production of standard homogeneous products until the marginal cost of production is equal to the market price of the product, determined by supply and demand independently of the company. The mathematics require that companies are so small as to have no individual influence on price – all sell at the prices determined by 'the market'. In neoclassical theory 'the firm' is largely a matter of cost curves in a diagram. Companies have no problems related to product innovation or acquisition of information.

The manifest deficiencies of the basic neoclassical account of 'the firm' has given rise to many attempts by writers regarding themselves as within the neoclassical theory group to bridge the gulf between the reality of companies and the neoclassical model of companies. The best-known theory is that of Robert Coase, regarding transaction costs, mentioned in the previous chapter and discussed further in Chapter 4.[32] Other economic theories of the firm are contrasted with the above account of companies in an article 'Companies and Markets: Economic Theories of the Firm and a Concept of Companies as Bargaining Agencies'.[33] There is no escaping the fundamental incapacity of neoclassical theory to accommodate the major agencies of money-bargaining systems, which are at the same time necessarily major factors in the evolution of economies. This lack of understanding of companies in neoclassical economics has clouded interpretations of crucial historical events, such as the British industrial revolution. Some redress is provided in Chapter 5.

The article 'Companies and Markets' summarises the requirement of companies to achieve their money-making purpose as a matter of ensuring that revenues are greater than costs, or that:

Sales × Price > Production × Unit Cost

The four factors of this viability condition are interdependent:

- Sales depend on the extent to which a product incorporates features fitting to the requirements of buyers. This includes, as a matter of major importance, the fit of the price to buyers' budgets. Sales depend heavily on price. A sufficient number of buyers must be able to afford the product if the viability condition is to be fulfilled.
- Price depends on unit cost. Price will be based on a 'mark-up' or 'cost-plus' pricing procedure. Strong anticipated or realised bargaining position (i.e. high sales) will result in higher mark-ups on unit cost.
- Unit cost depends substantially on the level of production. The level of production and unit costs will be related to the technology used. Technological characteristics often mean that unit costs vary markedly with different levels of production. In general, high levels of production have the lowest unit costs. Other unit costs, such as unit distribution costs, will be affected by the volume of product to be sold.
- Sales should be equal to production. A certain 'break-even' level of sales is necessary to make the format viable. Production will depend on the potential for sales at the price dictated by the unit cost at the proposed level of production.

Companies need to format from the start with capacity that enables them to meet, as a minimum, this viability condition. Some adjustments will be possible, but if the initial set-up falls well short of the viability condition, a company will fail. Companies will subsequently make continuous efforts to adapt their format to increase profitability. In particular, there will be ongoing efforts to reduce the unit costs of production, giving them the option to increase sales and profitability by reducing price, or to maintain price and take increased profitability at the same level of sales. Unit costs will fall if the price of inputs is reduced. They will also fall if the ratio of output to inputs is increased – that is, if productivity is increased.

It is not necessary, of course, that a company meets the viability condition in all phases of its operations. Products typically have a life cycle, and the viability condition has to be met across the cycle. Few firms produce just one product, so there is normally scope for toleration of losses for a period on one product which are made up by profits on another. Overall the company sustains viability. The assessment of unit costs may also be affected by discretion in the allocation of overhead costs.

Companies have the limitations implicit in their role as specialist money-bargaining agencies. They can provide employment and incomes. They can provide goods and services to people and organisations that have the budgetary resources to pay for them. They cannot provide goods and services without payment. In consequence, unless communal interest can be given substance through a money budget, companies may ignore communal interest.

Companies are, however, creations of support-bargaining systems. What they can and cannot do is established by political support-bargaining processes. Their existence is conditional on their maintenance of support, which means performing useful social functions. In general, the advantages of having strong competing specialist money-bargaining agencies have been seen as outweighing the disadvantages of their operations. They create incomes and employment, and the evolution of economies, to the widespread benefit of their societies. They also provide the means by which their disadvantages can be countered. Taxation of incomes and expenditures generated by companies permit the formation of communal budgets, which can then buy goods and services from companies. Companies respond to communal needs when there are communal expenditures. Communal budgets are established in the context of communal organisation. Health, education, sanitation and welfare services increase with the expansion of companies, provided communal organisation is sufficient to manage properly a communal budget.

Companies themselves have a communal interest in the provision of infrastructure and services necessary to the functioning of money-bargaining systems. Roads and commercial law are essential to the functioning of companies. Education and training are essential for a productive workforce. Companies alone cannot provide these requirements to desirable levels, so they have an interest in ensuring that communal budgets are used to make the necessary provisions.

Companies have thus to be understood as operating not as isolated and independent money-bargaining agencies, but as components of a support-bargaining and money-bargaining system. The support-bargaining system has to determine how it will regulate these specialist money-bargaining agencies. It was emphasised in the preceding chapter that support-bargaining and money-bargaining systems are closely intertwined. This is, of course, in marked contrast to the neoclassical insistence on a separate and self-sufficient model of economic activity.

Chapter 6 describes the evolution of the support-bargaining system in Britain alongside the accelerated evolution of the money-bargaining system that constituted the industrial revolution.

Notes

1 Kropotkin, Peter, 2008/1902, *Mutual Aid: A Factor of Evolution*, Hong Kong: Forgotten Books. See also Spread, Patrick, 2013, *Support-Bargaining, Economics and Society: A Social Species*, Abingdon and London: Routledge, pp. 5, 33, 141–3.
2 Menger, Karl, 1892, 'On the Origin of Money', *The Economic Journal*, Vol. 2, No. 6, pp. 239–55.
3 Davies, Glyn, 1994, *A History of Money from Ancient Times to the Present Day*, Cardiff: University of Wales Press, p. 27.
4 On the importance of symmetry, see Spread, 2013, Chapter 10, Social Symmetries.
5 Davies, 1994, pp. 61–2.
6 Spread, 2013, pp. 200–6.
7 Arrow, Kenneth J., 1950, 'A Difficulty in the Concept of Social Welfare', *Journal of Political Economy*, Vol. 58, No. 4, pp. 328–46. See also Arrow, Kenneth J., 1970, *Social Choice and Individual Values*, 2nd edition, New Haven, CT, and London: Yale University Press.
8 Barry, Norman, 2000, *An Introduction to Modern Political Theory*, 4th edition, London: Palgrave, pp. 291–2.
9 See Spread, Patrick 2011, 'Situation as Determinant of Selection and Valuation', *Cambridge Journal of Economics*, Vol. 35, No. 2, pp. 335–56, p. 342. Reprinted in Spread, Patrick, 2015b, *Aspects of Support-Bargaining and Money-Bargaining*, E-Book, World Economics Association.
10 For more comment on public choice theory see Spread, Patrick, 1984, *A Theory of Support and Money Bargaining*, London: Macmillan, pp. 32–41, and Spread, Patrick, 2004, *Getting It Right, Economics and the Security of Support*, Sussex: Book Guild, Footnote 5, pp. 200–1.
11 Backhouse, Roger, 1993, *Economists and the Economy: The Evolution of Economic Ideas*, New Brunswick, NJ, and London: Transaction, pp. 120–1.
12 Backhouse, 1993, pp. 152–3.
13 Coleman, D. C., 1977, *The Economy of England 1450–1750*, Oxford: Oxford University Press, p. 24.
14 Backhouse, 1993, pp. 110–1.
15 Backhouse, 1993, p. 128.
16 Spiegel, Henry William, 1991, *The Growth of Economic Thought*, Durham, NC, and London: Duke University Press, pp. 102–4.
17 Backhouse, 1993, p. 113.
18 Quoted by Spiegel, 1991, p. 108.
19 Spiegel, 1991, pp. 106, 112–13.
20 Spiegel, 1991, pp. 100–1.
21 Spiegel, 1991, pp. 106–7.
22 Backhouse, 1993, pp. 114–15.
23 Backhouse, 1993, pp. 116–17.
24 Coleman, 1977, pp. 141–2.
25 Coleman, 1977, p. 142.
26 Backhouse, 1993, p. 117.
27 Thornton, Henry, 1802, *An Enquiry into the Nature and Effects of the Paper Credit of Great Britain*, London: J. Hatchard.
28 Backhouse, 1993, p. 124.

29 Backhouse, 1993, pp. 131–2, 121.
30 Mathias, Peter, 2001, *The First Industrial Nation: An Economic History of Britain 1700–1914*, London and New York: Routledge, p. 329.
31 On organisational hierarchies, see Spread, 1984, paras 1.28, 3.116, 5.20, 37, 48–66, etc.
32 Coase, R. H., 1937, 'The Nature of the Firm', *Economica*, Vol. 4, No. 16, pp. 386–405.
33 Spread, Patrick, 2015a, 'Companies and Markets: Economic Theories of the Firm and a Concept of Companies as Bargaining Agencies', *Cambridge Journal of Economics*, Advance Access published 2 June 2015, doi:10.1093/cje/bev029. Reprinted in Spread, 2015b, *Aspects of Support-Bargaining and Money-Bargaining*, E-Book, World Economics Association. See also Spread, 2008, Chapter 4: Organisations: Function and Format.

3 Macroeconomics and money-bargaining

The neoclassical model is a 'microeconomic' model, covering transactions involving consumers, 'resources' and firms. If the model is a good one, the 'macroeconomy', the national economy, should be merely the sum of all the micro-transactions. There are, however, immediate problems. The term 'national' implies a government and a territory, neither of which can be accommodated in the neoclassical microeconomic model. Other characteristics of the neoclassical model mean that macroeconomies are notably different from what neoclassical theory suggests they might be.

These incompatibilities have led to the development of two different strands in macroeconomic research. One strand takes neoclassical microeconomic theory as its starting point. Much academic macroeconomic research is devoted to the analysis of the macroeconomic equilibrium that should emerge, given the tendency of neoclassical markets to equilibrium with an optimal allocation of resources. The second strand is more pragmatic. It focuses on the observed working of macroeconomies, seeking responses to problems arising in the management of economies, in the form of practical policy recommendations. In this strand, the neoclassical model still provides a theoretical framework, but there is also a more pragmatic understanding of how macroeconomies function. National accounts, which measure and record the functioning of macroeconomies, have theoretical foundations in neoclassical theory, but they also embody more pragmatic ideas of how economies function, not least the role of government and the implications of distance.

Clearly, if a microeconomic theory is to explain the evolution of a whole economy, the microeconomic theory must be wholly compatible with the macroeconomic theory. This chapter is concerned with the links between micro- and macroeconomic theory. It shows also that macroeconomic theory, largely as it now stands, while incompatible with neoclassical microeconomic theory, is consistent with the understanding of economic processes provided by the theory of money-bargaining. The usefulness of macroeconomic theory in its pragmatic forms derives from its broad consistency with the idea of money-bargaining.

A system of national accounts has been central to both the theoretical and applied development of macroeconomic analysis. National accounts perform something like the function of company accounts, although the concepts behind them and their coverage are markedly different. They have provided a conceptual and quantitative basis for the monitoring of economic performance and all the developments in economic policy worldwide since the Second World War. One central measure, 'gross domestic product', or GDP, has gained public prominence through its use in the media as a summary measure of economic performance. Its related measure, 'gross national product' (GNP), is GDP plus net property income from abroad. Subtracting an estimate of depreciation from GNP gives 'national income'. Roger Backhouse's *History of Economics* provides a brief history of the development of national income accounting in Europe and the USA in the twentieth century.[1]

Backhouse records the attempts of William Petty in the seventeenth century to estimate the national income of England and Ireland.[2] Petty draws firm conclusions from his analysis. Chapter 8 of his *Political Arithmetik* is titled: 'That there are spare Hands enough among the King of England's Subjects, to earn two Millions per annum more than they now do; and that there are also Employments, ready, prope, and sufficient, for that purpose'.[3] It seems that 'welfare to work' programmes are not an innovation of recent years. Later in the same century Gregory King produced an account of national income for 1688 which is regarded as providing a useful guide to levels of income at that time. King's account is used in Chapter 5.

The development of national accounting gathered pace in the twentieth century. In 1915 Willford King published *The Wealth and Income of the People of the United States*.[4] A national Bureau of Economic Research was established in the USA in 1921, providing national income estimates for 1909 to 1919. This work was taken up by Simon Kuznets, who produced estimates for 1929 to 1932. The term 'gross national product' was first used by Clark Warburton at the Brookings Institute in 1934. In Britain A. L. Bowley produced estimates of national income based on tax returns, data from the 1907 census and other sources. Colin Clark published British *National Income and Outlay* in 1937. In 1940 James Meade and Richard Stone began work at the Central Economic Information Service of the War Cabinet, constructing national income accounts for 1938 and 1940.[5] They adopted concepts introduced by John Maynard Keynes in the *General Theory* as the basis of national accounts construction.[6] They also adopted the double-entry approach to national accounting. In the 1950s these concepts and techniques became the international standards for preparation of national accounts. In both Britain and the USA national accounts were developed during the Second World War for the pressing purpose of assessing the levels of production of war materials and war-related materials that were feasible. In this work there was no question of allowing theoretical convenience to take precedence over realism, so the accounts are a practical formulation, well adapted to tracking the performance of economies. Macroeconomic accounts are highly relevant to actual economic performance.

National accounts provide three basic aggregates of economic activity for any period: the aggregate of incomes earned by the 'factors of production', labour, land and capital; the aggregate of expenditures by consumers, investors and government, plus exports (the expenditure of foreigners on home-produced goods) less imports (the expenditure of home buyers on foreign-produced goods); and the value of output, as the 'value added' in each industry. 'Value added' in an industry is the value of the output of the industry less the value of its inputs. It consists of the incomes derived from the factors of production used in the industry, in the form of wages and salaries, income from self-employment, rents, interest and profit. The components of the accounts are defined in such a way as to make the three measures necessarily equal – expenditure is equal to income, which is equal to the value of goods and services produced. National accounts measure economic activity in 'nominal' terms, the money terms in which transactions are conducted, and in 'real' terms, which are measures of 'volume' derived from data on volumes of production of different products and adjustment of nominal data to take account of changes in prices.

GDP provides a central measure of the income, final expenditure and output of a country, permitting comparisons of economic performance from year-to-year and between countries. It is almost universally used to track economic performance. Growth in GDP is closely related to growth in employment, and consequently changes in GDP have implications for support-bargaining. Rapid growth in GDP generates employment and incomes. Governments which sustain economic growth and the employment that goes with it tend to attract support. Governments unable to stimulate economic growth, and hence unable to provide employment, commonly find that they lose support. Expenditures on investment give indications of the prospective future growth in output and consumption in an economy. Comparative performance in the different industrial sectors indicates the industries in which a country is comparatively strong, and those in which it is comparatively weak. The relative strengths and weaknesses have implications for the design of education and training programmes.

National accounts capture in monetary terms the evolution of national economies. Many nations have evolved from situations in which agriculture is the dominant occupation to a stage where industrial production has taken over as the major source of employment and source of incomes. Western nations experienced this evolutionary process mainly in the nineteenth century. Chapter 5 describes the evolution of the British economy through the industrial revolution in terms of the evolution of a money-bargaining system, revealing some aspects of the evolutionary process that are not apparent from analysis based on mainstream economic theory. Some economies then evolve further to a state in which service industries are prominent. This evolutionary development was especially apparent in Western nations in the second half of the twentieth century.

The evolution of economic structures affects the evolution of societies more generally. In nineteenth-century Britain the development of industry brought employment opportunities in factories and movement of population to urban centres. The social dynamic of urban centres – with people located close together, getting in each other's way, but also offering great scope for social support-bargaining – radically changed society and the political system through which it was governed.[7]

The pragmatic element in 'national accounts' includes the sense of national confines to an economy. Economies and economic change are conceived in terms of national groups and national territories. Each group and territory comes under the jurisdiction of its own political support-bargaining system. Economies are conceived as specific to formal support-bargaining systems. They are managed by national governments and the national accounts provide much of the basic information necessary to national economic management. The spatial dimension can be varied to cover regions of a nation. Different parts of a country may have different rates of growth. Population will normally move to areas where the economy is growing and offering opportunities for employment. The preparation of regional expenditure accounts is complicated by the difficulties of identifying imports and exports. National accounts have a spatial dimension that is notably lacking in the neoclassical microeconomic model.

Besides the territorial boundary, the national income concept is also bounded by the neoclassical concept of scarce resources. The factors of production are conceived as being in scarce supply at any time and augmentable only within limits and within time constraints. The size of GDP is limited by the availability of the factors of production. The growth of GDP depends on increases in the available factors of production and on productivity improvements.

The territorial boundaries involved in national accounts are explicitly those bounding the support-bargaining system through which the money-bargaining system is regulated. Formal support-bargaining systems subdivide the territory over which the support-bargaining system is operative into spatial bargaining sets or constituencies. Formal support-bargaining systems also determine those entitled to participate in the formal support-bargaining system. The agents of formal support-bargaining systems – those entitled to vote – are largely also the agents of the money-bargaining systems that come under the jurisdiction of the support-bargaining systems. The theory of money-bargaining understands people as agents of the money-bargaining system, rather than as the 'labour' resource, or factor of production, of neoclassical theory.[8] Some of these agents derive all or part of their incomes from ownership of land and provision of capital, the other neoclassical factors of production. Income accrues to people, the agents of the system, rather than to factors of production. Their numbers constitute a limit on the size of the money-bargaining system.

The use of the term 'resources' for factors of production in neoclassical economics led to confusion over the status of 'natural' resources. The resource 'land' was originally conceived as covering land proper and all the natural resources that were available on land and in the sea. But as economics became increasingly concerned with mathematical formulations, it became unacceptable, even to a self-indulgent theory group, that 'land' should be understood in so very broad a manner. 'Resources' for purposes of mathematical economics had to be precise and homogeneous. Natural resources were consequently excluded from the concept of land as a resource. No satisfactory alternative place was found for them in the model. In money-bargaining natural resources are taken up as required, subject to the viability of the company that takes them up on the terms at which they are available. In some cases ownership of the resources will mean that payments must be made to the owners, but in other cases natural resources have no owner-agents and can be used without charge. While this presents no problem when the natural resources in question are, like wind and rain, eternally renewable, problems arise when natural resources such as fish and timber are taken freely. The failure of economists to recognise the damage arising from depletion of natural resources is in part a consequence of their ambiguous treatment in the neoclassical model.[9]

National accounts and companies

While national accounts are useful in tracking movements in aggregate incomes, production and expenditures, they foster neglect of the significance of companies. As was seen in the previous chapter, neoclassical theory conceives companies as small and responsive automatically to prices. This concept has influenced the preparation of national accounts and the analysis derived from them. The USA has about 5.7 million firms and the UK about 4.9 million, so it might seem reasonable to expect the effects of individual firms to cancel out in the aggregates.[10] But in December 2004 Microsoft paid a dividend of US$33 billion, making up 6 per cent of the increase in Americans' personal disposable income for that year. *The Economist* remarks that:

> These kinds of firm-specific shocks are typically excluded from economists' models, which assume that individual businesses' ups and downs tend to cancel each other out. Yet to understand how things like trade and GDP evolve, tracking the biggest companies is essential.[11]

In Britain in 2014 Lloyds Bank announced that it was setting aside nearly £10 billion for compensation payments to people who were sold unsuitable payment protection insurance by the bank. This payment is also of sufficient size to have significant implications for macroeconomic performance.

The influence of large companies is even more marked in international trade than in changes in GDP. A study of trade balances of OECD countries by the Bank of Spain showed that trade flows are strongly concentrated. The top five Japanese companies account for 20 per cent of Japanese exports. Samsung alone accounted for 17 per cent of South Korean exports in 2011.[12] Nokia accounted for 20 per cent of exports from Finland between 1998 and 2007. It also accounted for 25 per cent of GDP growth.[13] In earlier times companies were even more prominent. It was seen in the previous chapter that the export of silver bullion by the East India Company to Asia in the seventeenth century had a major impact on the English economy.

The case for the importance of large companies was made more comprehensively by Alfred Chandler in his account of the development of US, British and German companies in the later nineteenth century through to the Depression of the 1930s. Chandler emphasises the importance of management as the force behind economic growth, rather than the 'invisible hand' of the market. He sees large companies as the foundation of modern economies, harnessing people and technology for the provision of goods and services across economies increasingly linked by transport and communications, and providing opportunities for smaller companies to thrive.[14] He implies that neoclassical theory has been detrimental to the proper understanding of economic processes by diverting attention away from the role of companies, particularly large companies. Far from being the drivers of economic success, the neoclassical perspective gives companies negative connotation:

> Economists, particularly those of the more traditional mainstream school, have not developed a theory of the evolution of the firm as a dynamic organization. For many of them, the modern industrial enterprise is little more than an extractor of monopolistic or oligopolistic rents ... But in the history just told the modern industrial enterprise played a central role in creating the most technologically advanced, fastest growing industries of their day ... Therefore the enterprises whose collective histories have been reviewed here provided an underlying dynamic in the development of modern industrial capitalism.[15]

The largest money-bargaining agencies have important impacts on their economies that are easily neglected in conventional economic analysis. Relatively large companies can have significant impact on their local economies. The more countries trade internationally, the more they are impacted by the operations of large companies. Money-bargaining focuses attention on companies, while neoclassical theory focuses attention on aggregates, because neoclassical 'markets' assume many small companies. In terms of money-bargaining theory, all neoclassical 'companies' have the weakest possible bargaining positions. This blind spot in neoclassical theory for the significance of companies, particularly large companies, dates back to Adam Smith's understanding of small-scale 'masters' and 'master-manufacturers' as the operative agents of economies. As will be seen in Chapter 8, it has caused neoclassical theorists to produce a particularly distorted account of international trade.

It is not only important analytical elements that are lost through the neglect of companies in macroeconomic analysis. The whole character of the process of economic change is lost. William Nordhaus and James Tobin commented in 1973 on neoclassical growth theory:

> The steady equilibrium growth of modern neoclassical theory is, it must be acknowledged, a routine process of replication. It is a dull story compared to the convulsive structural, technological, and social changes described by the historically oriented scholars of development mentioned above. The theory conceals, either in aggregation or in the abstract generality of multi-sector models, all the drama of the events –the rise and fall of products, technologies, and industries, and the accompanying transformations of the spatial and

occupational distribution of the population. Many economists agree with the broad outlines of Schumpeter's vision of capitalist development, which is a far cry from growth models made nowadays in either Cambridge, Massachusetts, or Cambridge, England. But visions of that kind have yet to be transformed into a theory that can be applied in everyday analytic and empirical work.[16]

As will be seen in Chapter 5, the idea of money-bargaining gives companies a prominent role in the evolution of economies. In conjunction with support-bargaining, it may also offer vision equal to actual events.

Money-bargaining and the social accounting matrix

Along with the more familiar national accounts, Richard Stone and Alan Brown developed a matrix of monetary inputs and outputs relating to the different agencies of the economic system – households, companies, government and the 'rest of the world'.[17] While the focus of standard national accounts is on final demand and value added, Stone and Brown's 'social accounting matrix' (SAM) shows the expenditures on intermediate goods and services, and the involvement of households with government and companies. A SAM contains much information about the internal workings of an economy; the penalty is that it is more difficult to follow and cumbersome in use. The data requirements to construct a SAM are very substantial. Data is seldom so accurate as to produce the necessary balance of row and column totals. Adjustments have to be made. These are sometimes so substantial as to call into question the overall reliability of the data. They are invariably more substantial than those which balance income, expenditure and output measures of GDP. SAMs normally display data relating to a single year over several pages, offering a static overview of an economy. Year-to-year changes are more difficult to read than year-to-year changes in GDP. SAMs represent better than standard national accounts the idea in money-bargaining of agents engaged in a network of transactions, while standard national accounts reflect more the neoclassical concept of resource allocation. Because of their emphasis on money flows, measurement of money-bargaining would imply greater prominence for SAMs, though their complexity and data requirements are impediments.

Improvement of national income accounts

There have been numerous proposals for the improvement of national accounts. The prominence of 'GDP' has given it importance over and above its importance as a component of national accounts used by specialists for monitoring of economic performance. In February 2008, on the initiative of Nicholas Sarkozy, President of France, a 'Commission on the Measurement of Economic Performance and Social Progress' was established under the chairmanship of Joseph Stiglitz, with Amartya Sen as adviser to the chairman, to consider the weaknesses of GDP as an indicator of economic performance and social progress and to consider what remedies might be required.[18]

The Report of the Commission is prominently concerned with the limitations of GDP as a measure of the well-being of nations. One theme of the report is 'that the time is ripe for our measurement system to *shift emphasis from measuring economic production to measuring people's well-being*'.[19] Various recommendations are made to achieve this, relating, for example, to non-paid household work, quality of life, income distribution and the requirement for sustainability. The concept of resource allocation that underpins the accounts makes it appropriate to consider all activity, whether specifically paid for with money or undertaken without monetary payment. In developing countries a large amount of food is still produced on a subsistence basis. Estimates of the monetary value of these activities are difficult and potentially involve large errors and uncertainties in the accounts – adding to those already present.

Much of the pressure for modification and supplementation of the accounts comes from concerns of mainly left-wing interest groups that the prominence of GDP measures in public reporting gives too much emphasis to the economic side of life, at the expense of proper attention to the social and humanitarian side. It is an aspect of the fundamental tension between individual and group which is the basis of support-bargaining. Group interests are seeking to give GDP a more social content and hence make it less a measure that promotes material production as the way to the 'good life'. The recognition of GDP as a measure of something important has led to demands for the incorporation of elements in it that people other than economists see as important.

The idea of support-bargaining and money-bargaining makes it clear that there is a second and generally more important bargaining system operative besides the exchanges that involve money. With this understanding, GDP necessarily becomes a measure of a particular facet of human well-being. The benefits and costs identified through support-bargaining do not need to be assigned money values and loaded into accounts tracking the performance of the money-bargaining system. GDP can be confined almost entirely to transactions that specifically involve money payments from the budgets of money-bargaining agents. It is likely to be more readily comprehensible in that form, especially if the private and public sectors are more prominently distinguished.

Some of the pressure for changes to GDP may arise from popular misunderstanding of the nature of GDP. Comment seems sometimes to assume that GDP covers only private exchange, and is consequently a matter of purely 'capitalist' endeavour. This misunderstanding may be prompted in part by impressions derived from the neoclassical model that economists are only concerned with private exchange. GDP is, of course, concerned with a great range of communal expenditures, on, for example, defence, public health, educational services, police and environmental services. The public sector accounts for about 20 per cent of output in many OECD countries.[20] Furthermore, much private consumption expenditure derives from government provision to private individuals and households in the form of pensions and other welfare payments.

The Commission takes up the idea of William Nordhaus and James Tobin regarding the 'defensive' nature of a substantial part of GDP or, as Nordhaus and Tobin have it, 'instrumental expenditures'.[21] Governments have to spend on prisons and crime prevention, not so much to enhance the well-being of their people as to protect them from harm. People have to spend money on commuting to work, which is not of immediate benefit, but is rather a cost necessarily incurred in getting to where they can earn a living. Since these are not expenditures that contribute to human well-being, and on the assumption that GDP is intended as a measure of improvements in well-being, it would be logical to remove these and similar expenditures from GDP. In terms of money-bargaining, however, all requirements are situation-related. GDP is devoted to meeting the needs that arise from current situations. Situations evolve through these expenditures. The support-bargaining system will define situations, and the agents of the bargaining system will take steps to improve adverse situations. The support-bargaining system will, for example, determine when there is an enhanced threat from terrorists, and government will undertake the necessary expenditures to combat the threat. 'Well-being' involves 'response to situations', rather than a simple sense of pleasurable acquisition. This means, of course, that there will always be potential for sustained growth in GDP because there will always be situations to respond to. The perception that GDP growth is 'unsustainable' means that GDP growth can be sustained by combating those elements that threaten to stall it. Environmental damage is just one of the situations identified through the support-bargaining system that has to be remedied through expenditures that will contribute to growth in GDP. The more the accounts are diluted with estimates of values relating to concepts deriving from support-bargaining the less useful the accounts will be for monitoring changes in the performance of a money-bargaining system and the sooner will accounts appear dated as evolutionary changes take place in both support-bargaining and money-bargaining. Confining the accounts as strictly as possible to monetary transactions would eliminate much ambiguity, potentially make them more accurate, and might also reduce the costs of preparing them.

The understanding of GDP as a 'response to situations' implies that the more fundamental measurement issue is how far situations have been improved. As regards private agents, their expenditures will indicate their expectations of improvements to their situations. Trial and error will, to a large extent, inform them of where expenditures are best directed to improve their situations. Even so, there will be disappointments.

As regards the public sector, improvements to situation may be more difficult to identify, both because of the nature of the situations and because of the absence of payments for particular services provided by the public sector. The long-standing and almost universal situation of nation states is the threat of attack from other nation states, or combinations of them. Most nations spend large sums on armed forces to deter such threats. If defence expenditure deters invasions, it clearly improves the national situation, but measurement of the improvement is difficult, if not impossible. The sort of trial and error that can be applied in the private purchase of, say, groceries, entails high risk in the context of defence. The absence of certain knowledge of outcomes in default of the expenditures undertaken means that measures of improvements in situation are often nigh impossible. The only indicator of achievement in the public sector may be the expenditure in GDP, but it is essentially a measure of input rather than improvement. Economies evolve through these assessments of situation and corresponding expenditures.

In some cases, expenditures made to improve one identified situation can inadvertently create new situations that are seen to require remedial action. Overconsumption of alcohol by individuals can create addictions, giving rise to crime. Treatments are necessary to deal with the new situation. Release of CO_2 from industrial plants and vehicles seems to have affected the upper atmosphere and brought about increases in global temperatures. Extensive regulation and expenditure have been introduced to remedy the situation. Depletion of natural resources from industrial usage has given rise to protective legislation and expenditures aimed at sustaining the natural environment. These sequences imply an intricate and unpredictable evolutionary process.

The importance of situation as determinant of interests and expenditures is readily apparent in the different expenditures that arise in different climates. People in high latitudes spend large sums of money protecting themselves against cold weather. People in lower latitudes have built-in warmth. Adjustments for defensive or 'instrumental' expenditures, as suggested by Nordhaus and Tobin, would necessarily involve deducting all expenditures on heating, insulation of buildings and warm clothing from the GDPs of countries in the high latitudes. If warmth is regarded as a positive benefit, an estimate might be added to the GDPs of countries in the lower latitudes to represent the value they receive from their climatic conditions. Otherwise, it is necessary to recognise that different situations generate different expenditures. Different nations have different situations, and their expenditures will not be straightforwardly comparable.

The Stiglitz Commission presents its report as 'opening a discussion rather than closing it'.[22] The issues remain very substantially those covered in Nordhaus and Tobin's 1973 article. It seems possible the debate is maintained as a better option than the implementation of proposals that people are reluctant to pronounce unhelpful. The comment in the quotation at note 16, by Nordhaus and Tobin, that visions of a more expansive kind 'have yet to be transformed into a theory that can be applied in everyday analytic and empirical work' makes clear that the first priority is to establish sound theory, which can then be used with confidence as the basis of a measurement system.

Microeconomics and macroeconomics

It was noted in the second paragraph of this chapter that a first strand of macroeconomic research has been strongly oriented towards the identification of the macroeconomic equilibrium that should emerge through the functioning of neoclassical markets. While it has been seen that the second strand of macroeconomic research, being of a more pragmatic type, is not too much concerned by its divergence from neoclassical theory, the divergence of the first strand is a matter of considerable embarrassment to neoclassical macroeconomists.

Macroeconomic research on the basis of neoclassical microeconomic theory centres around 'General Equilibrium Theory' (GET) – the analysis of the process by which different sectors of an economy come into equilibrium. Abu Turab Rizvi's study of the microeconomic foundations of GET suggests that the foundations are insecure:

> This paper examines the status of the microfoundations project in general equilibrium theory. The basic conclusion derived is that one can say that there is no strict microfoundations approach to macro-level phenomena based on general equilibrium theory of the Walrasian Arrow–Debreu–McKenzie type.[23]

Efforts to link microeconomics and macroeconomics have failed. Later, Rizvi summarises the observations of other economists on the disparity between neoclassical microeconomics and macroeconomics:

> The main impetus to the very recent efforts to provide microfoundations for macroeconomics stems from several developments of the 1960s onwards concerning problems with the neoclassical synthesis and its associated econometrics, and these are very well known: Clower's (1965) observation that the textbook consumption function was inconsistent with GET; Arrow's (1967) statement that it was a 'major scandal' that standard microeconomics was not yet compatible with macroeconomic phenomena such as unemployment; and Lucas and Sargent's (1979) critique of the neoclassical synthesis as being 'fundamentally flawed' since it was without adequate microfoundations (Howitt, 1987). Thus there came to be a wide agreement with Drazen's (1980, p. 293) statement that '[e]xplanations of macroeconomic phenomena will be complete only when such explanations are consistent with microeconomic choice theoretic behaviour and can be phrased in the language of general equilibrium theory'.[24]

Richard Nelson and Stanley Winter, in their study of economic evolution, argue that the disparity between macroeconomic and microeconomic theory arises in large part because of the incapacity of neoclassical theory to deal satisfactorily with technological change. Neoclassical theory 'stands as an obstacle in thinking about microeconomic phenomena and macroeconomic phenomena within the same intellectual frame'.[25] Understanding of technology would certainly rank among the major disparities between micro- and macroeconomic theory. Of equal, or perhaps even greater, importance is one of the least remarked disparities: neoclassical microeconomic theory cannot accommodate spatial issues, whereas macroeconomics, as noted above, necessarily takes account of the division of the world into national territories, of the spatial distribution of economic activity within nations and the substantial resources allocated to transport of goods within and between nation states.

A further major disparity arises with regard to the agents involved at micro- and macro-levels. The neoclassical model is concerned purely with private individuals. Macroeconomics necessarily has to take account of the very large role of governments in economic systems. Agencies whose primary concern is political support-bargaining play a major role in macroeconomic systems.

Economists have not been able to reconcile neoclassical microeconomics with macroeconomics, even to their own satisfaction. The fact is, as Rizvi notes, macroeconomics emerged as a separate study from microeconomics, and had to be reconciled subsequently with an existing microeconomics.[26] An alternative macroeconomic theory was developed for practical purposes, tied closely to statistical measures of economic performance.

Rizvi gives the incompatibility of micro- and macroeconomics a broader social setting of particular relevance to the present context. He quotes John Stuart Mill's comment that, 'Human beings in society have no properties but those which are derived from, and may be resolved into, the laws of the nature of the individual man.'[27] The group is merely the sum of its individual members. Rizvi notes that John Hicks, in his well-known work *Value and Capital*, treats the relationship between individual and group in the same way: 'that the behaviour of a group of individuals, or a group of firms, obeys the same laws as the behaviour of a single unit'.[28] The suggestion in Rizvi's article, drawing on the work of several writers, is that there may be a fundamental incompatibility of macroeconomic theory and neoclassical microeconomic theory arising from the differences in individual behaviour as conceived in neoclassical theory and the behaviour of people as members of large social groups. It is possible that 'systematic macro-phenomena have some intrinsic macro-component, contrary to the purely "compositive" view of John Stuart Mill'.[29] The idea of support-bargaining shows how individual opinion sometimes fuses into and sometimes conflicts with the opinions of social groups. Economic theorists have no understanding of the dynamic of support-bargaining. The preferences of all individuals will be influenced by their group associations, as they seek to gain group support. The pursuit of support is intertwined with the pursuit of money and material advantage. Such being the case, a system based on purely individual preferences cannot be aggregated to describe a system operative in society as a whole. The consequences of this include the presence of government as an 'intrinsic macro-component' among 'macro-phenomena'.

Micro-, macro- and Depression in the 1930s

The assumption that the tendency towards equilibrium at microeconomic level implies a macroeconomic tendency towards equilibrium lay behind the paralysis of economic theory in the Depression of the 1930s. Economic theory indicated that depression should not happen, since 'the market' would redress imbalances automatically. Yet all too clearly, unemployment was affecting large numbers of people around the world. Several economists, along with many non-economists, in Europe and North America, identified a deficiency of demand in the economy as the root of the problem, and proposed government expenditure as the remedy. Laughlin Currie, in the USA, worked in the mid-1930s on the idea that it was necessary for governments to 'prime the pump' through deficit spending to stimulate private spending.[30]

The particular exposition that assembled the greatest support in the intellectual support-bargaining of the time was that of John Maynard Keynes in his *General Theory of Employment, Interest and Money*. Backhouse asks, given that governments were already spending on infrastructure programmes, and recovery was apparent, why the *General Theory* had the impact it did. He continues, 'The conventional answer is that economists had the policies but not the theory to back up those policies; that there was an element of schizophrenia amongst economists, whose theoretical system ruled out the possibility of unemployment.'[31] Backhouse acknowledges that the conventional answer was an oversimplification, but sees it as not entirely devoid of truth. Keynes's theory provided a theoretical explanation, easily presented in mathematical terms, to account for lack of macroeconomic equilibrium corresponding to microeconomic equilibrium. Because of the special considerations relating to savings, investment and income levels, the equilibrating mechanism of microeconomics was not to be expected in a macroeconomic context. Hence the economy had got out of equilibrium, and government expenditure was necessary to restore it. Keynes saved economic face by providing a technical argument as to why savings might equate to investment at levels of economic output that did not sustain full employment. A part of the neoclassical system was sacrificed to save the whole. So the *General Theory* had the impact it did because it restored the confidence of the theory group, gave it a technical framework of endless mathematical interest and gave the green light to governments to do what they had in any case determined to do, and were in some cases doing. The technicalities of the *General Theory* are contested in Chapter 7.

Keynes seemed to reconcile neoclassical microeconomic theory with macroeconomic theory, albeit at some cost to the purity of the microeconomic system. He gave a new lease of life to the application of conventional market theory to trade in goods and non-financial services. It made it possible to continue ignoring the bigger deficiencies of neoclassical microeconomic theory – it was not compatible with macroeconomic theory, or with the observable behaviour of those engaged in ordinary economic activity. Backhouse remarks, 'One of the main problems with the state of macroeconomics around 1980 was that the new classical macroeconomics appeared to be based on rigorous microeconomic foundations, but its models were implausible, whilst Keynesian macroeconomics had no satisfactory microeconomic foundations.'[32] The concept of national income and the national accounts have provided a good foundation for the formulation of economic policy, but the most advanced macroeconomic theory, the many man-years of research centred on GET, have produced little of value because it assumes the macroeconomy behaves in accordance with microeconomic principles.

Micro-, macro- and the Harrod–Domar model

The *General Theory* focused on the relationship between savings, investment and incomes as the critical element in the stabilisation of the system at full employment. The relationship was the basis of the 'Harrod–Domar' model of economic growth. Originating in 1939 with a model by Roy Harrod, it was developed in 1946 by Evsey Domar, and became staple fare of economic development theory for many decades. Because it assumed markets were perfectly competitive, as in neoclassical microeconomic theory, it was known as 'neoclassical' growth theory.[33] The model demonstrated that growth depended on the propensity to save and the 'incremental capital–output ratio' – the ratio of additional capital expenditure to the output it generated. The implication was that policy should be directed towards increasing savings and raising the incremental capital–output ratio.

The model chiefly demonstrates the surreal world in which many economists were content to operate. It is difficult to imagine the chief executive of a company welcoming advice from his accountant to the effect that all he had to do to ensure the growth of his firm was to increase his investment and the output from it. Backhouse comments:

> The Harrod–Domar model was the starting point for an enormous literature on the theory of economic growth. In this literature theoretical issues were without question dominant. Beyond the concern to explain what came to be called certain 'stylized facts' about long-run growth ... there was only limited concern with facts about the real world.[34]

The Harrod–Domar model reflects at macroeconomic level the faith of neoclassical economists at the microeconomic level in the infallibility of mathematical formulations and their relevance in the real world. That sort of thinking did not elevate the Harrod–Domar model alone. It gave rise to a general emphasis on model building and mathematical formulations that arguably did little to advance the well-being of developing countries. It distracted from a host of far more important issues relating, for example, to education, infrastructure, credit provision and the format of companies. Money-bargaining directs attention to the issues that are really important for the enhancement of material well-being. Backhouse concludes his chapter on 'Growth and Development' with the reflection that,

> Of particular importance has been a certain tension between formal models of the process of economic growth and much wider, and more informal, discussions of the factors causing economic growth. The problem is that formal models can show only the 'mechanics' of growth: the relationship between inputs and outputs; between saving, investment and the growth of output. The determinants of productivity (and hence the 'causes' of growth) are left unanalysed by such formal models.[35]

Neoclassical microeconomic theory remains detached from macroeconomic theory. Attempts to bring them together in GET and in growth models such as the

Harrod–Domar model have not advanced the understanding of either. Macroeconomics, centred on the development and use of national accounts, has been remarkably fruitful in providing a focus for the formulation of economic policy and the monitoring of economic performance. But it has been useful despite rather than because of its neoclassical microeconomic connections.

The Arrow–Debreu theory

That is perhaps most particularly true in relation to the most sophisticated theoretical link established by neoclassical theorists between microeconomics and macroeconomics, the Arrow–Debreu theory, mentioned by Rizvi above, in association with the contribution of L. W. McKenzie.[36] Its sophistication makes it the most inaccessible. It is known *of* by virtually all economists because it is held to prove that most attractive claim of neoclassical theory, that the market allocates resources with Pareto optimality – so that no redistribution of goods or productive resources can improve the position of one individual without making at least one other individual worse off.[37] John Geanakoplos writes of the Arrow–Debreu model:

> The Arrow–Debreu model of general equilibrium is relentlessly neoclassical; in fact it has become the paradigm of the neoclassical approach. This stems in part from its individualistic hypothesis, and its celebrated conclusions about the potential efficacy of unencumbered markets.[38]

While the theory is accepted by neoclassical economists as an essential part of the neoclassical concept, very few are in a position to check it thoroughly, since to do so requires familiarity with some arcane mathematical techniques: mathematical convexity theory (separating hyperplane theorem), fixed point theory and differential topology theory.[39] According to Geanakoplos the first two techniques are 'the most important mathematical devices in mathematical economics'.[40] But that is perhaps a reflection of the rarefied environment in which such work is carried on. Geanakoplos was Director of the Cowles Foundation for Research in Economics at Yale University, where Arrow and Debreu worked on their theory, when he wrote the article referenced here. Judging by the content of the leading economics journals, calculus is at least the more common technique. It is doubtful whether knowledge of the mathematical techniques relevant to the Arrow–Debreu model is widely distributed across the neoclassical theory group. It is more the preserve of a small specialist sub-group. Those equipped to evaluate the model have a professional interest in sustaining it, so their evaluations will tend to be supportive of it.

The Arrow–Debreu theory raises, in acute form, questions regarding the use of mathematics in economics, for it is in this theory that mathematical formulations are given the fullest rein. Mathematics is conceived as defining the reality more than the reality determining the necessary mathematics. In physics maths keeps station alongside empirical evidence. Any disparities of mathematical formulations or implications with empirical evidence have to be reconciled. It may be that the empirical observations have been wrongly recorded or misunderstood, in which case the empirical evidence is reassessed and reconsidered in the light of the mathematics. If the empirical evidence is unassailable, then the mathematics has to be reconsidered. But in mathematical economics there is a sense of 'mathematical infallibility'. If the real world does not accord with the mathematics, then so much the worse for the real world. Geanakoplos remarks, 'the model of Arrow–Debreu, with its idealization of a separate market for each Arrow–Debreu commodity, all simultaneously meeting, is the benchmark against which the real economy can be measured'.[41] The real economy may perform well or badly against the theory, but it is the theory that sets the standard of what is. The illusion is in the human understanding of reality.

While very few can check the mathematics of the Arrow–Debreu theory, it can still be seen that it is not well conceived to do what it claims to do. It does not give a realistic account of economic exchange. The distance between the mathematics and the reality, at least the reality of common theory, becomes alarmingly apparent in a list of some of the assumptions and positions of the Arrow–Debreu theory, taken from the article by Geanakoplos (figures in brackets are page numbers):

- Each commodity has an objective, quantifiable and universally agreed upon description (116). There is no scope for product innovation.
- The transactions that allocate resources take place at one moment in time (116). 'In the Arrow–Debreu model, all trade takes place at the beginning of time. If markets were reopened at later dates for the same Arrow–Debreu commodities, then no additional trade would take place anyway' (122). At least some commodities exist at the opening of the instantaneous trading (122).
- Arrow–Debreu commodities – that is, the commodities to which the model applies – have such precise descriptions that further refinements cannot yield imaginable allocations that increase the satisfaction of agents in the economy (116). At the same time, according to Geanakoplos, it is acknowledged that there is ambiguity over the descriptions – for example, whether apples of different sizes are different commodities (116).
- Descriptions of Arrow–Debreu commodities include their location and temporal status (116). The incorporation of location in commodity definition makes it possible to deal with transport costs as part of the single transaction (116).
- The descriptions of Arrow–Debreu commodities depend also on the state of nature – what is happening elsewhere. Because of this, the general equilibrium theory of the supply and demand of commodities at one moment in time can incorporate the analysis of the optimal allocation of risk (116). Because of this, there is no market for insurance in the Arrow–Debreu model (121).
- However, no agent takes into account what other agents know – for example, about the state of nature (122).
- Bankruptcy is not allowed in an Arrow–Debreu equilibrium (121).

- Consumers make choices between entire consumption plans, not between individual commodities. 'A single commodity has significance to the consumer only in relation to the other commodities he has consumed, or plans to consume' (117).
- Consumer preferences, including preferences over savings, do not change according to the role he plays in the production process – that is, whether he is a capitalist or a landowner (117).
- Consumer preferences do not depend on the preferences of other consumers, or the supply of commodities (117).
- Every agent spends all his income (the nonsatiation hypothesis) (117, 120).
- Commodities are infinitely divisible (the convexity hypothesis). 'When commodities are distinguished very finely according to dates, so that they must be thought of as flows, then the convexity hypothesis is untenable' (117).
- There are no increasing returns to scale, or gains from specialisation (118, 121). '[W]hen there are significant increasing returns to scale, the model of competitive equilibrium that we are about to examine is simply not applicable (118) ... increasing returns to scale over a broad range is definitely incompatible with equilibrium' (121).
- Every individual is endowed with a share of ownership in every firm (117).
- Prices are strictly relative prices, of one commodity to another. Nevertheless, a price is specified for each commodity, for mathematical convenience (118). Money is not necessary to the model, though it can be conceived as incorporated in the model (122).
- Every agent knows all prices. '[A]t each date each agent is capable of forecasting perfectly all future prices until the end of time' (119). There is no asymmetric information (122).

The very tight definitions of Arrow–Debreu commodities mean that 'it is very rare to find a market for a pure Arrow–Debreu commodity',[42] since there are unlikely to be many buyers and sellers. The real world is seen as defective in that it cannot accommodate Arrow–Debreu commodities:

> More commonly, many groups of Arrow–Debreu commodities are traded together, in unbreakable bundles, at many moments in time, in 'second best' transactions. Nevertheless, this understanding of the limitations of real world markets, based on the concept of the Arrow–Debreu commodity, is one of the most powerful analytical tools of systematic accounting available to the general equilibrium theorist.[43]

The real world is 'second best' to the model. Real world markets are regarded as limited because they do not deal in the hypothetical commodities of the theory. In the Arrow–Debreu theory, the concept of a 'commodity' is stripped down to fit the theory. In money-bargaining commodities are seen as having many features designed to fit them to the bargaining sets of consumers. Potential buyers 'strip down' the commodities to those features which fit their situations. The commodities with features that fit their situations form their bargaining sets. A consumer bargaining set may comprise just one supplier of a commodity with the required features, so that, as with the stripped down Arrow–Debreu commodity, there is no 'market' in the neoclassical sense of many buyers and many sellers.[44] Arrow–Debreu creates a 'commodity' that fits the mathematical requirements, whereas money-bargaining describes the reality of market choice. It is impossible to trade Arrow–Debreu commodities in real-world circumstances. Through the looking glass, things look different – Lewis Carroll was a mathematician.

Arrow–Debreu incorporates a location and time in all commodity definitions. In money-bargaining location and time are features associated with products. The Arrow–Debreu conception represents, however, a rejection of the common notion of time. All transactions in the Arrow–Debreu model are instantaneous, so temporal position in the commodity definition is merely a matter of mathematical notation. The commodities are not given a time dimension because transactions do not take place in dimensional time. This time compression applies also to incomes: 'The income that could be obtained from the sale of an endowed commodity, dated from the last period, is available already in the first period.'[45] The absence of a time dimension means that budgeting, savings, credit and other financial services have no place in an Arrow–Debreu world.

Similarly, the 'locational' designation attaching to Arrow–Debreu commodities is mathematical artifice. It involves none of the characteristics associated with real-world locations. Ships in the real world do not move instantaneously from place to place, and on to other places. Trade takes place over distances and over time, and Arrow–Debreu commodities, in spite of their mathematical attributes, have no place in these dimensions. The theory adopts notions of location and time that can be accommodated with the mathematical techniques employed.

The Arrow–Debreu theory assumes a convexity hypothesis that rules out increasing returns to scale. This is acknowledged to be 'The empirically most vulnerable assumption to the Arrow–Debreu model.'[46] As was seen in Chapter 2, the viability condition for a company in money-bargaining (sales × price > production × unit cost) links scale of production to unit cost as something often fundamental to corporate viability. Geanakoplos excuses the assumption by reference to the 'traditionally important cases of decreasing and constant returns to scale in production'.[47] The 'tradition' is the neoclassical assumption of the 'perfect market'. Even mathematical economists feel justified in appealing to the traditions of their forebears in extenuation of their current odd behaviour. The Arrow–Debreu model proves the existence of a Pareto equilibrium when there are no economies of scale. Since it shows also that a Pareto equilibrium is incompatible with increasing returns to scale, it proves that no Pareto equilibrium can be achieved in the real world. Far from demonstrating the existence of Pareto equilibrium, Arrow–Debreu proves that no such equilibrium is possible. Geanakoplos rates the exclusion of increasing returns to scale as the empirically most vulnerable assumption of the Arrow–Debreu model, but the assumption that all transactions take place in an instant must be close behind.

The Arrow–Debreu model is conceived as a process of barter. It does not involve the use of money. On money:

> all the reasons for its real life existence: transactions demand, precautionary demand, store of value, unit of account, etc. are already taken care of in the Arrow–Debreu model ... There is no point in making the role of money explicit in the Arrow–Debreu model, since it has no effect on the real allocations.[48]

The definitions of commodities and the concepts of prices and transactions in the Arrow–Debreu model subsume the functions of money. Yet, as was seen in the previous chapter, the character of money and factors relating to its supply have been of great importance in the promotion of economic expansion and in the destabilisation of economies. Money accommodates the time disparities between revenues and expenditures. Just as there is no role for budgeting, savings, credit and other financial services in a model without a time dimension, there is no role for money. The lack of money in the neoclassical economic model undoubtedly has a bearing on the emergence of the global financial crisis in 2007. It is hard to see enlightenment in evasion of an important aspect of economic exchange.

The Arrow–Debreu model wholly excludes any possibility of the economic evolution that is the subject of this book. Geanakoplos remarks:

> Similarly when the world has a definite beginning, so that the first market transaction takes place after the ownership of all resources and techniques of production, and the preferences of all individuals have been determined, one cannot study the evolution of the social norms of consumption in terms of the historical development of the relations of production.[49]

Arrow–Debreu, in some ways, takes precisely the opposite directions to the theory of money-bargaining in that it dispenses with money, whereas money is central to money-bargaining. It contracts transactions to a single instant, whereas money-bargaining understands an endless process of evolution. It requires an objective view of commodities, and rolls into the concept of objective commodities the minutest detail of them, including notions of spatial and temporal characteristics, though they are then exchanged in an instant that would seem to belie their spatial and temporal qualities. In money-bargaining, products have features that are discernible to potential buyers as fitting to their situation. The features include the locations and times of their availability. Perception is crucial to the determination of what is bought and sold. The purpose of the Arrow–Debreu theory group is to prove that an equilibrium exists in macroeconomic transactions. It claims to achieve its purpose, though since it is achieved at the expense of realistic representation of the transactions process, it might be regarded as conclusively failing in its purpose. The theory of money-bargaining offers an explanation of the observable process of monetary exchange.

For most people the assumptions of the Arrow–Debreu model, as summarised above, will be enough to demonstrate conclusively that it is not a model with any concern for the everyday world of work, shopping and trade. Backhouse remarks, 'No one who understands the Arrow–Debreu model has ever claimed that it describes any actual economy.'[50] But perhaps because there are very few who understand the Arrow–Debreu model, there are many who think it is concerned with an actual economy. Even Geanakoplos, who is certainly among the few, frets over its limitations. As was seen above, he is concerned that the exclusion of increasing returns to scale is 'empirically most vulnerable'. He writes further, 'The major crisis of labour market clearing in the 1930s, and again recently, argues strongly that there are limits to the applicability of equilibrium analysis.'[51] Such statements clearly indicate disappointment that a theory intended to explain an actual economy does not do so. Within the theory group, it has not been uncommon to treat the Arrow–Debreu model as reflecting the behaviour of actual economies.

While Backhouse's premise is doubtful, his question, immediately following the above quotation, is apt: 'so why do economists pay any attention to it?' In the first edition of *Economists and the Economy*, published in 1988, he provides three answers: 1) because supply and demand theory is used to analyse many problems, and the Arrow–Debreu model shows equilibrium is possible, so the analysis is not vacuous; 2) it shows how stringent the conditions are for equilibrium to be optimal. In particular there must be a complete set of futures and insurance markets. It must be possible to buy any commodity for delivery any time in the future and insure against any eventuality. Backhouse notes that such markets do not exist, but nevertheless continues to, 3) the Arrow–Debreu model provides a framework for thinking about economic problems. By the 1993 edition he has realised that his reasons are not good reasons at all, and they are excised.[52] Offering such reasons implies that Arrow–Debreu has something to do with real economies. Economists may not claim specifically that the Arrow–Debreu model describes any actual economy, but they insistently cite it as evidence for the claimed resource allocation function that free markets are supposed to produce. It is claimed to give strict mathematical backing to the more accessible formulations of neoclassical theory. If Arrow–Debreu does not model actual economies, it is not possible to draw any conclusions from it about the behaviour of actual economies.

A theorist of intellectual support-bargaining might suggest reasons for the attention it has received relating to the assembly of support and the bargaining position of the theory group: 1) it has been effective in sustaining the claim that free markets produce optimal allocation of resources, even though this is contrary to its true import; 2) it purportedly demonstrates that free markets move to equilibrium, and hence justifies the pursuit of GET; 3) it provides scope for interesting mathematical speculation; 4) it promotes the idea of arcane but vital expertise in a small theory group, enhancing the bargaining position of the theory group in intellectual support-bargaining; 5) with the neoclassical theory group securely institutionalised, consent to Arrow–Debreu enhances prospects of advancement in institutions concerned with economic theory formation. The Arrow–Debreu model has assembled support among economists because it answers interests other than those regarding the truth about the functioning of human society.

There is a remarkable mixture in this kind of work of the clever and the myopic. The mathematical prowess is dazzling, but its premises are bizarre. Gérard Debreu was a mathematician before he was an economist. Some of his pronouncements suggest a degree of myopia with regard to the broader concerns of the social sciences.[53] In the neoclassical theory group mathematical prowess is accorded great esteem, so that the inclination is to affirm support for such work, particularly when it confirms central tenets of the group. The Arrow–Debreu theory became firmly institutionalised in universities. While it seems entirely divorced from the real world, the weight of support attaching to it has given it influence in the real world. Backhouse's reconsideration seems nevertheless to have been part of a broader reconsideration of its status.

The Arrow–Debreu theorem has, as noted above, been the basis of research on macroeconomic GET and the forging of links between microeconomics and macroeconomics. Understood as above, however, it separates microeconomics even more completely from the macroeconomic world of employment, companies, education, government deficits, trade cycles, export promotion, finance and currency fluctuations. The separation arises fundamentally because, as suggested above, neoclassical microeconomics was developed to fulfil mathematical ideals and interests, while macroeconomics, centred on national income accounts, was developed for the pragmatic purpose of monitoring economic change and formulating economic policies. Once a realistic theory of microeconomics is developed, formulated to take account of the observed functioning of economies, a seamless linkage between microeconomics and macroeconomics can be established. That is what Nordhaus and Tobin yearn for in the quotation at note 16.

Money-bargaining and macroeconomics

Money-bargaining is both a macroeconomic and a microeconomic theory. The macroeconomy is conceived as a network of monetary transactions, involving private agents, composite agents in the form of companies and agents concerned mainly with support-bargaining but engaged in money-bargaining in response to the requirements of support-bargaining. The microeconomics of money-bargaining includes the situation-related assessment of interests by all agents in the system, and the pursuit by companies of viable formats, described in the previous chapter. Existing macroeconomic theory is, as has been seen, ostensibly based on neoclassical economic theory, but is inconsistent with it. It is more consistent with the theory of money-bargaining. The national accounts which measure macroeconomic performance are largely compatible with the understanding of money-bargaining. Concepts change, but few significant changes of substance are necessary to adapt the accounts to the idea of money-bargaining.

Money-bargaining conceives individuals as the basic agents of money-bargaining systems. They control, with varying degrees of attention, their monetary transactions through budgets. The sums of their budgetary revenues constitute the macroeconomic aggregate of personal income, while their outlays on goods and services constitute consumers' expenditure. Individuals save part of their revenues, in various forms. A part of their revenue goes to government in taxation, which government expends through its budget on communal services.

In national accounts personal savings are treated as the residual after consumption. Keynes defines savings as the residual of income after consumption. In the theory of money-bargaining, however, savings are positive budgetary responses to situations. They are used to reconcile revenues with anticipated expenditures over time. The implications of this conceptual difference are considered in Chapter 7 in the context of Keynes's *General Theory*.

Individuals derive their incomes from employment, self-employment, rent, interest and dividends. Classification of the incomes to the sectors in which they are earned gives the output structure of the economy. Since the budget revenues of individual agents correspond to the 'factor incomes' of established accounts the change is more a matter of conception or classification than of content.

While individuals are the basic agents of money-bargaining systems, they are also engaged in support-bargaining. The major agents of money-bargaining systems are the specialist agencies of money-bargaining – companies. Companies generally develop the strongest money-bargaining positions. Companies finance capital investment from their own budget revenues, from the sale of shares and from borrowing. It is mainly companies which provide individuals with their budget revenues. It is also mainly companies that are the recipients of the expenditures of individuals on goods and services. Their capital requirements absorb, through share issues or borrowing, most of the savings set aside by individuals. The flows of money through company budgets end up in the budgets of private individuals. But companies constitute the central agents of money-bargaining and the driving force behind economies. Their pursuit of viability and, beyond that, profitability drives them to product development and the reduction of unit costs. As was seen earlier, large companies strongly influence the performance of whole economies. The evolution of economies, as will be seen in Chapter 5, is dictated to a considerable degree by the performance of leading companies. A SAM matrix shows the value of intermediate transactions as companies acquire inputs necessary to their format from other companies.

Among companies, financial services companies have a distinctive role as agents of money-bargaining systems. National accounts include 'financial accounts' which are essentially concerned with transactions involving financial services companies. These companies enable individuals and companies to reconcile time differences between the receipt of budgetary revenues and requirements for expenditure. An important part of this function is the provision of facilities for savings with certain time profiles and provision of credits for investment with different time profiles. Companies, as was seen in the previous chapter, must establish the facilities for a viable format before they start trading. In the case of a manufacturing format, a company must establish buildings and machinery that in operation will meet the viability requirement. Companies need significant sums of money before they start trading, or to expand their trading. Financial services companies enable them to raise the necessary finance, either by assisting with the issue of shares or by provision of loans.

Financial services are needed by all agents of a money-bargaining system. They consequently have central positions in money-bargaining networks. The security of the funds they hold is widely perceived as linked to the size of their assets, so that there is a strong tendency for financial services companies to grow very large in deposit liabilities and credit provision. Like other companies, financial services companies develop 'products', in the form of financial instruments, that accommodate the situations of potential investors. They mix returns, charges, risk, periods, derivations and conditionalities in a way which they anticipate will establish a place for the products in the bargaining sets of potential investors. The operations of financial services companies are normally regulated by a central bank, deriving its authority from government. In particular, banks must conform to regulations regarding the relationships between different types of assets and liabilities in their balance sheets. When the solvency of several large banks became questionable in the financial crisis beginning in 2007, it was found that the implications of their failure for whole economies was, in many cases, so great that it was necessary to provide public funds to sustain their operations. Some aspects of the financial crisis are considered in Chapter 7.

Role of government in money-bargaining

Governments, national and local, also function as agents of money-bargaining systems. Formal support-bargaining systems establish governments to advance communal interests. Part of this function requires that they engage in money-bargaining. Their earliest engagement was in providing communal defence, with an associated requirement for large sums of money and many military employees. Expansion of their role has expanded their budgets, so that they now raise large revenues through taxation and expend large sums on a variety of communal amenities and services. Their employment has increased accordingly, providing substantial revenues for the budgets of private agents.

Much of their expenditure relates to essential provision for the conduct of business by private companies. Substantial capital investments are made in transport infrastructure. Societies commonly require that their governments operate education systems – again a service essential to the functioning of a sophisticated money-bargaining system. But much government budgetary outlay consists of social welfare provision made in fulfilment of communal recognition that in certain circumstances people should be given financial support. This provision, including pensions, unemployment benefits and general benefit payments, constitutes revenues for the budgets of private individuals, enabling them to maintain expenditures on the maintenance of themselves and their families. As was seen earlier, a significant proportion of aggregate economic output, or value added, is attributable to governments. But even that understates their prominence. Direct expenditures by governments on goods and services, along with the welfare payments made to private individuals, take government budgetary outlays in aggregate to the equivalent of more than 40 per cent of total final expenditure in OECD countries.[54] A SAM matrix shows the flows of funds into and out of government budgets and to the budgets of households and companies. The evolution of government as part of the evolution of money-bargaining systems is described in Chapter 6.

Neoclassical theory, as mentioned above, is entirely concerned with transactions between private individuals. The involvement of governments is seen mainly as intrusive and unhelpful to the optimal allocation of resources. Part of the motivation behind the development of neoclassical theory seems to have been the desire to stop governments from intervening in business affairs, or at least to limit their intervention. The debate over the appropriate extent of government involvement in money-bargaining can be related to the conflict between individuals and the community that is fundamental to the idea of support-bargaining. Some seek support for the predominance of individuals, while others favour the ascendancy of the group. Neoclassical theorists have long been champions of the individualist cause.

While governments have a prominent role in money-bargaining, their primary role as support-bargaining agencies gives them distinctively different motivation and consequently a different role to that of other agents of money-bargaining. The inclination of governments is to assemble support by providing as much as possible in the way of services while minimising the loss of support that is likely to accompany the raising of taxes. Through this balancing of support, revenues and costs are linked in the public sector. It is, however, a balance achieved at a high level of aggregation. In a formal support-bargaining system, people are obliged to vote for overall programmes, not for the provision of individual services. People pay taxes, rather than choosing and paying for specific services. Governments do not charge people on the basis of their usage of each specific service. The absence of direct discretionary payments for specific services means no close link is established between the costs involved in provision of the service and the revenues received for it. Budget revenues are one big pot, rather than a series of returns for each specific service. Without direct and discretionary money payments for services, it is difficult to establish the degree to which any particular provision is valued. The lack of linkage between provision of specific government services and revenue returns means that governments have limited information about the valuation of their services and limited incentives to expand the money-bargaining system in accordance with valuations through service innovation, expansion of provision and improvements in productivity. Instead of valuations by monetary expenditures, governments have to judge their allocations of expenditure to different services in accordance with their assessments of the support voiced for the different services through the general communal debate. The nature of this communal debate is considered in Chapter 9.

Valuation by support is, on the one hand, necessarily imprecise and easily mistaken. Money payments, on the other hand, are good indicators of valuation.

The extent to which buyers choose products at the prices at which they are offered indicates the value attaching to the products in terms of their fit with the buyers' situations, including their budgetary situations and their valuations of other products. Strong sales indicate that a product is improving the situations of numerous buyers. Companies will respond by improving products with the features identified as attractive to buyers, expanding output and reducing unit costs so as to accommodate the budgetary situations of more potential buyers. It is the business of companies to identify what is valued in money terms and can be provided through a viable format.

In some circumstances governments opt to provide certain products or services for specific payments by users. In effect, they adopt company formats. When they do this, they normally accord themselves the strong bargaining positions of sole suppliers. Since they regard themselves as providing what is essentially a communal service, governed by accumulation of support, competition with private specialist money-bargaining agencies is inappropriate. People then have no choice but to buy such services from government and, consequently, government need have little concern for loss of revenues if service is poor. The format is viable because alternative sources of the products or services are eliminated. Government-owned companies have limited incentives to strengthen their formats through product and service innovation and reduction of unit costs. They are consequently likely to contribute less to the growth of an economy. Fears of loss of support may mean that government companies are reluctant to introduce new technologies or cost-cutting measures if they involve reductions in employment.

While governments and companies act under different motivations in money-bargaining, governments are nevertheless dependent on strong money-bargaining systems for their revenues. Successful government, in the sense of successful accumulation of support, depends in large measure on expenditures for communal purposes, implying the need for substantial and growing budgetary revenues. Governments consequently try to ensure that their engagement encourages the expansion of money-bargaining. Large expenditures are made on infrastructure, health and education, all important to the functioning of money-bargaining systems. Governments also have mostly come to recognise that companies are effective in money-bargaining and, unless the communal interest is of overwhelming importance, provision of goods and services is most effectively achieved when left to these specialist agencies, in competition with one another. Regulation of the private provision is generally sufficient to safeguard the communal interest. Their primary concern with the assembly of support can nevertheless cause governments to take measures that significantly impede the growth of money-bargaining.

This contrasting dynamic of public and private sectors is reflected in the accounting conventions used in the compilation of national accounts. Because governments do not get paid for the health, education and other services they provide, these services can only be valued in money terms by reference to the wages, salaries and other payments outlaid in providing them. The work of the public sector is valued in national accounts by reference to the value of inputs. Growth in the value of public sector output is then entirely the consequence of increased inputs. In contrast, the output of the private sector can be valued by what is paid for it. With an output measure, it is possible to identify increases in productivity. As has been seen, companies have strong incentives to increase productivity, which normally equates to reductions in unit costs. Growth in GDP is driven by increased engagement of agents, product and service innovation, and increases in productivity. Because changes in productivity and service innovation in the public sector cannot readily be measured in money terms, all the GDP growth arising from improvements in productivity and innovation has to come from the private sector.

The lack of the discretionary user payments for public sector output that permit identification of productivity improvements in the private sector does not mean there are no productivity improvements in the public sector. With many services it is possible to identify reductions in unit costs, such as expenditures per pupil in an education system, with the same quality of education, or costs per mile in road construction, with the same quality of road. These reductions in unit costs imply improvements in productivity. The report of the Stiglitz Commission notes that the valuation of government contributions to GDP are understated if there are productivity improvements and recommends increased attention to measurement of government outputs.[55] The implication is that GDP data might be adjusted in accordance with estimates of improvements in government productivity. However, if GDP measurement is confined to monetary transactions, as advocated above, the only measure of government output is the total of tax and other revenues that is made over to government in exchange for the services it provides.

The lack of immediate monetary productivity measures for the public sector and the estimation of public sector growth by reference to inputs constitute important reasons for distinguishing sharply between public and private sectors in the accounts of a money-bargaining system. While both public and private sectors are engaged in money-bargaining, and their engagements are closely interdependent, the predominant concern of the public sector with support-bargaining means that its money-bargaining is carried on with notably different incentives from those of private agents. Growth in private sector GDP has a notably different dynamic and different implications to growth in public sector GDP.

Attaining full employment

The assumption that neoclassical theory identified the underlying dynamic of a macroeconomy made it difficult to understand why economies did not reach equilibrium at full employment. As has been seen, in the early 1930s in particular, recession and high levels of unemployment were difficult to explain. The theory of money-bargaining implies no inevitable movement of an economy to equilibrium at full employment, or at any other level of employment. The process is evolutionary, moving from situation to situation. There are, nevertheless, elements of money-bargaining systems that suggest movement towards high levels of employment.

In their pursuit of profitable format, businessmen will develop products suited to the requirements of potential buyers. Products and services are continuously adapted to accord with the changing situations of potential buyers. Businessmen will also be seeking to fit their products more readily to the budgets of potential buyers by reducing unit costs so that they can reduce prices. Reducing unit costs may mean reducing levels of employment, but falling prices suggest increased sales, and increased sales imply increased employment. Experience, tough for many at certain periods, has established that product innovation, productivity increases and reductions in unit costs bring growth in money-bargaining systems and expansion in employment. The activities of companies in pursuit of the viability condition tend to bring about net increases in employment. At the same time, individual agents will increase their chances of employment by adapting their skills to the requirements of employers. They may also, if they encounter difficulties in obtaining employment, reduce their requirements for income. In this way, companies and individual agents of a money-bargaining system, acting together, will tend to increase employment. Much of the vigour, or evolutionary strength, of money-bargaining systems arises from their ready adaptation to unfolding situations.

There is, however, no inevitability about this tendency to employment. Reductions in unit costs and prices by a company may reduce employment but fail to expand sales. Reductions in employment by one company may not be offset by increases in employment in another. Innovations may not be made, or being made may not bring about a net increase in employment. Mistakes and misjudgements in companies, particularly large companies, can affect the overall performance of an economy. Overconfidence and lack of confidence arising from support-bargaining within a trading community can cause a system to evolve in such a way as to reduce employment opportunities. Technological innovation in one country may weaken the bargaining positions of companies in another, and bring about unemployment. Losses in one company are likely to be transmitted through the money-bargaining network to other companies in the form of reductions in their revenues, and potential loss of viability. Interventions arising from political support-bargaining can adversely affect the evolutionary expansion of a money-bargaining system. Money-bargaining requires well-motivated, skilled and energetic agents, both as individuals and as managers of companies. The performance of a money-bargaining system depends on the skills and energy of its agents.

Large companies often contribute significantly to the stabilisation of economies. They employ skilled and experienced managers who can be expected to evolve their companies along paths favourable both to the companies and to the money-bargaining systems in which they operate. Large companies are commonly diversified, so that downturns in sales in some product lines are made up by expansion in others. They also accumulate substantial reserves that can sustain them through periods of poor trading. But, on occasions, poor performance or failure of large companies can have resounding consequences across economies. Large size generally means a central role in a wide network of monetary transactions, so that consequences of failure are widely transmitted. Local economies are susceptible to failure of companies with significant local roles. Mistakes in financial companies can be particularly severe in their effects on other agents, as recent experience has demonstrated.

The network of money-bargaining makes agents interdependent. Any particular company depends for expansion on the availability of the right inputs. Hence the rapid growth of an economy and employment depends on the harmonious evolution of its component agents. Lack of people seeking employment with the skills relevant to the expansion of companies in a particular industry may inhibit the growth of such companies. Lack of transport facilities may constrain what might otherwise be rapid growth in a particular region. Governments derive support from the provision of communal services, but if the pursuit of support gives rise to measures that reduce business incentives or otherwise impede the functioning of the private sector, growth can slow, with a resulting slower growth in government revenues and slower growth in the provision of services. Evolution of public provision has to proceed in harmony with private provision.

Confidence and business cycles

In the neoclassical understanding of economic performance, steady economic growth can be expected, as the productivity of resources improves. The observed reality is, however, that growth is unsteady, with periods of rapid expansion and periods of slower growth, moving sometimes even into recession. Business cycles have attracted a great amount of research, with generally inconclusive results regarding their causes and the nature of the cycles. Because it is difficult to explain in terms of neoclassical theory, economists working in the neoclassical tradition have sometimes underestimated the importance of the phenomenon.

In bargaining theory, confidence and the lack of it are outcomes of support-bargaining. Businessmen will not make decisions as isolated individuals, but as part of a support-bargaining process. Businessmen as a group are likely to assess situation in a similar way and come to certain common understandings of their situation and the appropriate action to improve it. Businessmen as a group will share the confidence to format companies, or expand existing companies, at certain times, and will share the lack of confidence that causes them to restrain their activities at other times. They will run, as it were, in unison from side to side of the ship, and the ship will rock; that is, the ship will move cyclically.

A cyclical movement of this kind will be tied in with changes in bargaining positions. Those seeking employment at a time of confident expansion and high aggregate employment will find themselves in a strong bargaining position and will raise their requirements for wages. At a certain point, employers are likely to find the viability of their formats at risk with rising unit costs, and will defer additional employment. When unemployment is high, those seeking work will be prepared to accept lesser payments and employers will find that business formats are viable. Ups and downs in economic growth are to be expected in money-bargaining systems, but the variety of factors that influence confidence, and the further variety of factors that influence growth directly, mean that the regularity associated with cyclical motion may not be clearly apparent. It is probably important that businessmen share some common movement because a company formatting for expansion when others foresee contraction may find that it has overestimated the sales potential of its products. Business cycles are considered further in Chapter 7.

Compatibility and national accounts

National accounts are formulated to measure the overall performance of an economy. As was seen above, the accounts, largely as formulated, measure very well the transactions of a money-bargaining system, as conceived in the theory of money-bargaining. The compatibility derives from the foundations of both accounts and theory in observation of the actual functioning of economies. The disparities of macroeconomic performance with the neoclassical model arise because the neoclassical model was designed more for methodological convenience than for realism.

Money-bargaining implies neither equilibrium nor optimal allocation of resources. An economy evolves by reference to situations, with no conceivable point of equilibrium. There are evolutionary impulses to growth, but there are also possibilities of evolutionary contraction. The idea of optimal allocation of resources in neoclassical theory arises because the theory implies a single measure of value, which can be maximised. In bargaining theory value depends on situation. All agents are in different situations, and conceive situations differently, so all make different valuations, so it is not possible to conceive an optimal position. The valuations are made both by reference to general situations and budgetary situations. People with large budgets are likely to spend on luxury goods, but their valuations are specific to their situation. The money expended by people with small budgets will express valuations relative to their different situation.

The 'resources' of neoclassical theory – land, labour and capital – are associated with the 'agents' of a money-bargaining system. The 'labour resource' comprises in money-bargaining the individual agents of the money-bargaining system. Land and capital are controlled by their owners, giving them a role as agents of the money-bargaining system. Economies are conceived in terms of national territories and the people of a nation – that is, coterminous with formal support-bargaining systems. The agents of a support-bargaining system are generally also the agents of the associated money-bargaining system. The limits of the system are the limitations of agents in numbers and capacities. 'Agents' in money-bargaining take over the functions of 'resources' in neoclassical theory and, because of that, national accounts require little adaptation to represent the activity in national money-bargaining systems.

Notes

1 Backhouse, Roger E., 2002, *The Penguin History of Economics*, London: Penguin, pp. 240–5.
2 Backhouse, 2002, pp. 69–72.
3 Hull, Charles Henry (ed.), 1899, *The Economic Writings of Sir William Petty, together with The Observations upon Bills of Mortality, more probably by Captain John Graunt*, 2 Vols, Cambridge: Cambridge University Press. Petty's papers originally produced 1662–87. Available online at The Online Library of Liberty: http://oll.libertyfund.org/index.php?option=com_staticxt&staticfile=show.php%3Ftitle=1677&Itemid=27. Accessed 23 July 2015.
4 King, Willford, 1915, *The Wealth and Income of the People of the United States*, New York.
5 Meade, James, Stone, Richard and Stone, Giovanna, 1944–72, various editions of *National Income and Expenditure*, varying authorship and contributors, published variously by Oxford: Oxford University Press; Cambridge: Bowes and Bowes; London: Bowes.
6 Keynes, John Maynard, 1961, *The General Theory of Employment, Interest and Money*, London: Macmillan, New York: St Martin's Press.
7 On group formation in a factory environment and the formation of trade unions, see Spread, Patrick, 2008, *Support-Bargaining: The Mechanics of Democracy Revealed*, Sussex: Book Guild, pp. 129–32.
8 See Spread, 2008, Chapter 7, Resources and Dimensions.
9 On the treatment of land and natural resources in economic theory, see Spread, 2008, pp. 191–8.
10 US data source: Statistics of US Businesses. (Data for 2012.) Available at: www.census.gov/econ/susb/. Accessed 25 August 2015. UK Data source: Department for Business Innovation and Skills, Business Population Estimates for the UK and Regions 2013. Available at: www.gov.uk/government/uploads/system/uploads/attachment_data/file/254552/13-92-business-population-estimates-2013-stats-release-4.pdf. Accessed 25 August 2015.
11 *The Economist*, 22 June, 2013, p. 80.
12 Canals, Claudia, Gabaix, Xavier, Vilarrubia, Josep M. and Weinstein, David, 2007, 'Trade Patterns, Trade Balances and Idiosyncratic Shocks', Banco de España, Documentos de Trabajo. Referenced by *The Economist* at www.economist.com/bigfirms13. Accessed 3 February 2014.
13 Ali-Yrkkö, Jyrki (ed.), 2010, 'Nokia and Finland in a Sea of Change', ETLA – Research Institute of the Finnish Economy, Helsinki: Taloustiete Oy. Referenced by *The Economist* at www.economist.com/bigfirms13. Accessed 3 February 2014.
14 Chandler, Alfred, 1977, *The Visible Hand: The Managerial Revolution in American Business*, Cambridge, MA, and London: Belknap Press. See also Chandler, Alfred, 1990, *Scale and Scope: The Dynamics of Industrial Capitalism*, Cambridge, MA, and London: Belknap Press.
15 Chandler, 1990, p. 593.
16 Nordhaus, William D. and Tobin, James, 1973, 'Is Growth Obsolete?', in *The Measurement of Economic and Social Performance*, National Bureau of Economic Research. Available at: http://www.nber.org/chapters/c7620.pdf. Accessed 3 February 2014.
17 Stone, Richard and Brown, Alan, 1962, *A Computable Model for Economic Growth*, London: Chapman and Hall.
18 Stiglitz, Joseph E., Sen, Amartya and Fitoussi, Jean-Paul, 2009, Report by the Commission on the Measurement of Economic Performance and Social Progress. Available at http://ec.europa.eu/eurostat/documents/118025/118123/Fitoussi+Commission+report. Accessed 25 August 2015.
19 Stiglitz *et al.*, 2009, p. 12. Original emphasis.

20 Stiglitz *et al.*, 2009, p. 12.
21 Nordhaus and Tobin, 1973, p. 8.
22 Stiglitz *et al.*, 2009, p. 18.
23 Rizvi, S. Abu Turab, 1994, 'The Microfoundations Project in General Equilibrium Theory', *Cambridge Journal of Economics*, Vol. 18, No. 4, pp. 357–77, p. 357.
24 Rizvi, 1994, p. 360. Rizvi's references: Clower, R. W., 1965, 'The Keynesian Counterrevolution: A Theoretical Appraisal', in Hahn, F. H. and Brechling, F. (eds), *The Theory of Interest Rates*, London: Macmillan; Arrow, K. J., 1967, 'Samuelson Collected', *Journal of Political Economy*, Vol. 75, pp. 730–7; Lucas, R. E. and Sargent, T. J., 1979, 'After Keynesian Macroeconomics', *Federal Reserve Bank of Minneapolis Quarterly Review*, Vol. 3, No. 1; Howitt, P., 1987, 'Macroeconomics: Relations with Microeconomics', in Eatwell, J., Milgate, M. and Newman, P. (eds), *The New Palgrave*, Vol. 3, pp. 273–6, New York: Stockton; Drazen, A., 1980, 'Recent Developments in Macreoeconomic Disequilibrium Theory', *Econometrica*, Vol. 48, No. 2.
25 Nelson, Richard R. and Winter, Stanley, 1982, *An Evolutionary Theory of Economic Change*, Cambridge, MA, and London: Belknap Press, p. 232. See also pp. 230, 272, 413.
26 Rizvi, 1994, p. 359.
27 Rizvi, 1994, p. 359.
28 Rizvi, 1994, p. 359, quoting Hicks, J. R., 1939, *Value and Capital: An Inquiry into some Fundamental Principles of Economic Theory*, Oxford: Clarendon Press, p. 245.
29 Rizvi, 1994, p, 370.
30 Backhouse, 2002, p. 242.
31 Backhouse, 1993, p. 180.
32 Backhouse, 1993, p. 189.
33 Backhouse, 1993, p. 42.
34 Backhouse, 1993, p. 42.
35 Backhouse, 1993, p. 59.
36 McKenzie, L. W. 1954, 'On Equilibrium in Graham's Model of World Trade and other Competitive Systems', *Econometrica*, Vol. 27, pp. 54–71. McKenzie, L. W., 1959, 'On the Existence of General Equilibrium for a Competitive Market', *Econometrica*, Vol. 27, pp. 147–61.
37 Arrow, Kenneth and Debreu, Gérard, 1954, 'Existence of an Equilibrium in a Competitive Economy', *Econometrica*, Vol. 22, pp. 265–90. The definitive account is recognised as Debreu, Gérard, 1959, *Theory of Value: An Axiomatic Analysis of Economic Equilibrium*, New York: Wiley.
38 Geanakoplos, John, 2004, 'The Arrow–Debreu Model of General Equilibrium', *Cowles Foundation Paper No. 1090*, Cowles Foundation for Research in Economics at Yale University, p. 122.
39 Geanakoplos, 2004, pp. 119, 121.
40 Geanakoplos, 2004, p. 116.
41 Geanakoplos, 2004, p. 117.
42 Geanakoplos, 2004, p. 116.
43 Geanakoplos, 2004, pp. 116-17.
44 See Spread, Patrick, 2011, 'Situation as Determinant of Selection and Valuation', *Cambridge Journal of Economics*, Vol. 35, No. 2, pp. 335–56. Reprinted in Spread, Patrick, 2015b, *Aspects of Support-Bargaining and Money-Bargaining*, E-Book, World Economics Association. See also Spread, 2008, pp. 71–87, 107–13.
45 Geanakoplos, 2004, p. 120.
46 Geanakoplos, 2004, p. 118.
47 Geanakoplos, 2004, p. 118.
48 Geanakoplos, 2004, p. 122.
49 Geanakoplos, 2004, p. 122.
50 Backhouse, 1988, *Economists and the Economy: The Evolution of Economic Ideas*, Oxford: Blackwell, p. 180.

51 Geanakoplos, 2004, p. 123.
52 Backhouse, Roger E., 1993, *Economists and the Economy: The Evolution of Economic Ideas*, 2nd edition, New Brunswick, NJ, and London: Transaction, pp. 215–16.
53 Backhouse, 2002, p. 261; Backhouse, 1993, pp. 17–18.
54 Stiglitz *et al.*, 2009, p. 12.
55 Stiglitz *et al.*, 2009, pp. 11–12, 26.

4 Evolutionary economics

The dynamics of neoclassical theory imply that economies will tend towards equilibrium. Yet economic history indicates that economies change over time in an irreversible process. At one time people may earn their living predominantly by growing cereal crops and tending sheep and cattle; then, 100 years later, a large proportion are coal miners and workers on production lines in manufacturing; and, after another 100 years, large numbers are office workers, shop assistants and specialists in information technology. The incapacity of neoclassical economic theory to accommodate an evolutionary process has meant that the evolution of economies has largely been ignored in mainstream economics. Economic historians have found it difficult to use the neoclassical model in a historical context. It has, however, remained their formal theoretical reference, causing them, as will be seen in the following chapter, to miss important features of historical change. Response to the crying need for an evolutionary theory of economic activity has been largely left to institutional economists.[1]

The first theorist to work on evolutionary economic theory was also the first institutional economist. Thorstein Veblen asked, in an article published in 1898, 'Why is Economics not an Evolutionary Science?',[2] developing his ideas further in his best-known work, *The Theory of the Leisure Class: An Economic Study in the Evolution of Institutions*, published in 1899.[3] Veblen suggested that changes in habits of thought constituted the essential evolutionary process, though because people retained the habits of thought appropriate to earlier times they might impede the evolution of economies. Veblen's answer to the question 'Why is economics not an evolutionary science?' was broadly that economists lacked the habits of thought necessary to develop an evolutionary science. Veblen's approach to evolutionary economics is discussed in *Support-Bargaining, Economics and Society*.[4]

The idea of certain broad generalities, such as 'habits of thought', being selected in social evolution, as 'variations' are selected in natural selection, forms the basis of evolutionary institutional theory. 'Rules', 'routines' and 'habits' are the 'institutions' of institutional theory and are understood to govern social and economic change. The immediate difficulty with such factors is that they are, as institutional economists acknowledge, more factors that bring stability and order to society than factors promoting change. Even Veblen's 'habits of thought' are as much impediments to evolution as evolutionary impulses. Rules, routines and habits lack any inherent dynamic of change, let alone a dynamic of evolutionary change. Institutional economics is arguably just as ill-equipped to deal with evolutionary theory as neoclassical economics. Some 'change' or evolutionary dynamic has to be associated with rules, routines and habits.

Institutional-evolutionary theorists have generally followed Veblen in adopting Darwin's theory of natural selection as the appropriate dynamic.[5] Darwin's theory suggested that biological variations occur in species, making them more or less able to meet the exigencies of their environment. Those fortunate in having variations that suit them to their environment survive, while those with variations that are unsuitable become extinct. Teeth and claws are obvious physical variations that have enabled certain species to gain advantage in the struggle for survival. They successfully reproduce, so that the advantageous variations are propagated from generation to generation. Over many generations new species may emerge by this process, all fitted in some way to their environment. Darwin was unable to explain the origin of the variations that came to be selected or rejected, but later biological research established that genes mutate, producing variations that function in a way comparable to those postulated by Darwin. Modern science has confirmed the essentials of Darwin's theory of natural selection. Reduced to essentials, the process may be understood in terms of variation, selection and inheritance.

In the *Origin of Species* Darwin described how pigeon breeders select birds with the qualities they seek – strong homing sense and speed on the wing – and breed from them, bringing into being birds in which those qualities are yet more pronounced. Darwin used the example of pigeon breeding to introduce the idea of selection. On the face of it, the pigeon model provides a better analogy or parallel with a competitive economy than natural selection itself. Humans compete to produce the best homing pigeons. They 'make' good pigeons by ensuring that the opportunities to reproduce go to the pigeons with what humans regard as desirable characteristics. The process is one of human competition, and the same competitive process is apparent in society. Darwin's presentational expedient is closer to social evolution than his substantive theory. But institutional theorists have preferred the model of natural selection, in which the role of 'selector' goes to the environment. Those species that meet the requirements of the environment survive, breed and prosper. Those that do not are eliminated.

Institutional economists, like other social theorists, may have preferred a connection with Darwinian natural selection, rather than a connection with pigeon breeding, partly because it allies their theory with what has come to be regarded as secure natural science. Darwinian natural selection is a sure foundation. It seems, however, to have been in some ways counterproductive because the parallel between biological natural selection and social selection is hard to maintain.

The process 'variation–selection–inheritance' provides the foundation for the association of natural selection with the social sciences. Stanley Metcalfe identifies:

> the three widely accepted ideas that, jointly, define an evolutionary process (see Lewontin, 1974, and Brandon, 1990). These are: the principle of variation, that members of a relevant population vary with respect to at least one characteristic with selective significance; the principle of heredity, that there exist copying mechanisms to ensure continuity over time in the form and behaviour of the entities in the population; and the principle of selection, that the characteristics of some entities are better adapted to prevailing evolutionary pressures and, consequently, these entities increase in numerical significance relative to less well-adapted entities.[6]

Numerous concepts have been created to make the connections between social processes and variation–selection–inheritance, including 'replicators', 'interactors', 'transmitters', 'propagators' and 'vehicles'. Numerous 'units of selection', the 'variations' that are 'selected', have been proposed, including Veblen's 'habits of thought' and, in an economic context, 'business units'.[7]

Geoffrey Hodgson and Thorbjørn Knudsen try to refine and firmly substantiate this idea of 'generalised Darwinism': 'The basic argument ... is that the core Darwinian principles of variation, inheritance and selection apply to social as well as biological phenomena.'[8] They acknowledge that the details of evolutionary processes in natural selection and social evolution are very different, but still argue that connection at a high level of abstraction, or 'metatheoretical' level, is useful to the understanding of social processes.[9] Generalised Darwinism is claimed to highlight the importance of rule-like dispositions in society, characterised as 'program-like', through the programmes involved in the creation of biological genotypes. Hodgson and Knudsen conclude: 'In sum, the emerging ontology of social reality as consisting of systems of rule-like dispositions – described as *institutions* – fits perfectly into a generalized Darwinian framework. The links between institutional and Darwinian ontologies are established.'[10]

The application of theory developed in one sphere to the phenomena of another is fraught with problems. To fit the new phenomena with the theory may require that they be understood or interpreted in ways that distort their nature, as commonly understood. In so far as there is a common understanding of the formation of biological genotypes and the formation of social rules, it probably distinguishes very sharply between them. The codes that form biological genotypes are very different from the social processes that produce social rules: so different as to make it potentially misleading to associate them. Metatheoretic and ontological levels can embrace too much. The advantages of making such connections between biological science and social theory are apparent from an understanding of support-bargaining. The association potentially assembles around the social science some part of the massive support already established around the biological science. If the latter is recognised as sound, then the former, being like it, can also be claimed as sound. Social theory is authenticated in the theory group by association with natural scientific theory.

Institutional-evolutionary theory versus neoclassical theory

Institutional economics may be said to have come off second best to neoclassical economics in the intellectual support-bargaining of the twentieth century. Evolutionary economists suffered in much the same theory group. In the early years of the century neoclassical economists were advancing the marginal model as scientific and rigorous, and consequently requiring the commitment of those who were serious about the advance of economic knowledge. Evolutionary economics was stigmatised as lightweight and possibly frivolous. The prominence of Thorstein Veblen, a decidedly radical theorist, probably did much to retard the cause. Stephen Sanderson writes:

> the first decades of the twentieth century represented a sort of 'dark age' for evolutionism. During this time evolutionism was severely criticised and came to be regarded as an outmoded approach that self-respecting scholars should no longer take seriously. Evolutionary theories did not die out completely, but they were seldom seen, and even the word 'evolution' came to be uttered at serious risk to one's intellectual reputation.[11]

The suppressive effects of the neoclassical theory group and the institutionalisation of theory-making (in the sense of establishing it in universities and similar institutions) are apparent. It might be said that evolutionism became 'intellectually incorrect' in the intellectual support-bargaining of the period. 'Reputation' can be read as a euphemism for 'prospects for promotion'.

In the later years of the twentieth century a 'new' institutional economics emerged, as attempts were made to develop an alternative to neoclassical theory, or at least improve on it. Malcolm Rutherford, writing in 2001, describes the distinction as follows:

> During recent years the term 'institutional economics' has been applied to an ever-increasing variety of economic approaches or schools of thought. Most people recognise the terms 'institutional economics' or 'American institutional economics' or 'old institutional economics' (sometimes now 'original institutional economics') as applying to the tradition of economics associated with Thorstein Veblen, John R. Commons, Wesley Mitchell, and Clarence Ayres. Until quite recently this was the only meaning given to 'institutional economics'. But in recent years, the term 'new institutional economics' has become well-established as referring to the tradition of work stemming primarily from the transactions costs approach of Ronald Coase, Oliver Williamson and Douglass North.[12]

Both old and new institutional economics are concerned with rules, routines and habits as factors shaping economic exchange. They differ, however, in their understanding of the nature of economic exchange. Old institutionalists reject neoclassical theory. Geoffrey Hodgson provides an extended critique of neoclassical theory in *Economics and Institutions*.[13] For old institutionalists, exchange is something carried on in 'markets', understood as institutions. New institutional economists accept neoclassical theory as a basic account of economic exchange, but supplement it with various arrangements necessary to offset the risks and costs of engaging in economic exchange. The supplements are, in many cases, inconsistent with the assumptions of neoclassical theory, or imply the impossibility of neoclassical exchange, so that the commitment to neoclassical theory is more a matter of form than substance. For economists working in academic institutions there are decided advantages in retaining membership of the mainstream neoclassical theory group.

While old institutionalists, as noted above, turn to Darwinian theory for a dynamic of evolution, new institutionalists see Darwinian theory as lacking the human intention that is an essential element in human endeavour. Douglass North writes in *Understanding the Process of Economic Change*, 'In contrast to Darwinian evolutionary theory, the key to human evolutionary change is the intentionality of the players.'[14] He prefers, in effect, the pigeon selection model to natural selection in the social sphere. North suggests that institutions are the source of change. He also suggests that 'path dependence' is an important factor governing change. But in the end he acknowledges that he can provide no satisfactory theory of evolutionary economic processes, and even foresees little prospect of developing one: 'By now it should be clear that no dynamic theory of change is advanced in this study and I hope that it is equally clear that no such theory that could be useful is likely to evolve.'[15]

Old institutional economics: rules, routines and habits

In recent decades Geoffrey Hodgson has been one of the leading exponents of evolutionary economics in the context of old institutional economic theory. Hodgson champions Thorstein Veblen, albeit with reservations, as the originator of evolutionary economics and institutional economics.[16] His many books and articles trace the development of institutional and evolutionary theory, and argue its relevance to current issues in social and economic theory. In an article titled 'What are Institutions?' Hodgson responds to an immediate query of those approaching institutional economics:

> Without doing much violence to the relevant literature, we may define *institutions* as systems of established and prevalent social rules that structure social interactions. Language, money, law, systems of weights and measures, table manners, and firms (and other organizations) are thus all institutions.[17]

The function of these institutions is given as follows: 'Generally, institutions enable ordered thought, expectation, and action by imposing form and consistency on human activities'.[18] Rule is specified in the same article: 'The term *rule* is broadly understood as a socially transmitted and customary normative injunction or immanently normative disposition, that in circumstances X do Y ... Rules include norms of behaviour and social conventions as well as legal rules.'[19]

Habits derive from institutions, or rules: 'Insofar as institutions lead to regularities of behaviour, concordant habits are laid down among the population, leading to congruent purposes and beliefs.'[20] In the same vein:

> Rules do not essentially have a self-actuating or autonomic quality but clearly, by repeated application, a rule can become a habit. Typically it is easier to break a rule than to change a habit ... However, habits still have the same general form: in circumstances X, action Y follows.[21]

Institutions are rules and rules may become habits. Rules are generally followed with conscious recognition that a rule is being followed, while habits are automatic or reflex responses.

In an earlier article, 'The Approach of Institutional Economics', Hodgson aligned institutional theory with Darwinian natural selection and evolutionary processes, in the same way as Veblen treated 'habits of thought'. Habits and routines are selected in a manner analogous to Darwinian selection. He writes:

> Habits or routines may adapt slowly or 'mutate' as agents attempt purposeful improvements. In addition, there is some selection process by which some habits and routines are retained and imitated, and others fall out of use. Institutionalism is congenitally an 'evolutionary economics'.[22]

The institutions listed in the quotation above – language, money, law, systems of weights and measures, table manners and firms – are not obviously systems of rules, except in the case of law. Institutionalists are generally reticent regarding the actual rules, routines or habits they have in mind, preferring to work at the level of abstract generality. The following are examples of rules in the six institutions which would presumably gain acceptance as rules in institutional theory. They are all of the form: if X, do Y.

> **Language:** If I see someone being robbed, I can communicate my experience to others in the form 'There is a man being robbed', but not in the form 'There are a men robbed being'.
>
> **Money:** This coin is marked 'one pound' and by law it must be accepted in payment for goods priced at one pound. So on receipt of this coin I must hand over such goods.
>
> **Law:** This person stole that man's property, so the thief will be incarcerated for two years.

Weights and measures: Society has established through its government that this piece of brass is one pound in weight. So when I require a pound of beef, the butcher must ensure that the beef he gives me balances with this piece of brass on a scale.

Table manners: I need some salt, which is on the far side of the table, so I must ask someone to pass it to me, rather than reaching across the table to get it.

Firms: Here is an order for a ton of cement, so I record it in the order book, stamp it as received, make up an order form in triplicate, pass one copy to accounts, one copy to dispatch and retain one copy on file.

These are all commonplaces of human behaviour. A great range of activity is routine following of a variety of rules, and many of them are assimilated as habits. The rules are, however, established for the specific purpose of giving stability, consistency, dependability and even permanence to the operation of certain functions. They establish what can and cannot be done in the context of these functions. If the butcher gives me 8 ounces of beef instead of a pound, he is flouting the rules. Routines similarly establish stable activity and stable expectations around certain functions. Being stabilising, rules and routines are not conducive to change and, consequently, lack something essential as foundations for a theory of social and economic evolution.

Habits also suggest repetition and permanence. They too constitute a poor foundation for a theory of evolutionary change. But, unlike rules and routines, they suggest an element of psychological compulsion and, consequently, an underlying psychological impediment to change.

The abstraction of rules, routines and habits, and the reluctance to make them more specific, suggests a reluctance to engage with the underlying functions to which the rules, routines and habits apply. Making specific the functions leads to questions about the functions, and to the suggestion that the evolutionary process lies in the evolution of the functions rather than in the rules, routines and habits which they have brought into being. Thus, for example, changes in a firm's trading may result in changes to its internal rules and routines. Political change may result in changes in the rules regarding weights and measures. Changes in public attitudes to crime may result in changes to rules governing the punishment of theft. The evolution is in the functions, subsequently embodied in changes to rules and routines.

The association of these different institutions on the basis of their all having rules and routines belies their fundamental differences. Dealing with an order for a ton of cement is different to communicating in language, even if they have rule-compliance in common. Both language and firms have many other features that distinguish them very markedly from each other. Incarcerating a thief according to a rule is the culmination of a long social process dealing with disorder and insecurity in society. Associating the law against theft with a rule of language seems to ignore the differences between them more than is warranted. For purposes of theory-making it may be tempting to classify functions together as instances of rule-compliance, but as a matter of common experience the unification is strained. At a high level of abstraction, common features can be identified, but, at a less rarefied level, language is different to law and to firms.

For the purpose of realistic theory-making it is necessary to take these observable differences of function into account. A theory of social and economic evolution requires a focus on the evolution of the functions, for it is in the different functions that evolutionary change takes place. Agricultural activity gives way to industrial employment; people move from industry to services. Each activity generates the forms of behaviour and the rules appropriate to its acceptable functioning. Rules and routines have an important role, but as stabilisers and regulators of functions.

This includes an important coordinating role. In a company, if deliveries of inputs arrive routinely at 9.00 a.m., then the acceptance and checking of the inputs will follow routinely after 9.00 a.m., and a sequence of routines involving payments, storage and usage will follow. People sometimes refer to themselves as 'mere cogs in the wheel' – the routines mesh together to coordinate functions like cogs in a wheel.

Individual habits and habits of the group

While rules and routines are matters of public or common recognition, habits are not necessarily so. Habits are perhaps most commonly associated with individuals, and may, as remarked above, be understood as involving some degree of psychological compulsion. Changes in habits may reflect changes in psychological dispositions rather than changed attitudes to the substance of the habit. But there are also collective habits. Here too there is an important sense of psychological engagement, but the psychology of groups has been less well understood even than the psychology of individuals, so that collective habits have not been well understood. Veblen's 'habits of thought', as units of selection, are presumably collective habits of thought. Only in this form could they be regarded as significant factors in the evolution of a society. A collective Marxist habit of thought, or a collective neoclassical habit of thought, can clearly influence the evolution of a society. They have different implications to the ordinary run of individual habits, such as sweeping the doorstep when visitors are expected, or doodling at meetings.

While individual habits may be no more than the consequences of individual psychological quirks, related primarily to idiosyncrasies of the brain, collective habits, involving something like a herd instinct, may be understood as deriving from support-bargaining. As with rules and routines, important evolutionary changes are likely to arise from the matter to which a collective habit relates, rather than from the habit in itself. Marxism and neoclassical theory are, in terms of support-bargaining, creations of theory groups. Their adherents are members of a group, understanding their interests as bound up with one or other of the theories. Their habit has purpose. The support generated in each theory group reassures members that the triumph of the proletariat or the optimal allocation of resources is the appropriate social objective. It is not commitment to a theory of the straightforward type, 'if X do Y', but a commitment to observe and interpret the social situation in terms of one or other of the theories, and to prescribe correctives for society in accordance with the understanding in the theory of the actions necessary to improve the social situation. The significant evolutionary changes in the theories are likely to derive from observation that is not accommodated by the theories and cannot be interpreted satisfactorily within the adopted theoretical context. Marxists found it difficult to understand why the economy of the Soviet Union was weak while Western economies flourished. Collective habits will change with changes in the circumstances that generate the habits. This complexity of habits – their individual and collective forms, their psychological content and their relationship to circumstances – make them awkward explicators of social behaviour, especially when these aspects of their complexity are not all recognised.

Geoffrey Hodgson and Thorbjørn Knudsen nevertheless treat habits as the central variants in their generalised theory of Darwinian evolution:

> Here, the concept of habit is crucial. Habits are essential psychological mechanisms in learning and skill development (Dewey 1922). They are the individual building blocks of customs, routines, and all higher level social replicators in organizations. Habits and routines are persistent, they replicate, and they contain ready-made solutions to frequently occurring problems. Their persistence means that organizational evolution often stubbornly resists corporate or government initiatives.[23]

Habits are chosen because they seem to meet the criteria for a Darwinian unit of selection. And after all, Darwin could not explain how 'variations' varied. A heavy weight of explanation is placed on them, when they are perhaps no more than superficial expressions of underlying processes and functions.

The quotation itself concedes the further difficulty with habits, remarked on earlier, as the focus of evolutionary explanation. The habits and routines are conducive to persistence and inertia, rather than evolutionary change. Veblen's account of the role of 'habits of thought' recognises that they can impede evolutionary processes, implying either that some 'habits of thought' impede the evolution of others, or that they impede some other process of evolution. The above quotation suggests that the more important dynamic concerns the changes a company or government wishes to bring about, and why, for these constitute the evolutionary process. Hodgson and Knudsen, as has been seen, describe generalised Darwinism as pitched at a 'metatheoretical' level of high abstraction. At that level, the 'habit' provides some association. But it misses the importance of changes in the functions to which 'habits' relate. They do not probe the nature of habitual behaviour with specific illustrations; rather they acknowledge that generalised Darwinism is not easily applied to the detail of social behaviour.[24] Societies observably evolve at a functional level, and a theory of economic evolution has to deal with the evolution of functions.

Besides rules, routine and habits

Hodgson recognises that institutional theory risks missing some essentials of an evolutionary process. Towards the end of his article on 'The Ubiquity of Habits and Rules' he writes:

> This does not necessarily mean that all action is driven by habits and rules. Indeed, as Peirce, Veblen and Commons noted, account has to be taken of novelty and creativity as well. Creativity may itself emerge from the clash or combination of rival languages or rules, or it may be essentially undetermined or 'uncaused'. These questions are not raised because an answer is possible here, but to indicate that the ubiquity of habits and rules should not be taken to mean that such factors are excluded. On the contrary, a theoretical focus on habits and rules should include explanations of their origin, evolution, breakdown and replacement.[25]

Incapacity to accommodate novelty, creativity and innovation is obviously a serious drawback in a theory of evolution, since evolution is likely to be conditioned by such factors. Habits, rules and routines suggest the regular aspects of life, the bureaucratic aspects, whereas evolution is necessarily concerned with what is changeable. It reflects the incapacity of institutional theory to deal with the underlying functions of which rules, routines and habits are the indicators or expression. The 'origin, evolution, breakdown and replacement' of habits and rules lie in the underlying functions. What is decided at a monthly board meeting is likely to be more important with regard to the evolution of a company than the routine of a monthly board meeting.

The importance of creativity and innovation is apparent in the hierarchies of companies. Those at the top of hierarchies are expected to be creative and take initiatives. Those at the bottom of hierarchies perform the routine tasks, and will be instructed in what routines to follow by those higher up. The routines are dictated by the functional creativity and innovation of those at the top. Pay-scales will reflect the same priorities as the hierarchy – the innovators at the top of the hierarchy will be paid more than those who follow routines at the bottom end. There is probably a good inverse correlation between the rule-following or routine content of jobs and the level of pay.

Because routine jobs can be done by employees at relatively low rates of pay, there is an incentive for companies to design tasks so that they involve routine. As a matter of minimising unit costs, and hence meeting the viability condition, tasks in a company will be reduced as far as possible to routine. Hence routines become common in companies. This again reflects the dependence of routines on the underlying functions. Other functions, besides companies, will involve concern for costs, and routines will be used to minimise costs.

Pricing in old institutional economics

While old institutional economics rejects neoclassical theory, it retains a sense of market exchange. Rules, routines and habits are understood as moderating the

Evolutionary economics 77

dynamism of market exchange. They channel market dynamism into socially acceptable courses. The way 'market exchange' functions is, however, left unspecified. The lack of understanding of market exchange makes it difficult for institutional economists to account for price formation. The institutional account of price formation focuses on administrative aspects of price formation. The emphasis shifts from the dynamic mechanism of neoclassical theory to the rules followed by organisations in setting prices.

Institutional economists themselves recognise that they lack a comprehensive theory of price formation. Hodgson acknowledges that, 'Institutionalism has no general theory of price but a set of guideline approaches to specific problems.'[26] A general theory of pricing is reckoned beyond what is feasible, given the variety and complexity of price formation in the real world. Prices are regarded as 'social conventions, reinforced by habits and embedded in specific institutions ... A theory of price must in part be a theory of ideas, expectations, habits and institutions, involving routines and processes of valuation.'[27] The bureaucratic aspect of institutional theory is very evident. Prices are set within organisations through following habits and routines. Hodgson provides a string of questions that arise with the application of institutional guidelines to specific pricing problems:

> What are the costs and how are they evaluated? What routines govern the calculation of prices? What information is available and what is unknown? By what routines is information obtained and used? What routines are used to revise prices in line with the experience on the market? What is the strategy concerning competitive pricing? How does this relate to market structure?[28]

Just as the earlier quotation refers incidentally to 'corporate or government initiatives', as being outside the range of rules, and potentially thwarted by them, the questions refer to feedback from 'the market' whose nature is unspecified and which functions outside the range of institutional theory. Prices are set by following rules and routines, using information taken from market experience, but the processes that generate market experience are taken as given, or understood, or beyond the scope of institutional theory. The administrative routines are adjuncts to a market dynamic operating 'out of focus'. Hodgson's questions will provide information regarding the rule-following procedures of an institution, but they are unlikely to explain the interactions of buyers and sellers.

Marc Tool, in his 'Contributions to an Institutionalist Theory of Price Determination', confirms the centrality of exchange: 'Since all modern economies are, and will remain, monetary exchange economies, theoretical explanations of ratios of exchange – prices – and their determination must constitute a major area of inquiry.'[29] Tool provides a summary account of the centrality of price formation for neoclassical theory and the inadequacy of its supposed explanations. He suggests, 'Institutionalists, in contrast, argue that the more inclusive and descriptively accurate theory must be one of discretionary pricing and that instances of free-market determination are exceptionally rare.'[30] The neoclassical market concept is seen as dependent on primary institutions of private ownership of property and legally enforceable contracts.[31] It does not reflect 'the breadth and complexity of behaviour actually correlated in markets'.[32] By contrast, 'Institutionalists recognise that modern markets are comprised of a large number of usually complex, correlated patterns of behaviour, all of which, though typically habitual, are initially creations of people as discretionary agents.'[33] Limitations of information are identified as the major reason for departure from the neoclassical concept of price formation.[34] Companies deal internally with uncertainty through routine procedures, which become habits.

Tool's conclusion implies, like Hodgson, that any general theory of price formation has to be abandoned; the process can only be explained in terms of the specific pricing routines in large companies:

> *only enquiry into the complexities of the structural fabric involved can disclose the particular pricing power centres, who the price-setting agents are, the criteria reflected in their decisions, and the consequences that flow therefrom.*[35]

Tool's analysis is nevertheless consistent with the idea of companies as bargaining agencies seeking to meet a viability criterion, as described in Chapter 2. He notes, in particular, the extensive use of 'mark-up' or 'cost-plus pricing', which is integral to the concept of a viability condition.[36] The switch of emphasis from market interactions to company price-setting routines in Tool's analysis suggests, however, as with Hodgson's analysis, the loss of a 'market' dynamic. With the concept of companies as agents of money-bargaining systems the interaction of seller and buyer in price formation remains central. Companies design their products and their selling arrangements by reference to consumer situations, including consumer budgetary situations. Companies use 'mark-up' calculations for pricing, but they also adjust prices in accordance with their assessed bargaining position, or, for products already on sale, the bargaining position revealed by the level of sales at current pricing. Whatever the internal procedures or routines of buyers and sellers in a money-bargaining system, it is their interaction that constitutes the market dynamic and the dynamic of price formation.

In this way also institutional economics is as unsuited to evolutionary theory as neoclassical economics. There is at least a dynamic to neoclassical theory, even if it is a rarefied abstract dynamic, and a dynamic implying equilibrium rather than evolution. Failure to develop an alternative theory of dynamic exchange, of dynamic interaction between buyers and sellers, leaves a hole in old institutional theory. In large measure, it accounts for the triumph of neoclassical theory in the intellectual support-bargaining of the twentieth century. It also accounts for the failure of institutional theory to provide a satisfactory account of economic evolution.

Institutions, players and definitions

It was suggested above that institutions – rules, routines and habits – shape functions to desirable forms and give them an element of stability, even a degree of permanence. They are contingent on the functions they relate to, rather than primary phenomena. This distinction is important to the debate between Geoffrey Hodgson and Douglass North over the nature of firms. Hodgson records the debate, including extracts from North's communications to him, in his article, 'What are Institutions?'.

Hodgson regards firms as institutions, albeit with additional features relating to their boundaries and their designation of someone 'in charge', with a chain of command.[37] North makes a sharp distinction between institutions and players: 'Institutions are the rules of the game in a society or, more formally, are the humanly devised constraints that shape human interaction ... Conceptually, what must be clearly differentiated are the rules from the players.'[38] For North, organisations, including firms, are players:

> It is the interaction between institutions and organizations that shapes the institutional evolution of an economy. If institutions are the rules of the game, organizations and their entrepreneurs are the players. Organizations are made up of groups of individuals bound together by some common purpose to achieve certain objectives.[39]

North sees 'business' as being carried on by 'players' operating in an institutional framework, while Hodgson conceives companies as institutions.

Hodgson bases his view that firms are institutions on the existence of rules within firms. The existence of internal rules makes it inappropriate to claim that firms are players. Firms have internal conflicts, and 'internal mechanisms by which the organizations coerce or persuade members to act together to some degree. Crucially, these mechanisms always involve systems of embedded rules.' The existence of rules governing the internal behaviour of organisations makes them institutions: 'The unavoidable existence of rules within organizations means that, even by North's own definition, organizations must be regarded as a type of *institution*.'[40]

Hodgson seeks to accommodate North's view by recognising that it is possible to conceive firms acting as players from the particular point of view adopted by North: 'There is nothing in principle wrong with the idea that under some conditions organizations can be treated as single actors.' He suggests that North is 'abstracting' from organisations by treating them as players, but not 'defining' organisations as players. As long as no 'definition' of organisations as players is involved, there is no objection to treating them as players. Definition is a step too far:

> However, a problem arises if we *define* organizations as actors. This would amount to an unwarranted conflation of individual agency and

organization ... The treatment of the organization as a social actor abstracts from such internal conflicts, but an abstraction should not become a fixed principle or definition that would block all considerations of internal conflict or structure.[41]

Hodgson's definition of organisations as institutions stands, but North is permitted to treat them as players. North accepts the compromise; he acknowledges that he is not interested in the internal processes of organisations, but in their 'macro aspects'.[42]

The debate illustrates the limited view that old institutional theory provides of social phenomena. It requires its adherents to focus on the rules that are operative in some sphere of action, and insists that they are the defining features of the action. It easily overlooks what to other theorists will appear as the more critical features, the features that make something functional in society. These are what North is concerned with – the action itself or the 'play'. Firms and other organisations have trading functions – functions such as money-bargaining agents – that are more important than the rules by which they expedite their business; the rules arise from the determination that certain functions are to be fulfilled. A focus on the rules distracts from the important features. The distinction is more sharply apparent in the context of games, where 'the rules of the game' can be clearly distinguished from the game itself. The 'Rules of Football' govern the game of football. They will be a focus of attention for those administering the game, including referees. But, for the players, the game itself will be the focus of attention – the teams, the goal scoring, the pitch, the skills, the strategies. The rules of the game coordinate the approach of players to the game, but they are derived from the actual play. Without the game, there would be no rules. If the players want to modify the way the game is played, they will seek changes in the rules. Without trade, there would be no companies and no internal rules.

The debate illustrates more broadly the function of definition. Hodgson observes conscientiously in all his work the traditional academic obligation to 'define your terms', and insists that others do so. The ostensible aim is to make clear what is under discussion; to ensure that all participants agree on the basics and do not become distracted by semantic debates. But in social bargaining theory definition is a means of securing group support for a particular concept conducive to the interests of the theory group. Definition selects those features of a phenomenon that accord with the group concept, and makes them the essential features of the phenomenon. Theory groups share a particular vision or concept that sustains the group interest. The more their concepts can be established in the minds of others, the more the features they see are seen by others, the more the group interest is likely to prevail. When a group member defines, he or she will select by reference to the group concept. Definition by a theory group excludes concepts that are not regarded as being in the interests of the group. Hodgson is anxious that organisations should be defined in accordance with his concept of institutional economics.

Hodgson's insistence on definition seems inconsistent with his understanding of cognitive processes. He writes:

> Our knowledge of the world does not spring alive from the sensory data as they reach the brain. To derive information it is necessary that a prior conceptual framework is imposed on the jumble of neurological stimuli, involving implicit or explicit assumptions, categories or theories which cannot themselves be derived from the sense data alone[43] ... In order to gain knowledge of the world we require prior clues and cognitive frames that are provided in part through social interaction with others.[44]

We understand in accordance with our preconceptions and the preconceptions of our group. We pick out those features of phenomena that conform to our preconceptions, or which are relevant to our interests. We understand such features as the defining features of the phenomena. The more we can get others to accept such features as defining, the more our own preconceptions will be confirmed and the more likely it is that the interests tied up with them will be advanced.[45] If North is allowed to *define* organisations as players, they are taken out of the old institutional paradigm and potentially erode the support assembled in the old institutional theory group.

It is the more surprising that Hodgson should define with such nescience when he is well aware that his own institutional school has suffered from definition. Alfred Marshall opened his *Principles of Economics* with a definition of economics:

> Political Economy or Economics is a study of mankind in the ordinary business of life; it examines that part of individual and social action which is most closely connected with the attainment and with the use of the material requisites of wellbeing.[46]

Economics was, on this basis, a broad field of study. Hodgson records that:

> In 1929, Lionel Robbins was elected to the LSE chair that had been vacated by Young. This youthful appointee was to steer LSE economics in a very different direction. Immediately, Robbins set about the task of ridding it of its institutionalist and historicist ballast. His famous *Essay* was published in 1932. In a masterly stroke, he simply redefined economics in terms that would exclude institutionalism and historicism from within its disciplinary boundaries.[47]

Robbins's definition was: 'Economics is the science which studies human behaviour as a relationship between ends and scarce means which have alternative uses.'[48]

It received extensive support among economists, being adopted as a standard definition. It is what the neoclassical theory of economics is about. It means that the study of economics is confined to neoclassical theory and the neoclassical theory group. The posts designated for economists in the faculties of economics in universities have to be filled by neoclassical economists if they are to be filled by economists. Hence, Robbins's definition marginalised institutional economists. Such are the effects of definition. It seems innocuous, even exemplary, but it can separate combatants on a battlefield. Religious faiths have long divided on the basis of definitions that can have no empirical foundation. Hodgson's defining is more benign. He is prepared to make concessions to keep North in the institutional fold; but not to the extent of sacrificing the institutional definition of organisations. The loss of organisations in that way would constitute too great an erosion of the subject matter of old institutional economics. Hodgson is attempting the kind of 'Robbins coup' that excluded institutional economics from the mainstream of economic theory-making.

The role of definitions should be immediately apparent to institutional theorists, since they function like rules. Obedience to a definition is like obedience to a rule. The definition stabilises or gives permanence to certain concepts and closes down others that might take speculation in a new or different direction. If the rule is 'economists must study scarcity', economists who want to take a broader approach to economic activity cease to be members of the economists' theory group and will not enjoy the perks of membership. The 'game' is studying scarcity. Anyone studying 'institutions' can be ruled offside, and can be given a red card after repeated offences. When the game is a career, that is serious. As with rules, it is necessary to attend primarily to the activities or concepts associated with the establishment of definitions. Definitions in social science are never a starting point. Very often they are the closure of alternative views.

'Assumptions' perform much the same function. They may seem innocuous, a mere prelude to the main business. But they are established by reference to preconceptions of a theory group, and close down options. Thus, the assumptions of neoclassical theory close out many aspects of human motivation. They effectively define humanity, or, rather, they take the humanity out of humans. The rule is, 'humans must act rationally to maximise their return from the resources they use'. Human behaviour defined in this way is amenable to mathematical treatment. Neoclassical theory is the mathematical implications of the rule. All the critical business is complete before any mathematics is introduced. But the conclusions of the mathematics are accepted without regard to the assumptions. It was seen in the previous chapter that the Arrow–Debreu model has been accepted as demonstrating that macroeconomic equilibrium is possible, even though it depends on assumptions, such as the absence of economies of scale, that are certainly not valid, so that it effectively demonstrates that macroeconomic equilibrium is not possible. Assumptions as definitions and as rules are important, but, as with rules in general, their function is to make positions permanent, to inhibit change, to block the evolutionary processes that might otherwise occur in the thinking from which they derive.

Coase and transaction costs

New institutional economists accept neoclassical theory as the rational foundation of their work, but seek to provide a context: 'Defining institutions as the constraints that human beings impose on themselves makes the definition complementary to the choice theoretic approach of neoclassical economic theory.'[49] The idea of transaction costs, first formulated by Ronald Coase, identifies failings of neoclassical theory that are potentially resolved through new institutional theory. Coase argued that neoclassical theory takes no account of the costs incurred in undertaking market transactions. In 'The Nature of the Firm', an article published in 1937, he attributed the formation of firms to these costs of transactions. Firms allocate resources by direction because by doing so transaction costs are reduced. Coase subsequently argued in 'The Problem of Social Cost', published in 1960, that government direction of industry could similarly be used to reduce transaction costs.[50]

These articles form the foundations of new institutional economics, so that, while they have no specific concern with the evolution of economies, some account of their content and significance in the light of the theory of support-bargaining and money-bargaining is appropriate. Coase's theory of the firm provides also a modification of the neoclassical account of the firm which, for many economists, maintains the acceptability of neoclassical theory. The idea of companies as money-bargaining agencies pursuing a viability condition is quite contrary to Coase's account of firms. It forms an essential element in the account in the following chapter of the evolution of economies. For this reason also it is appropriate to give an account of Coase's theories.

Neoclassical theory offers an automatic system for an optimal allocation of resources through a price mechanism. In a firm, resources are allocated by direction of the owners or managers of the firm. The reason for this supersession of the market, according to Coase, is that there are costs involved – 'transaction costs' – in using the price mechanism. Contracts committing employees to work under direction are used instead of reliance on the price mechanism. For Coase, the element of 'direction' defines the firm, as a master directs his servant. The discomfort of direction for the directed means that there must be some reason for imposing it, which for Coase is the avoidance of transaction costs.

Coase rejects the explanations of Maurice Dobb and F. H. Knight for the existence of firms. Dobb argued that the complexity of trading, involving extensive division of labour, requires the coordinating functions of a firm. Knight argued that the assumption of perfect information in neoclassical theory eliminates uncertainty, and real-life uncertainty requires the use of firms. In a firm, the entrepreneur assumes responsibility for uncertainties, and pays a guaranteed fixed sum to employees, contingent on their agreeing to work by direction.[51] It was suggested in *Getting It Right* that these explanations are too easily dismissed by Coase. In spite of his avowed commitment to realism, Coase accepts uncritically the abstract rationale of the neoclassical model.[52] He assumes it is an accurate reflection of the realities of economic exchange, except that, in reality, there are additional 'transaction costs'.

Coase is remarkably ambiguous regarding the precise nature of transaction costs, given the central role they play in his theory. They are initially identified as the reason for imposing direction on people who dislike it. If transaction costs associated with neoclassical markets are the reason for the formation of companies, it should be easy enough to identify them. Coase designates transaction costs as 'the costs of using the price mechanism',[53] or as 'marketing costs'.[54]

Coase elaborates further on the costs of using the price mechanism:

> The main reason why it is profitable to establish a firm is that there is a cost of using the price mechanism. The most obvious cost of 'organising' production through the price mechanism is that of discovering what the relevant prices are. This cost may be reduced but it will not be eliminated by the emergence of specialists who will sell this information. The costs of negotiating and concluding a separate contract for each exchange transaction which takes place on a market must also be taken into account.[55]

Transaction costs are, first, costs relating to acquisition of information about the prices involved in market transactions and, second, costs relating to the negotiation and conclusion of a contract for every exchange transaction. Information about prices can be partly, though not wholly, obtained through market transactions. The costs of many market contracts can be reduced by forming a company and concluding longer term contracts providing for work under direction, within certain limits. This contractual relationship is seen by Coase as the defining feature of a firm: 'When the direction of resources (within the limits of the contract) becomes dependent on the buyer in this way, that relationship which I term a "firm" may be obtained.'[56] The consistency of this relationship with the contractual relationship between a master and servant is regarded by Coase as confirmation that his concept of a firm is realistic.[57]

The identification of the first type of transaction cost is, in effect, a repudiation of the neoclassical theory on which his argument is based. Perfect information, including information about prices, is an essential assumption of the neoclassical model. Rejecting this assumption of the model means rejecting its mathematics and the 'optimisation' in the allocation of resources that it is claimed to produce.

Coase is also repudiating his own argument against Knight's contention that uncertainty is the reason for the formation of companies. Coase argues against Knight that uncertainty can be eliminated by buying advice on the (neoclassical) market: 'We can imagine a system where all advice or knowledge was bought as required.'[58] But, on his own admission, in the above quotation, it cannot be entirely eliminated. As Knight contends, a neoclassical market cannot exist in conditions of uncertainty. Coase seems to concede Knight's argument when he remarks earlier in his article, 'It seems improbable that a firm would emerge without the existence of uncertainty.'[59] Coase's transaction costs cannot be supplementary to neoclassical costs when they imply rejection of the neoclassical model.

Coase assumes further that neoclassical transactions require contracts, and the costs of negotiating these contracts constitute transaction costs that can be reduced by the formation of companies. This implies that the neoclassical system is not the independent self-optimising price mechanism that it is supposed to be. Exchanges have to be made under negotiated contracts. In his critique of Dobb, Coase asserts that the neoclassical market is sufficient in itself to allocate resources.[60] Dobb's point is that actual trading is more complex than is conceived in the neoclassical model, and Coase's attribution of contracting costs to neoclassical exchange confirms this point. Again, Coase's account of transaction costs, such as it is, invalidates the neoclassical concept that it is supposed to supplement. If acquisition of price information and negotiation of contracts are to be accounted transaction costs involved in using the neoclassical price mechanism, then there is no neoclassical price mechanism. Coase demands that Dobb and Knight recognise the realism of a pure neoclassical model that he himself shows to be invalid.

There is, of course, an easy distinction between production costs, which may be read as constituting neoclassical costs, and all the other costs that trading companies must meet, including costs of marketing, transport, advertising, administration, research, legal procedures and conformance to regulations. Coase's use of the term 'marketing costs' for transaction costs suggests this division. But Coase also designates 'marketing costs' as 'the costs of using the price mechanism', implying that they are not simply 'non-production costs'. Awareness of such a distinction may, nevertheless, have helped to sustain the idea that the need to reduce transaction costs offers a rationale for the existence of firms.

In the understanding of money-bargaining, companies function as specialist money-bargaining agencies. They aim to meet a viability condition by formatting production, or any sort of output, so that products fit the situations of potential buyers, while keeping unit costs of production at a level that permits prices acceptable in the budgetary situations of a sufficient number of buyers to generate viable sales and revenues. They adapt or develop technology to this requirement, and in many cases adopt a scale of production that gives low unit costs and, hence, prices best fitted to the budgetary situations of a large number of buyers. This, as has been seen, is totally different to the understanding of neoclassical theory. Neoclassical markets do not have supplementary costs arising from the use of the system. There is just no counterpart in reality to the conceptions of the neoclassical model. 'Firms' perform a quite different function governed by mathematical formulation. They equate marginal costs to marginal revenues, and such a function makes sense only if the equation involves all costs. Transaction costs are a chimerical explanation for the operation of companies in a chimerical neoclassical system. Companies operate on very different principles.

Coase's theory of transaction costs has been extensively taken up by economists anxious to provide a more realistic account of firms than is provided in neoclassical theory, while remaining within the neoclassical theory group. As noted in Chapter 2, some of these economic theories, and other economic theories of the firm, are discussed in the article 'Companies and Markets'.[61]

Social costs and transaction costs

Coase's 1960 article on social cost suggests that transaction costs of the sort that give rise to firms may, in a social context, imply a requirement for government regulation. Coase describes various legal cases involving the imposition of damage by one agent on another – for example, through straying cattle, smoke nuisance, exhaust of damaging chemicals, or emission of noxious odours. The accepted economic understanding of such situations derives from the work of Arthur Pigou, whose 'smoking chimneys' provide the classic example of an 'externality' in the economic literature.[62] Pigou's conclusion, widely accepted by economists, is that the originators of such damage should pay compensation for the damage they do, or should pay taxes to the value of the damage caused. Coase examines the case of a cattle-raiser whose herd damages the crops of a neighbouring farmer. He concludes that production can be maximised, in the absence of transaction costs, either by the cattle-raiser paying compensation to the farmer, or by the farmer paying the cattle-raiser to reduce the size of his herd.[63] He maintains that, 'The economic problem in all cases of harmful effects is how to maximise the value of production'.[64]

Coase argues that whether or not the damaged farmer actually pays does not affect the outcome. If he does not pay, the cost still falls on the cattle-raiser in the form of 'revenue foregone'.[65] Coase is treating the cattle-raiser as a 'resource allocator', in accordance with the requirements of the neoclassical model. But in real life, a cattle-raiser is a money-bargaining agent seeking viability. He will not take account of hypothetical revenues. It makes a difference to incentives and production if the farmer does not pay to protect his crops against threatened damage from a cattle-raiser.

The farmer is unlikely to pay. Damage, or harm, cannot be traded in a money-bargaining system. As a 'commodity' or 'service', a 'negative benefit', it cannot be sold; no one buys damage. Those threatened with damage will recognise also that if they pay to protect themselves from impending damage, they give the damager an incentive to provide more. Paying burglars to desist from burglary would merely expand their threat. Those threatened with damage will be likely to appeal to the community for protection – that is, threats of damage will be dealt with through the support-bargaining system. There is, of course, the possibility of extortion and protection rackets, but that implies rejection of support-bargaining and resort to violence.

Coase notes the economic arguments regarding resolution of the issue of damage would not be accepted by the judiciary: 'The reasoning employed by the courts in determining legal rights will often seem strange to an economist because many of the factors on which the decision turns are, to an economist, irrelevant'.[66] The judiciary has to determine who has the legal right to do what. According to Coase, its decisions can always be modified through market transactions, and if such market transactions are costless, they will always be made. Production will be restored to a maximum.

Where there are transaction costs, however, the market transactions may cost more than the benefits they bring, and the maximisation of production will not be achieved. In Coase's 1937 article, the incidence of transaction costs is seen as minimised by the establishment of a firm. In the case of social costs, however, such a course may not be feasible. The alternative is to impose 'direction' through government:

> In the standard case of a smoke nuisance, which may affect a vast number of people engaged in a wide variety of activities, the administrative costs might well be so high as to make any attempt to deal with the problem within the confines of a single firm impossible. An alternative solution is direct Government regulation. Instead of instituting a legal system of rights which can be modified by transactions on the market, the government may impose regulations which state what people must or must not do and which have to be obeyed.[67]

In such circumstances, according to Coase, 'The government is, in a sense, a super-firm (but of a very special kind) since it is able to influence the use of factors of production by administrative decision.'[68] Coase makes a distinction between legal rights and government regulation, the former being distinctly a matter for judges to determine. Those who find judgment on legal rights going against them can remedy the situation through money payments to their adversary. But government regulation is imposed without the option to buy a way out, just as a firm can direct its staff to carry out certain actions.

Coase is clearer with regard to the nature of transaction costs in his 1960 article than in his 1937 article:

> In order to carry out a market transaction it is necessary to discover who it is that one wishes to deal with, to inform people that one wishes to deal and on what terms, to conduct negotiations leading up to a bargain, to draw up the contract, to undertake the inspection needed to make sure that the terms of the contract are being observed, and so on.[69]

Such costs certainly do not feature as costs in the neoclassical model, where there is 'perfect information'. It is a reflection of the inadequacies of the model that Coase's transaction costs seem no more than the minutiae of many transactions, yet are designated a special category of costs, requiring special theoretical accommodation. They are clearly costs associated with a bargaining process. The bargaining process is further evident from the comment: 'What payment would in fact be made would depend on the shrewdness of the farmer and the cattle-raiser as bargainers.'[70] Resources are being allocated through a bargaining process superimposed on neoclassical transactions, without any recognition that the bargaining system rules out the operation of the neoclassical model. The 1960 theory of social costs has the same failing as the 1937 theory of the firm: if the analysis is correct, the neoclassical model is not operational. Coase concludes that government action is required to ensure the maximisation of production.

Coase sees the economic objective as the maximisation of production, but this only constitutes an optimal allocation of resources within the confines of the model, where consumers' choice ensures that production values correspond to the valuations of consumers. In the wider context of smoking chimneys and industrial smells the idea of optimal allocation of resources is difficult to pin down because there is no market mechanism through which consumers can express, in monetary terms, their preferences for clean air, nor any mechanism for the expression of communal valuations in monetary terms of many specific communal provisions. Production becomes divorced from the choices of consumers or citizens regarding what they will spend their money on, and hence is no indicator of optimal value. Whatever it is, optimal allocation certainly does not lie in maximisation of production.

Bargaining systems extend beyond money-bargaining into support-bargaining. Or rather, since support-bargaining is generally the primary system, due to the connections of support with security, money-bargaining is a subordinate bargaining process to support-bargaining. The values of the two systems are different. In support-bargaining the implied question is, 'How hard would you fight for this?' while in money-bargaining the question is 'How much would you work for this?' People do not actually have to engage in physical combat because, under a support convention, their support is proxy for violent capacity. But the principle is apparent. Governments would be unlikely to regulate simply for the maximisation of production. Their interests lie in the assembly of support, and their policies and actions will be directed to accommodation of the interests of existing and potential supporters. Companies, as was seen above, operate on different principles to those designated for them in the neoclassical model. Governments similarly operate on different principles to those of the neoclassical model. Governments can regulate because they are established through formal support-bargaining systems, meaning normally that they have the support of more people than other contenders for government. Governments can 'lay down the law' because if they are not obeyed they can impose penalties. Money-bargaining constitutes an offshoot of support-bargaining, falling under the direction of the support-bargaining system. Where the transactions of money-bargaining adversely affect third parties, those injured will turn to the support-bargaining system for redress.

This will normally mean turning to the judicial system for judgments in accordance with laws made through formal support-bargaining systems. A judiciary is required to apply relevant outcomes of support-bargaining to disputes. Laws cannot take into account all the circumstances that may arise, so in many cases a judiciary has scope for interpretation of their application in any particular circumstances. Laws are often drafted in such a way as to require the exercise of judicial discretion if cases are to be brought to conclusions. Where the law establishes rights that conflict, the judiciary has to determine which rights shall be regarded as predominant. This judicial discretion will sometimes extend to assessment of the economic impact of any judgment. As has been seen, the health of a money-bargaining system is important in support-bargaining. People out of work are more inclined to make demands on political systems. Judges may accept that the costs of enforcing a right to quiet or to clean air are in some cases too high to be accepted. They are, in effect, mixing the formal expressions of support that create law with their own less formal sense of where support lies. Subject to the obligation to follow formal law, judges will commonly exercise discretion by making rulings that they anticipate will have the support of most people in their society.

Their rulings may be made in the light of local distributions of support. Coase records that a British judge expressed the opinion in the nineteenth century that noxious smells from tanneries might be acceptable in Bermondsey while they would not be acceptable in Belgravia. The implication is that the poor people of Bermondsey would, on the whole, in the substantial majority, be likely to say 'yes' to noxious smells in order to sustain the industry on which many of them depended. In posh Belgravia, by contrast, there would be no tolerance of the smell of tanning and no support for anyone engaged in that business.[71]

Coase and social bargaining theory

Coase's analysis lacks understanding of political processes and the status of laws and regulations. It is a mistake to suppose that a judiciary or government will want to supplement the functioning of a neoclassical market by imposing solutions based on economic theory when the outcomes seen as desirable in economic theory are threatened. Government functions as a support-bargaining agency. Coase's administrative alternative is not an alternative, but a primary process, involving the enactment and enforcement of laws and regulations through the process of support-bargaining.[72] As was seen in Chapter 2, a money-bargaining system of any extent cannot function without the regulation provided by support-bargaining. The important valuations are made through the support-bargaining system. Coase remarks that problems of welfare economics ultimately dissolve into questions of aesthetics and morals – that is, into support-bargaining.[73] Support-bargaining governs the operation of money-bargaining systems. This has resulted in extensive protection for third parties from damage incurred as a result of the activities of companies, but not to the extent of giving them unconditional protection from such damage. Businesses which pollute the surrounding countryside for their own profit are widely condemned, but some degree of pollution is accepted in order to gain the benefits of money-bargaining.

As in his 1937 article, Coase takes the neoclassical market and its values as the reference point or touchstone of what is desirable in the social context of his 1960 article. He treats the neoclassical price mechanism not just as an abstract model but as a representation of how economic exchange actually takes place. But, more than that, in both articles he assumes that even when he introduces processes that are incompatible with the neoclassical model, the neoclassical model remains operational. The neoclassical concept exists only in the mind and is not affected by actions of companies or any other agents that are clearly incompatible with it.

Coase's intricate analysis of firms and social costs is the inevitable consequence of adopting a paradigm that cannot accommodate the phenomena it is supposed to explain. He takes neoclassical theory beyond the lecture theatre, where it reigns, but shows only that it cannot cope. Coase recognises that his analysis of social costs is unsatisfactory: 'The discussion of the problem of harmful effects in this section (when the costs of market transactions are taken into account) is extremely inadequate.'[74] Coase complains about Pigou that, 'it is impossible to be sure that one has understood what Pigou really meant' because Pigou had not thought his position through.[75] But Pigou suffered from the inherent deficiencies of the paradigm he used as reference. Coase suffers from the same problem, with similar consequences.

Coase's analysis of firms and social costs has formed the basis for the new institutional economics. Coase remarks, 'the problem is to devise practical arrangements which will correct defects in one part of the system without causing more serious harm in other parts'.[76] 'Institutions' constitute the necessary arrangements. It could be accounted a Pigovian origin, for Coase notes, 'Pigou goes on to say that if self-interest does promote economic welfare, it is because human institutions have been devised to make it so.'[77]

North's new institutional economics

Douglass North builds on Coase's idea of transaction costs. Transaction costs give rise to institutions: 'My theory of institutions is constructed from a theory of human behaviour combined with a theory of the costs of transacting.' For North transaction costs are costs of measurement and costs of enforcement:

> The costliness of information is the key to the costs of transacting, which consists of the costs of measuring the valuable attributes of what is being exchanged and the costs of protecting rights and policing and enforcing agreements. These measurement and enforcement costs are the sources of social, political, and economic institutions.[78]

Costs of measurement are the costs of assembling information relating to particular transactions – for example, information on the amount of vitamin C in an orange drink, or the precise specifications of an automobile.[79] Enforcement costs include the costs of a legal system and, in societies where formal legal systems are little developed, other means of enforcing agreements on exchanges.[80]

While North takes up Coase's idea of transaction costs, he does not align his transaction costs with those of Coase. Rather, he remarks that, 'Neither Coase nor many of the subsequent studies of transaction costs have attempted to define precisely what it is about transacting that is so costly.'[81] North's 'measurement costs' are, nevertheless, similar to Coase's price information costs. As with Coase, North's postulate of a requirement for measurement information constitutes a rejection of the neoclassical model; and enforcement costs are not part of the neoclassical model. Since the agents of the neoclassical concept are purely rational, they accept the enforcement implied by economic loss.

North nevertheless accepts some underpinning of neoclassical theory, even if he qualifies his assent so strongly that it is questionable whether it is any assent at all. The foundation in human behaviour of his theory of institutions involves something very like rejection of neoclassical theory:

> The condition of the world throughout history provides overwhelming evidence of much more than simple rational noncooperative behaviour. The behavioural assumptions of economists are useful for solving certain problems. They are inadequate to deal with many issues confronting social scientists and are the fundamental stumbling block preventing an understanding of the existence, formation, and evolution of institutions.[82]

If neoclassical theory is a 'stumbling block', it would seem appropriate to set it aside altogether. North draws on neoclassical theory, but, as the above quotations make clear, he draws also on information theory, behavioural theory and transaction costs theory. Neoclassical theory appears as a particularly obstructive stumbling block with regard to historical development. This comment appears on the first page of his final chapter:

> we have paid a big price for the uncritical acceptance of neoclassical theory. Although the systematic application of price theory to economic history was a major contribution, neoclassical theory is concerned with the allocation of resources at a moment of time, a devastatingly limiting feature to historians whose central question is to account for change over time.[83]

North's own purpose is to account for economic change, so this feature of neoclassical theory has fundamental relevance to his work. He retains enough of neoclassical foundations to severely constrict his understanding of the evolution of economies. The commitment to neoclassical theory, when it is so much at odds with his understanding of social and economic processes, suggests that concern for retention of membership of the mainstream economic theory group has been allowed to override concern for provision of an accurate explanation of the functioning of human society. It is the legacy of Robbins – if scholars do not give their assent, however qualified, to neoclassical theory, they are not economists, and not entitled to positions in scholarly institutions as 'economists'.

Institutions are the rules that structure the behaviour of individuals, or make them behave in socially acceptable ways. This has the important effect of reducing uncertainty. North remarks that, 'The major role of institutions in a society is to reduce uncertainty by establishing a stable (but not necessarily efficient) structure to human interaction.'[84] This uncertainty relates to a great variety of social and economic circumstances:

> They [institutions] are a guide to human interaction, so that when we wish to greet friends on the street, drive an automobile, buy oranges, borrow money,

form a business, bury our dead, or whatever, we know (or can learn easily) how to perform these tasks.[85]

Rules and informal practices inform people what actions are acceptable in the society under given circumstances.

Though institutions have this stabilising effect, they are themselves conceived as the sources of social change: 'Institutional change shapes the way societies evolve through time and hence is the key to understanding historical change'.[86] North does not deal with the basic institutionalist problem of how the essentially stabilising institutions are at the same time the sources of change. As with the old institutionalists, he accounts the 'institutions' as the variants, rather than the functions to which they relate. Institutions evolve, though the mechanism of their evolution is not identified. North stresses the importance of 'path dependence', but what is apparently the main mechanism of institutional change is referred to only incidentally. The emphasis is on institutions as cultural constraints determining the evolution of societies:

> These cultural constraints not only connect the past with the present and future, but provide us with a key to explaining the path of historical change. The central puzzle of human history is to account for the widely divergent paths of historical change.[87]

The institutions constitute 'constraints' on people or processes, implying that they are not the fundamental determinants of change.

Path dependence

North sees 'path dependence' as an important factor in explaining how the past links with the future. Path dependence is a state in which what happens is determined by what has already happened. The best-known example of path dependence is the retention of the QWERTY typewriter keyboard, as described by Paul David.[88] It is claimed that the QWERTY keyboard has been retained because, once established, it became necessary for those wishing to work as typists to train on a QWERTY layout, even though the Dvorak layout, developed in the 1930s, was ergonomically more efficient.

North bases his account of path dependence in *Institutions, Institutional Change and Economic Performance* on the work of Brian Arthur.[89] Arthur's theory of path dependence was developed in the context of experience with different technologies producing increasing returns to scale.[90] A particular technology could achieve market dominance because it was the first to produce a satisfactory product on a scale that gave lower unit costs than its rivals, and hence could be sold more cheaply. Once established the product would be difficult to displace. Users could find themselves 'locked in' to a particular technology.

North seeks to adapt Arthur's technological path dependence to the development of institutions, with direct analogies to Arthur's elements of technological path dependence. In his later book on *Understanding the Process of Economic Change*, North takes a broader approach to path dependence:

> How the past connects with the present and future is the subject of path dependence – a term which is used, misused and abused. It could mean nothing more than that choices in the present are constrained by the heritage of institutions accumulated from the past ... A step toward a more comprehensive understanding of the term is to recognize that the institutions that have accumulated give rise to organizations whose survival depends on the perpetuation of those institutions and which hence will devote resources to preventing any alteration that threatens their survival. A great deal of path dependence can be usefully understood in that context. The previous chapter suggests a still more complex view of path dependence. The interaction of beliefs, institutions, and organizations in the total artifactual structure makes path dependence a fundamental factor in the continuity of society.[91]

This gives the concept of path dependence a much more general application and links it with the maintenance of organisational ascendancy. North concludes that, 'A major frontier of scholarly research is to do the empirical work necessary to identify the precise sources of path dependence so that we can be far more precise about its implications.'[92] While the conceptual scope of path dependence is expanded, it is not greatly augmented in detail. 'Path dependence' is a compelling metaphor, but the reality behind it is not well established – that, of course, is why the metaphor is useful. Path dependence is considered further below.

North's stifled dynamic

North asserts, as in the quotation above at note 15 ('By now ... likely to evolve'), that his institutional theory has no dynamic, and he sees no prospect of there being one. But, on close inspection, he does provide an institutional dynamic – a dynamic that is clearly akin to support-bargaining. An idea of bargaining is sustained throughout his book as a kind of sub-text or incidental explanation of what happens. Beneath the analysis of institutions there is a more fundamental dynamic of bargaining. His comments assume that we all know about 'bargaining power' and 'bargaining strength'. It is as if North knows there is something going on that he cannot pin down and elevate to its proper place in the hierarchy of explanatory ideas. It is supplementary, but it might clearly be primary. It is appealed to as a kind of 'common theory' that everyone knows about but which is not formally recognised as theory.

Some examples of North's references to bargaining in *Institutions, Institutional Change and Economic Performance* are:

- Institutions are not necessarily or even usually created to be socially efficient; rather they, or at least the formal rules, are created to serve the interests of those with the bargaining power to devise new rules.

- Moreover, it is the bargaining strength of the individuals and organisations that counts. Hence, only when it is in the interest of those with sufficient bargaining strength to alter the formal rules will there be major changes in the formal institutional framework.
- And because much of human economic history is a story of humans with unequal bargaining strength maximising their own well-being, it would be amazing if such maximising activity were not frequently at the expense of others.[93]

North uses the idea of bargaining strength as a simple means of accounting for the observation that some people gain ascendancy, political and economic, over others. The origin of institutions lies in bargaining processes, and those with the strongest bargaining positions determine the institutions. The rules are made by the ascendant. So the evolution of societies depends not so much on changes in institutions but on the bargaining processes that determine the institutions.

North's work could be regarded not so much as institutional theory as social bargaining theory. A title such as *Bargaining and the Creation of Institutions* would scarcely misrepresent the content, even as it is. If adopted as a working title, it would surely have forced the author to elucidate his sub-text. But he remains wedded to the neoclassical framework, in which bargaining is at best anomalous. Without a proper understanding of political and economic bargaining processes he is obliged to subordinate the idea of bargaining to that of institutions. Neoclassical theory is a stumbling block upon which North falls flat.

Schumpeterian evolutionary theory

While most evolutionary theory has been produced by institutional economists, Joseph Schumpeter worked on evolutionary theory based on his own ideas of economic change driven by technological innovation. Schumpeter was an ardent admirer of Leon Walras and his mathematical account of economic processes, which formed the foundation of neoclassical theory.[94] Nevertheless, he recognised that the Walrasian approach gave a very poor account of the observable performance of economies. The business cycle seemed to display an inherent instability in economic activity. Technology clearly influenced economic development in a way that Walras's equations could not accommodate. Walras had, nevertheless, recognised that periodic crises disrupted the tendency to equilibrium.[95] Schumpeter suggested that economies evolve with periods of equilibrium interspersed with sudden spurts of technical innovation. Esben Andersen abstracts Schumpeter's account of the evolutionary process to:

1. A system of routine behaviour
2. is radically challenged by the innovative behaviour of the few,
3. but sooner or later the equilibrating forces will establish a *new* system of routines.
4. And then the story starts once more.[96]

Schumpeter's theory merges Walrasian equilibrium with his own theory of 'creative destruction' by supposing that each operates at different periods.

Schumpeter rejected any association of economic evolution with biological evolution, thus distancing himself from Veblen's evolutionary theory.[97] The differences between Darwinan evolution and social processes were too great for Schumpeter to accept that the latter could derive anything constructive from the former. Schumpeter's dynamic rested on the (non-biological) selection that is implicit in his idea of 'creative destruction'. The old institutionalists responded to the purely biological theory of natural selection, not recognising that it missed the vital support-bargaining mechanism for group formation. Schumpeter simply rejected natural selection altogether as a basis for economic evolution. Both might have done better with pigeon theory, which involves a kind of creative destruction. Pigeon fanciers determine among themselves what the ideal pigeon will be, and select for breeding those that display the right characteristics, while discarding those that do not.

Schumpeter's dynamic of 'creative destruction' is markedly different to the Walrasian mathematical dynamic that takes economies towards equilibrium. Schumpeter cannot be said to have satisfactorily reconciled the two systems. In terms of bargaining theory, there is no reconciliation to be made. Even accepting some relevance of Walrasian theory, the two systems are, as Hodgson points out, deeply incompatible: 'His [Schumpeter's] endless emphasis on leaps and discontinuities is an anathema to any true marginalist'.[98] Accepting Schumpeter's dynamic means rejecting that of Walras. Schumpeter, like Coase, claims allegiance to neoclassical theory even when espousing theories that are destructive of it. Neoclassical theory is again a stumbling block in the provision of a realistic account of economic change.

Evolution of the firm

Interest in evolutionary economic theory was rekindled in 1982 with the publication of *An Evolutionary Theory of Economic Change* by Richard Nelson and Stanley Winter.[99] Their aim was to produce a mathematical model of the evolution of the firm and industries. They describe their theory as 'neo-Schumpeterian', and it is because of this self-selected affiliation that their work is treated here, rather than in the context of the 'old institutional economics', where it might otherwise be included, by virtue of its Darwinian content.

Nelson and Winter seek to incorporate Schumpeter's theory of technological change in their model of company and industry evolution. The institutional element is central to their theory in that they specify 'routines' as the explicators of company evolution. Companies succeed or fail according to the fitness of their routines. Nelson and Winter conceive the routines as units of selection or 'variants' in the Darwinian mould. Searching turns up 'mutations' of routines that are then subject to selection. They initially present their theory on Darwinian foundations, though with a strong commitment to Lamarck's theory of inheritance of acquired characteristics. The connection with natural selection is, however, loosely made and superseded by an avowed primary commitment to neo-Schumpeterian evolution.

Martin Fransman questions whether 'routines' are useful as the central explanatory factor in a context in which non-routine events are likely to be of primary importance.[100] This is the same objection as was raised above to the idea of 'institutions' in general as the variants on which evolution might depend. Routines are essentially stabilising factors. They constrain rather than promote change. They derive from underlying functions and processes. A 'neo-Schumpeterian' approach necessarily involves accommodating 'innovation'. The use of routines in companies can also be readily explained in terms of coordination and reduction in unit costs. As noted above, routines are used to ensure that different functions mesh together. If tasks are reduced to simple routines, they can be performed by relatively low-paid employees.

One notable feature of the work of Nelson and Winter, both staff of Harvard University, an oracular institution of the neoclassical economic theory group, is a forthright rejection of neoclassical economic theory. The rejection of orthodox theory and commitment to evolutionary economics seemed to mark the opening of a new era. However, Nelson and Winter were committed to construction of a mathematical model, in the neoclassical tradition, and found themselves obliged by that commitment to adopt much of the neoclassical framework. Neoclassical assumptions lend themselves to model-building; Schumpeterian and institutional frameworks are not mathematically tractable. Difficulties in modelling technical innovation meant that they were obliged to omit that part of Schumpeter's theory that deals with product innovation, even though new products are a vital part of economic evolution.

Nelson and Winter's account of the evolution of firms brings together neoclassical theory, institutional routines, Darwinian natural selection, Lamarckian inheritance and Schumpeterian evolutionary theory. All these theories have serious flaws and some are incompatible with others. They themselves reject neoclassical theory. Schumpeter specifically rejects Darwinian natural selection as a foundation for evolutionary economic theory. Lamarck's theory runs counter to Darwinian theory and is largely discredited. Nelson and Winter make little attempt to resolve the differences, preferring instead to select from each in accordance with the requirements of their model-building. Their theory is considered in more detail in *Support-Bargaining, Economics and Society*.[101]

Esben Andersen notes that Nelson and Winter's work is only loosely a work of evolutionary economics. In 1996 he wrote:

> While frequently used, the notion of evolutionary economics is still lacking a widely agreed upon definition and we are still waiting for an authoritative exposition of 'the elements of evolutionary economics'. In this situation the inclusion of the term evolutionary economics into the title of a book or paper gives little indication of its contents ... But in what is probably the most well-known work in the area, the book by Nelson and Winter (1982), we find only more modest formulations like an 'approach' or 'an evolutionary theory of economic change', while the name 'evolutionary economics' is first met

in the index of the book (p. 432) where it suddenly becomes a designation of the Nelson and Winter research programme which combines ideas of Alchian, Simon and Schumpeter and a number of novelties.[102]

It was perhaps advantageous that evolutionary economics was not confined in a definition. It seems almost implicit in the name that 'evolutionary economics' should have the space to evolve. But the weakness of the formulations is apparent from Andersen's comment.

Path dependence and evolutionary processes

It was seen above that Douglass North stresses the importance of path dependence in social evolution but has difficulty in giving it substance. The metaphor of 'path dependence' suggests 'one thing leading to another', or 'one situation leading to another'. In North's treatment it is more a matter of continuity and entrenchment of interests rather than change. But it suggests the evolutionary mechanism of support-bargaining and money-bargaining.

Economic geographers have taken up path dependence as part of an increased interest in recent years in the evolutionary element of regional and urban development.[103] They aim to use evolutionary economic theory to assist in the understanding of the role of geographical factors in economic development as a whole, but also 'to demonstrate how *geography matters in determining the nature and trajectory of evolution of the economic system*'.[104] Three main approaches to the study of evolutionary processes are identified: generalised Darwinism; complexity theory; and path dependence theory.

Boschma and Martin understand path dependence as being specifically the idea that the economic landscape – that is, the spatial organisation of economic production, circulation, exchange, distribution and consumption – does not tend towards any equilibrium state. However, the concept is not without problems. They draw on Ron Martin and Peter Sunley to comment:

> For one thing, there is the problem of defining what it is about regional economies that follows a path dependent trajectory of development – the region's firms, its industries or the regional economy as a whole? Can multiple paths co-exist, and how do they interact? Second, what are the processes that allegedly engender path dependence in the economic landscape? Further, where do new paths come from, and why do they emerge where they do? And how do old paths come to an end?[105]

Such questions are impossible to answer in the context of neoclassical theory. Martin and Sunley see its insistence on the tendency of economies to equilibrium as a significant impediment to the emergence of a clear account of path dependence:

> we find that despite its declared emphasis on the importance of history, path dependence theory as formulated by its leading architects – David, Arthur,

and others – retains elements of equilibrium thinking, which we contend is in tension with the idea of path dependence as an evolutionary concept.[106]

As with North, neoclassical theory is a stumbling block. Martin and Sunley conclude that a rethinking of the notion of path dependence is necessary if it is to function as a core concept of evolution of the economic landscape.

Paul David emphasises the importance of an historical approach to economic theory, yet he also designates his approach as 'path-dependent equilibrium analysis'.[107] He reconciles path development with equilibrium theory by suggesting multiple possible equilibria. Which path is taken determines which equilibrium emerges. An economy becomes 'locked in' to a certain path and the equilibrium associated with that path. Exogenous shocks break the lock-in and initiate new paths. Other writers have reconciled path dependence with equilibrium by suggesting that the equilibria that emerge are temporary. They last so long as it takes for an endogenous innovation or exogenous shock to displace them and initiate a new path dependence.[108] Martin and Sunley, in contrast, suggest that a path-dependent historical process is incompatible with a tendency to equilibrium.[109] As with Schumpeter's evolutionary theory, the insistence on neoclassical equilibrium alongside path dependence involves tolerance of serious inconsistencies.

Support-bargaining and money-bargaining dispenses with any ideas of equilibrium and, as noted in Chapter 1, describes the evolutionary process as change from situation to situation, with each situation identifying interests and actions that lead on to a following situation. This, it is suggested, constitutes the reality behind the metaphor of 'path dependence'. The movement from situation to situation traces out a sequence that can have the appearance of inevitability. This is especially so when particular elements of situation play a critical part in the identification of the interests or actions necessary to take an overall situation forward.

The attention accorded by economic geographers to path dependence reflects the common experience that geographical features frequently play the role of 'critical feature' in a situation and give rise to paths of evolution. In the geographical context, the metaphorical 'path' is close to the reality of geographical features. A natural sea inlet, for example, can provide a safe anchorage for ships and give rise to evolutionary paths of development. Ship owners of necessity establish their businesses around the harbour. Those dependent on ships and shipping services will establish themselves near the harbour. However the situation evolves, the harbour remains a critical feature attracting people into the vicinity and discouraging them from going elsewhere. Man-made infrastructure can also constitute a critical feature. A bridge over a river provides the means by which people on one side of the river can connect with people on the other side. Paths, bridleways and carriageways will necessarily converge on the bridge. Businesses established on one side of the river can sell goods and services to people on the other side of the river. The bridge creates an evolutionary path. Settlements develop around the bridge rather than in those areas where crossing the river is difficult.

Bridges have played an important role in the evolution of societies and economies. Bridges over the Thames facilitated the growth of London. Cambridge was first called Grantabrycge. The name changed to Cambridge and the river was renamed the Cam, but the bridge suffix was retained. In Oxford, the existence of a ford over the Isis played a similar role. 'Oxenaforda' was a place where oxen could ford the Isis river. Guildford became prominent as the site of a ford across the River Wey, possibly across sands of a yellowish, or 'gilded', appearance. Natural geographic features and man-made infrastructure commonly constitute permanent or semi-permanent features of situation that constrain social and economic evolution to particular locations and particular forms.

Much of the movement from situation to situation is dictated by the format requirements of businesses. Businesses locate near bridges because the bridges extend vendor sets, giving greater scope for sales and better chance of meeting the viability condition. Concentrations of population are important to the formats of many businesses, so that an initial concentration of population can provide opportunities for business formats that establish new situations of greater concentration of population, attracting more businesses to format in that location. The 'paths' of evolution are often the consequences of business format centred on particular opportunities provided by an evolving situation. Imperatives of locational format based on natural geographic features, including deposits of natural resources, and on man-made infrastructure, including canals, roads and railways, have some prominence in the following chapter.

In Arthur's account of path dependence the technological format of a particular company gives it lower unit costs than other companies producing the same product. Consumers who conceive their budget as central to their situation, and are concerned for economies in expenditure, find themselves bound to buy from the company offering the lowest prices. Other companies formatted on a smaller scale, with higher unit costs, are likely to have difficulties in achieving viability. Where the budget is conceived as the predominant component of situation, there is 'lock-in' to the low unit cost and low-price producer.

In the case of the QWERTY keyboard, it was the capacity of typists to use the layout that came to be seen as critical by employers. Their format required that all typists could use the QWERTY keyboard. All aspiring typists found it necessary to acquire skill in the use of a QWERTY keyboard. To break dependence on the QWERTY layout required a large number of employers ready to accept typists trained on a different layout. If employers could be convinced that typists trained on an alternative keyboard had such high productivity as to markedly reduce their unit costs, then the lock-in might be broken. It was claimed, on the basis of 'naval studies', that the Dvorak layout raised the productivity of typists. Unfortunately, the 'naval studies' turned out to have been conducted by a Lieutenant Commander August Dvorak.[110] That perhaps explains why the claimed advantages in productivity did not register with employers.

The simple case of lock-in arising from path dependence is the case of individuals who have bought, say, a car or a computer printer. Their situation is such that they are likely to be locked in to buying spare parts from the car manufacturer or ink cartridges from the printer manufacturer. Their situation reduces their bargaining set to a single supplier. Alternative spare parts or printer ink may be available, but the risks and penalties attached may be regarded as unacceptable. The path of dependence is short but compelling.

In the case of the individual lock-in, escape depends only on the individual decision to change car or change printer, or take the risks of alternative sources of spare parts or ink. In the case of the economies of scale and the QWERTY keyboard escape is not so easily achieved, since the situation facing buyers and typists arises from the decisions of many agents, and escape depends on the coordinated decisions of many agents. Many buyers make feasible economies of scale, and many buyers must turn to alternatives to eliminate the economies of scale. Similarly, many employers make the QWERTY keyboard standard and, to change the standard, it is necessary that many employers change. Changes in the situation concepts and hence in the choices of many buyers or many sellers requires a process of support-bargaining. Assembly of support requires that many see the existing situation as unsatisfactory. And even if they do, the potential rewards may be insufficient to make acceptable the effort involved in change.

The high constraints on alternatives arising in path dependence may result in strong bargaining positions. Owners of land around the bridges of London would have had strong bargaining positions and would have gained higher rents than those with land distant from the bridges. Because of the way buyers see their situation, the company having economies of scale in Arthur's example has a strong bargaining position. Those buyers, limited in choice by their budgetary situation, have correspondingly weak bargaining positions. They are likely to obtain goods that are significantly less well fitted to their general situation than those they could obtain with a lesser budgetary constraint.

A bridge and the QWERTY layout provide standardisation, or enforce similar behaviour among many people. That is the nature of the 'path'. This standardisation has advantages in situations where uncoordinated behaviour is socially uncomfortable or dangerous. The convention that everyone drives on the left in Britain constitutes a standardisation of behaviour that eliminates the confusion and danger that would arise if there were no convention. It would be difficult to change the standard, since it works to the advantage of so many. It pre-empts many other decisions. Cars for sale in Britain need right-hand drive; road signs must be visible from the left; people learning to drive must learn to drive on the left.

It was seen in Chapter 1 that the value and use of money is dependent on its communal support. In Britain the 'pound' and 'pence' constitute the standard currency. Many decisions, regarding, for example, accounting and vending machines, are pre-empted by the standardisation of the currency.

A de facto standard was established in the early years of personal computing with the use of Microsoft's Windows operating system and its associated software. The standard was convenient to many. However, while the QWERTY layout was generic, and driving on the left is customary in Britain, neither giving any particular company a bargaining advantage, the acceptance of Windows software as standard gave Microsoft a strong bargaining position, by which it became very profitable. It imposed constraints on the software development of others. With many individual users, the standard remained effective for a long period. But, in time, those left in weak bargaining positions, and resentful of the 'path dependence' that brought it about, became sufficiently well organised, and assembled sufficient support, to gain passage of legislation that opened opportunities for alternative suppliers of operating and other software.

The understanding of what is critical in a situation can be straightforward, as in the case of an individual owning a computer printer, but it can also be complex. The critical feature of situation may be a matter of common assent, usually involving some material presence, but it may be the idiosyncrasy of an individual, or even the idiosyncrasy of a group. As was seen in Chapter 1, understanding of situation is subject to group influence, and identification of critical features will similarly be subject to group influence. All that is required is that there be sufficient recognition that a certain feature of situation is critical to impose that feature as an ongoing determinant of choice. Because of the diverse influences on the understanding of situation, many factors can be seen as critical and impose a certain evolutionary sequence. Some groups become 'locked in' to a particular brand of shoe, scarf, handbag or car because it is conceived as a critical indicator of membership of a group.

Martin and Sunley draw a parallel between the lock-in of path dependence and the intellectual lock-in that binds much of economics, including much evolutionary economics, to the idea of equilibrium.[111] This intellectual lock-in can be seen as an aspect of intellectual support-bargaining. The predominance of the neoclassical paradigm constitutes a critical component of situation for economists. Many interests and opportunities are tied up with such reference. It is a dependence shored up by very material interests of employment and career. Breaking the dependence involves intensive support-bargaining to formulate a better alternative, gain its acceptance by many individuals and bring about its adoption in the dominant institutions of learning and instruction. An alternative will be better when it shows greater explanatory capacity than the existing theory, and hence gives its adherents a greater sense of intellectual security. But while this greater explanatory capacity can go so far in generating increased intellectual security, the full sense of intellectual security is only achieved when the new theory is adopted by a large theory group. It is communal endorsement that gives most people the sense that they are right.

The path dependence and lock-in arising from acceptance of theory is apparent also in the acceptance of 'definitions', 'rules' and 'assumptions', as described above. These constrain users to certain understanding, and eliminate alternative understanding. They impose certain frames on their adherents. They lock in their adherents to certain modes of thinking, setting them on certain evolutionary paths of thought. Theoretical frames and definitions capture minds just as surely as a bridge captures the attention of businessmen.

Economic geographers have been remarkably tolerant of a paradigm that cannot accommodate spatial considerations any more than it can accommodate historical change. As Martin and Sunley point out, the preconception of equilibrium is incompatible with an evolutionary approach, but some economic geographers retain commitment to it. It seems another fallout from Robbins. With the theory of support-bargaining and money-bargaining, spatial evolution gets the central role that it plays in reality.[112]

The idea of path dependence has taken evolutionary theorists closest to the evolutionary process identified through support-bargaining and money-bargaining. It implies the compelling nature of existing situations and the evolution of societies from situation to situation. Existing situations, the selections they imply, the constraints they impose and the opportunities they offer are at times so compelling as to leave little choice but to proceed in accordance with their prompting. Natural geographical features such as fords and man-made features such as bridges can determine the evolution of whole regions. The understanding of the evolution of economies requires understanding of their spatial evolution. 'Path dependence' presents, in metaphorical form, an evolutionary process driven by support-bargaining and money-bargaining – the reality behind the metaphor.

Foundations of evolutionary economics

The attempts to develop an evolutionary theory of economics have suffered from shaky foundations. Perhaps most notably, Darwinian natural selection, potentially the most secure foundation of all, is incomplete, omitting just the process that is most particularly relevant to cultural evolution and hence to the evolution of economies. Hodgson and other old institutionalists cannot successfully adapt the variation–selection–inheritance sequence to social and economic processes. Nelson and Winter, though sketching their foundations rather loosely, also suffer from this particular deficiency of Darwinian theory.

The other popular foundation is neoclassical theory. North well recognised it as a stumbling block, particularly with regard to historical account. He is unable to see beyond it to the bargaining process that is lodged so unobtrusively in his work. Schumpeter, dismissive of the Darwinian approach, is so devoted to neoclassical theory, or at least to Walras, that he is prepared to tolerate it as alternating with the wholly incompatible process of evolution by innovation. The old institutionalists properly reject it, but then find they can give no alternative account of monetary exchange and pricing. Nelson and Winter reject it, but are obliged to reinstate large parts of it as necessary to their model-building. Even prominent geographical economists, who might be expected to be the first to reject a theory that lacks any concept of space, sustain the notion of equilibrium.

The neoclassical model is the more insidious a stumbling block because it is a purely mental block. There is little connection with the real world, and certainly none of the empirical evidence necessary to maintain the hypotheses of a science. The 'consumers', 'firms' and 'markets' of the economic model are mathematical formulations, only connected by nomenclature with the real world.[113] For members of the neoclassical theory group there is a 'neoclassical system' that runs whether you can see it or not. The mathematical model is projected onto the reality, so that it seems real. If you cannot see it, you are not an economist. Such is its hold on the minds of the theory group it can be projected as a reality despite any amount of evidence that it is false. It is an article of faith. Firms and governments may function in direct contradiction to its precepts, but still it is there. The obscurities of Coase, Schumpeter and the new institutionalists arise from this 'projected reality', which always has to be accommodated. Theorists tolerate the most extreme inconsistencies and evasions to maintain their allegiance to the model. Identification of the actual system as a matter of money-bargaining reveals the full extent of the neoclassical illusion.

The explanation of this quasi-religious commitment to neoclassical theory lies in the institutionalisation (in the sense of organisation) of economics on the basis of Robbins's definition of economics as concerned with the allocation of scarce means for competing purposes.[114] The neoclassical theory group established itself as the dominant group in the institutions teaching economics, so that professional advancement in these institutions required commitment to 'mainstream' theory. The mainstream exercised its ascendancy through appointments, promotions, research finance, teaching curricula, journal publication and book publication. For all but a few, leaving the mainstream meant something like professional oblivion. Because of this constraint, the theory group came to accept that members could stretch neoclassical theory to extremes and still be admitted as members. Only outright rejection of neoclassical theory would bring expulsion from the theory group.

This lingering commitment to neoclassical theory, and the failure to find an alternative, is evident in a conspicuous feature of the theories of economic evolution. They confine themselves almost entirely to theoretical issues. They are concerned mainly with abstractions and hypotheses. There are few examples of how actual historical events are explained by the evolutionary theory. There is no attempt to provide a systematic account of the evolution of economies in accordance with the theories. As noted in the Introduction, the observable evolution of economies requires that evolutionary processes are a central feature of any economic theory. But the theory must also be shown to apply to the actual historical evolution of economies. The following chapter seeks to explain the evolution of economies, particularly the British economy in the period of the industrial revolution, in terms of support-bargaining and money-bargaining.

Notes

1 Cf. Andersen, Esben Sloth, 1996, *Evolutionary Economics: Post-Schumpeterian Contributions*, London and New York: Pinter, n. 22, pp. 24–5.
2 Veblen, Thorstein, 1998/1898, 'Why is Economics not an Evolutionary Science?' *Cambridge Journal of Economics*, Vol. 22, No. 4, pp. 403–14.
3 Veblen, Thorstein, 1899, *The Theory of the Leisure Class: An Economic Study in the Evolution of Institutions*, New York: Macmillan.
4 Spread, Patrick, 2013, *Support-Bargaining, Economics and Society: A Social Species*, London and New York: Routledge, pp. 210–16.

5 For an account of Veblen's development of institutional and evolutionary economic theory, see Hodgson, Geoffrey, 2004, *The Evolution of Institutional Economics: Agency, Structure and Darwinism in American Institutionalism*, London and New York: Routledge, pp. 143–94.
6 Metcalfe, Stanley J., 2005, 'Evolutionary Concepts in Relation to Evolutionary Economics', in Dopfer, Kurt, 2005, *The Evolutionary Foundations of Economics*, Cambridge: Cambridge University Press, pp. 391–430, p. 394. Metcalfe's references: Lewontin, Richard, 1974, *The Genetic Basis of Evolutionary Change*, New York: Columbia University Press; Brandon, Robert N., 1990, *Adaptation and Environment*, Princeton, NJ: Princeton University Press.
7 Metcalfe, 2005, p. 411. An 'interactor' is distinguished from a 'replicator' in the way that, in Richard Dawkins's theory (Dawkins, Richard, 1976, *The Selfish Gene*, Oxford: Oxford University Press), a gene is distinguished from its vehicle. The vehicle, or interactor, is the visibly active element, while the replicator, or gene, gains replication or annihilation, dependent on the performance of the interactor or vehicle. The distinction corresponds roughly to the distinction between the genotype and the phenotype (see Hodgson, Geoffrey and Knudsen, Thorbjørn, 2010, *Darwin's Conjecture: The Search for General Principles of Social and Economic Evolution*, Chicago and London: Chicago University Press, p. 24. See also p. 228).
8 Hodgson and Knudsen, 2010, p. 23.
9 Hodgson and Knudsen, 2010, pp. viii, 26, 37.
10 Hodgson and Knudsen, 2010, p. 231. Original emphasis. See also pp. 42, 44–5.
11 Sanderson, S. K., 1990, *Social Evolutionism: A Critical History*, Cambridge, MA, and Oxford: Basil Blackwell, p. 2. Quoted by Andersen, 1996, n. 20, p. 24. See also Andersen, 1996, pp. 3–4, 16–17.
12 Rutherford, Malcolm, 2001, 'Institutional Economics: Then and Now', *Journal of Economic Perspectives*, Vol. 15, No. 3, pp. 173–94, p. 173.
13 Hodgson, Geoffrey, 1988, *Economics and Institutions*, Cambridge: Polity Press.
14 North, Douglass C., 2005, *Understanding the Process of Economic Change*, Princeton, NJ, and Oxford: Princeton University Press, p. viii.
15 North, 2005, pp. 125–6.
16 Hodgson, Geoffrey, 2004, *The Evolution of Institutional Economics: Agency, Structure and Darwinism in American Institutionalism*, London and New York: Routledge, pp. 124–282.
17 Hodgson, Geoffrey, 2006, 'What are Institutions?', *Journal of Economic Issues*, Vol. 40, No. 1, pp. 1–25, p. 2. Original emphasis.
18 Hodgson, 2006, p. 2.
19 Hodgson, 2006, p. 3. Original emphasis.
20 Hodgson, 2006, p. 7.
21 Hodgson, Geoffrey, 1997, 'The Ubiquity of Habits and Rules', *Cambridge Journal of Economics*, Vol. 21, No. 6, pp. 663–84, quotation p. 664.
22 Hodgson, Geoffrey, 1998, 'The Approach of Institutional Economics', *Journal of Economic Literature*, Vol. 3, No. 1, pp. 166–92, p. 175.
23 Hodgson and Knudsen, 2010, p. ix. Hodgson and Knudsen's reference: Dewey, John, 1922, *Human Nature and Conduct: An Introduction to Social Psychology*, 1st edition, New York: Holt.
24 Hodgson and Knudsen, 2010, pp. viii, 3, 22–3, 26, 45, 224.
25 Hodgson, 1997, p. 679. Hodgson's references: Peirce, C. S., 1934, 'Pragmatism and Pragmaticism', Vol. V, in Hartshorne, C. and Weiss, P. (eds), *Collected Papers of Charles Sanders Peirce*, Cambridge, MA: Harvard University Press; Veblen, 1899; Veblen, T. B., 1919, *The Place of Science in Modern Civilisation and Other Essays*, New York: Huebsch.
26 Hodgson, 1998, p. 170.
27 Hodgson, 1998, p. 169.

28 Hodgson, 1998, p. 170.
29 Tool, Marc R., 2002, 'Contributions to an Institutionalist Theory of Price Formation', in Hodgson, Geoffrey, M. (ed.), 2002, *A Modern Reader in Institutional and Evolutionary Economics*, Cheltenham and Northampton, MA: Edward Elgar, p. 3.
30 Tool, 2002, p. 5.
31 Tool, 2002, p. 5.
32 Tool, 2002, p. 6.
33 Tool, 2002, p. 6.
34 Tool, 2002, pp. 7–8.
35 Tool, 2002, p. 9. Original emphasis.
36 Tool, 2002, pp. 7, 9, 22.
37 Hodgson, 2006, p. 18
38 North, Douglass C., 1990, *Institutions, Institutional Change and Economic Performance*, Cambridge: Cambridge University Press, pp. 3–4.
39 North, Douglas, 1994, 'Economic Performance through Time', *American Economic Review*, Vol. 84, No. 3, pp. 359–67, p. 361. Quoted by Hodgson, 2006, p. 9.
40 Hodgson, 2006, p. 10. Original emphasis.
41 Hodgson, 2006, p. 10. Original emphasis.
42 North, letter to Hodgson, quoted in Hodgson, 2006, p. 19.
43 Hodgson, 1997, p. 673.
44 Hodgson, 1997, p. 678.
45 For the process of theory formation see Spread, Patrick, 2008, *Support-Bargaining: The Mechanics of Democracy Revealed*, Sussex: Book Guild, Chapter 10, Intellectual Support-Bargaining.
46 Marshall, Alfred, 1920, *Principles of Economics*, 8th edition, London: Macmillan.
47 Hodgson, Geoffrey, 2001, *How Economics Forgot History: The Problem of Historical Specificity in Social Science*, London and New York: Routledge, p. 207.
48 Robbins, Lionel, 1932, *An Essay on the Nature and Significance of Economic Science*, London: Macmillan, p. 15.
49 North, 1990, p. 5.
50 Coase, R. H., 1937, 'The Nature of the Firm', *Economica*, Vol. 4, No. 16, pp. 386–405; Coase, R. H., 1960, 'The Problem of Social Cost', *Journal of Law and Economics*, Vol. 3, pp. 1–44.
51 Coase's references: Dobb, Maurice, 1928, *Russian Economic Development since the Revolution*, London: Routledge; Knight, Frank, *Risk, Uncertainty and Profit*, Boston: Houghton Mifflin.
52 For further comment on Coase, 1937, see Spread, Patrick, 2004, *Getting It Right: Economics and the Security of Support*, Sussex: Book Guild, pp.58–66.
53 Coase, 1937, p. 403.
54 Coase, 1937, pp. 392, 394, 395, 405.
55 Coase, 1937, pp. 390–1.
56 Coase, 1937, p. 392.
57 Coase, 1937, p. 404.
58 Coase, 1937, pp. 400–1.
59 Coase, 1937, p. 392.
60 Coase, 1937, p. 398.
61 Spread, Patrick, 2015a, 'Companies and Markets: Economic Theories of the Firm and a Concept of Companies as Bargaining Agencies', *Cambridge Journal of Economics*, Advance Access published 2 June 2015, doi:10.1093/cje/bev029. Reprinted in Spread, 2015b, *Aspects of Support-Bargaining and Money-Bargaining*, E-Book, World Economics Association.
62 Pigou, A. C., 1932, *The Economics of Welfare*, London: Macmillan.
63 Coase, 1960, pp. 6–8.
64 Coase, 1960, p. 15.

65 Coase, 1960, p. 7.
66 Coase, 1960, p. 15.
67 Coase, 1960, p. 17.
68 Coase, 1960, p. 17.
69 Coase, 1960, p. 15.
70 Coase, 1960, p. 5.
71 Coase, 1960, pp. 20–1.
72 Coase, 1960, pp. 17–19.
73 Coase, 1960, p. 43.
74 Coase, 1960, p. 18.
75 Coase, 1960, p. 39.
76 Coase, 1960, p. 34.
77 Coase, 1960, p. 29.
78 North, 1990, p. 27.
79 North, 1990, pp. 28–9.
80 North, 1990, pp. 31, 55.
81 North, 1990, pp. 28.
82 North, 1990, p. 24.
83 North, 1990, p. 131.
84 North, 1990, p. 6.
85 North, 1990, pp. 3–4.
86 North, 1990, p. 3.
87 North, 1990, p. 6.
88 David, Paul A., 1985, 'Clio and the Economics of QWERTY', *American Economic Review*, Vol. 75, No. 5, pp. 332–7.
89 North, 1990, pp. 93–5.
90 Arthur, Brian W., 1989, 'Competing Technologies, Increasing Returns, and Lock-In by Historical Events', *Economic Journal*, Vol. 99, No. 394, pp. 116–31.
91 North, 2005, pp. 51–2.
92 North, 2005, p. 77.
93 North, 1990, pp. 16, 68, 134. Further references to bargaining are on pp. 47, 48, 49, 63, 65, 79, 82, 84, 89, 90, 101, 104, 109, 136.
94 Andersen, 1996, p. 1.
95 Andersen, 1996, p. 9.
96 Andersen, 1996, p. 29. Original emphasis.
97 Schumpeter, Joseph A., 1934/1911, *The Theory of Economic Development: An Enquiry into Profits, Capital, Credit, Interest and the Business Cycle*, London: Oxford University Press, pp. 57–8. See also Andersen, 1996, Note 20, p. 24. See also Spread, 2013, pp. 218–19.
98 Hodgson, Geoffrey, 1996, *Economics and Evolution: Bringing Life Back into Economics*, Ann Arbor: University of Michigan Press, p. 147. See also Spread, Patrick, 2012, 'The Evolution of Economic Theory: And some Implications for Financial Risk Management', *Real-World Economics Review*, No. 61, 26 September, pp. 217–19.
99 Nelson, Richard R. and Winter, Stanley G., 1982, *An Evolutionary Theory of Economic Change*, Cambridge, MA: Belknap Press.
100 Fransman, Martin, 1994, 'Information, Knowledge, Vision and Theories of the Firm', *Industrial and Corporate Change*, Vol. 3, No. 3, pp. 713–57, p. 741.
101 Spread, 2013, pp. 216–19. See also Spread, 2015a.
102 Andersen, 1996, Note 21, p. 24. See also Note 22.
103 Boschma, Ron and Martin, Ron, 2010, 'The Aims and Scope of Evolutionary Economic Geography', in Boschma, Ron and Martin, Ron (eds), 2010, *The Handbook of Evolutionary Economic Geography*, Cheltenham and Northampton, MA: Edward Elgar, p. 3.

104 Boschma and Martin, 2010, p. 6. Original emphasis.
105 Boschma and Martin, 2010, p. 8. See Martin, Ron and Sunley, Peter, 2010, 'The Place of Path Dependence in an Evolutionary Perspective on the Economic Landscape', in Boschma and Martin, 2010, p. 68.
106 Martin and Sunley, 2010, p. 64.
107 David, Paul A., 2005, 'Path Dependence in Economic Processes: Implications for Policy Analysis in Dynamical System Contexts', in Dopfer, 2005, pp. 151–94, pp. 151, 153.
108 Martin and Sunley, 2010, pp. 71–4.
109 Martin and Sunley, 2010, pp. 69, 72–3, 84, 86.
110 Liebowitz, Stan J. and Margolis, Stephen E., 2000, 'Path Dependence', in Bouckaert, B. and De Geest, G. (eds), *Encyclopaedia of Law and Economics*, Cheltenham: Edward Elgar and Ghent: University of Ghent, 0770, pp. 981–98, p. 992.
111 Martin and Sunley, 2010, p. 86.
112 On locational format of companies, see Spread, 2008, Chapter 5, Locational Format.
113 Spread, 2013, pp. 194–5. See also Spread, 2008, pp. 331–2.
114 On institutionalisation, see Spread, 2013, pp. 165–6, 168–71.

5 The evolution of money-bargaining

The dominance of landowners

Spoils of conquest

Throughout human history some of the strongest bargaining positions have been established through possession or control of land. It is quite commonly possible for a single individual or family to own or control all the land in a locality. Everyone needs land, or the food that derives from it. Possession of land and the dependence of others on access to land, or the produce of land, has given strong bargaining positions to some, with correspondingly weak bargaining positions for others. Many people have found themselves dependent on landowners for their sustenance. Such dependence has often obliged them to make returns to landowners, through provision of services and displays of deference, as a matter of survival.

Land has been historically of such vital interest that its allocation has commonly been determined by violence. People fight for territory. Once the group, the tribe, or the nation has secured its territory, land is allocated by leaders to those deemed to have merited it or to those strong enough to demand it. Such allocations normally have regard to the part played by recipients in the original fight for the territory, at least in the immediate aftermath of the territorial acquisition. The land of England was distributed in this way in the eleventh century. William of Normandy, claimant to the English throne over Harold, won the battle of Hastings in 1066 and occupied the territory. In the aftermath of conquest and consolidation the land was substantially redistributed to the Norman knights that had helped with the conquest, subject to their continued provision of military services. The Domesday Book of 1086 showed that half the value of land and property in the whole country was in the hands of fewer than 200 men, mostly Norman barons. There were only two surviving English lords of any account, while more than 4,000 thegns had lost their land.[1]

The Domesday Book records that over 90 per cent of the people earned their livelihood from the land. There were no significant alternative sources of employment. 'The king and a tiny group of powerful men' lived in style on the revenues of their great estates. Ranged under them, and heavily dependent on them, were the 'free men' or 'sokemen', who comprised about 14 per cent of the population and held about 20 per cent of the land; the 'villani', comprising about 41 per cent of the population and holding about 45 per cent of the land; the 'bordars' or 'cottars', comprising 32 per cent of the people and holding just 5 per cent of the land; and the slaves, who comprised about 9 per cent of the population and held no land.[2] Ownership and access to land thus stratified the population into those who dominated the society, a large number of middle-ranking people who held land roughly in proportion to their numbers in the population and a large number having very little land or no land at all. This stratification by reference to land ownership and access produced a social hierarchy that would largely enforce the interests of the ascendant group. The middle-rankers, with a significant stake in retention of their good access to land, would be inclined to discourage disruption from those with lesser status. Order and a degree of stability could be achieved. The lowest were obliged to proffer their support, heartfelt or not, to those in superior positions in order to ensure that they were not cut off entirely from any means of sustenance. The ascendant group held almost a monopoly of effective violence and could bolster the hierarchical order through violence and the threat of violence.

The ascendancy of the landed was reinforced by their capacity to make and enforce laws. The ascendant group makes the laws, taking care, if it is wise, to maintain the support of the critical levels of the landed hierarchy that sustains it. The makers of law in England following the conquest seem naturally to have regarded laws as a means of keeping the conquered populace under control. The laws did not necessarily apply to themselves. Their ascendant bargaining positions, and their capacity for violence, extensively ensured that those appointed to enforce the law did so selectively. It was centuries before the ruling group was forced to recognise that the law applied to its own members. King John was reminded of it in Magna Carta but took no notice. Most spectacularly, Charles I was executed under laws that he might have thought were his, interpreted and applied by a newly ascendant group.

The continuity of landowning life in England was assured through the custom of primogeniture, whereby estates passed intact to the eldest son of the proprietor. It was up to the eldest son to expand his inheritance by marrying a daughter of some other proprietor. Marriage constituted for many centuries the major means by which landowners under stress could revive their fortunes. Among the more spectacular marital coups was the seventeenth-century marriage of the Duke of Somerset to Baroness Percy, a daughter of the greatest northern family. Petworth House in West Sussex was built on the proceeds.

Bargaining positions and the Black Death

The social order based on land ownership and control, originally imposed by violence, was sustained as a social order that delivered a degree of security to all, without the necessity for high levels of violent enforcement. Freedom to go about the daily business of earning a living and raising a family without imminent threat of death or dispossession has always been much prized, even if the arrangements that bring it about do not accord with modern principles of social justice. There was, however, a serious jolt to the system in the mid-fourteenth century with the loss of perhaps one third of the population from the Black Death in 1348–9. This, coupled with several serious subsequent outbreaks of plague in the fourteenth century, brought about a radical change in the situations of landowners and those dependent on land. Bargaining positions were dependent on the options open to landowners and to their potential tenants and labourers. Bargaining positions changed markedly. Landowners found themselves short of tenants and labour. The lower orders found they could choose among landlords vying for their services. Ralph Griffiths records that,

> For many peasants, this became an age of opportunity, ambition and affluence ... The peasant in a smaller labour market was often able to shake off the disabilities of centuries, force rents down, and insist on a better wage for his hire ... Landowners, on the other hand, were facing severe difficulties.[3]

Some landowners intensified the exploitation of their tenants to revive their revenues, while others enclosed land for their use that had previously been open to common usage.[4]

For the most part, the evolution of society was a matter of small changes in situation from day-to-day and year-to-year, deriving from and bringing about small changes in behaviour, adding up to a slow evolution of society. The Black Death marked a sudden and radical change in situation, an interruption of the slow evolution that was normal experience. Behaviour changed markedly in response to the new situation. People found it was no longer necessary to pay such deep deference to landowners. Their new bargaining positions meant they could assert their own interests more strongly.

The Black Death might be regarded as an 'external shock', rather than a consequence of a characteristic 'situation-to-situation' evolution. For most English people it would appear as 'a bolt from the blue'. But it arose in the course of evolution of a wider bargaining process. The Black Death was a consequence of England's engagement in international trade. The fleas that transmitted the plague infested the rats that came in on ships from foreign ports. The wildlife, pursuing its own survival, availed itself of the opportunities arising from human trade.

The links between support-bargaining, governed by concerns over security, and money-bargaining, concerned mainly with material interests, were clearly very close under the feudal order – in fact, scarcely separable. Access to the necessities of life depended on access to land in some form. People were obliged to work for their access. They also had to behave in accordance with the expectations of the ruling group. A very weak money-bargaining position meant people had to retain support through support-bargaining. The elite could take advantage of such dependence. What there was of an economy was a political and social economy.

At the same time, political ascendancy required the buttresses of money revenues derived from land ownership and control.

The evolution of a full support-bargaining system in Britain from the violent society of the eleventh century is described in *Support-Bargaining: The Mechanics of Democracy Revealed*.[5] The limitation of voting rights under a support convention to people holding land or other property, right up to the Representation of the People Act of 1918, reflects the continued hold on people of the land-based system of social, political and economic order.

Population growth and alternative revenues

After the several incidents of plague in the fourteenth century the population had fallen from between 4 and 5 million prior to the 1348–9 visitation to about 2.5 million in 1377.[6] Growth in population only resumed around 1525. In the following years of the sixteenth century the bargaining positions of landowners changed again, this time for the better, with corresponding weakening of bargaining position for everyone else. According to John Guy:

> Land hunger led to soaring rents. Tenants of farms and copyholders were evicted by business-minded landlords. Several adjacent farms would be conjoined, and amalgamated for profit, by outside investors at the expense of sitting tenants. Marginal land would be converted to pasture for more profitable sheep-rearing. Commons were enclosed, and waste land reclaimed, by landlords or squatters, with consequent extinction of common grazing rights.[7]

Many of these 'business-minded landlords' would presumably have been, after 1536–7, the buyers of former monastic lands expropriated by Henry VIII. The expropriation of the land and treasure of the monasteries constituted a major accrual of wealth to the Crown, sufficient in normal circumstances to relieve the Crown of any necessity for taxation, and hence any necessity to negotiate with landowners. Henry's debts, however, and his further pursuit of dynastic honour on the battlefield in the 1540s, meant that the wealth accrued from the monasteries was rapidly disbursed. The change of ownership of substantial landholdings, just at a time when population growth augmented the demand for land, seems to have hastened the emergence of new approaches to land management.

Enclosure played a significant part in the adoption of a more commercial approach to agriculture. Enclosure increased the scope for agricultural improvement. Livestock and crops could be alternated, to the benefit of yields in both activities. Land alternating between pasture and arable use was more productive than land that was permanently used for one or the other. The advantages of the alternating land use meant that rents of enclosed land diverged increasingly from rents of unenclosed land. Tudor landowners exercised the bargaining position still inherent in ownership of land by extending their enclosure of land.

The weakness of the bargaining positions of ordinary people was reflected in the extinction of common rights through enclosure. The changes were not, however, in any way a reversion to the highly divergent bargaining positions that obtained prior to the Black Death. D. C. Coleman notes that enclosure was limited in the latter half of the sixteenth century.[8] Given the advantages of enclosure, its limited extent suggests that there was no longer any substantial number of people with the status of 'bordars', 'cottars' or slaves, with little or no defence against the ambitions of landowners. Those lower down in the social hierarchy retained bargaining position. Coleman records substantial opposition to enclosure, including the passing of a statute against enclosure in 1489 and Thomas More's *Utopia*, in which an encloser is rated a 'covetous and insatiable cormorant'.[9] Ideas were gaining support that moderated the inclination to enclosure of land.

Population change may go unrecognised as the origin of social change by those immediately involved. It may constitute a hidden element of situation, affecting bargaining positions but not understood as the origin of such effect. A farmer might find himself presented with a rent increase. He would know from gossip around the market that other farmers were facing similar demands. If he refused, he would lose his tenancy. He would perhaps lament that times had changed since his grandfather's day, when landowners were only too pleased to get a good tenant like himself. The landowner and his steward would know that it was easy to find new tenants. They might have enquiries coming in from men with good records. They would perhaps congratulate themselves on making the estate so attractive, when their grandfathers had difficulty in getting tenants. Both landowner and farmer would assess the situation, their interests and their bargaining position, and rents would rise. The higher rents would establish a new situation, perhaps stimulating some to think that they might be better off buying and selling grain as an intermediary, rather than growing it. They would scarcely be aware of the demographic changes that were affecting the situation. They would respond in accordance with their immediate experience of situation change, producing in aggregate the evolution of whole societies. The changes in the body of society will affect the distribution of support in society. Hence, they will influence the behaviour of the ruling elite, whose decisions affect events more directly, and who are consequently the stronger focus of attention in history books.

People dependent on land could always experience sharp changes from year-to-year in their situations and bargaining positions as harvests were bountiful or bad. The first half of the seventeenth century ended with a sequence of bad harvests and 'rocketing food prices':

> Amongst a people of whom many lived around the level of bare subsistence, such catastrophic weather – and there are suggestions of a general worsening of climate in northern and north-western Europe in the late sixteenth and early seventeenth centuries – brought scarcities which could hardly have failed to exacerbate the results of chronic malnutrition.[10]

The effects of bad harvests can so change bargaining positions as to contribute to the breakdown of whole bargaining systems. In 1783–4 volcanos in Iceland erupted for eight months, spreading ash clouds over Europe and beyond. The eruptions brought famine in Iceland. In Europe they brought a period of bad weather and bad harvests, contributing to the unrest that culminated in the French Revolution of 1789. The people of Iceland no doubt knew the origin of their misfortunes, but Europe experienced it only as extraordinary weather and atmospheric conditions. People finding themselves in situations in which they could not maintain themselves demanded more of governments that were, in some cases, ill-prepared to deal with such emergencies. European society, and French society in particular, evolved in new directions

Coleman notes that in the period 1450 to 1750 immense prestige attached to the ownership of land and played a major role in political and social advancement:

> Wealth made in trade, finance, or the law was invested in land, at the most practical level because it provided the safest outlet for profits, and at another level because it conferred social status, provided a base for family advancement, and offered a lever for political power.[11]

But clearly, there is an implication that the predominance of land had declined. Wealth made in trade, finance and the law was invested in land, implying that land was not so overwhelmingly the source of wealth that it had been up to the fourteenth century. A more extensive money-bargaining system had developed alongside land ownership. For some, land was becoming a status symbol, associating them with the traditional exercise of power in the land, rather than a matter of basic livelihood. They played the landed gentleman, but were assuming second persona, rather than being tied in to a way of life rooted in the land.

The hierarchy of land in the seventeenth century

Peter Matthias portrays landowning and land access in the period 1750–1850 as a hierarchical structure not entirely unlike that given above for the mediaeval period. He describes three main groups directly concerned with the land. The landowners were concerned with rents rather that engaging themselves directly in agricultural production. There was also an element of show: 'Magnates wanted the technically best animals and seeds – just as they wanted the fastest horses – for prestige more than for profit.' The second group comprised those having rights over land. This included small freeholders, owner-cultivators, the rent-paying peasantry not employing labour, the farmer who paid rents and employed labour, the smallholders, and squatters, the last of whom had no legal title to land but had rights of customary usage. The third group comprised landless farm labourers working for wages. The land still sustained a hierarchy, even though it did not have the steep differentials of bargaining position that were apparent in the mediaeval arrangements for land usage. Mathias remarks that, 'No sharp divisions existed here between rural groups. A characteristic of English society as a whole was exactly the lack of sharp frontiers between classes. No formal boundaries existed: landowners did not form a caste'.[12] Situation plays a large part in the determination of bargaining position, and the bargaining positions of the lower orders were sustained in part by the availability of alternative sources of income. Many people engaged in both agriculture and industry, since industry in its early stages was a matter of people working in their own cottages at spindles and looms, supplementing their agricultural earnings. Such occupations could fit in well with variations in demand for agricultural labour and the availability of female labour. During the period there arose more and more opportunities for leaving agriculture altogether for work in industry in the growing towns.

The lack of formal boundaries did not mean there were no significant differences of interests. 'English landowners had a particular interest in agricultural improvement, with the transcendent object of increasing their rent rolls'.[13] The movement for agricultural improvement was strongest among the landed gentry, the large owner-occupiers and tenants with substantial farms, rather than the aristocratic landowners. Enclosures and engrossing were the foundation of improvement. The enclosure movement gathered momentum in the second half of the eighteenth century and reached its peak in the first decade or so of the nineteenth, coinciding with the requirements of wartime.[14] Coleman records that prevailing anti-enclosure sentiment abated in the mid-seventeenth century.[15] Small proprietors and peasants suffered in the process. 'Much more ruthless elimination occurred of persons without ownership of land sufficient to support a family, but who had made ends meet by their rights of common over fens, commons, wastes, woods, heaths and moors'.[16] The returns on land were raised at the heavy expense of common people.

Accounting the change

The growth of industry and trade resulted in growing recognition that a money-bargaining system was developing alongside the old integrated order of land as both security and source of income. Sir William Petty, born in 1623, was one of the first to recognise that this new sphere of activity could be described and its changes tracked in quantitative terms. His *Political Arithmetic*, as was seen in Chapter 3, was a first exercise in macroeconomic accounting. Petty recognised the possibility of aggregating the value and volume of individual transactions to provide an account of the monetary transactions of the nation.

The first statistics that were adequately researched and sufficiently detailed to be useful for modern analytical purposes, albeit with significant reservations, were produced by Gregory King in 1688. An adaptation of King's statistics is shown in Table 5.1, with the categories of occupation shown in descending order of size. An 'affluence indicator' has been calculated as the ratio of the share of income of each group to its share of population. The category 'High titles and gentlemen' is mainly 'gentlemen' and 'esquires', but also temporal lords, spiritual lords, baronets and knights. It comprised 2.8 per cent of the population but received 14.1 per cent of the income, giving it an affluence indicator of 5.0.

Table 5.1 Occupations and incomes in England and Wales, 1688, based on the compilations of Gregory King

	Number of families	Persons per family	Number of persons	% of total persons	Yearly income per family (£)	Total income of group (£)	% of total income	Affluence indicator (%income/%persons)
Cottagers and paupers	400,000	3¼	1,300,000	23.6	6.5	2,600,000	5.8	0.2
Labouring people and out servants	364,000	3½	1,275,000	23.2	15.0	5,460,000	12.2	0.5
Freeholders	180,000	5.4	980,000	17.8	57.6	10,360,000	23.2	1.3
Farmers	150,000	5.0	750,000	13.6	44.0	6,600,000	14.8	1.1
Artisans and handicrafts	60,000	4	240,000	4.4	40.0	2,400,000	5.4	1.2
Common soldiers and seamen	85,000	2.6	220,000	4.0	17.5	1,490,000	3.3	0.8
Shopkeepers and tradesmen	40,000	4½	180,000	3.3	45.0	1,800,000	4.0	1.2
High titles and gentlemen	16,586	9.3	153,520	2.8	379.0	6,285,800	14.1	5.0
Law, science and liberal arts	26,000	5.8	150,000	2.7	90.8	2,360,000	5.3	1.9
Persons in offices	10,000	7.0	70,000	1.3	180.0	1,800,000	4.0	3.2
Merchants and traders	10,000	6.4	64,000	1.2	240.0	2,400,000	5.4	4.6
Clergymen	10,000	5.2	52,000	0.9	48.0	480,000	1.1	1.1
Naval and military officers	9,000	4.0	36,000	0.7	71.1	640,000	1.4	2.2
Total excluding vagrants	1,360,586		5,470,520	99.5	32.8	44,675,800	99.9	1.0
Vagrants			30,000	0.5	2	60,000	0.1	0.2
Total			5,500,520	100.0		44,735,800	100.0	1.0

Notes: 'High titles and gentlemen' covers temporal lords, spiritual lords, baronets, knights, esquires, gentlemen. Some of King's categories have been combined and for the combinations the Persons per family are derived from the Total persons and Number of families. Decimal figures indicate combined groups.

Source: Adapted from Mathias, 2001, p. 24. Mathias notes that his calculations are from Harleian MS 1898 (British Library).

Its affluence was rivalled only by the 'Merchants and traders', a much smaller group. Broadly speaking, these were the land-affluent and the business-affluent in the late seventeenth century. King's table gives two categories of merchants and traders, 'Merchants by sea' and 'Merchants, lesser'. The former comprised 2,000 families with 16,000 persons and a total income of £800,000, giving them an affluence indicator of 6.1. A part of the income of the 'High titles and gentlemen', probably a substantial part, would be in the form of rents, but King does not identify rental income separately.[17] At the middle level, freeholders and farmers, comprising about 31 per cent of the population, received little more than their 'par' income from working on the land. What can be taken as nascent industry and commerce, in the form of 'Artisans and handicrafts' and 'Shopkeepers and tradesmen' accounted for just under 8 per cent of the population and received a return very similar to that of the freeholders and farmers. The major occupational groups, 'Cottagers and paupers' and 'Labouring people and out servants' comprised nearly 47 per cent of the population, but received very much less than their 'par' return. 'Cottagers and paupers', as implied by the name of the category, were seriously deprived. They were dependent on charity for survival.

King did not distinguish between agricultural and industrial sectors, no doubt because of the mixed occupations of large numbers of the working families referred to above. The categorisations that would best capture the changes taking place had not yet been established. King had only the contemporary 'common theory' to direct his researches. King's economic unit was the 'family' or 'household', which included domestic servants and apprentices. N. F. R. Crafts notes that domestic servants were a very important occupational group, to which King did not give adequate coverage. Manufacturers are usually referred to by King as 'poor manufacturers' and are low-paid domestic artisans and cloth workers. Very few people depend on subsistence, in the sense of growing and consuming their own food, without significant other source of income.[18] The economy of the time was more monetised than the economies of most continental countries. Mathias notes that King did not cover non-distributed corporate income for the Crown, the church, trading companies and other organisations. This and the inadequate coverage of domestic servants leads Mathias to conclude that the data on income per head within groups is meaningless.[19] The comments on relative incomes in the previous paragraph must therefore be read with reserve.

While King's figures do not distinguish between agriculture and industry as separate categories of economic output, modern writers have used his data to create estimates.[20] Deane and Cole, publishing in 1962, estimated that between 60 and 80 per cent of the occupied population was primarily engaged in agriculture, though many of them would have had secondary occupations in industry and trade.[21] They estimate, however, that agricultural output was only 43 per cent of total output in 1700. King's data for 1688 suggests around 40 per cent.[22] The publication in 1981 of population estimates, based on parish records for the whole period 1581 to 1871, by E. A. Wrigley and R. S. Schofield made necessary substantial reassessment of King's statistics.[23] Using the new population data and other sources, and adjusting for the limited coverage of domestic service, Crafts suggests an upper limit for employment in agriculture in 1688 of 55.6 per cent of the labour force.[24] This figure implies that the move from agriculture to industry was already well advanced in 1688 compared to other European countries. Crafts comments: 'even in Gregory King's time modern research indicates that England and Wales was already substantially non-agricultural'.[25]

Of particular interest in the present context is that King did not distinguish any corporate sector. Deane and Cole remark that the omission of the corporate sector was probably unimportant because the total paid-up capital of British joint-stock companies was not much more than half a million pounds at the time, giving them a negligible share of national product.[26] In King's time, companies were not such prominent forms of organisation for engagement in money-bargaining as to earn them coverage in his statistics. The omission of the undistributed incomes of corporate bodies such as the Crown and church was probably more detrimental to the overall significance of the statistics than the omission of the profits of business organisations.

Gregory King's artisans were engaged in some particularly significant metal-work. They were developing skills in scientific instrument making, watch-making, clock-making and mechanical toys. Mathias notes that these skills developed most markedly in Restoration England, for navigation instruments, astronomical instruments and microscopes. Some of the development was a consequence of initiatives by the Royal Society and the Admiralty, but some also served a luxury market for watches and performing dolls. Watch-making became a large trade in eighteenth-century England, utilising an extreme division of labour, with 'rationalized production and interchangeable parts' using specially developed tools, such as slide rests, screw cutting lathes and pre-set lathes.[27] Watch-makers had developed skills in precision engineering that would evolve into the essential skills needed later on to make steam engines function efficiently. They had also adopted available technology and skills into business formats that met the viability condition and generated profits.

The English economy evolved over the period 1066 to 1750 from a situation in which all agents were heavily dependent on land, with few alternative sources of income, but with very different terms of access to land – resulting in very sharp differentials in bargaining positions between agents – to a situation in which many agents were still largely dependent on land, but had emerging options in industry and commerce. Land ownership still conferred strong bargaining positions, but the options available in industry and commerce reduced the differentials in bargaining positions across the community. People at all levels were straddling land-based occupation and industry-based occupation. Wealth acquired in industry and commerce was increasingly used to acquire land for status and influence. Less affluent people were supplementing agricultural incomes with incomes from industrial and commercial activities. Distinct businesses were established in a range of trades, including construction and retailing. Watch-making and other precision metal-work represented advanced technology. Land was declining in relative importance; industry and commerce were growing more important. Incomes from industry and commerce imply the independence of the money-bargaining system from the social and political dependence inherent in the land-based hierarchies. Money-bargaining was becoming more sharply differentiated from the support-bargaining system.

Attitudes, interests and bargaining positions

It was noted in Chapter 1 that the situations that determine interests and bargaining positions are, in large measure, shaped by the social associations of those who use them as references. The elements of a material and personal situation that are regarded as important, and those which can be ignored, depend on the social attitudes generated through social support-bargaining. Group values and tastes are brought to bear on the assessment of situation. People will have the support of their group if they choose in accordance with group understanding of situation and interests.

There are also more objective elements of situation that can change, and in doing so change the attitudes of all concerned. The enclosure of common land, or the closure of a factory, will constitute a radical change of situation for many, and both are likely to change attitudes. Ideas and attitudes emerge from the circumstances in which people find themselves, both in the objective sense and in the sense of their subjective understanding of their circumstances. The ideas and attitudes point the way to advantage. It is an area in which the social support-bargaining described in Chapter 1 elides with intellectual support-bargaining. Support assembled around certain ideas and attitudes translates readily into support for certain political policies and actions. As was seen in Chapter 1, support-bargaining over ideas constitutes an essential characteristic of bargaining societies.

The links between situation and attitudes created through support-bargaining form an evolutionary process. Assessments of situation generated by one set of attitudes give rise to actions that change situations, generating new interests, new attitudes and further action. There is an evolution of attitudes inseparable from the understanding of changing situations. Attitudes are assimilated in different groups of society in accordance with their interests, through the support-bargaining process. The more contact between different groups in a society, and the more groups interlock with common membership, the greater the scope for evolution. Group situation assessments, interests and attitudes evolve to attract and retain support. In societies of rigid groups such evolutionary processes are inhibited.[28] Coleman identifies the importance of changing attitudes to economic change in societies, without being able to identify how the changes are wrought: 'Social structure and attitudes influenced the working of the economy in various ways, and their interaction poses many questions for the historian'.[29]

Society-wide attitudes are caught up in what has been referred to as 'common theory'[30] or the 'mindset'[31] of a people. 'Common theory' encompasses 'common observation', 'common sense', 'common experience' and 'common understanding'. People generally attune their attitudes to their circumstances and way of life, and to the groups that form from shared circumstances. Attitudes and group support reconcile most people to the circumstances in which they find themselves. They consequently function to a considerable degree as conservative constraints on change. Yet certain subgroups will often regard their circumstances as intolerable and set about assembly of the support that will enable them to achieve change. Subgroups advocating change are often in part defined by age. Typically, older people have come to accept the status quo, but the young want change. The latter inevitably outlast the former, though their ascendancy lasts only so long as it takes to become old.

The early period in Britain, in which landowners dominated society politically, socially and economically, was a period in which Britain was most characteristically a violent society rather than a support-bargaining society. Attitudes were attuned to that state of society. They were the attitudes appropriate to effectiveness in violent confrontation. People needed to acquire and hold territory, and cultivated attitudes in society that were best suited to attain those objectives. Loyalty was the most valued virtue.[32] People of high status defended their 'honour' above all else. Social hierarchies, like military hierarchies, were authoritarian. The ascendant group developed elaborate codes of conduct and family honour, elevating the importance of military virtues and military performance. Later on, in more peaceable times, the way of life of country gentlemen involved a code of conduct that defined the group almost as distinctively as their place of residence.

Property, work and incentives

The central role of land ownership in the political, social and economic life of Britain up to and largely into the nineteenth century dictated also veneration for property. Land and the property on it were what people fought for, and no one could take it away without a fight. Owning land was a badge of honour in the community, and there was dishonour in losing it. The adoption of a support convention whereby support substituted for violence in the formal governance of the country was possible only with continued assurances that rights of property would be recognised. If support was to be substituted for violence, its use had to preclude the appropriation of land. People would still fight for land. After the first English Civil War, Cromwell's General Ireton pressed those debating constitutional issues at Putney in 1647:

> All the main thing I speak for, is because I would have an eye to property. I hope we do not come to contend for victory – but let every man consider with himself that he do not go that way to take away all property. For here is the case of the most fundamental part of the constitution of the kingdom, which if you take away, you take all by that.[33]

Even to a leader of an anti-royalist army, land ownership was the foundation of social order. As noted above, property qualifications for voting were not abandoned until 1918. Ideas of ownership and possession are important to money-bargaining.

Institutional economists generally see 'property rights' as the most important 'institutions' that sustain economic exchange.[34] The significance of property is considered further in the following chapter.

Military organisation invariably involves steep hierarchies of command, structured bargaining positions that ensure orders from 'above' are obeyed without question. Civil society based on ownership of land reflected the hierarchical military structure. People took their places in the hierarchy in accordance with the rights of access they held to land. Societies were imbued with a strong sense of order deriving from dependable and widely accepted understanding of hierarchy, perhaps reinforced by the idea of a social 'pyramid', with a monarch at the top and rising numbers at each level of the hierarchy below.

The receipt of rents meant that a landowner could live at leisure. Much of the administrative business of an estate could be contracted to a steward, leaving the proprietor to enjoy his wealth in hunting, shooting, fishing and the social delights of London, with an occasional grand tour when the European continent was at peace. Idleness was appropriate to wealthy men; paid employment certainly demeaning. Military service and politics were the only activities regarded as honourable for persons of substance. Not surprisingly, many aspired to such a life. There was, however, nothing but condemnation for the idleness of everyone else. The poor were required to work, even if there was a lack of opportunities to work. Underemployment, endemic in pre-industrial economies, looked like idleness to those predisposed to see it as such. At least until the mid-eighteenth century the common view among the superior classes was that wages had to be kept down if employees were to be kept at work. Coleman quotes Arthur Young's comment in the 1770s: 'Everyone but an idiot knows that the lower classes must be kept poor or they will never be industrious'.[35] Any rise in wage rates risked inducing a reduction in work in favour of increased leisure. It was feared that payments under the Poor Laws would merely increase idleness. The attitudes conducive to industrial routines of work had not been established. Yet they were making headway. A study of court records for the second half of the eighteenth century suggests that there was a marked reduction in leisure time in that period.[36] The adjustment was not easy – employers in factories had to impose strict discipline to ensure their work was done.[37] One of the big changes that took place was probably in attitudes to work and workers. Deane and Cole comment:

> From about the middle of the eighteenth century it is possible to discern a significant change in the attitude of contemporaries towards the labouring population. Complaints of the recalcitrance of labourers diminished and some writers began to argue that high, not low, wages provided the greater incentive to industry.[38]

Mathias similarly notes that changes in attitudes became more common at this time with the recognition that mechanisation could so raise productivity that it became possible to pay higher wages while maintaining low prices.[39] A strong technological format could accommodate higher wages within the viability condition.

The change of attitude to labour seems to coincide with another important change of attitude or understanding. A land-based economic situation suggests that there is a fixed product from a fixed acreage of land. People who wanted to improve their income are then obliged to do so at the expense of others. A 'fixed cake' economy means fighting for the 'lion's share', or exercising a superior bargaining position to ensure a good share. Coleman notes that concepts of change, innovation and growth were alien to Tudor and early Stuart England. Land, status, lineage and family were the obsessions.[40] Ideas of improved productivity and growth mean that the 'cake' can expand, and there is the possibility of everyone getting more than before.

Coleman records that in the period 1650 to 1750 various improvements in productivity were instituted. Landowners and farmers found themselves squeezed between falling prices and rising costs, and sought to maintain or increase their profits by reducing costs, rather than simply increasing their cultivated area and employing more cheap labour. Coleman recognises that such behaviour had great economic significance.[41] Among other things, it led to recognition of the need for wage incentives to labour if people were to raise their productivity. The search for greater productivity was sustained through the agricultural 'improvement' movement developing in the mid-eighteenth century.

The changes in attitudes to labour exemplify the interaction of situations and attitudes. Attitudes dictated how people interpreted and understood what they observed and experienced. Labour conceived as idle was observed to be idle, whatever the opportunities open to workers. There was no need to agonise over the condition of labourers and their families if their poverty was the consequence of their own innate idleness. As innovations were introduced into money-bargaining, the old observations were less exclusively prominent. People began to recognise that employees could and would work under the right opportunities and incentives. Working in conjunction with capital equipment, employees became more productive and could be paid more without destroying the viability of an enterprise. A positive attitude to the potential of labour meant greater readiness to invest in businesses that would employ labour. A social support-bargaining system develops attitudes consistent with the interests of different social groups. Situations are defined by reference to the interests of the groups. In general, the groups assembling the greatest support are recognised as entitled to the changes they advocate, though with the proviso that they do not thereby damage other groups to any significant extent, and certainly not to an extent that threatens adherence to the support convention. Those who see things differently seek to assemble the support that will enable them to prevail. As situations change, the distribution of support changes and the attitudes of newly prevalent groups gain acceptance.

Religion with attitude

The most widely held attitudes in British society were those associated with the belief that humans were the creation of a supernatural being and that eternal life would be the reward for those who behaved in accordance with the teaching of his son Jesus Christ. Attitudes were derived from interpretations of the teaching within the faith group. Those at the head of society could not ignore the influence of such a group because of its concentration of support. Church teaching had to be suborned to the service of temporal order. The desired role of churchmen was that of convincing the people that their share of the cake was ordained by God, and was to be accepted with humility and gratitude. Monarchs established, effectively by right of superior force, their right to appoint those who would lead the church. Since church endowments often made ecclesiastical appointments very lucrative, the power of appointment constituted a choice instrument of patronage. Monarchs appointed men who had been of service and who could be expected to continue to render service. Even so, the relationship between church and monarch was often fractious. The mediaeval church in England might, albeit controversially, look as much to the Pope as to the king for supreme authority. Loss of papal support for a king would mean loss of local support and potential revolution. The wealth of the church meant also that it was a force to be reckoned with. People dependent on the church for their livelihoods could be expected to support the church, over and above the obligations of faith. William Rufus (William II) sought to strengthen his hand financially by intercepting some part of the church revenues. With the 'ingenious aid of a quick-witted and worldly clerk', he deferred appointments to church positions and kept the associated revenues for himself. For such service, the clerk was appointed Bishop of Durham.[42]

People sometimes wonder how it is that churchmen can espouse the highest principles of love, compassion and humility yet at the same time behave in a manner that is markedly inconsistent with such principles. The answer seems to be that piety is important only to the extent that it assembles support – that is, it is important in a support-bargaining system only in so far as it effectively assembles the support necessary to keep a faith group together. Once a church has become institutionalised and an established part of a state, it is, of necessity, engaged in the support-bargaining that sustains the interests of the state. An established church takes on part of the responsibility for the ordering of state affairs. Stepping out of line means risking the displeasure of the leaders of the state. Supporting the temporal power means enjoyment of temporal advantages. When Christianity became the established church of the Roman Empire under Constantine, it changed from an obscurely pious, even fanatically pious, sect into an important player in the evolution of the Empire.[43] Its piety still served a purpose, but it was diluted in accordance with the necessity of sustaining support in 'affairs of state'. The Vatican today maintains the grandeur and political machinations of a major player in international support-bargaining. Its budget is opaque but functional. It remains concerned with love, compassion and humility, but not to the extent of eschewing the trappings of power. It maintains its position in international support-bargaining rather than conforming itself to the uncomfortable teachings of Christ. In Britain, the Archbishop of Canterbury was embarrassed to find in 2013 that the Church Commissioners had invested, albeit indirectly, in a money-lending company that he had specifically condemned. The Archbishop acknowledged in extenuation that it would be difficult to invest only in companies that were entirely free from sin. Lesser Christians still espouse the highest principles while adapting their behaviour to the maintenance of support in a support-bargaining world. If the churches moved too far from the temporal way, if they lost too much support, they would be forgotten.

Extreme conflict between church and state in the sixteenth century in England led to the establishment of the Church of England, with the monarch at is head. The division of the church into two institutions ended the idea of a unitary church and unitary doctrine. Many new interpretations of the precepts of Christ arose and new churches were established to propagate the new interpretations. In the mid-seventeenth century religious contention exacerbated constitutional dissension, resulting in civil war. The new political order emerging after the Glorious Revolution of 1688 was of Tories contesting government with Whigs. By the end of the seventeenth century the Anglican Church was closely associated with the Tory faction in the country. Anglicanism 'truly established itself as the landowners badge'.[44] Tory landowners appointed Tory Anglicans to the best livings in the land, ensuring that appropriate attitudes were fostered from the pulpit. The nineteenth century was an era of great prominence and prestige for the Church of England, deriving from its association with the most politically powerful in the land.

The Whigs were similarly associated with faith groups. Their supporters came extensively from the emerging industrial-commercial community – Gregory King's 'Artisans and handicrafts', 'Shopkeepers and tradesmen', 'Merchants and traders', and probably a good number of the lesser 'Freeholders' and 'Farmers'. Many of them were of non-conformist faith. Their teaching moved with the changing situation from 'accept your lot and be grateful' to acceptance that there was virtue in the exercise of business initiative, so long as the rewards were well used in the service of God and fellow men.[45] With that attitude, people could take up new economic options without compromising their membership of their faith group. Unitarians and Quakers were prominent in the economic changes of the eighteenth century.[46] As with attitudes to work and workers discussed above, the social support-bargaining that dictates attitudes and situation concepts, and with them the requirements for action, and hence the evolution of the bargaining system, is apparent in the changing attitudes of churchmen to business and investment. Money-bargaining could evolve with favourable attitudes towards business among believers. Eight talents in hand might be invested for a return, with no lesser chance of salvation.

Changes in the understanding of faith or doubts about its truth were the origin of broader changes in social attitudes. The Reformation, beginning in the fifteenth century, ended the hegemony of the Catholic Church over the thinking of both high and low on religious matters in northern Europe, giving rise to a more independent, querulous and inquisitive approach. The European Enlightenment of the eighteenth century brought into question the authenticity of the Christian scriptures and with it their status as the basis of human understanding. A more reasoned approach to human affairs was seen as offering potentially better outcomes. The reassessment of faith gave rise to some displacement of faith. If there were no grounds for determining which particular doctrine was correct, there might be no grounds for any faith at all. These changes of attitude represented major shifts in intellectual support and consequently major shifts in what political initiatives would assemble support.

Joel Mokyr traces the implications of the Enlightenment in *The Enlightened Economy: Britain and the Industrial Revolution 1700–1850*. He remarks that:

> The literature on the Industrial Revolution to date has paid little heed to the Enlightenment, in large part because scholars trained in the hard-nosed facts of the beginnings of economic growth in Europe were reluctant to deal with phenomena that were hard to measure and explain, such as beliefs and ideas.[47]

Lacking an understanding of social and intellectual support-bargaining, scholars have found it difficult to account for the way in which thought affects political and economic actions. Coleman makes a similar point, referring to an earlier period, in the quotation at note 29 above (Social structure ... the historian). Mokyr notes that the famous names of the European Enlightenment are mainly French and Scottish rather than English. He suggests that the Enlightenment in England took place within the Protestant religion, rather than against religion.[48] People did not have to leave their faith group to assimilate new ideas; the faith groups assimilated enough new ideas to permit retention of membership. The changes in religious attitudes described above contributed to industrial change, alongside the thinking of the secular Enlightenment.

Education and attitudes

While support-bargaining shapes attitudes within a society, its greatest effect on attitudes is probably indirect, through its determination of educational provision. Education clearly has the most profound effect on attitudes. It opens minds to a range of information far beyond what can be derived from immediate experience. It potentially alters people's understanding of themselves and their situation, thus altering also their understanding of their interests and their bargaining positions. Education can also open the way to engagement with the 'high theory' groups that order and extend information in certain ways, implying again certain interests and assembling support for or against those interests. Theories about governance and economics have materially influenced distributions of political support and through that the establishment of governments and their actions. Because of this impact of education, attitudes towards education itself have always been among the most important influences on societies and the most contested aspects of political support-bargaining.

Most education of young people has historically been provided by or through religious institutions. Belief in the omnipotence of God and in the goodness of God implies that what happens in earthly society is ordained by God, and consequently not to be questioned. Church teaching consequently tends to assemble support for an existing social and political order. Children, where they were taught at all, were taught in schools and Sunday schools that the existing dispensation was an expression of God's will, and beyond human dispute. If the lower classes of society were slow to change their attitudes, it was partly because they were denied broader forms of education. The upper classes appreciated the support of religious teachers in inculcating into the lower classes attitudes supportive of the existing order. In many cases appointments of religious teachers were made for just that purpose. The lower classes unwittingly condemned themselves to weak bargaining positions by accepting the definitions of situation provided by the ascendant.

Society in general discouraged learning among the lower classes. Jonathan Rose's study of *The Intellectual Life of the British Working Classes* describes how the intellectual ambitions of working-class individuals were discouraged and suppressed.[49] There are instances of the intellect of working class men being recognised and nurtured, but for the most part learning was discouraged among those of inferior social status. Even within the working class learning was frequently disparaged. Parents might stigmatise book-reading as effeminate; real men used their muscles. Nevertheless, there were determined efforts within the working class to advance the education of working-class people. It came to be understood among some working-class leaders that, 'Economic inequality rested on inequality of education: hence, monopolies on knowledge had to be broken by any means necessary.'[50] The 'mutual improvement' movement gave opportunities for a great number of working-class men to gain at least the rudiments of education.[51] Negative attitudes to education did not prevent the emergence of an industrial revolution in England, since although the technology of the revolution required education, intellect and ingenuity, the factories required largely unskilled labour. The later weakness of Britain in the face of competition from Germany, France, the USA and other countries seems to have been attributable, in some measure, to the limited education of the British workforce.[52]

Attitudes gain potency when they are shared across large numbers in a society. Widely enough shared, they become 'obvious' – see the comment of Arthur Young above. They are generated through social, political and intellectual support-bargaining, the last of these being pre-eminent in the development of the 'high theory' by which certain types of information are ordered and 'understood'. The evolution of social attitudes thus derives from the support-bargaining process. The industrial revolution involved evolution in social attitudes both as contributing cause and as consequence. It gave rise to unprecedentedly vigorous support-bargaining in all its aspects. That vigour has been maintained ever since. Chapter 9 considers further the way information and theory are used in bargaining processes.

The rise of companies

Gregory King's 'Merchants and traders' were clearly doing well in 1688. With 1.2 per cent of the population, they accounted for 5.4 per cent of the income, giving them an affluence indicator of 4.6, not far short of the 5.0 of the 'High titles and gentlemen'. The 'Merchants by sea' were doing particularly well, with an affluence indicator of 6.1. Many of these would, in all probability, be merchants running chartered companies. Such companies were in possession of a royal charter giving them a monopoly of trade in one or more parts of the globe. Most of them bore the name of some geographical location in which they held the monopoly – East India, Muscovy, Hudson's Bay, etc. The monopoly granted was necessarily a monopoly in relation to competing British traders only. But since trade was understood in terms of international conflict,[53] the charter was also recognition that the company had authority to carve out the best trading rights it could against rival traders of other nations. The Dutch and French, successively Britain's main enemies in the period 1650–1713, were according their own merchants similar charters. The instructions given for the first venture of the Dutch East India Company included, 'Attack the Spanish and Portuguese wherever you find them.'[54]

The Muscovy Company was the first British chartered joint-stock company, gaining its charter in 1555. It was, however, the Dutch East India Company that became the trendsetter among chartered companies. It gained its charter in 1602. Whereas British chartered companies initially issued shares for each specific voyage, the Dutch company issued shares on the basis of voyages over a period of 21 years. The Dutch company also explicitly told its investors that their liability was limited to their investment in shares. Dutch investors could trade their shares on a stock exchange in Amsterdam, near to the company's offices.[55]

The concept of trade as international conflict meant that the competitive aspect of trade was understood to involve at least diplomatic competition, with the threat of violence, if not actual violence, underlining the import of diplomatic initiatives. Winning that sort of competition might make it possible to establish a trading monopoly with a controlled territory. As far as possible, the controllers of territory tried to exclude competing traders. These circumstances meant that trade development required substantial involvement of governments in the opening of negotiations with prospective trading partners and the conclusion of trade treaties. The capacity to enforce trade agreements by armed force counted in negotiations. Commerce and state were necessarily locked together. Coleman remarks, of the arrangements governing regulated companies and chartered companies, 'Whatever the financial form, however, it was the collection of rights and privileges which reflected the deal between the State and the merchants.'[56] The companies gained government support in the establishment of trade treaties and monopoly access to markets, while governments gained money in the form of tax and loans, required most pressingly to sustain their wars. The undercurrents of violence and extent of actual violence take the trade of the chartered companies beyond the bounds of bargaining systems. They make clear that engagement in foreign trade was as much a matter of politics as money-bargaining. The politics involved too much violence to be regarded as wholly a matter of support-bargaining. Companies remained substantially dependent on political involvement even after violence was eliminated from normal foreign trade. The regulation of foreign trade became a matter of international support-bargaining. Money-bargaining between nation states is considered further in Chapter 8.

The best 'high theory' of the time in economics, given the name 'mercantilism' in the late eighteenth century, held that the aim of overseas trade was to accumulate 'treasure' in the form of bullion.[57] Since their discovery and occupation of South America, Spain and Portugal had been the successful nations because they had succeeded in accumulating treasure. The theory seems, in large measure, a 'merchant's theory', in that it designates state 'profit' as the objective, in much the same way as merchants seek profit. The state had a 'format' in much the same way as a company would have a format. Acquiring bullion by exporting and impeding the outflow of bullion by impeding imports brought about an accumulation of bullion. Accumulation of bullion was seen as an end in itself, though it was noted that Spain and Portugal had acquired significant territory on the back of their accumulation of bullion. The unacknowledged link implicit in mercantilist theory is, then, the use of trade for the enhancement of violent capacity. The violent capacity was, in many cases, necessary to the expansion of trade. And states, or their rulers, were always short of money to pursue their territorial ambitions through war. As was seen in Chapter 2, David Hume pointed out that the mercantilist ambitions for accumulation of bullion might be self-defeating, since an inflow of bullion would be likely to raise prices, render a nation uncompetitive and give rise to an outflow of bullion.[58] It was seen also, however, that the mechanism was not always fully functional in a timescale that mattered.

As also noted in Chapter 2, silver was the favoured commodity in Asia. Because of the perceived importance in Britain of the amassing of bullion, the merchants of the chartered companies could not acquire all their requirements for silver in Britain, and were obliged to acquire large amounts on the continent. Silver was supplemented for trading purposes on outgoing vessels by lead, tin, mercury, corals, ivory, armour, swords, satins and broadcloths. Most of this was traded in India for cotton textiles, which were then traded in the Spice Islands for pepper, cloves and nutmeg. Part of the spice cargo might then be traded in India on the way back for tea, which was in demand in Europe.[59]

The importance to trade of territorial control meant that expeditions were often strongly oriented towards conclusion of treaties and the protection of whatever trading rights were established. Military capacity was necessary to deal with rivals and encourage potential partners to conclude treaties. Displays of force made clear what lay behind the diplomatic courtesies. The Dutch East India Company gained control of the Spice Islands. The British East India Company gained its charter in 1600 with a monopoly on trade not just over the East Indies, but also over a very wide area, including Africa, Asia and America. It became what might be called, perhaps euphemistically, an 'integrated trading organisation', controlling a large fighting force, military and naval, along with such governmental and administrative elements as were necessary to secure the territories with which it was to trade. It appointed resident 'factors' to manage its local trading posts. Through the efforts of Robert Clive and the East India Company, India was added to the British Empire. Clive joined the company as a clerk but transferred to its military division, becoming famous for his military exploits. He committed suicide in 1774 in the wake of a trial in which he was cleared of alleged malpractices. The Governor General of India, Warren Hastings, was impeached by parliament but eventually also cleared of the allegations against him. The company continued to run India until the mutiny of 1857. By that time its role was under severe attack. Britain ruled the waves and its empire without the need for a buccaneering company. The violence had largely been separated from the trade. A new concept of companies had evolved. The East India Company's charter expired in 1874.[60]

The trade of chartered companies was conceived as trade with 'territories' rather than trade with other business organisations or individual businessmen. All the associations of 'territory' or 'land' were involved, including most particularly the idea of land as something that was acquired and held by force. Just as the early order in England under landowners was a political, social and economic order based on ownership of land, so the international trade of the chartered companies was a political and economic order based on the control of territories. The violence necessary to control territory was necessary also to the advancement of trade. The domestic order evolved in such a way as to diminish the importance of land and the incidence of the violence associated with landholding. The use of violence for the acquisition and control of foreign territory remained prominent, but trade with secure territories was increasingly conceived in terms of trade with trading agencies. While diplomatic initiatives remained essential to the maintenance of trade, the extent of actual violence diminished. As in domestic circumstances, money-bargaining, decreasingly associated with territory or land, became increasingly separable from support-bargaining.

The introduction of chartered companies added in important ways to the organisational formats available for the conduct of business. They were the immediate origin of the joint-stock limited liability companies that later came to dominate economic activity around the world. Their immediate predecessors were the 'regulated companies' that also held monopolies in overseas markets. The regulated companies were associations of independent merchants, like guilds, which engaged in and regulated the trade in their chosen markets.[61] Prominent among them was the company of Merchant Adventurers, which controlled the trade with the Low Countries in the sixteenth century and was 'the most powerful English business organization of the time'.[62] The English Merchants of the Staple controlled the wool trade with Calais. Access to such markets was dependent on commercial treaties negotiated by the king.

The guilds held monopolies of trade in particular localities in exchange for payments to the sovereign. In law they were 'corporate persons' – legal entities that existed independently of the persons that from time to time worked in them and controlled them. The 'corporate' personality was adopted by a great range of undertakings, including towns, universities and religious communities, as well as guilds. The guild was the most important form of business organisation during the Middle Ages. According to Micklethwait and Wooldridge, 'The guilds were often more like trade unions than companies, more interested in protecting their members' interests than in pursuing economic innovation'.[63]

The perception that the guilds were too much concerned with their own interests played a large part in their decline.[64] Partnership, in which two or more partners invested, rose in importance as the common form of business organisation. Much of the slave trade was undertaken by partnerships.[65] This trade was the foundation of the sugar and tobacco plantations in the West Indies and the cotton plantations of the southern USA. Partnerships were generally regarded as more dependable and more ethical than joint-stock companies, on the understanding that partners would be fully engaged in their business and look to its integrity, while shareholders, particularly shareholders with limited liability, would not be so conscientious. The advantages of joint-stock and limited liability arrangements were apparent in the high-risk and long-duration voyages undertaken by the chartered companies. They again became apparent as the levels of capital required for certain types of business grew in the nineteenth century.

The reputation of joint-stock companies in Britain was seriously damaged by the collapse in the value of the shares of the South Sea Company in 1720. The company was established in 1711 under the auspices of Robert Harley, Chancellor of the Exchequer and then Lord High Treasurer, as a means of financing some part of the national debt and wresting control from the Whiggish Bank of England of the financing of engagement in the War of the Spanish Succession. The company was also accorded a monopoly of trade with South America, though returns from this trade depended on relations with Spain. The prospects of the company were heavily promoted, while official involvement seemed to guarantee security. By offering its shares in exchange for government debt it was able to take over a proportion of that debt. In 1719 the company was authorised by parliament to take over a further portion of government debt. In the following year, with the company authorised to take over further debt, in preference to the Bank of England, enthusiasm for the company's shares drove their value to great heights. Other joint-stock companies were launched on a wave of speculative excitement. To staunch the competition for investment funds, the South Sea Company persuaded the government to pass the Bubble Act of 1720, which made it very difficult to set up joint-stock companies. The implicit suggestion that joint-stock companies were risky backfired on the South Sea Company. Its trading prospects came under closer scrutiny and its shares declined precipitately in value, bringing substantial losses for its investors. Many people from many different walks of life, including many celebrities of the time, lost money. The government prevented more serious losses by effectively taking over the company.[66] It transpired that the company had risen largely on the strength of misrepresentation, bribery and fraud, with political and financial 'insiders' profiting from prior knowledge of the company's acquisitions of government debt, and various helpers of the company's cause being handsomely rewarded. The company nevertheless survived into the nineteenth century. The experience meant that joint-stock arrangements were looked on with suspicion in Britain for the next 100 years. The Bubble Act was only repealed in 1825. The tribulations of the joint-stock format were even greater in France, where a similar financial collapse was experienced, involving the Compagnie d'Occident, with the crucial difference that the Banque Royale, the equivalent of the Bank of England, was closely involved with the Compagnie d'Occident. The failure of the company brought severe damage to French national finances.[67]

The behaviour of guilds, regulated companies and chartered companies all reflect an acute awareness of bargaining position, particularly when understood in terms of the exclusion of alternatives to themselves as traders. The guilds excluded from trade in their appointed towns anyone who had not fulfilled a prescribed term of apprenticeship or who failed to meet other qualifications for membership of the guild. The regulated and chartered companies sought monopolies imposed by law to protect themselves against competition. The approach reflected the 'fixed cake' concept of trade – once a share of the cake had been obtained, it had to be protected. Bargaining position was based on the suppression of alternative sources of whatever a company had to offer.

The guilds faded in importance as governments and people questioned the justice and usefulness of guilds that protected their own interests to the detriment of others. A similar reaction against the monopolies of the chartered companies developed in the late seventeenth century, just the time when the Glorious Revolution trimmed the power of the monarch. Monopoly rights were ended, 'So by *circa* 1700, it can be said that most English foreign trade was open to all comers.' The associations of individual traders in guilds or regulated companies imposing monopolistic arrangements in their spheres of trade had given way to distinct trading organisations competing with similar organisations of their own state on reasonably level terms, though still protected against competition from foreign companies by tariffs, navigation laws and commercial treaties.[68] Attitudes to business evolved as new groups became ascendant over the course of the seventeenth century, particularly in the wake of the Glorious Revolution. These groups saw the existing situations as inimical to their interests and had the support necessary to change them.

Adam Smith in the *Wealth of Nations*, published in 1776, restated the case for competition as the means of serving the interests of the community. His study emphasised the importance of productivity, achieved through division of labour. Improvements in productivity meant higher output and lower prices for consumers. In terms of bargaining theory, producers should establish their bargaining positions with buyers not through the suppression of alternatives but through competition that would determine which products were most favoured by consumers and ensure the lowest possible prices. There is, nevertheless, lacking in Adam Smith's account of economic behaviour any sense of the organisation necessary to combine technology with specialist labour in a production process that provides what buyers want at prices they can afford. The technology and division of labour among the watch-makers referred to above involved organisation.

The evolution of money-bargaining 131

Smith's pin factory involved organisation to acquire the appropriate technology and assign tasks to labour in accordance with the requirements of the pin-making technology. It was not the division of labour of itself that raised productivity, but the technology, and the adaptation of work to the requirements of the technology. Factories were the consequence of organising work around technology. Smith was arguing against monopoly, but he seems to have associated monopoly with organisation. Guilds, regulated companies and chartered companies were all 'organisations' and all sought bargaining position through the suppression of alternatives to themselves. 'Organisation' seemed synonymous with monopoly. For Smith, small-scale 'masters' and workers seemed most likely to create the sort of competitive trading that would bring social benefit. While the association of organisation with monopoly is understandable, it caused him to miss the necessity of building bargaining position on a different basis through organisation.[69] Bargaining position based on accommodation of the requirements of buyers is achieved through the format of companies. Companies focus inputs, including technology, to the purpose of meeting consumer requirements. Improved productivity remains important because it reduces unit costs, and hence helps establish a format that achieves viability or profitability. Because maximising output is no longer the principle objective, productivity is not so important simply as a means of increasing output.

The success of the chartered companies, particularly the East India Company, marked a reorientation of British trade away from Europe and towards the rest of the world, and the expansion of British influence, in conjunction with its trade, around the world. Both imports and exports were increasingly linked with non-European countries:

- In 1622 imports from Europe to London were 94 per cent of the total, and only 6 per cent derived from America and Asia. In 1752–4, imports to England and Wales from Europe were 54 per cent of the total, while imports from America were 33 per cent and from Asia 13 per cent.
- Exports from London to Europe in 1663/9 were 91 per cent of the total and to America and Asia 9 per cent. In 1752–4 exports from England and Wales to Europe were 72 per cent of the total, while exports to America were 20 per cent and to Asia 8 per cent of the total.

A corresponding change took place in the commodity structure of trade.

- Imports of textiles had been 41 per cent of the total in 1622, but fell to 21 per cent in 1752–4, while imports of sugar and tobacco rose from 2 per cent to 23 per cent of total in 1752–4. (The 1622 data relates to London only, while the 1752–4 data relates to England and Wales.)
- Exports of wool textiles fell from 74 per cent of total in 1663/9 to 47 per cent in 1752–4, while exports of foodstuffs rose from 3 to 17 per cent, and of 'Other manufactures' from 11 to 29 per cent. (The 1663/9 data relates to London only, while the 1752–4 data relates to England and Wales.)

132 *The Evolution of Economies*

A significant evolution of trade by geographical origin and destination and in traded commodities took place from the mid-seventeenth to mid-eighteenth centuries, based mainly on the geographical orientation and trading engagements of the chartered companies, and the development of slave plantations for sugar and tobacco in the West Indies.[70]

This reorientation of trade involved expansion of the shipping fleet and requirements for new forms of trade finance and insurance. London began to catch up with Amsterdam in the provision of these services. The development of more sophisticated financial services for international trade was accompanied by developments in domestic banking services.[71] Evolution in provision of credit and in British shipping services is considered further in Chapters 7 and 8.

The acceleration in economic evolution

In the eighteenth century and into the nineteenth century the pace of economic evolution in Britain accelerated. The acceleration started in particular industries or sectors of economic activity, with limited impact in the early decades on the aggregate measures of economic performance. Technology and the companies that used technology took on new forms. As companies using the new technologies grew larger and their linkages with other companies grew, they increasingly had their impact on the aggregate measures of growth.

The acceleration took place in a context of renewed growth in population. As has been seen, population change is an important undercurrent to social evolution. Favourable economic circumstances tend to give rise to population growth, and population growth in turn produces opportunities for economic growth. Population change is an important component of the evolutionary movement from situation to situation.[72] Population had been in decline in the period 1650–1700 but growth resumed at a slow rate, 0.25 per cent per year for England, over the next 50 years. A marked acceleration in the rate of growth, to 0.77 per cent per year, set in around the middle of the eighteenth century, and a further acceleration, to 1.32 per cent per year, occurred in the first half of the nineteenth century. The population of England grew from about 5.9 million in 1750, to 16.7 million in 1850. Improvements in agriculture no doubt played a part in this acceleration in growth of population, while the increased opportunities in cottage industries may also have contributed in some areas. Provisions of the Poor Laws may also have been a factor, through reduction in the financial burdens imposed by children on families.[73] The growth over the century 1750–1850 implies a notable change in the situation with regard to requirements for employment and the potential for consumption. Volume of sales is important to the viable format of companies, and population is necessarily a major determinant of volume of sales. The expansion of the population of England implied increased scope for the format of companies. The emergence of format opportunities is, as was seen in the previous chapter, an important element in the process of economic evolution.

The expansion also gave England a population closer to those of France and Germany. The population of England in 1850 was nearly three times its 1750 level, while that of Germany was about twice its 1750 level (17.0 to 35.4 million) and that of France about one and a half times its 1750 level (24.6 to 36.3 million).[74] The population of England was still less than half the population of Germany and that of France, but in 1750 it was less than a quarter that of France. Without the growth of population in Britain it seems likely that continental countries would have led the world in the acceleration of economic evolution.

Early acceleration was most apparent in the cotton, wool and textiles industries, in coal production, and in output of iron. From about 1830 railway construction and operation expanded rapidly, and from the 1840s growth in shipbuilding was strong. Steel production grew rapidly from the 1850s. Table 5.2 shows data on the value of output of major industries, derived from Chapter VI in Deane and Cole on The Growth of the Nineteenth Century Staples.

Cotton overtook wool in annual value of net output in the first quarter of the nineteenth century. Annual output reached a peak value of about £66 million around 1875. Annual output of textiles made from cotton, wool, worsted, linen and silk reached £84.5 million around 1875. Annual value of coal output expanded to £121.7 million around 1900, with rising exports and increasing use in shipping, gas and electricity production.[76] Iron and steel production rose throughout the century, with demand for capital equipment, urban infrastructure, railway construction, railway rolling stock, shipbuilding and domestic products. Rail services developed strongly from about 1830. Shipbuilding expanded from the 1840s on as iron replaced wood and steam replaced sail. Production tonnage of steam-powered vessels overtook tonnage of sail-driven vessels in the 1870s.[77]

Three industries are of particular interest with regard to the acceleration in the evolution of money-bargaining. The cotton industry introduced a company format that had far-reaching implications for the evolution of economies around the world. Formats in the iron and steel industry reduced the costs of capital equipment made from these materials and made possible the format of companies for a variety of other outputs. The introduction of rail services extended the whole domestic money-bargaining network. A fourth industry, shipbuilding, along with provision of shipping services, impacted international trade later in the nineteenth century with something like the effect the railways had on domestic trade – they extended international vendor sets. The evolution of international trade is considered in Chapter 8.

The cotton format

Three technological innovations in cotton production in the late eighteenth century were of central importance to the acceleration in the evolution of the British economy. Robert Arkwright's water frame, patented in 1769, made possible the production of cotton yarn of unprecedented strength, permitting it to be used for warp as well as weft in the weaving of cotton textiles. John Hargreaves's spinning jenny, patented in the following year, contained 16 spindles and

Table 5.2 Value of output of major industries

£ million per year

	Cotton Value added to raw material	Wool Net value added	Linen Net output at 60% of gross output	Textiles Net output	Coal Value at pithead	Iron and steel Value of gross product	Rail traffic Receipts	Shipping Value of tonnage built
Early 1770s	0.6		3.4	12.0	2.8	16.2		2.3
Early 1800s	11.0	12.8	4.3	32.9	6.9	17.9		1.8
Around 1825	26.7	16.8	7.5	49.6	10.3	35.7		3.5
Mid-century	30.2	20.3	9.1	57.1	46.2	102.4	12.6	16.3
Around 1875	66.0	18.0	10.8	84.5	121.7	123.9	55.4	18.7
Around 1900	57.2	23.2	7.2				83.2	
Indices (first year of data above = 100)								
Early 1770s	100.0		100.0	100.0		100.0		100.0
Early 1800s	1,833.33	100.0	126.5	274.2	100.00	110.4		78.3
Around 1825	4,450.00	131.3	220.6	413.3	246.43	220.4		152.2
Mid-century	5,033.33	158.6	267.6	475.8	367.86	632.0	100.0	708.7
Around 1875	11,000.00	140.6	317.6	704.2	1,650.00	764.0	439.7	813.0
Around 1900	9,533.33	181.3	211.8		4,346.43		660.3	

Note: See notes and comment by Deane and Cole on specifications and provenance of data.

Source: Adapted from Deane and Cole, 1962[75].

multiplied the output of a single operative by about the same number. Samuel Crompton's mule, patented in 1789, combined the functions of the two and produced a smoother and finer yarn.[78] Adopted by companies, mostly partnerships, this technology brought about a rapid expansion in cotton production at low unit cost.

Producers had hit on a format that has proved exceptionally rewarding ever since. It was possible to meet, and in some cases handsomely exceed, the viability condition of 'sales × price > production × unit cost'. The new technology made volume production possible with unskilled labour. The cost of labour, though relatively high in international terms, combined with the technology, gave a low unit cost of production;[79] the low unit cost of production meant that a low price was feasible for the finished product; the availability of overseas markets made it possible to sell the volume output at the price necessary for viability. High volume and low unit costs, with sales to large markets overseas, has been a highly successful format for many businesses around the world ever since. All the large international conglomerates and transnational corporations follow this basic format. Companies establish high-volume production in countries where labour costs for unskilled and semi-skilled labour are low, and sell the output into countries with large numbers of consumers and budgets strong enough to meet the prices required for viability. The format has been particularly important in the manufacture of textiles and clothing. Relatively simple technology and the requirement for substantial unskilled labour have made it a favourite 'entry-level' industry for industrialisation around the world. Hong Kong, Singapore, South Korea and China all first embarked on industrialisation through export of textiles and clothing. It was the evolutionary course of the British economy that first brought into being this durable format.

The rapid growth of cotton production and the importance of overseas markets in the late eighteenth century and through the nineteenth century are shown in Table 5.3.

Average annual production nearly tripled in the period 1784–6 to 1801–3. In 1760 the proportion of a relatively small output going to export was as high as 50 per cent. Production grew up to 1784–6 on sales in the domestic market, with exports falling as a proportion of output to 17 per cent. Exports reached an early peak share of output, at 66 per cent, in the first decade of the nineteenth century. That export proportion was exceeded only in the later years of the century.

International trade was important to the cotton industry not only because of export sales but because its main raw material, raw cotton, became available in large volume from plantations in the southern USA. Up to 1780 this raw material came mainly from the West Indies. The scope for expansion of supply from that source was, however, limited. The US plantations and their slave labour were crucial to the expansion of the British cotton industry.[80] But technology also played a part. The cotton gin, a machine for separating cotton from seeds, invented by Eli Whitney in the USA in 1793, greatly reduced the price of imported raw cotton.[81] Slavery on the plantations was abolished following the

136 *The Evolution of Economies*

Table 5.3 Gross value of cotton output and cotton exports as proportion of gross output

£ million per year

Years	Gross value of output	Value of exports	% export
1760	0.6	0.3	50.0
1784–86	5.4	0.9	16.7
1801–3	15.0	9.3	62.0
1805–7	18.9	12.5	66.1
1819–21	29.4	15.5	52.8
1839–41	46.7	23.3	49.8
1859–61	77.0	49.1	63.8
1879–81	94.5	69.9	74.0
1899–1901	89.2	70.3	78.8

Notes: Figures are annual averages; gross output estimates based on retained imports of raw cotton; from 1819–21 'Value of final product'; for 1819–1901 the 'Value of exports' is derived from the proportion exported given in Deane and Cole, Table 43; see also the extensive notes and sources given by Deane and Cole for their two tables.

Source: Adapted from Deane and Cole, 1962, pp. 185, Table 42; 187, Table 43.

defeat of the Confederate southern states in the American Civil War, fought from 1861 to 1865. The war disrupted supplies of cotton to Britain and affected production,[82] but the ending of slavery did not incapacitate the British cotton industry, which resumed its expansion after the war.

The evolution of the cotton industry was dramatic and exciting to contemporaries. It was a new phenomenon in the business and economic world. Cotton became the most important manufacturing industry in the British economy by the first decade of the nineteenth century. It accounted for between 4 and 5 per cent of national income.[83] Substantial though it was, however, it could have only limited impact on growth rates of the economy as a whole.

Deane and Cole published estimates of growth in national income per head in 1962 that suggested strong and accelerating growth rates for the whole period 1700 to 1870. In 1986 Crafts published revised estimates showing much slower growth rates for the period 1700 to 1830, but confirming the estimates of Deane and Cole for the period 1830 to 1870. The revised figures show a particular reduction in the estimate for the period 1760 to 1800, reducing it from 0.52 per cent per head per year to 0.17 per cent. Crafts' revised estimates have been generally accepted.[84] Growth up to 1800 was significantly slower than previously thought. After 1830 there was a 40-year period of rapid growth – nearly 2 per cent per year. Crafts writes, 'As such the new estimates of national-output growth add further to the arguments for abandoning the view that at the macrolevel we are going to find a marked discontinuity.'[85] Wrigley notes that the earlier and later estimates of national income per head for 1831 agree, implying that output in the mid-eighteenth century was significantly higher than the earlier estimates.[86] This is consistent with the modern reassessment of the extent of engagement in industry at the time of Gregory King's estimates of income. The revised estimates reflect, in part, the new estimates for population and population growth provided by Wrigley and Schofield.[87]

Growth in the cotton industry accelerated after the Napoleonic Wars and its output came to account for more than 5 per cent of national income. In the period 1820–40 cotton production switched almost entirely from water power to steam power. The weaving process took much longer to be mechanised in a commercial form. Edmund Cartwright patented a power loom in 1785.[88] His invention, however, required a long period of development, never wholly successful. It was only around the 1830s that steam-powered looms were available for effective use in a factory format. Few handloom weavers remained operative after 1850.[89]

The viability condition focuses attention on the unit cost of production as the basic determinant of price and hence of sales. The strength of the cotton format is apparent in the price movements of cotton. Price data is scant for the eighteenth and nineteenth centuries.[90] However, Crafts provides indices of prices for various output groups, based on his estimates of volume output and value added for the same output groups. They are implied price trends rather than directly documented price trends, with the original statistics subject to considerable margins of error.[91] Nevertheless, they give some indication of the reductions in prices that made the cotton format so effective. Table 5.4 shows Crafts' price data. The column on the right is an addition, showing prices relative to cotton for 1801.

The price of cotton output rose by 23 per cent in the period 1770 to 1801, but then fell through to 1831 to a level nearly 34 per cent below its price in 1770. It is the largest fall of any product except iron, the other great evolutionary influence of the late eighteenth/early nineteenth century. Although the price of cotton rose in the period 1770 to 1801, the additional column on the right shows that the

Table 5.4 Relative prices of industry output

Indices 1770 = 100				
	1700	1801	1831	1801 prices relative to cotton
Cotton	100	123.6	66.2	100.0
Wool	100	125.6	113.4	101.6
Linen	100	101.0	99.3	81.7
Silk	100	200.0	144.4	161.8
Building	100	150.0	178.8	121.4
Iron	100	59.2	30.1	47.9
Copper	100	256.2	129.2	207.3
Beer	100	135.3	255.9	109.5
Leather	100	129.3	123.8	104.6
Soap	100	161.9	115.5	131.0
Candles	100	134.5	94.8	108.8
Coal	100	116.7	133.3	94.4
Paper	100	300.0	193.8	242.7

Source: Crafts, 1986, p. 25, Table 2.5 (last column added).

increase was generally less than that incurred by other products. Only linen, iron and coal showed slower growth in price. The Napoleonic Wars brought price increases across the economy. Over the period 1770–1831 the price data suggests a marked reduction in the unit costs of cotton output, giving scope for expansion in sales. The fall in cotton prices continued. The average value of cotton piece goods exported in 1821 was 11.73 pence per linear yard; by 1850 it was 3.63 pence; in 1900 it was 2.50 pence.[92]

The successful company formats of the cotton industry contrast with the unsuccessful attempt to establish a viable format for mechanised silk production in the early eighteenth century. What Mathias calls the first genuine factory was a silk throwing mill on the River Derwent in Derby. Thomas Lombe patented the mill in 1718 and established the factory in 1720. Water power was harnessed to production through a paddle wheel on the river, driving 25,000 movements. Raw silk was imported. While there was innovative technology and factory organisation, the venture could not achieve viability. Overseas markets were closed to British silk because higher-quality and cheaper silks were produced overseas. To make any sales at all on the domestic market the venture required protective tariffs against imports. Even with protection, sales on the domestic market were insufficient to meet the viability condition.[93] Cotton production, by contrast, had overseas markets to give high-volume sales, if the price was right. The production technology gave high volume of production with low unit costs, and a good-quality product. The imported raw material did not add excessively to unit costs because of slavery and, from 1793, the cotton gin. The combination produced a viable format for many cotton mills.

The iron format

The second major evolutionary acceleration of the late eighteenth and early nineteenth century was in iron. The iron industry received its technological boost in the early 1780s when Henry Cort's puddling and rolling technique made it possible to refine pig iron into the more malleable wrought iron using coke. The process had previously been carried out in numerous small forges at high cost and with poor quality.[94] James Watt's steam engine, the ubiquitous driver of machinery, developed in 1765 as a modification of Newcomen's engine but applied to blast furnaces for the first time in 1776, made generally available the strong blast necessary to the coke smelting process.[95] With Britain's large deposits of coal and iron ore, these innovations made it possible to establish iron production in new high-volume and low-cost formats. The effects on prices of iron products are shown in Table 5.3. Prices of iron in 1801 were 40 per cent below those of 1770, and by 1831 they were 70 per cent below.

Iron was a key material in the acceleration of the evolution of the money-bargaining system. It was the material used in the making of much of the capital equipment required in other industries, including mining, manufacturing, railways and shipbuilding. Iron was essential to the steam engines that powered most of the machinery of the period and, in particular, the new railway engines. The fall in the price of products made of iron opened up new opportunities for the viable format of businesses to produce many other products and services. In this way, the new format in iron production transmitted an evolutionary impulse across the money-bargaining system.

Iron also stimulated evolution of the infrastructure that supported economic change. The transport infrastructure, including canals and railways, required substantial ironware. Urbanisation required urban infrastructure, including drains, railings and water and sewerage systems. The state expended large sums on military hardware. Cannons and cannonballs, chains and anchors were in demand for the war against Napoleon. Throughout the nineteenth century iron was in demand to furnish the navy that protected international trade routes.

Reductions in the unit cost, and hence the price, of iron gave rise to product innovation. Companies could increase sales by modifying established products or introducing new products made from iron. Mathias notes that, 'The catalogue of the 1851 Exhibition is highly instructive in revealing the great expansion in the iron markets as more and more objects were being contrived from metal'.[96] The scope for product innovation meant that a variety of company formats could fulfil the viability condition. Small workshops could be set up fairly easily. Many became established around Birmingham, Sheffield and in Lancashire villages. Around Sheffield knives and cutlery were produced from steel made in many small furnaces in the area prior to Bessemer's invention of the converter in the 1850s.[97] With that innovation steel production moved to a new format, involving a larger scale of production to achieve lower unit costs.

Output of iron rose rapidly from the mid-eighteenth century on. Total output of pig iron is estimated to have doubled between 1760 and 1788 and to have reached around 250,000 tons in 1805. Growth was strongest in the period leading up to the middle of the nineteenth century. There are problems in the valuation of output, but in 1805 it is estimated that the iron industry accounted for about 5.9 per cent of national income. The proportion fell in the post-war period to about 3.6 per cent and stayed at that level for about three decades. James Nielson's 'hot blast' technique, perfected in 1829, reduced fuel consumption in blast furnaces by two-thirds, hence reducing unit costs and reinvigorating growth in iron output. At about the same time, the construction of railways began, with attendant demand for iron products. In 1851 iron industry output is estimated to have accounted for over 6 per cent of national income; by 1871 the share had risen to 11.6 per cent.[98] The format opportunities it opened up in other industries, through scope for product innovation and its role in capital investment, meant that it played an even more important role in accelerating the evolution of the economy than its share of national income suggests.

The reduction in unit costs and improvements in quality arising from the technological innovations resulted in the increasing exclusion of imports from the domestic market. In the decade 1787–96 average annual imports of bar iron had been 45,000 tons per year; in the period 1801–5 they were 31,000 tons per year; and in the period 1806–10 they had fallen to 19,000 tons. The fall in imports was accompanied by a rise in exports, as foreign buyers, attracted by the low prices, acquired iron capital equipment, iron infrastructure, iron armaments and iron products for the consumer market. Around 1805 exports are estimated to have been about 23.6 per cent of gross output, staying roughly at that share until mid-century. In the early 1850s exports achieved a 38.7 per cent share, and held roughly that level to the end of the century.[99]

Henry Bessemer's invention of the converter for steel production in 1856 made it possible to format steel production on a large scale. The method was technically superseded in 1866 by the Siemens–Martin open hearth method of production, though British steel producers were relatively slow to convert to a new technique that produced higher-quality steel at a lower price. Production of steel quadrupled from the 1870s through to the 1890s as railways converted from iron to steel rails and shipbuilders adopted mild steel plate and girders as the foundations of their vessels.[100]

As with cotton, technological innovation made possible the format of companies for iron and steel production on a substantially increased scale, with substantially lower unit costs. The low prices possible with the low unit costs made it possible to sell the large volumes produced, displacing higher-priced imported products and permitting the export of a large proportion of output. The particular importance of iron lay in its use for the manufacture of capital equipment. By improving the specifications and lowering the cost of capital equipment, as well as generating a new range of capital equipment, the new formats of the iron manufacturers stimulated the evolution of new formats across the money-bargaining system.

The new formats liberated many people from the old regimes of land-based servitude, but they did not liberate people from hierarchy. Mathias writes:

> In the iron towns, like Merthyr Tydfil, massive technology had brought the iron masters into the position of being lords of their communities, as the cotton lords of Lancashire mill towns, with an absolute divide separating the owners of capital in the industry and their workers ... Class consciousness always and class bitterness in bad times ran high in these places. But such an extreme local industrial class structure was as unusual as was the massive technology in the national economy of 1851.[101]

Many landowners owed their positions and attitudes to heredity and upbringing. While their forebears might, in many cases, have had the driving energy and determination needed to take possession of their land and hold it, their successors did not necessarily inherit the same temperament. The early iron masters and cotton lords were, however, for the most part self-made men. They were first-generation masters, with the force of character and single-mindedness necessary to build their businesses. Company formats for money-bargaining created dependence comparable to the dependence created in earlier centuries by ownership of land, and the masters of company formats reacted in much the same way as the landowners. They exercised power in their communities.

The railway format

The third major industry of the evolutionary acceleration became prominent after 1830. At this time, as was seen above, aggregate growth rates of the British economy were rising. Though iron products and steam engines were available earlier, a range of technical innovations was necessary before it became possible to format viable companies using steam locomotives for provision of rail services. Cort's puddling and rolling process was necessary to make rails strong enough to bear the weight of locomotives. Stronger and lighter metal casings were required to withstand the pressures in higher-powered steam engines and yet remain light enough to maintain an acceptable power to weight ratio. Richard Trevithick dispensed with Watt's external condenser. George Stephenson and Timothy Hackforth simultaneously discovered that by exhausting steam up the boiler-fire chimney the power of an engine was much increased. George and Robert Stephenson created a 'revolutionary multi-tubular boiler'.[102] These innovations gave steam engines the greater power and lighter weight necessary to pull commercial loads. They gave railway companies a viable format, and gave railways a starring role in the economic drama of the nineteenth century.

The new service was markedly different from the transport services available from canals and coaches. The Stockton and Darlington line initiated the use of steam power on rails, though carriages were mostly hauled by cable and stationary engines, with steam locomotives used only for a small stretch of line. The line was open for use by carriers using their own waggons and horses, in the same way as canals were used. Experience acquired on the Stockton and Darlington line was applied in the development of the 35-mile double-track Liverpool–Manchester line, inaugurated in 1830. Three hundred and eight shareholders from Liverpool, Manchester and London took up 4,233 shares in the Liverpool and Manchester Railway Company. Their holding gave them a yield of around 10 per cent per year. The Act of Parliament authorising construction of the railway was passed on 5 May 1826. The directors were uncertain whether to use locomotives or stationary engines on the line. They arranged a trial of locomotives at Rainhill in 1829. The *Rocket*, designed by George and Robert Stephenson, won the £500 prize and convinced the directors that locomotives would be superior to stationary engines. The company format was established on the basis of steam locomotives. The line linked the cotton and textile mills of Manchester to the docks of Liverpool. Apart from 1¼ miles along the Wapping Tunnel from Liverpool Docks, and another much shorter tunnel, where cable haulage was used, steam locomotives did all the pulling. Its construction was pushed by its promoters with the argument that the proprietors of the Liverpool–Manchester canal were exploiting their monopoly of freight between the two towns by setting high freight rates. It cost 15 shillings per ton to move cotton from Liverpool to Manchester, and took 36 hours, by canal and river. Reactions to the line seemed to validate, for once, the arguments of the promoters, since the canal proprietors cut their freight rates to 10 shillings per ton as soon as the railway opened. The Liverpool–Manchester rail link increased the use of Liverpool Docks.

Mathias records that average freight rates on the canals were subsequently lower than those on the railways, and freight carried on canals continued to rise through much of the nineteenth century. But the railways were able to meet the logistical requirements of industry much more extensively than canals. The railways generated new business in freight transport that could not be accommodated on the canals.[103]

The railways gained additional revenues from the unexpected enthusiasm of passengers for rail travel. The Liverpool–Manchester line provided the world's first regular passenger rail service. Coach services ceased to be viable on routes where railways offered an alternative, though railway stations opened opportunities for horse-drawn 'taxi' services to carry people from origin to station and from station to final destination. Companies using the long-distance coach format contracted, but new companies with a local format increased in number.

The potential of railways gripped the public imagination and its budgets at an early stage. Large capital sums were made available to railway companies for construction. Much of it was raised locally. Requirements for rail capital meant that rail shares were the most important factor behind the expansion of the London Stock Exchange and the establishment of provincial exchanges.[104] Merchants and landowners were prominent investors.[105] Some landowners accepted shares in exchange for permission for a railway to pass over their land. Even with the substantial demand for investment funds, capital was cheap. It could also be secure. Over two-thirds of the capital of railway companies was in the form of preference shares carrying a guaranteed return, regarded by many as giving security comparable to that of gilt-edged securities.[106] The open taps of capital were no doubt one of the reasons why rail construction was so much more expensive in Britain than in other countries. At about £40,000 per mile it was three or four times as expensive as in the USA and continental countries. Much of the capital was used to pay off parliamentarians and the opponents of lines. Landowners also had to be compensated. The funds available meant that railway buildings and bridges could be built in something more than purely functional style. Investment was mainly concentrated in particular periods, starting with the 'mania' of 1825. Further concentrations of investment occurred in 1834–7 and 1844–7.[107]

Rail track grew rapidly across the country. By 1847 3,505 miles were open. Ten years later 8,942 miles were open. By 1860 the mileage had topped 10,000 miles. The immediate economic impact of railway expansion was the employment of many men for construction. At the peak of construction in 1847 around 257,000 men were employed, compared with 47,000 employed in the operation of railway companies. The total in railway employment topped 300,000 in a money-earning population estimated at around 12 million.[108] The first year in which those employed in operating the railways outnumbered those employed in constructing them was 1850. By that time the construction force had fallen to 59,000, while operational staff had risen to 60,000.

Railway construction and railway operation were important components in themselves, in terms of net output, in the money-bargaining system of the nineteenth century. As with iron, however, their importance extended much further. The railways made it easier to format companies to meet the viability condition because they extended the vendor sets of producers. Instead of being confined to buyers in a particular locality, either by the lack of transport or the high unit cost of the available transport, companies could sell to distant buyers, enabling them to produce and deliver at a larger scale and at a unit cost commensurate with distant sales. Company vendor sets, the bargaining sets comprising those buyers whose situations would incline them to purchase a company's products at the price they could be offered at, suddenly expanded and created new format opportunities. The unit cost of production plus the unit cost of transport still made feasible a price at which the corresponding volume of production could be sold. Potential buyers previously regarded as beyond commercial range now came within range. Deane and Cole remark that, 'The accelerated growth of the iron and steel and coal industries in the late 1840's and the 1850's ... can clearly be related to the construction of new transport facilities and the consequent expansion of capacity.'[109] Rail transport changed the situation in which companies were formatted. Many opportunities opened up for larger-scale company formats.

While much of the expanded scale would likely have been new business, there is an implication that opportunities for small-scale, localised format were lost. Local monopolies with high unit costs would not be viable when goods were coming in from companies outside the locality, producing at lower unit cost and newly able to distribute at low unit cost, to sell at lower prices than were feasible for incumbent suppliers. Buyers would choose the lower prices of the distant supplier, other features of the transaction being equal. At the same time, as with the rail passengers mentioned above, new local opportunities would arise in the distribution of products arriving by rail. Locational aspects of format are considered further below.

Railways and companies

The period 1820 to 1860 that saw the evolution of railways into technically and commercially viable form was also a period in which companies evolved into what might be regarded as their modern form. The two lines of evolution were certainly connected, but the influence of railway development on company legislation is debated. Micklethwait and Wooldridge see the requirements of the railways as the major factor in acceleration of the reform of company law. Incorporation, the establishment of a legal entity for trade or some other purpose, required an Act of Parliament or a royal charter. The rush to invest in railway companies meant incessant Acts of Parliament. There were five a year from 1827 to 1835, and 29 in 1836. In 1845 there were 120 railway acts, 272 in 1846 and 170 in 1847. Reformers were pressing for laws that would provide for the establishment of companies outside the immediate jurisdiction of parliament. According to Micklethwait and Wooldridge, 'The crucial change was the railways, and their demands for large agglomerations of capital.'[110]

Mathias recognises the effects of railway requirements for capital on the growth of stock exchanges across the country. He also recognises the constraints of the Bubble Act: 'There was virtual prohibition of company flotation and publicly raised capital in manufacturing industry after the Bubble Act of 1720.'[111] However, he doubts the extent to which laws impeded the growth of business organisations, and doubts the impact of the changes in law when they came. He writes:

> There was also virtual prohibition of incorporation in manufacturing business between 1720 and the early nineteenth century. All attempts to incorporate a firm by letters patent, royal charter or private Act of Parliament had to run the gauntlet of a Parliament hostile to anything thought productive of speculation and open to challenge by all rivals with friends at Westminster and at Court. But it remains doubtful how important a blockage to enterprise this hostility by the law created. No great pressure was put on Parliament by frustrated manufacturers or an industrial lobby. Very little institutional pressure built up and no great flood of applications for incorporation resulted after the repeal of the Bubble Act in 1825.[112]

He suggests that legal means were found of setting up business organisations with what were, in effect, the advantages of incorporation. Business organisations evolved around the existing law, circumventing the impasse in the formal support-bargaining system. He writes:

> Forms of enterprise demanding incorporation in order to share risks and to assemble very large and pre-mobilized capitals developed their own appropriate legal forms allowing such investment as transport undertakings, insurance companies, shipping, mining and land improvement.[113]

At least as far as railway investment was concerned, the legal arrangements were clearly not sufficiently accessible after 1830 to prevent the rise of applications to parliament for incorporation. It seems reasonable to conclude that the heavy demands on parliament, lucrative as they may have been to many members, were a significant factor in the emergence of a new procedure for incorporation. The new procedure could not, however, entirely replace the parliamentary process in all circumstances. Railways required land, and land with very precise specifications with regard to location and extent. The incorporation process through parliament involved resolution of issues concerning provision of land, with authorisation of compulsory purchase if necessary.

Mathias suggests that any impediments to incorporation set by the intricacies of law were probably beneficial, since when incorporation with limited liability did become available in the mid-nineteenth century, there were very high rates of company failure. In the eighteenth century, 'open access to incorporation could have brought chaos'.[114] The implication is that the legal arrangements prevented many people from starting companies which were likely to fail. It is, however, perhaps preferable that companies are formed and given the opportunity to succeed, rather than prevented from forming altogether. New companies frequently fail today, but no one suggests that their formation should be impeded.

Whatever the impulses behind them, the mid-years of the nineteenth century saw the passage of the Acts of Parliament that are widely seen as having created the modern company. In 1844 a Joint-Stock Companies Act allowed companies to incorporate through simple registration, though it did not provide for automatic limited liability. Limited liability was still looked on with grave suspicion. Nevertheless, its supporters contrived to gain passage in 1855 of the Limited Liability Act, granting limited liability to companies incorporated under the 1844 Act. In the following year a second Joint-Stock Companies Act removed some of the constraints in the 1855 Act on the application of limited liability. Companies could now be formed as distinct legal trading entities with limited liability by seven people signing a Memorandum of Understanding, registering an office and designating their creation 'ltd'. The 1862 Companies Act consolidated the measures of the earlier acts, with minor modifications, into one.[115]

Company formats clearly evolved around the legal situation when the law did not permit a straightforward approach. Lawyers facilitated the formation of companies to do what their investors wanted them to do, in forms that suited their investors, while remaining within the letter of the law. The rapid succession of acts from 1844 to 1862 indicates that the interest groups wanting more straightforward processes for the formation of companies, no doubt including many of the large numbers that wanted to invest in railways, gained the necessary parliamentary support for passage of new legislation. A 'catch-up' evolution occurred that established in law the sort of arrangements that had earlier evolved despite the law. The 'rules', as understood by institutional economists, impeded the evolution of the underlying functions, until the efforts of those who were impeded gained sufficient support to alter the rules in accordance with the required evolution of the functions. The longevity of the new legal arrangements is the best evidence for their genuine response to pressing needs of business and their positive role in the evolution of the British economy. The acts may be seen as marking the emergence of companies as fully fledged specialised bargaining agencies of money-bargaining systems. The support-bargaining system sanctioned the establishment and operation of such agencies, giving businessmen the freedom to sustain the evolutionary process that had already markedly accelerated the economic evolution of the country.

Evolution of technology

The emergence of the vital cotton, iron and railway formats was, to some extent, fortuitous in that it was technology in just those products or services that evolved to a state in which viable format became feasible. But the evolution of the technology was also purposeful. Technicians with an eye to business opportunities could see the value of certain technologies in industries that had recognisable potential to underpin further economy-wide expansion. They concentrated their efforts on the development of the most auspicious technologies. Mathias remarks, 'Everyone knew that the greatest strides in technical progress lay in applying the steam engine and iron machinery to more and more processes in more and more industries.'[116]

The idea of evolution as a passage from situation to situation is perhaps more clearly apparent in the evolution of technology than in the more general process of social and economic change, since technology involves transition from one clear physical situation to another, with the required situation also readily defined in physical terms, with much less subjective assessment of situation than is apparent in processes of political, personal or social evolution. If the casement of an engine is insufficiently strong to withstand the steam pressures required to drive a locomotive, then interest focuses on the production of a stronger casing. With the stronger casing, a new situation is created, offering new opportunities and generating new interests. Mathias records this sort of evolutionary sequence. The vibration set up by steam engines was found to splinter wooden machinery. Iron machinery could withstand the shaking. Once effectively substituted for wood, it was seen that iron machinery could be made larger, with the capacity to withstand the vibrations of more powerful engines. So higher-powered steam engines were developed.[117] Hence, production could be faster and a company format strengthened. Mathias also records that the precision engineering skills developed in the seventeenth century for making watches and scientific instruments were, in evolved form, important to the engineering of James Watt's steam engines. They made it possible to engineer pistons that fitted with sufficient precision in their cylinders as to contain the necessary steam pressures.[118] Loss of steam pressure required a closer fit of pistons to cylinders, and the engineering skills to meet this requirement were available because of an associated evolution of skills among engineers. The development of the bicycle from hobby-horse through the penny-farthing to the chain driven wheel shows clearly an evolution from deficient situation to less deficient situation to a technology that well serves its purpose.

The replacement of wooden machinery with iron machinery was acceptable because the cost of iron had been reduced through the emergence of the Cort process and the establishment of new low unit cost formats for production of iron. The evolution of the physical state of technologies is carried on in conjunction with interests in the format viability of the technology. An engine casement may be designated 'weak' because it is insufficiently strong to power a locomotive that will haul commercial freight – the situation is understood in terms of opportunities for company format. Technologies have to be developed so that they not only function in the physical sense, but also have the cost characteristics that permit their incorporation in a viable business format. Thomas Newcomen's steam engine was a direct response to the costs of lifting water from mines using horses turning a windlass.[119] The technology is an essential element in the capacity of a viable company.

These commercial considerations are an important factor in the relationship between 'technology' and 'natural science'. Some remarkable developments in natural science took place in the seventeenth century, most notably the many revelations of Isaac Newton. T. S. Ashton, in his 1948 history of the industrial revolution, portrays science and technology as closely connected in the eighteenth century:

> there was much coming and going between the laboratory and the workshop, and men like James Watt, Josiah Wedgwood, William Reynolds, and James Keir were at home in the one as in the other. The names of engineers, ironmasters, industrial chemists, and instrument-makers on the list of Fellows of the Royal Society show how close were the relations between science and practice at this time.[120]

Recent economic historians have been inclined to distinguish technological development more sharply from natural science. Many of the major technological developments of the eighteenth and nineteenth centuries came from individuals with no deep scientific training. George Stephenson, for example, one of the most celebrated technological innovators, was entirely self-taught in engineering. He referred mathematical calculations to his son Robert. His lack of credibility among trained engineers meant that the Liverpool and Manchester Railway Company had a rough ride in the parliamentary hearings involved in obtaining passage of its enabling Act of Parliament. Mathias comments that, 'By and large innovations were not the result of the formal application of applied science, nor a product of the formal educational system of the country'.[121] They were achievements of instinctive technical innovators, drawing what they needed as and when they could from sources open to them. Mokyr is more inclined to recognise close links between science and technology, though 'the connections between science and industry in this age were multiple and often roundabout'.[122] Science in some cases did not have the answers to questions posed in the course of technological development: 'Improvement and refinement of new techniques were usually slow in this period because often the underlying knowledge (or "epistemic base") was still quite limited in the early stages of the Industrial Revolution'.[123] The idea of a sophisticated natural science providing leadership and inspiration to mere technicians is inappropriate. The technicians were, in some cases, in advance of science. They employed a recognisably similar technique to that of scientists. Like Ashton, Mokyr recognises, 'The legitimation of systematic experiment as a scientific method carried over to the realm of technology.'[124]

Technological evolution might be said to have its own path, distinguished from the evolution of natural science in part by the purpose of enquiry. Natural scientists seek universal laws regarding relationships between natural phenomena, while technologists are concerned with functionality. But the distinction arose also from the requirement in technological evolution, referred to above, that whatever evolves should have characteristics of functionality and costs that suit it to incorporation in a business format. A large part of the interest associated with technological 'situations' is the interest in opportunities for format of companies. Economies evolve through the format of companies, with many format opportunities arising from the evolution of technology. Evolution of technology is an integral part of the evolution of companies and of economies.

The pragmatic approach to technological development served well in the earlier stages of technological evolution. In those stages, eye and instinct, trial and error, could generate technological evolution. But the natural scientific approach gave more detailed accounts of technological 'situations', identifying, in particular, operative causes and their effects that could not be identified through the procedures usually followed by technologists. Understanding of causation makes it easier to identify what has to be done to resolve impediments in the evolution of technology. James Watt, for example, learned from his scientific friend William Cullen that water under low pressure boiled at a much lower temperature than under atmospheric pressure. Even tepid water would boil at low pressure, and the vapour released would spoil a vacuum. This scientific knowledge led to Watt's conclusion that a steam engine needed a separate condenser.[125] If that scientific knowledge had not been available, evolution of the steam engine would have been delayed. As the 'low-hanging fruit' of technical evolution was exhausted, understanding of the underlying science became more important. Britain's substantial reliance on artisanal instinct became something of a weakness. In the latter half of the nineteenth century a shortage of trained chemists impeded British performance in the chemicals industry.[126] In the modern era detailed knowledge of the science underlying natural phenomena, whether biological, electronic, chemical or physical, is almost prerequisite for technological advance. Governments and companies undertake scientific research to underpin the technological evolution that will sustain viable company formats.

While scientific ideals held that discoveries should be widely disseminated, technology was a different matter. Much technological development was undertaken with an eye to profitable investment in the format of companies. If the technology were widely propagated, it would be difficult to build a money-bargaining position based on the technology. Many sources of a similar product at a similar unit cost meant substantial competition and, for some, incapacity to meet the viability condition. Developers often tried to keep their technology secret, but inevitably much technological innovation was copied.

Patents offered a means of protecting a technology from copiers and imitators. The provision for protection of technology by patent was an important spur to invention. As Coleman remarks, 'Patents were (and still are) potential money-spinners, because of the monopoly rights they confer.'[127] For some, patents made their fortunes. But while patents, for the most part, were a spur to innovation, the patents system could also inhibit the evolution of technology by denying to others the use of a basic technology. Technology could be effectively 'frozen' in a particular situation, with aspiring developers denied the chance to take it forward because of potential infringement of a patent. It is suggested that James Watt's patents on the steam engine delayed its evolution for a time.[128] Patents were not necessarily advantageous to inventors. For the grant of a patent, it was necessary to reveal the technology, and risk its adoption by others. Enforcement of a patent was potentially expensive, and some minor modification to a patented idea might be sufficient to get round the patent.

The famous names mentioned in relation to the various technologies are useful markers of key points in the evolution of technologies that made possible their adoption into viable company formats. But the descriptions of technological innovation make clear that the achievements of the particular 'names' are set amid evolutionary currents involving many ingenious people working independently on many aspects of technological change, many of whom might have achieved the 'breakthroughs' that made their rivals famous, and whose work, in many cases, contributed to the fame of others. Mathias notes that:

> It was far from being the work of brilliant individual inventors. The names that have reached the textbooks are those few out of a large crowd who were feverishly working on every one of the major inventions developed. The actual progress of every major innovation depended not only on basic advances made by the famous but on innumerable smaller developments made by the unknown ... An innovation evolves almost 'biologically' as a species slowly advances. This showed also in the high rate of simultaneous inventing by different people, making constructive reactions to similar problems. Each person was responding to the demand created by businessmen anxious to adopt a machine to solve a problem or make a fortune. [129]

Mathias notes that the steam engine, 'came out of an international struggle in the seventeenth century amongst amateur aristocratic inventors'.[130] Thomas Newcomen's steam engine was the first to be used commercially, beginning operations in 1712. It had little power, and was slow and expensive. James Watt's separate condenser greatly improved the efficiency of the Newcomen engine. Watt's engines benefited from the metal-working skills available at the Royal Arsenal at Woolwich and in Matthew Boulton's workshops in Soho, and from a device for the accurate boring of cannon developed by John Wilkinson.[131] Richard Crompton's 'mule', combining the functions of Arkwright's 'throstle' water frame and Hargreaves's 'jenny', was introduced in 1779, but up to 1850, 'endless mechanical problems in its operation were resolved by ingenious mechanics and technicians, most of whom remain obscure'.[132] The evolution of technology involves response to 'big situations', but it also involves attention to many incidental problems: a valve may not open and close sufficiently rapidly as to give a machine smooth high-speed function; a wheel may buckle too easily because the material it is made from is too weak; brakes may overheat and make a machine unreliable.

International copying was commonplace because patents did not have international recognition. The technology used in Thomas Lombe's 1720 silk mill was of Italian origin. Britain led in some of the technologies that were most important to the acceleration of economic evolution, including the use of coal, steam, metals and textiles, but lagged in other technologies, particularly chemical, glass, paper and high-end textiles. British technicians were, nevertheless, adept in refining imported technologies.[133] The broad evolution of technology in Britain involved streams of foreign innovation, with the same smattering of famous names among many unknowns.

This evolutionary process is apparent also in the delays that occurred between an initial 'breakthrough' and the adoption of a technology in a viable company format. Mokyr notes that new technologies often needed to be 'tweaked' before they could be successfully used. The 'tweaking' involved adapting the technology to local environments and requirements, ironing out functional shortcomings and aligning operational requirements with the capacities of labour and management.[134] In some cases application had to wait on some complementary technology being brought to a usable state. Steam power underwent decades of modification and development before it was extensively used. It was first used in a cotton mill in 1785, and usage increased from that date. But still there was an increase in the number of water-powered mills up to 1830. Improved performance of steam engines meant that 80 per cent of cotton mills used steam power by 1838, and 90 per cent by 1850.[135] Mokyr notes also that Abraham Darby's use of coke for iron smelting and Edmund Cartwright's power loom both took time to become established.[136] Darby smelted iron ore with coke in Coalbrookdale from 1709, but it was not taken up widely until later in the century when Cort's puddling and rolling technology became available.[137] In the case of the power loom, Cartwright's invention never became fully operational: 'The Revd Edmund Cartwright took out the first power-loom patents as early as 1786–8 but commercial success did not follow until Horrocks and other Stockport manufacturers developed other models after 1813.'[138] The above quotation from Mathias, at note 129 ('It was far ... make a fortune'), makes it clear that technology also had to be 'tweaked' so that its output and costs were commensurate with incorporation in a viable format.

Locational format and urbanisation

All companies must, of necessity, format in a certain location. The choice of location may be critical to the viability and profitability of a format. A company's location must be such that it gives the company access to vendor sets in sufficient volume as to make its format viable. Some companies, especially retailers, will establish something like a local monopoly by locating where there are no rival suppliers for the surrounding community. Others will locate amid their rivals, on the reckoning that the agglomeration of sellers will attract buyers in sufficient volume to make numerous suppliers viable. Companies need also a variety of raw materials and other inputs. Calculations are made regarding the relative advantages of locating near sources of inputs and transporting outputs to their buyers, or locating near buyers and transporting inputs.[139] Some companies achieve viability by ensuring first that they are located in an area where a ready supply of workers with the skills necessary to their operations is available. Larger companies may realise the advantages of different locations through their organisational structure. In a mining company, the mineral must be mined where it occurs; processing of ore can be done away from the mine in a different division where the necessary power supplies are available; another division is located where specialist labour requirements are available to shape the mineral into final products.

The importance of location to viability means that locational factors play a prominent part in the evolution of economies. For most companies, their initial choice of location fixes them for an extended period. Whatever the disadvantages of an existing location, the high costs of moving are likely to deter change of location unless there are very strong reasons to move. In some cases, companies are tied to a particular location by specific features of the location, such as a harbour or a bridge. Spatial 'path dependence' is established, as described in the previous chapter.

Strong reasons to change location include the exhaustion of an essential raw material, or a switch to a new raw material. In the eighteenth century iron smelting in Britain moved from the Weald of Sussex and Kent to more remote areas of the country with the depletion of timber in the Weald. The industry relocated again when Cort's puddling and rolling process was introduced. The use of coke for the production of wrought iron freed ironmasters from the necessity of locating their works near woodland. They moved to four main areas where the new requirements for fuel could be met – Staffordshire, South Yorkshire, the Clyde and South Wales.[140] Fortunately for the ironmasters, iron ore was often located in the vicinity of coal.[141]

Locational format is intimately connected with the availability and costs of transport. Companies typically buy in raw materials and other inputs, employ staff in various numbers and types, make a product and deliver the product to a range of buyers. Both inputs and finished goods will normally have to be transported, but there will be choices to make over how far each is transported. Transport costs are normally set in terms of a charge per tonne or per cubic metre. Commodities that are heavy or bulky in relation to their value are consequently liable to incur transport costs that constitute a significant proportion of total cost per unit. The nature of the product can then have a critical bearing on the viability of a locational format. Analysis will normally show that the most advantageous locational format is that which minimises the transportation of commodities with high weight or bulk to value ratios. Unit costs were reduced in cotton and woollen mills by moving close to coalfields when the adoption of steam power meant a requirement for coal, with a high weight to value ratio. Iron works, as noted above, also moved close to coalfields. The combinations of factors relevant to locational format are apparent in a passage of Mathias on the location of the early Coalbrookdale iron works:

> Only after 1709 did coal begin to exercise its influence on the location of the iron industry ... Shropshire was perhaps chosen by Abraham Darby for his iron works because it gave access to the Severn, immediately adjacent, and water carriage from there to the sea. There was good 'sweet' coal and iron ore in the vicinity (he smelted with coke from his first year at Coalbrookdale

152   *The Evolution of Economies*

in 1709) and a good stream ran by to work his bellows. Canals were soon to give greater mobility to water carriage, and thus encourage siting at coal and ore more completely.[142]

Costs of transportation of coal inhibited the operational use of Newcomen's steam engine of 1712. The engine was highly inefficient as a pump, consuming large tonnages of coal per gallon of water raised. Numerous uses were proposed for it, but in the event it was used almost entirely for pumping water out of the coal mines that provided its fuel.[143] Used elsewhere, the cost of transporting its fuel raised unit costs beyond what could be accommodated in any company format.

Because of these locational imperatives in the format of new companies, the industrial revolution was, in its early stages, as Mokyr points out, mostly a local phenomenon.[144] Industry became concentrated in and around the major coalfields, which were conveniently located near the sea. The Northumberland and Durham coalfield was virtually on the coast; the Lancashire coalfield was close to Liverpool; the South Wales coalfield was close to the sea; Glasgow was within the Lanarkshire coalfield and on the Clyde. The locational characteristics of British coalfields and river systems offered important advantages in the format of companies.[145] Most of the country proceeded in much the same old way, most people knowing only by occasional report of the dramatic changes that were taking place around the coalfields. Only the arrival of railway trains, from the 1830s on, spread the revolution around the country, along with the recognition that radical changes were taking place. It also changed the calculations relating to locational format.

Of necessity, people looking for work migrated to the locations where employment was available. People changed their places of residence to establish locational situations that permitted them to take up the employment offered. As companies format in response to the opportunities of situation, so people also respond to opportunities for employment. In England in the nineteenth century those looking for work included large numbers of Irish, who 'could underlive the native English just as they traditionally outworked them'.[146] Concentrations of population developed in the areas of textile production and iron works. This involved not only the large numbers of operatives in the cotton and textile mills, but also the skilled engineers who maintained the equipment. Textile mills attracted firms to their vicinity with the skills necessary to keep machinery operational. With such a situation established, opportunities arose for the employment of others, and the format of other companies:

> The pull of Liverpool and Manchester also became important as marketing centres, the first for cotton buying, the other for sales. Very shortly other 'external economies' developed. Once a pool of skilled labour grew up in a mill town that added to the 'inertia' of location. It made it more worth while for expansion to occur in the same locality. A factory-trained labour force, of semi-skilled women and adolescents, was also an immense local advantage by the second generation.[147]

The evolution of money-bargaining 153

This dynamic of urban growth is important to the evolution of economies. Urban areas create favourable conditions for the format of companies. Where population is concentrated there is potential for sales. Costs of transport in time and money are minimised. The opportunities attract entrepreneurs, and each new company provides revenues for its employees, giving them budgets for disbursement on the products of other companies. The conditions give rise to extensive company formation, and hence relatively weak bargaining positions for all. Companies innovate in urban areas to strengthen their bargaining positions, giving urban areas a strong evolutionary impulse. Situations change more rapidly in towns than in rural areas. Company formats change with the changing situations. In rural areas there is no possibility of formatting viable businesses for provision of a large range of products and services.

But the situation in rural areas gives exclusive opportunities for the format of companies dealing in products that can only be rural in origin. Agriculture requires space. The people of urban areas have to be fed. There are, then, opportunities for company format in supplying towns with food grown in the country. Cities give rise to market gardening in their hinterlands, close enough to deliver perishable produce in good condition. Locational format is important to the interdependence of agriculture and industry. While urban areas provide the greatest opportunities for evolution of money-bargaining, there is also an important evolutionary dynamic in trade between urban and rural areas.

From landowners to companies

The Acts of Parliament from 1844 to 1862 relating to the establishment of companies in Britain may be seen as critical events in the evolution of the modern company. Companies of the kind made possible by these acts, albeit with extensive additional legislation in various parts of the world, still constitute the main vehicles for the conduct of business. Yet the development of companies has little prominence in the established understanding of the industrial revolution. The historians range widely in their analysis and explanations, but are, in many respects, bounded by the preconceptions of neoclassical economics, which has no place for companies in any realistic form. Crafts, for example, identifies two types of economic change, both of which have been labelled 'industrial revolution'. The first is the revolution in industrial structure, prominent in the textbook account of Phyllis Deane,[148] involving the movement from agriculture to industry. According to Crafts, this shows that there were, 'many signs of an efficient allocation of resources, investment was higher than ever before, the economy was heavily urbanized, and, in effect, Britain was exhibiting many of the features of a "developed" rather than a pre-industrial economy'. The second kind of change is that associated with technological change. In this, 'the picture evoked is of the spread of the factory system and steam-powered mechanization promoting faster growth of industrial output and faster structural change'.[149] This second kind of change Crafts identifies as his own definition, used in an earlier paper.[150] Technology, structural change, efficient allocation of resources, investment, urbanisation, the factory system, steam-powered mechanisation and faster growth are all recognised, but there is no mention of the role of companies. The neoclassical preconceptions are apparent, even if not wholly confining. Mokyr notes that economists take factories as something like a proxy for the firm, though technological change is identified as the critical element of the revolution:

> to economists interested in the microeconomics of the firm the rise of the factory system has remained the central event of the Industrial Revolution ... Yet at the end of the day there is more or less a consensus that the Industrial Revolution meant first and foremost that the engine of growth was to be found increasingly in technology, and that technology alone can propel a process that does not run into some kind of upper bound.[151]

Crafts is aware of the limitations of his analysis:

> An explanation of the industrial revolution in the second, technological, sense raises very difficult methodological and philosophical questions. As I argued in my earlier paper (1977), economic theory does not provide a suitable covering law to account for such phenomena.[152]

Neoclassical theory lacks the scope and realism necessary to guide investigations into historical development. It is not possible to understand the industrial revolution in terms of a system of optimal resource allocation, implying full employment of resources, through 'markets' for homogeneous products produced with given technology and sold at prices determined by supply and demand independently of any particular seller. Neoclassical theory requires also, if optimal allocation of resources is to be achieved, that unit costs do not vary with scale of production. Nor can neoclassical theory comprehend the spatial distribution of economic activity. Observed and recorded essentials of the industrial revolution are inconsistent with every element of such a model.

In terms of bargaining theory, companies are the dominant agents of modern money-bargaining systems and their emergence in something close to their present form is a crucial event in the evolution of money-bargaining systems. The chroniclers of the industrial revolution miss the revolution. Technology, growth, structural change and factories were all part of it, but the essential organisational and motivational component was companies. Without recognition of the role of companies the 'revolution' lacks its heartbeat. Companies made possible the practical application of the technology, the establishment of factories and the growth in output. Companies were the vehicles by which people could profit from their ingenuity and enterprise, and hence were the means by which much of the motivation behind the industrial revolution was harnessed. The revolution, if it is to be called a revolution, lay in the displacement of the old landed order by companies as the major source of the nation's livelihoods. The 1844 to 1862 acts marked a significant point in the evolution of the British money-bargaining system from a basis in landowning and land dependence to a situation in which companies were accepted as specialist money-bargaining agencies, consolidating their role as the dominant agents of the money-bargaining system.

Companies have been the major means by which material well-being has evolved subsequently around the world. People who prepared themselves in earlier times for agriculture or domestic service instead prepared themselves for work in companies. Before, people depended on land for their political, social and economic sustenance. With the emergence of companies, they became dependent on companies for their material well-being. Most individual agents found it necessary to acquire money revenues by reaching an agreement with a company for the use of their services. Their position in social support-bargaining might be influenced by their company employment, but might also have little or nothing to do with it. Their political support-bargaining position would be independent of their company employment. The money-bargaining system became a little less closely integrated with the support-bargaining system.

Companies have been the principal purveyors of innovations that advance material well-being. They have been the agencies by which technology is made available to ordinary people and affects their lives. The acceleration in economic evolution in the late eighteenth and nineteenth centuries was brought about by technological advance, but crucially it was technology adapted to the requirements of company formats. Technology had to be developed to a particular form, with particular characteristics, before it could be put into service through companies. It is perhaps because companies operate at 'arm's length' from the support-bargaining system that they do not receive vocal popular acclaim.[153] But many people are dependent on them directly for their standards of living, which, for the most part, at least in those countries which have allowed companies to operate with a fair degree of freedom, are higher than could have been dreamt of in past times. Virtually all the rest, in public service, are indirectly dependent on the success of companies in making money.

Sustaining the rate of evolution

The three formats described above as central to the industrial revolution have distinctive features that made them accelerators of the evolution of the whole British economy. The cotton format involved high volume and low unit cost, depending on foreign trade for high-volume sales of final product. As noted, this has proved to be a format of enduring success. The iron format made available low-cost capital equipment, making it possible for other companies to establish viable formats in the production of a range of other products. Product innovation, both in iron products and in products made with iron equipment, increased the volume of money-bargaining transactions. The railway services format opened up bargaining sets across the whole economy. Because sales could be made over wide geographical areas, it became possible to format higher-volume low unit cost companies in a way that had not been feasible before. The emergence of these three formats was a critical step in the accelerated evolution of the British economy and subsequently of other economies.

The idea of company format and a viability condition helps to explain also why it was that the more rapid evolution of economies was sustained. Mokyr writes:

> We can imagine a counterfactual world in which the economies of Western Europe reached a new equilibrium around 1800 or 1810, with the new cotton spinning mills, low-pressure steam engines, and puddling furnaces becoming the dominant designs to crystallize into a new but stable industrial set of techniques. Instead, technology continued to expand.[154]

Companies provided the necessary impetus to sustain the process of technological evolution. Company formats could themselves evolve along with the technology on which many of them were dependent. Entrepreneurs, employees and buyers all found their material well-being advanced through the operations of companies. Iron production and railway services involved formats that generated opportunities for the successful format of many other companies. Technological evolution on its own might have stalled, as Mokyr suggests. But the motivations tied up with company formats ensured that companies and technology together sustained a newly established rapid rate of economic evolution.

Companies and company format also help to explain Mokyr's 'big question' – why it was that Western Europe succeeded in sustaining an economic evolution which took millions of people out of the poverty that had engulfed the great majorities in previous generations, while other civilisations, such as the Ottoman world, China and India, all with remarkable achievements in science and technology, failed to achieve sustained evolution.[155] Western Europe developed support-bargaining systems that were sufficiently secure to permit the emergence of organisations that, because of their wealth, might have challenged the ruling groups. Company formats drove Western Europe forward to prosperity. Other civilisations, for all their arts and science, failed to establish the conditions, circumstances or situations that make acceptable the operation of companies. The theories, ideologies, beliefs, ideas and attitudes necessary to the tolerance of companies did not emerge. The aversion of a ruling class to business remains apparent in Britain. 'Trade' and the upstarts who engaged in it were treated as inferior by the social stratum that dominated British political life up to the start of the First World War. Their intellectual cousins in the universities formulated a neoclassical economic theory that totally ignored the evolution of business and technology that was taking place under their noses. Today, the study of companies has been segregated from 'true' scholarly investigation in outhouses known as business schools.

The viability condition is a commercial condition, involving concepts of investment, revenues, costs and profit. Meeting the viability condition involves product innovation, use of technologies, choice of location, marketing and cost-cutting. These concepts would not be prominent in the minds of those who worked the land in earlier centuries. There is a sense in which the viability condition is universal. Any farmer engaged in sales of produce for money must ensure that revenues exceed costs, and hence 'sales × price' exceeds 'production × unit costs'.

But traditional farming was more a 'way of life', understood in terms of working the land in accordance with the seasons and, for the most part, in the way it had always been worked. Farmers produced much the same output in much the same way. The price they received would depend on what they could negotiate with corn merchants or butchers, along with all the other farmers engaged in the same negotiations over similar products. They would deal with what was within their immediate oversight – the land area under cultivation and the yield from the land. Fine weather meant a good harvest for everyone. Bad weather meant shortages for everyone. Production levels were the focus of attention. Reductions in unit costs would have been only a largely unremarked consequence of their inverse relationship to yields. The viability condition of necessity underlaid the working of the land, but its understanding of farming was not the understanding of farmers. The evolution of economies from land-based organisation to companies involved also the evolution of concepts in money-bargaining from strong focus on land and its yields to the establishment of bargaining positions for industrial products through elimination of alternative sources of supply, and later for the establishment of bargaining position by meeting the requirements of buyers. The guilds and chartered companies depended on legislation and regulation – the support-bargaining system – for their ability to meet the viability condition. They cultivated their positions in support-bargaining to protect their money-bargaining positions. But as people became less tolerant of the disservice and expense imposed on them by such business arrangements, the legislation was changed and businesses were increasingly required to achieve viability by meeting the requirements of buyers. Businesses became independent money-bargaining agencies with the viability condition both the underlying determinant of their survival and the direct focus of their attention. Farmers were affected by the new approaches to industry. The growing relevance of the viability condition to farm management as the money-bargaining system evolved can be seen in the increased concern of farmers, remarked on above, for refined cost-cutting rather than extension of cultivable area or simple reductions in wages. The idea of 'improvement' involved a more commercial way of thinking and a stronger concern with the elements of the viability condition. Enclosures gave farmers opportunities to raise yields and reduce unit costs. The increasing use of technology in agriculture, including the use of steam engines, implies the same melding of technology into corporate format as is characteristic of industrial companies.

The twentieth and twenty-first centuries have brought remarkable further evolution, both in the technology used by companies and in their organisation. 'High-tech' companies have expanded incomes but their impact has perhaps been more marked in the way they have changed people's lives. People travel conveniently in cars. Very large companies, such as General Motors, Toyota and Volkswagen, have been formatted for provision of motor vehicles. Most households find space for radios, televisions, computers, smartphones and various other technologically sophisticated gadgets. Alfred Chandler designates the twentieth century 'the electronic century'.[156] In electronics company formats have become very large – giants like Panasonic, Samsung, Microsoft and Apple. The large company formats follow the high-volume and low-cost format of the nineteenth-century cotton industry in Britain, though their concept of high volume dwarfs that of the cotton companies. Motor vehicles have extended bargaining sets in the way that railways did in the nineteenth century. They extend the bargaining system into areas that railways cannot reach, in the way that railways extended the system to areas where canals could not reach. Electronic computers have changed company formats and created new format opportunities across the money-bargaining system, in a way that resembles the nineteenth-century impact of the ironmasters' company format. The internet offers new bargaining sets for consumers and new formats for companies. Information is available in great volume – and people can only buy what they know about. Apple, Facebook, Google and Amazon compete in a new cyber-linked money-bargaining that suffers much less from the format constraints of physical location. Aircraft construction and airline services have extended international money-bargaining sets in much the same way as shipping did in the nineteenth century. The use of containers in shipping has increased opportunities for high-volume and low unit cost formats in international trade. Technology has become much more closely integrated with natural science, especially in emerging fields such as biotechnology and nanotechnology. While new technologies have been the basis of new products and new processes, there has been no let-up in efforts to reduce unit costs, as the means of increasing sales through lower prices, securing the viability of a company in contested bargaining sets, or enhancing the profitability of a company.

The function of companies as the dominant agents of money-bargaining systems inevitably gives rise to disputes in support-bargaining systems over their benefits, their social impact, their ethical status and their desirability. The political dimensions of money-bargaining are considered further in Chapter 6.

Family and hierarchy

While the 1844–62 companies acts established a legal framework within which companies could operate with limited liability, they did not cover the organisation of firms for production. Alongside the evolution of the technologies that companies would incorporate, their internal organisation evolved. In *Support-Bargaining: The Mechanics of Democracy Revealed*, organisations in general and companies in particular are described as deriving their efficacy from hierarchies of control and the use of budgets.[157] Elements of hierarchical control can be seen in companies at all times. It is an easy transplant from or imitation of military control. But in the eighteenth century, as the rate of evolution began to accelerate, internal hierarchies were not so well established. The arrangements that companies could make with their employees had to take into account employees' understanding of work. People had become accustomed to the 'putting out' system. Under that system the head of a household controlled family work. Workers enjoyed a high degree of autonomy. Work was an adjunct of family life and utilised family hierarchy. Mathias notes that in the mills and mines of the late eighteenth and early nineteenth century family employment was customary: 'Family labour became a bridge between the conditions of employment in the old world of the putting-out system and the new factory world.'[158] Children worked in the mills and mines for their fathers and mothers, as they had done in the cottages. The disciplines of production were imposed by families rather than factory supervisors. The regulations of the Factory Act of 1802 applied only to pauper apprentices in the factories who operated outside the family employment system.

The family system of employment was gradually supplanted by direct employment of individuals. A different form of 'outsourcing' was, however, maintained. Many tasks were assigned to autonomous technicians:

> Many of the functions that were eventually to be carried out by management through a hierarchical structure of foremen and supervisors were still carried out in the first half of the nineteenth century by a 'labour aristocracy' of skilled, well-organized operatives and foremen.[159]

The advantages of hierarchical control within a confined unit meant that outsourcing diminished.

The adaptation of company formats to accommodate what is customary in a society can be seen in the twentieth-century practice in Japan of providing lifetime employment for employees. The major companies not only guaranteed employment, but provided a range of social amenities for employees and their families. These practices have diminished in recent decades with the need for reductions in unit costs to maintain viability. In Britain, in the later twentieth and early twenty-first centuries, companies have been required to accommodate aspirations of employees to improved 'work–life balance'. Companies have been required to adhere to more extensive regulations governing recruitment, treatment and dismissal of employees, including introduction of flexible working hours, accommodation of employees' needs for childcare and provision of maternity leave. Companies are also required to conform to extensive regulations regarding environmental protection and the employment of disabled people. While companies are conceived in bargaining theory as specialist money-bargaining agencies, they are, nevertheless, obliged to take into account as a matter of expedience the customary modes of behaviour established in societies through social support-bargaining. They are also obliged to conform to legislation established through political support-bargaining, with the prospect of financial sanctions against them if they fail to do so.

Companies brought together technology and business skills to accelerate the rate of evolution of the British economy. Those who created the technology only rarely had the business skills necessary to establish a format through which the technology could be profitably employed. To make money from their inventions, the technicians needed to associate with businessmen. There were some notable personal alliances. Mokyr mentions, among others: Matthew Boulton and James Watt, producing steam engines; Richard Roberts and the businessmen Thomas

Sharpe and Benjamin Fothergill, in engineering; the railway engineer George Stephenson allied with Henry Booth. In some cases notable technical innovators could not make the alliances that might have made their fortunes. Richard Trevithick, who dispensed with Watt's separate condenser in the development of a high-pressure and lighter steam engine, paving the way for George and Robert Stephenson's railway locomotive, is an example.[160] The technical genius and mechanical vision of Isambard Kingdom Brunel was difficult to constrain to a viability condition. As with the evolution of technology, the celebrities of business success are only part of the story. Many lesser people made important contributions. The hierarchies of companies successfully harness many people and many skills to company purposes. Matthew Boulton and James Watt were perpetually concerned with retention of their key employees.[161]

The idea of the company format explains also the survival of many small firms in the nineteenth century. The acceleration in the evolution of the British money-bargaining system was brought about mainly by the new, larger-scale formats in industries such as cotton and iron and steel. A neoclassical preconception of economic change would suggest that all production would necessarily change to this low-cost mode of production. But small firms remained the most characteristic mode of production in the mid-nineteenth century. Small-scale formats produced specialist output and had the flexibility to meet the changing requirements in their vendor sets. Many sold all or most of their output to the large companies. Even with the railways, there were severe constraints on the movement of goods and services, so small companies could operate with local vendor sets. Reference was made above to the many small metal-working companies operating in Birmingham, Sheffield and Lancashire. Most employment was in these smaller firms.[162] The establishment of 'factories' with high volume and low unit cost was, thus, an element in a corporate format that turned out to be of exceptional importance, but it was not the only viable format. Still today many small firms establish viable formats on the basis of special products or services, or with local vendor sets.

The rise of companies is apparent also in the changing spatial distribution of population. As has been seen, opportunities for viable format arise most copiously in areas of concentration of population – in urban areas. The social organisation based on landowning and land dependence necessarily functions where land is available and population cannot be concentrated. Hence the rise of companies in Britain has been accompanied by growth in the population living in urban areas, with the growth of towns quickening with the accelerated evolution of money-bargaining.

Cartels and combinations

As bargaining agencies companies are always seeking to strengthen their bargaining positions. This can be done positively by developing products that are better fitted to the interests of a wider range of potential buyers, by ensuring that the products are readily available and by ensuring that services associated with sales are well suited to the vendor set. But it can also be done in the more negative way, crucial to the operations of guilds and chartered companies, of constraining the choices open to potential buyers. Competition erodes the bargaining positions of companies, offering buyers many options for their purchases. Companies may act to reduce competition. They may take over rival firms. They may arrange cartels that fix prices for a certain type of product so that all companies remain profitable. Companies may also seek legislation through the support-bargaining system to reduce competition by imposing constraining conditions on newcomers seeking to set up as rivals to them, or by impeding the import of rival products from overseas.

As has been seen, up to the early seventeenth century monopolistic arrangements – that is, strong company bargaining positions consequent on the elimination of alternatives – were regarded as normal and even essential to acceptance of the risks associated with forming and operating a company, especially a company trading overseas. Strong money-bargaining positions in trade and commerce were also used to reward those whose service had helped to maintain royal ascendancy. The passing of power from king to parliament brought into question the king's right to make money from the grant of monopolies, bypassing the oversight of parliament in financial matters. In the late seventeenth century the tide of opinion moved against monopolies and the protection afforded by the state to companies was reduced. The benefits to buyers from strong competition among companies was recognised – in effect, strong bargaining positions for consumers began to be favoured above strong bargaining positions for companies. Opportunities to sell were opened to all with the lifting of the controls imposed by guilds and the protections given to chartered companies.

The advantages of free competition maintained their broad attraction into the eighteenth and nineteenth centuries. Mathias remarks that, 'one can still regard the period from 1830 to 1875 as they hey-day of the competitive economy in Britain'.[163] There were, nevertheless, many attempts to establish agreements that would keep prices at comfortable levels across an industry, or at least across an industry in a particular region. From the late 1870s, with weakening bargaining positions in their markets, companies were more inclined to seek stronger bargaining positions through the formation of agreements. Trade associations provided an institutional basis for the establishment of agreements. In some cases more formal agreements, or cartels, were established, with a shipping cartel probably the most effective.

Companies were also amalgamated, either by merger or takeover, or through the creation of a holding company to control a combination. Such amalgamations could invariably be justified on positive grounds by those promoting them. They potentially offered a format with reduced unit costs arising from a larger scale of production and the sharing of management and distribution services, and hence lower prices for buyers. The balance of positive and negative factors in the strengthening of corporate bargaining positions was, nevertheless, largely a matter of speculation and those involved invariably speculated in accordance with their interests. Claims to positive virtue in many cases masked the reality of recomposition of the money-bargaining network in favour of the claimant.[164]

Companies had recognised early on that their bargaining positions relative to their employees and potential employees could be weakened by combinations of those dependent on employment. Individually, each worker was dependent on gaining employment with a company for his or her budget revenues. But worker combinations meant that companies became, in large measure, dependent on securing agreement with a combination. Workers acting together could deprive companies of all their labour unless terms satisfactory to them were agreed. The prevalent opinion, that companies were of most benefit when in competition with each other, could be applied also to the relationship between companies and their employees. Free competition was desirable, implying constraints on freedom of combination. The principle was well established long before the formal legislation against combinations in 1799. The impact of the Combination Laws on bargaining positions was far less than that of the underlying situation in the money-bargaining system. Too many people were looking for budget revenues as a matter of survival for enforcement of laws about who could do what. The Combination Laws were repealed in 1824. Changing concerns amid changing situations were reflected in the passage of legislation in 1871 and 1875 protecting certain rights of trade unions.[165]

The accelerated evolution of economies has meant constant job losses and obsolescence of skills among workers, and the prominence of trade unions operating in both money-bargaining and support-bargaining systems to mitigate the hardships arising from such change. In many countries the relative bargaining positions of companies and employees has been central to divisions evolved under the formal support-bargaining process. The same conflict was central in the twentieth century to the ideological and political rivalry between the 'superpowers'. It remains prominent in the debate over the role of 'capitalism' and its contributions to the reduction of poverty in the developing world. In Britain the friction over bargaining positions of companies and workers has been especially prominent, since trade unions created and financed the Labour Party in the early years of the twentieth century.[166]

Accelerated evolution in the USA

While Britain was the first country to achieve marked acceleration in the rate of evolution of its economy through the integration of new technologies in company formats, it was in the USA that companies were permitted the greatest scope to define a society and advance its prosperity. The idea of 'freedom' that launched the American revolution was an idea of mercantile freedom as well as political freedom, involving escape from the impositions of colonial taxation and the Navigation Acts. Americans did not have to bother with a 'revolution' that replaced landowners with companies. Land was not in short supply and landowners did not have the history they had in Europe.

The evolution of money-bargaining   163

Leading US businessmen developed company formats to give the strongest possible bargaining positions based, first, on the low unit costs to be derived from large output volume and, second, on the reduction of alternative sources of a particular product. While in Europe technological innovation has been used to explain an industrial revolution, in the USA the development of corporate organisation and management – company format – have featured more prominently in accounts of the evolution of the US economy in the nineteenth and into the twentieth century. The approach to the evolution of the British economy has been conditioned by Britain's early record of technological evolution and the very apparent impact of such innovations as the steam engine. It has been conditioned also by theoretical preconceptions that have tended to distract attention from the role of companies. The USA, coming later to the acceleration in the evolution of its economy, was able to import much of the critical technology, including the steam engine, and use it as the basis of innovation in company formatting.

The size of the country and the rapid growth of its population suggested the high-output and low unit cost format would be profitable. But if that format was to be successful, goods had to be delivered to buyers. The dispersion of the population made transport a major factor in the success of the format and in the economic evolution of the country. In the mid-nineteenth century the railway network was expanding rapidly for the distribution of goods all over the country. Manufacturing companies were less prominent than wholesalers and retailers until the Civil War of 1861–5 boosted manufacturing output.[167] Thereafter, a stream of technical and managerial innovations sustained a rapid rate of evolution. By 1913 the USA was producing 36 per cent of world industrial output, compared with 16 per cent for Germany and 14 per cent for Britain.[168]

In a country where concerns with transport and distribution were of such high importance it is not surprising that many prominent technological innovations related to the management of large-volume company formats for distribution – the machinery of stock management and product movement. In the early twentieth century elevators, mechanical conveyers, endless chains, moving sidewalks, gravity chutes, conveyers and pneumatic tubes were used in the mail-order business of Sears, Roebuck.[169] The high-output low unit cost format also led to innovation in production processes. Henry Ford introduced conveyer belts to move parts to workers on a vehicle assembly line, reducing the time taken to assemble the Model T from 12 hours to two and a half hours,[170] with corresponding reduction in unit costs.

The interest of buyers in remote populations in acquiring products from the centres of manufacturing and East Coast importers gave opportunities for format of companies to build and operate railways. The railways extended the vendor sets of large companies over great areas. The rapid growth in the construction of railways in the mid-nineteenth century was undertaken by a large number of companies, many of which failed, as had happened in Britain. The capital requirements of railway investment were a major factor in the growth of the New York Stock Exchange. Access to large vendor sets made possible the high volume low

164   *The Evolution of Economies*

unit cost company format, so that, by the First World War, large corporations dominated the US economy.

Consolidation occurred also among the companies building and operating the railways. Small independent companies were at a particular disadvantage when it came to joining up the USA through railways. It was not just the inadequacies of the links, but the competition between links. Running two lines between the same settlements, with similar schedules, wastes land and finance to little public advantage. Collusion and consolidation were introduced into the railway system, pushed in particular by Cornelius Vanderbilt and J. P. Morgan.[171] Better services for clients and stronger bargaining positions for the leading railway companies to a considerable extent went hand in hand.

The positive aspects of consolidation in some areas could be argued in defence of other consolidations. When accompanied by technological innovation, it was easy to accept that large volume with low unit cost formats were beneficial to buyers. Mergers were common in many sectors: 'Integrated companies, which did not really exist in the 1860s, dominated America's most vital industries by the turn of the century.' The major vehicle for consolidation was the formation of trust companies, or holding companies, holding controlling shares in a number of erstwhile rival companies. John D. Rockefeller formed Standard Oil as a trust company. J. P. Morgan used holding companies to dominate banking on Wall Street. Morgan was instrumental in the metamorphosis of Carnegie Steel, the world's largest manufacturer, valued on sale at $480 million, into the United States Steel Corporation, valued at $1.4 billion, in the early 1900s.[172]

However much was owed to the positive impact of high volume and low unit cost, or to the negative impact of suppression of competition, the trust companies gained powerful bargaining positions. This was not, of course, to the liking of everyone. Trade unions, in particular, disliked such bargaining power when it was used to hold down or reduce their wages. Dramatic confrontations took place, with the state initially, as in Britain, protecting the interests of the companies. Anti-trust legislation, introduced mainly to regulate the use of trust companies, was used to outlaw combinations of workers. In 1914, however, unions were granted immunity from anti-trust actions.

The Sherman Anti-Trust Act of 1890 responded to more general public disquiet regarding the bargaining strength of major corporations. Using anti-trust legislation, Standard Oil was broken up in 1906 and action was instigated against the trust arrangements that enabled J. P. Morgan to dominate US banking. Micklethwait and Wooldridge nevertheless note that, on the whole, Americans liked strong companies. The benefits outweighed the costs. They really did improve the lot of ordinary Americans by providing a range of attractive products at affordable prices. Companies, for their part, took steps to demonstrate that they really were the friends of the American people, supplementing their economic benevolence with political and social initiatives.[173]

Americans have given more forthright support to companies as the dominant agents of money-bargaining systems than the British. Debates in Britain about the function and social role of companies have inhibited their activities. Trade unions and the Labour Party they created have, at times, been positively antagonistic to companies. Among the middle classes the lingering and still lingering taste for the life and culture of the landed gentleman made it difficult to admire people who so unashamedly devoted their lives to the accumulation of money.

There was clearly conspicuous evolution in the formats of companies in the USA. Much of the situation by which a company evolves can be identified in physical terms, so that the evolutionary process is readily apparent. The state of machinery, for example, can be defined, like technology, in physical terms. Engineers and works managers will determine the situation with regard to machinery, plant and buildings in use and recommend appropriate improvements. The locations of plant and offices will be readily apparent. Managers of local offices or plants will determine their local situation in terms of the physical state of the plant and local facilities. Human resource departments will provide accounts of the situation regarding employment with the company. Accounting departments will be able to define the budgetary situation of the company in essentially objective terms.

Other aspects of a company's situation will be more difficult to define. At the head of the company an individual or a board will determine the strategic direction of the company, involving the assessment of current situation, the improvements required and the opportunities it presents. Some individual entrepreneurs take it upon themselves to say where the company is, where it should go and what should be done to get there. Henry Ford took the Ford Motor Company where he wanted it to go in a highly idiosyncratic manner. The constitution of a board can be critical in determining the understanding of a company's situation that is adopted, and the prescriptions for improvement. A supervisory board of the kind required in German companies, incorporating a range of stakeholders, is likely to understand the company situation in broader terms than a more narrowly constituted board. A family-run firm is likely to define its situation with a different eye to that of a public company with a board of professional businessmen. In the latter, the assessments of situation by senior managers are likely to have a major bearing on the accepted definition of company situation and the actions taken in pursuit of stronger format. Micklethwait and Wooldridge attribute the stronger performance of US companies relative to those in Britain in part to the prominence of family firms in Britain. Sons and grandsons might not have the same capacity for shrewd assessment of the state of a company's affairs as their founding ancestor. The sons and grandsons of the first ironmasters might not be of the same stuff as their forebears. Mathias remarks that, 'By the second or third generation of owners sometimes the mill was mainly thought of as the provider of revenue for the landed gentlemen in the style of an estate rather than as the centre of ambitions of the industrialist.'[174]

Companies thus define and evolve their situations through the structure of their ownership, the structure of their organisation and the hierarchies they set up. In general, the higher up the hierarchy, the more subjective the assessment of situation, and the more crucial to the successful evolution of the format of the company. The many organisational structures and management procedures, and the range of interests incorporated in organisational structures, have a major bearing on the evolution of companies through their role in the definition of situation. The control of companies is understood in bargaining theory as a matter of support-bargaining among those occupying positions at the head of company hierarchies.[175]

Evolution and revolution

Many writers on the industrial revolution query the use of the term 'revolution' to describe what happened in the British economy from the mid-eighteenth century and into the nineteenth century. T. S. Ashton's account of *The Industrial Revolution*, published in 1948, which became for many years the accepted short account of what happened, states:

> Whether or not such a series of changes should be spoken of as 'The Industrial Revolution' might be debated at length. The changes were not merely 'industrial', but also social and intellectual. The word 'revolution' implies a suddenness of change that is not, in fact, characteristic of economic processes. The system of human relationships that is sometimes called capitalism had its origins long before 1760, and attained its full development long after 1830: there is a danger of overlooking the essential fact of continuity. But the phrase 'Industrial Revolution' has been used by a long line of historians and has become so firmly embedded in common speech that it would be pedantic to offer a substitute.[176]

The metaphor of 'revolution', like 'path dependence', is more compelling than the account of the reality behind it. But political revolutions are different from what happened in the industrial revolution. They mark a sudden changeover in the exercise of power, a sharp discontinuity in a nation's affairs. As Ashton notes, economic change does not conform to this pattern, and the industrial revolution was not, in this sense, a 'revolution'. Other writers note that recent research has made the metaphor even more dubious, since it shows that revolutionary characteristics were less apparent in the 'revolutionary' period than had hitherto been thought.[177] Change evolved in certain industries over time, bringing about gradual change overall in the economic circumstances of the nation. The idea of 'revolution' certainly caught on in popular understanding, but historians of the process, at least since the mid-twentieth century, though finding themselves obliged to use a term so well established, have been reluctant to recognise a 'revolution' in anything more than a metaphorical and potentially misleading sense.

As with the idea of 'path dependence', the use of metaphor may gloss over a lack of understanding of the reality. The idea of an industrial revolution substitutes for the lack of theoretical understanding of what happened. As has been seen, neoclassical theory cannot begin to accommodate the technological and locational changes that are evident in the industrial revolution. Economic historians comment on the general lack of satisfactory theoretical reference. Coleman, writing of the pre-industrial period, comments, 'there is no agreed theory of economic growth for this sort of pre-industrialized economy which could be tested for fit against the historical experience'.[178] Crafts' remark on the deficiencies of economic theory was quoted above at note 152 ('An explanation ... such phenomena'). Mokyr finds that the efforts of neoclassical theory to adapt to realities in recent decades have made matters worse rather than easier for economic historians, and is consequently inclined to look elsewhere:

> Economic history still looks at theoretical work for guidance, but the help we get from theory today seems less neat, less clear-cut, more equivocal ... It is perhaps for this reason that economic history is turning outside economic theory to look for its theoretical support.[179]

The historians do not generally allow neoclassical economic theory to restrict their scope – their history would certainly appear ludicrous if they did. But, all the same, most here and there imply their allegiance to mainstream economics, with references to 'opportunity cost', 'economic rent', 'division of labour', 'total factor productivity', 'external economies', 'efficient allocation of resources', 'comparative advantage', etc. This residual allegiance means they have difficulties in fully coming to terms with the realities of economic change. Some of the myopia of neoclassical economics is reflected in their analysis. They cannot properly trace the way the British economy evolved over the later eighteenth century and into the nineteenth century, nor the way its evolution in this period grew out of earlier evolutionary development and proceeded later with further evolutionary change. The reality behind the metaphor of an industrial revolution was the evolution of companies as agencies that could adapt and organise the new technology into forms which made money for innovators, investors, employees and governments.

Micklethwait and Wooldridge seem inclined to accept Ronald Coase's theory of transaction costs as the explanation of the existence and purpose of companies. Companies are appropriate if savings on transactions costs outweigh the costs incurred in running a hierarchy. 'The market' exists as an alternative to companies, albeit with transaction costs.[180] Yet it is scarcely credible that men like Cornelius Vanderbilt, John D. Rockefeller, Andrew Carnegie and the very thoughtful Alfred Sloan expended such effort in saving on transaction costs as an alternative to a 'market' like that conceived in neoclassical theory without realising what they were doing. Great faith is required in the superior insight of theorists, as opposed to practitioners, to accept the idea of 'transaction costs' as determinant of the need for companies. Economies of scale, at best an add-on to neoclassical theory, but integral to the idea of corporate format, were far more significant for American company-builders.[181] Fortunately, like the historians of the industrial revolution, Micklethwait and Wooldridge do not allow theoretical preconceptions to blinker too heavily their observations regarding the behaviour of businessmen or the functioning of companies. They write that Carnegie, 'ruthlessly exploited the advantages of scale. The more steel he could produce, the lower his costs; the lower his costs, the more he could sell.'[182] If 'unit costs' is substituted for 'costs', as is necessary to the sense, this is the high volume and low unit cost company format, and nothing to do with the burden of transaction costs in an otherwise neoclassical market. Carnegie and other business leaders also ruthlessly exploited mergers and trusts to strengthen their bargaining positions – again, nothing to do with transaction costs, but everything to do with the advance of bargaining position. Coase's dichotomy of 'markets' and 'companies' is misconceived. The neoclassical 'market' is a mathematical abstraction, with no real counterpart. Companies and other agents make money-bargaining systems. Companies format to reduce all kinds of costs so that their unit costs permit a price at which all their output can be sold. They try to avoid or eliminate competition to give themselves strong bargaining positions. Only with the theory of money-bargaining is it possible to understand the course of economic evolution.

With such theory it is possible to see also that the debates over the precise dates of the start and finish of the industrial revolution are potentially as misleading as the idea of revolution. An acceleration in the evolution of the British economy became visible in the eighteenth century when certain new attitudes and ideas were mingled with certain business practices and aptitudes in metal-working and mechanics. A higher rate of evolution has been maintained ever since. Newcomen's steam engine changed the format of coal production, permitting the mining of coal from deep seams. Thomas Lombe tried, albeit unsuccessfully, a new format for silk production, using technology derived from Italy. Abraham Darby began smelting iron with coke in Coalbrookdale. A range of other innovations appeared. The new coal and iron formats affected the formatting of other enterprises. A stream of technical innovation was established, closely allied with developments in company organisation. Harnessed together, the two streams accelerated and sustained the evolution of money-bargaining. Transport facilities and overseas trade sustained the viability of formats based on volume production and low unit cost, such as those of cotton mills and iron foundries. The changes took place in specific companies or specific sectors, and impacted only gradually on aggregate statistics of economic performance. Crafts notes that productivity increased very slowly in most sectors of the British economy in the period 1780–1860. He remarks, 'this chapter has indicated that the term [industrial revolution] should *not* be taken to imply a widespread, rapid growth of productivity in manufacturing'.[183] The technology and format changes represent the important evolutionary stream. There have been interruptions in the process, but, for the most part, there has been sustained evolutionary change based on the integration of new technologies in company formats. Similar acceleration and retention of the new pace of evolutionary change has been achieved in many other parts of the world.

As Ashton notes, the 'revolution' had important social and intellectual dimensions. These too cannot be understood with conventional theory. Mokyr understands the social and intellectual changes in terms of the effects of Enlightenment thinking on the institutions of society, citing Douglass North's account of the creation of institutions.[184] But, as was suggested in the previous chapter, the institutions, in the sense of laws, customs, conventions, etc., are outcomes of the social, political and intellectual support-bargaining that goes on across societies. It is the changing distributions of support, the support accorded to various ideas, and the bargaining strength developed through organisation, that determine the broad evolution of society and the part that money-bargaining plays in it. Money-bargaining was allowed to evolve in the eighteenth and nineteenth centuries to a new and enlarged role in society because certain ideas and attitudes gained support in British society.

Population growth in Britain gave an underlying need and potential for change. The dynamism of money-bargaining in urban centres, where much of the population growth was concentrated, was important to the evolutionary process. Urban centres provide fertile ground for support-bargaining as well as money-bargaining. New situations prompted the formation of new interest groups across the country, demanding that the value of their support should be recognised in the formal support-bargaining system. Companies were displacing landowners as the dominant economic agents. Their operations were also helping to bring about the displacement of landowners as the dominant political agents. The 'revolution' in national circumstances was the change from dependence on landowners for material and social well-being to dependence on companies specifically for material well-being, but it was a revolution brought about through an evolutionary process. It may have lacked the temporal attributes of a political revolution, but it was certainly a revolution in the sense of a transformation. Part of the transformation was the survival of more people even in the crowded urban environments that facilitated both group formation and the format of companies.

Landowners affected by these changes, perhaps in alliance with those displaced from employment by new technology, might conceivably have brought the changes to a halt. But evolution of the support-bargaining system, facilitated by revenues from the growing money-bargaining system, accommodated the conflicts of interest, forestalling major revolutionary violence. The support convention just about held. The political system was sufficiently sensitive to the changing distributions of support within the country to respond with legislation that met the demands of major interest groups opposed to the changes without bringing to a halt the evolution of the money-bargaining system. Political revolutions occur when evolving distributions of support in a society are ignored. Ordinary people craved communal response to the problems thrown up by economic change, and could look only to the state to organise the response. Because it was increasingly their state, the state obliged. The changes in the money-bargaining system have to be understood in the context of a support-bargaining system, and vice versa. These links are considered further in the following chapter.

Notes

1 Gillingham, John, 2001, 'The Early Middle Ages (1066–1290)', in Morgan, Kenneth O., 2001, *The Oxford History of Britain*, Oxford: Oxford University Press, pp. 121, 164.
2 Gillingham, 2001, p. 181.

3 Griffiths, Ralph A., 2001, 'The Later Middle Ages (1290–1485)', in Morgan, 2001, p. 215.
4 Griffiths, 2001, p. 216.
5 Spread, Patrick, 2008, *Support-Bargaining: The Mechanics of Democracy Revealed*, Sussex: Book Guild, Chapter 13, The Emergence of Bargaining Societies.
6 Guy, John, 2001, 'The Tudor Age (1485–1603)', in Morgan, 2001, p. 258.
7 Guy, 2001, p. 260.
8 Coleman, D. C., 1977, *The Economy of England 1450–1750*, Oxford: Oxford University Press, p. 39.
9 Coleman, 1977, pp. 35–6.
10 Coleman, 1977, p. 95.
11 Coleman, 1977, p. 10.
12 Mathias, Peter, 2001, *The First Industrial Nation: An Economic History of Britain 1700–1914*, London and New York: Routledge, pp. 47–8.
13 Mathias, 2001, p. 53.
14 Deane, Phyllis and Cole, W. A., 1962, *British Economic Growth 1688–1959*, Cambridge: Cambridge University Press, pp. 160–1, 276.
15 Coleman, 1977, p. 113.
16 Mathias, 2001, p. 55.
17 Crafts, N. F. R., 1986, *British Economic Growth during the Industrial Revolution*, Oxford: Oxford University Press, p. 12.
18 Mathias, 2001, p. 29; Deane and Cole, 1962, p. 3.
19 Mathias, 2001, p. 25.
20 Peter Mathias (2001, p. 24) provides an adaption of King's statistics. Crafts (1986, p. 13) provides a revision of King's statistics, based on the work of Lindert and Williamson (Lindert, P. H. and Williamson, J. G., 1982, 'Revising England's Social Tables 1688–1812', *Explorations in Economic History*, Vol.19, pp. 385–408), alongside data for 1759 and 1801/3, based on the work of other researchers. Deane and Cole (1962, p. 2) adapt King's statistics into a national accounts format.
21 Deane and Cole, 1962, pp. 3, 137.
22 Deane and Cole, 1962, pp. 77–8, 156.
23 Wrigley, E. A. and Schofield, R. S., 1981, *The Population History of England, 1541–1871: A Reconstruction*, Cambridge: Cambridge University Press.
24 Crafts, 1986, pp. 14–15.
25 Crafts, 1986, p. 17.
26 Deane and Cole, 1962, pp. 1, 3.
27 Mathias, 2001, pp. 125–7.
28 On rigid groups, see Spread, 2008, pp. 27–31. See also Spread, Patrick, 2015d, 'The Political Significance of Certain Types of Group', in Spread, Patrick, 2015b, *Aspects of Support-Bargaining and Money-Bargaining*, E-Book, World Economics Association.
29 Coleman, 1977, p. 10.
30 Spread, Patrick, 2013, *Support-Bargaining, Economics and Society: A Social Species*, Abingdon and New York: Routledge, Chapter 8, Common Theory and Personification.
31 Spread, Patrick, 2004, *Getting It Right: Economics and the Security of Support*, Sussex: Book Guild, pp. 177–81.
32 Coleman, 1977, p. 10.
33 Quoted by Thompson, E. P., 1991, *The Making of the English Working Class*, London: Penguin, p. 25.
34 See, for example, North, Douglass C., 1981, *Structure and Change in Economic History*, New York: Norton, pp. 6–7, 17–19, 21, 64, 83–4, 147, 159, etc.; North, Douglass C., 1990, *Institutions, Institutional Change and Economic Performance*, Cambridge and New York: Cambridge University Press, pp. 33, 51–2, etc.; Hodgson, Geoffrey M., 1988, *Economics and Institutions*, Cambridge: Polity Press, pp. 148–54, etc.; Hodgson, Geoffrey M., 2000, *Evolution and Institutions*, Cheltenham and Northampton, MA: Edward Elgar, pp. 37–8, etc.

35 Coleman, 1977, p. 104.
36 Voth, H.-J., 1998, 'Time and Work in Eighteenth Century London', *Journal of Economic History*, Vol. 45, pp. 29–58.
37 Mathias, 2001, pp. 138–9.
38 Deane and Cole, 1962, p. 93. Deane and Cole's reference: A. W. Coats, 1958, 'Changing Attitudes to Labour in the Mid-Eighteenth Century', *Economic History Review*, 2nd series, Vol. 11, pp. 35–51.
39 Mathias, 2001, p. 180.
40 Coleman, 1977, pp. 8, 10–11.
41 Coleman, 1977, pp. 122–3.
42 Gillingham, 2001, p. 130.
43 MacCulloch, Diarmaid, 2010, *A History of Christianity*, London: Penguin, Chapter 5, The Imperial Church (300–451).
44 Coleman, 1977, p. 108.
45 Cf. Coleman, 1977, p. 108.
46 Mokyr, Joel, 2011, *The Enlightened Economy: Britain and the Industrial Revolution 1700–1850*, London: Penguin, p. 362.
47 Mokyr, 2011, p. 31.
48 Mokyr, 2011, p. 32. Mokyr cites Roy Porter in connection with this idea: Porter, Roy, 2000, *The Creation of the Modern World: The Untold Story of the British Enlightenment*, New York: W. W. Norton, p. 99.
49 Rose, Jonathan, 2002, *The Intellectual Life of the British Working Classes*, New Haven and London: Yale Nota Bene, pp. 20–9.
50 Rose, 2002, p. 24.
51 Rose, 2002, pp. 58–91.
52 Crafts, 1986, pp. 163–4.
53 Coleman, 1977, p. 132–3.
54 Micklethwait, John and Wooldridge, Adrian, 2005, *The Company: A Short History of a Revolutionary Idea*, London: Phoenix, p. 28.
55 Micklethwait and Wooldridge, 2005, p. 28.
56 Coleman, 1977, p. 58.
57 Backhouse, Roger E., 2002, *The Penguin History of Economics*, London: Penguin, pp. 57–8.
58 Backhouse, Roger E., 1993, *Economists and the Economy: The Evolution of Economic Ideas*, 2nd edition, New Brunswick, NJ, and London: Transaction, pp. 120–1. See also Mathias, 2001, p. 82.
59 Micklethwait and Wooldridge, 2005, p. 31.
60 Micklethwait and Wooldridge, 2005, pp. 29–32.
61 Micklethwait and Wooldridge, 2005, p. 24.
62 Coleman, 1977, pp. 52–3.
63 Micklethwait and Wooldridge, 2005, pp. 23–4.
64 On the decline of British guilds, see Mokyr, 2011, pp. 118–21.
65 Micklethwait and Wooldridge, 2005, p. 47.
66 Ferguson, Niall, 2002, *The Cash Nexus: Money and Power in the Modern World 1700–2000*, London: Penguin, p. 118. Micklethwait and Wooldridge, 2005, pp. 40–1.
67 Ferguson, 2002, pp. 117–18.
68 Coleman, 1977, p. 149.
69 For further comment on the *Wealth of Nations*, see Spread, 2008, pp. 424–7.
70 Coleman, 1977, pp. 137–40, Tables 12–15.
71 Coleman, 1977, pp. 146–7.
72 Cf. Wrigley, E. A., 2010, *Energy and the English Industrial Revolution*, Cambridge: Cambridge University Press, p. 146.
73 Mokyr, 2011, p. 443.
74 Wrigley, 2010, p. 155, Table 6.1.

75 Deane and Cole, 1962, pp. 185, Table 42; 187, Table 43; 196, Table 47; 204, Table 49; 212, Table 52; 216, Table 54; 225, Table 56; 233, Table 61; 234, Table 62.
76 Deane and Cole, 1962, p. 219, Table 55.
77 Deane and Cole, 1962, p. 235.
78 Deane and Cole, 1962, p. 183.
79 On relatively high wage rates in Britain, see Mokyr, 2011, pp. 267–73.
80 Mokyr, 2011, p. 162.
81 Deane and Cole, 1962, pp. 183–4.
82 Deane and Cole, 1962, pp. 187–8.
83 Deane and Cole, 1962, p. 191.
84 Wrigley, 2010, p. 183.
85 Crafts, 1986, pp. 44–7; see also Mokyr, 2011, pp. 255–6, esp. Table 12.1.
86 Wrigley, 2010, pp. 183–5.
87 See Crafts, 1986, p. 9.
88 Mokyr, 2011, p. 82.
89 Deane and Cole, 1962, p. 191.
90 Deane and Cole, 1962, pp. 12–18.
91 Crafts, 1986, pp. 24–5.
92 Mitchell, B. R., 1988, *British Historical Statistics*, London: Cambridge University Press, p. 761. Mitchell's sources: 1821–84: T. Ellison, *The Cotton Trade of Great Britain*, London, 1886; 1885–1961: Annual Statement of Trade.
93 Mathias, 2001, p. 116.
94 Mokyr, 2011, p. 131.
95 Deane and Cole, 1962, p. 221.
96 Mathias, 2001, p. 247. For catalogue, see http://www.gracesguide.co.uk/1851_Great_Exhibition:_Official_Catalogue. Accessed 8 October 2012.
97 Mathias, 2001, p. 247.
98 Deane and Cole, 1962, pp. 221–6, esp. Table 57.
99 Deane and Cole, 1962, pp. 221, 225, esp. Table 56.
100 Mathias, 2001, pp. 378–80.
101 Mathias, 2001, p. 247.
102 Mokyr, 2011, p. 213; Mathias, 2001, p. 255.
103 Mathias, 2001, pp. 252–3.
104 Mathias, 2001, p. 260.
105 Mokyr, 2011, pp. 214–15.
106 Micklethwait and Wooldridge, 2005, p. 54; Mathias, 2001, p. 263.
107 Mathias, 2001, p. 257; see also Deane and Cole, 1962, pp. 230–3.
108 Deane and Cole, 1962, pp. 231–3.
109 Deane and Cole, 1962, p. 296.
110 Micklethwait and Wooldridge, 2005, p. 54.
111 Mathias, 2001, p. 32.
112 Mathias, 2001, pp. 35–6.
113 Mathias, p. 36; see also p. 352.
114 Mathias, 2001, p. 36.
115 Micklethwait and Wooldridge, 2005, pp. 55–8.
116 Mathias, 2001, p. 121.
117 Mathias, 2001, p. 128.
118 Mathias, 2001, pp. 122–3, 125–7.
119 Coleman, 1977, pp. 152–3.
120 Ashton, T. S., 1968/1948, *The Industrial Revolution 1760–1830*, Oxford: Oxford University Press, p. 13.
121 Mathias, 2001, p. 124.
122 Mokyr, 2011, p. 42.
123 Mokyr, 2011, p. 82.

124 Mokyr, 2011, pp. 42–3; Ashton, 1968/1948, pp. 12–13.
125 Mokyr, 2011, p. 59.
126 Mathias, 2001, p. 125.
127 Coleman, 1977, p. 154; see also Mokyr, 2011, p. 26.
128 Mathias, 2001, p. 123; Mokyr, 2011, pp. 92, 408; Ashton, 1968/1948, p. 10.
129 Mathias, 2001, pp. 123–4.
130 Mathias, 2001, p. 122.
131 Mathias, 2001, p. 122.
132 Mokyr, 2011, p. 128.
133 Mokyr, 2011, p. 106; see also Coleman, 1977, pp. 151–2.
134 Mokyr, 2011, pp. 82–3.
135 Mathias, 2001, pp. 120–1.
136 Mokyr, 2011, p. 82.
137 Mathias, 2001, p. 112; Ashton, 1968/1948, p. 54.
138 Mathias, 2001, p. 117.
139 For a fuller account of locational decisions, see Spread, 2008, Chapter 5, Locational Format, esp. pp. 156–60.
140 Ashton, 1968/1948, pp. 30–1, 54; Mathias, 2001, p. 112.
141 Mathias, 2001, p. 111.
142 Mathias, 2001, p. 112.
143 Mathias, 2001, p. 122.
144 Mokyr, 2011, p. 80.
145 Mathias, 2001, p. 99.
146 Mathias, 2001, p. 179.
147 Mathias, 2001, p. 120.
148 Deane, P., 1979, *The First Industrial Revolution*, Cambridge: Cambridge University Press.
149 Crafts, 1986, pp. 6–7.
150 Crafts, N. F. R., 1977, 'Industrial Revolution in Britain and France: Some Thoughts on the Question "Why Was England First?"', *Economic History Review*, Vol. 30, pp. 429–41.
151 Mokyr, 2011, pp. 81–2.
152 Crafts, 1986, p. 8. For 1977 article, see note 150.
153 On attitudes to companies, see Spread, 2008, pp. 140–3.
154 Mokyr, 2011, p. 62.
155 Mokyr, 2011, pp. 10, 83–4.
156 Chandler, Alfred, 2005, *Inventing the Electronic Century: The Epic Story of the Consumer Electronics and Computer Science Industries*, Cambridge, MA: Harvard University Press.
157 See Spread, Patrick, 2008, Chapter 4, Organisations: Function and Format; see also Spread, 2013, pp. 65–6, 206–10.
158 Mathias, 2001, p. 181; see also Mokyr, 2011, p. 341.
159 Mokyr, 2011, p. 353.
160 Mokyr, 2011, pp. 213, 349.
161 Mokyr, 2011, p. 346.
162 Mokyr, 2011, p. 347; Crafts, 1986, p. 69.
163 Mathias, 2001, p. 355.
164 Mathias, 2001, pp. 354–61.
165 Mathias, 2001, pp. 335–7.
166 For further comment on the role of trade unions, see Spread, 2008, pp. 129–35, 401–3.
167 Micklethwait and Wooldridge, 2005, pp. 67–8.
168 Micklethwait and Wooldridge, 2005, p. 63.
169 Micklethwait and Wooldridge, 2005, pp. 62, 67.
170 Micklethwait and Wooldridge, 2005, p. 69.

171 Micklethwait and Wooldridge, 2005, p. 66.
172 Micklethwait and Wooldridge, 2005, pp. 71–4.
173 Micklethwait and Wooldridge, 2005, pp. 78–82.
174 Mathias, 2001, p. 385.
175 Spread, 2008, pp. 135–40; Spread, Patrick, 2015a, 'Companies and Markets: Economic Theories of the Firm and a Concept of Companies as Bargaining Agencies', *Cambridge Journal of Economics*, Advance Access published 2 June 2015, doi:10.1093/cje/bev029. Reprinted in Spread, 2015b, *Aspects of Support-Bargaining and Money-Bargaining*, E-Book, World Economics Association.
176 Ashton, 1968/1948, p. 2.
177 Crafts, 1986, pp. 46–7; Deane and Cole, 1962, pp. 40–1. See also Mokyr, 2011, p. 144.
178 Coleman, 1977, p. 3.
179 Mokyr, Joel, 2005, 'Is there a Theory of Economic History?', in Dopfer, Kurt, 2005, *The Evolutionary Foundations of Economics*, Cambridge: Cambridge University Press, pp. 195–218, p. 198.
180 Micklethwait and Wooldridge, 2005, pp. 111, 175–7.
181 Cf. the discussion of the Arrow–Debreu model in Chapter 4.
182 Micklethwait and Wooldridge, 2005, p. 68.
183 Crafts, 1986, p. 86. Original emphasis.
184 Mokyr, 2011, pp. 63–4, 368–9.

6 The state and money-bargaining

In his study of *The Economy of England 1450–1750* D. C. Coleman writes:

> In our period State action in economic and social matters can be seen as having four main ends in view: the maintenance of social stability and order; the encouragement and regulation of the internal economy; the encouragement and regulation of overseas trade and shipping; and the raising of revenue.

He notes that these objectives sometimes involved conflicts and contradictions – for example, encouraging the development of the internal economy through movement of labour might conflict with the maintenance of social stability. Such conflicts, he notes, are still with us today.

On the process of policy formation he remarks:

> The modern debate differs from those of the sixteenth and seventeenth centuries in that they are informed by a body of distinct economic theories which provide the bases for various policy recommendations (only too often mutually incompatible). Those of the earlier period were far less informed by such theories because it was only in the course of the eighteenth century that the latter came to exist as recognizable, analytical entities. Instead, the actions of the State, as well as the policy recommendations which it received, drew upon a complex of prevailing assumptions about the nature of economic and social life and the proper role of the State within it. These, in turn, jostled with the lobbying of pressure groups, the clamour of courtiers, the growing power of a parliament jealous of its rights, and the persistent urgency of a State treasury forever short of cash, to determine the ultimate shape of practical policy.[1]

Coleman's comments suggest a support-bargaining system. In Chapter 1 the process of support-bargaining was divided for analytical purposes into 'political support-bargaining', 'social support-bargaining' and 'intellectual support-bargaining'. The 'political' side of support-bargaining is the kind of bargaining that assembles support for policies advantageous to certain groups. In earlier times political support-bargaining was conducted with strong awareness that support implied violent potential. The threat of violence was real and actual violence not uncommon. But a support convention was increasingly accepted, and violence increasingly shunned.[2] After the particularly severe bout of violence in the Civil War of the seventeenth century, politics was conducted predominantly under a support convention. The 'jostling' of pressure groups, parliament and courtiers is the political support-bargaining process under a support convention.

'Social support-bargaining' produces the morality, customs and conventions that ease social intercourse. It is important to the cultural evolution of societies. But social support-bargaining may also be taken as including that 'complex of prevailing assumptions about the nature of economic and social life' referred to above in the quotation from Coleman. It was noted in *Support-Bargaining, Economics and Society* that there is a collection of amorphous, varied and ill-defined theories, with similarly ill-defined theory groups, that may be lumped together as 'common theory'.[3] This is theory held by ordinary people about the nature of the world and humanity, and the proper conduct of humans in their society. It includes ideas regarding the significance of family, the importance of religion, the ownership of property, crime and punishment and the distinction between public and private life. Ideas about 'rightness', 'goodness' and 'fairness' are incorporated in common theory. People lose support in their community if they act in a manner contrary to the common theory. But more than governance of behaviour, common theory provides a means of understanding the world. Before the emergence of more formal theory, or 'high' theory, this common theory constituted the essential 'intellectual' focus of support, so that politicians would be keen to present themselves as upholders of common theory, and wary of showing opposition to widely acknowledged elements of common theory. Inevitably, there are conflicts in common theory. Religious doctrine has been a major bone of contention. Conflicts between the protection of privacy and the prevention of crime are apparent in modern societies. Common theory condemns crime and demands the prevention of crime, but it also rejects close state surveillance of the lives of individual citizens. There is recognition in common theory of both individual freedom and obligations to the group. Such tensions have to be resolved, or at least accommodated, through support-bargaining. Common theory assembles support in numerous ill-defined groups which must be courted by politicians. The calculus of support-bargaining is the art of politics: assembling support without losing more than is acquired.

The modern debate draws on the high theory that emerged in the eighteenth century. This is an outcome of 'intellectual support-bargaining', associated in particular with institutions of higher education. The high theory may be seen as an extension of particular aspects of common theory by agents specialising in theory formation and set apart from the rest of society for the purpose.[4] The teaching of the institutions engaged in theory formation means that the high theory is propagated in society and passed from generation to generation. Extensive groups are formed with allegiance to the different theories. Politicians draw support from these groups. Economists and socialist theorists will recommend and support certain economic policies implied by their theories. People who have been taught these theories and assimilated them will be inclined to interpret events in accordance with them and give support to measures consistent with them. They constitute important frames of reference for the understanding of situations and the identification of appropriate action. Many media commentators hold such theories and are inclined to propagate the views and, with them, the interests incorporated in the theories. They are important to the assembly of support in modern bargaining societies.

A support convention in its fullest sense, in which the support of all adult members of a society is recognised as politically significant, is only possible when political support-bargaining is prominently concerned with ideas and theories. Where ideas and theories are not prominent, political support-bargaining tends to be concentrated within a relatively small ruling group, distributing material benefits within the group and to its close associates. The emergence of a state based on a full support-bargaining system is thus dependent on evolution in modes of thought; or on evolution through intellectual support-bargaining. As was seen in the previous chapter, education plays an important part in this evolution. The educational process subjects common theory to scrutiny and develops more formal theory from it. The formalisation of social scientific theory in the eighteenth century owed much to the important steps taken in the seventeenth century in formalisation of the understanding of the natural world.

The 'distinct economic theories' or 'recognizable, analytical entities' of the eighteenth century in the Coleman quotation above emerged as part of a more general development of theory commonly referred to as the Enlightenment. As was seen in the previous chapter, Mokyr's study of *The Enlightened Economy* stresses the importance of Enlightenment thinking in the changes associated with the industrial revolution in Britain.[5] The Enlightenment was a loose body of thought with a loose international support-group. Its leading thinkers included Rene Descartes, Jean d'Alembert, François-Marie Voltaire, Denis Diderot, Jean-Jacques Rousseau, David Hume, John Locke, Adam Smith and Immanuel Kant, though, as with the technological evolution of the industrial revolution, the intellectual evolution associated with the revolution involved a host of lesser names. The Enlightenment was, to a considerable extent, a reaction against the predominance of religious belief and superstition in public and private affairs. It emphasised reason and logic, science and scientific method, as the basis of human understanding. It emphasised also the application of individual intellect. Rather than passive acceptance of what was taught by 'authorities' it advocated a sceptical and investigative frame of mind. Enlightenment thinking influenced the evolution of society into and through the industrial revolution, though, as was noted in the previous chapter, religious attitudes were not entirely inimical to commercial engagement.

The commitment to reason and science in Enlightenment thinking sustained the idea, implicit in religious theory, that humans could have access to absolute knowledge. But the commitment to scepticism and questioning implied a continuing state of uncertainty. The insistence of Enlightenment thinkers on tolerance of the views of others was consistent with the idea of intellectual support-bargaining.

Our theories are sustained most fundamentally by the support of others. It is always possible to misread evidence, even the most apparently objective evidence, when there are interests at stake. As noted in Chapter 1, this tolerance and flexibility constitutes an essential foundation for an open support-bargaining system. If groups are too rigid and absolute in their understanding, there is no scope for movement of support between groups, and a support convention is likely to be broken.

Economic theory and government

The distinct body of theory relating to the functioning of money-bargaining systems emerged from Enlightenment thinking mainly through Adam Smith in the *Wealth of Nations*. Smith drew together and added to the work of many earlier writers, including William Petty and François Quesnay. His study of wealth was an extension of his study of morality. His principal concern was to show that people acting in their own self-interest in pursuit of wealth would bring benefits to society as a whole. The public good would be achieved through the free expression of private interest. This thesis was clearly potentially advantageous to many aspiring business people who sought unfettered freedom to pursue their material interests. It helped to assemble support for the changes associated with the industrial revolution, including the evolution of companies. As was seen in the previous chapter, the state did not, in general, stand in the way of the advances that constituted the industrial revolution. Prevailing modes of thought, in which the theories of Adam Smith were prominent, meant that the changes were adequately well supported. Late in the nineteenth century, Smith's theory of the social benefit arising from individual freedom in economic exchange was adapted to formal mathematical expression in neoclassical economic theory. Smith's account of the functioning of an economy was coloured by his thesis regarding self-interest and social benefit. In the hands of the later theorists observation gave way to mathematics and the colouring became outright distortion.

In his account of the role of the state, Mokyr specifically adopts an approach based on standard economic theory. He opens his chapter on Formal Institutions: The State and the Economy with:

> The relations between the state and its citizens were at the heart of the Enlightenment discourse, embodied in ideas reflected in famous book titles such as *The Social Contract* and *The Civil Society*. Economists have a rather more sober and technical theory of the state, and for the present purpose, it seems logical to follow the latter. Most economists recognize that the state's activities in the economy can be reduced to two basic types. One is to do for the economy things that the free market cannot do on its own or cannot do well. Among those, the state needs to impose and monitor obedience to the 'rules' of the economic game, such as property rights and contract enforcement, as well as to maintain peace and the rule of law ... It also provides 'public goods' such as infrastructural investments and national

defense where problems of excludability and non-rivalrousness make private provision ineffective ... The other type of activity the state was engaged in was the redistribution of wealth and income. The British state in the eighteenth century was a mechanism of rent-seeking in which powerful groups and members of the political elite used the power of the state in their own interests to gain certain privileges and exclusionary rights, such as monopolies, import prohibitions, and other regulations whose purpose it was to generate income for a few at the expense of the many.[6]

It was seen in Chapter 3 that the neoclassical model is incompatible with macroeconomic processes, not least because the former is based purely on individual behaviour, while macroeconomic processes involve the realisation of very substantial communal interest. Realisation of the communal interest involves heavy involvement of governments in money-bargaining. Neoclassical economists have been obliged, in the interests of realism, to find means of incorporating this government engagement into their model. Given the rational individualism that forms the basis of the neoclassical model, and the claims to optimal allocation of resources that are made, it is impossible to reconcile the model with a system of communal interest without discrediting its foundations. Nevertheless, the theory group has succeeded, at least to its own satisfaction.

The reconciliation has been effected through the use of definitions. What the state provides is characterised as 'public goods'. A 'public good' is a product or service that being provided to one individual is unavoidably provided to all, and whose use by one individual does not diminish what is available of it to others. If the state provides defence against attack for one citizen, it necessarily provides defence for all, and providing defence for the one does not diminish the defence that is available to others. The characterisation makes it appear plain that government must make provision where it is objectively apparent that a market based on individual interest and initiative will not be effective. Neoclassical theory assimilates state provision into its conceptual framework by defining state provision in such a way that it is compatible with the model. This 'assimilation by definition' process was identified in Chapter 4 in the context of the definition of an organisation in institutional economic theory, and the more far-reaching definition of economics itself by Robbins. Definitions are used to appropriate phenomena to particular frames of reference, or paradigms. Accepting the definition means assenting to or adopting the paradigm.

What states provide can, at least in part, plausibly be understood, given the inclination to do so, in terms of excludability and non-rivalrousness. But clearly the great range of public provision involves goods and services that do not conform to the definition of a public good. Public provision arises from a sense of communal interest – that is, from the process of support-bargaining. People form groups to pursue group interests. Governments are formed for the purpose of advancing group interests. Governments establish budgets, raising taxes and making expenditures, in pursuit of group interests established through support-bargaining. Defence is not provided by governments because it is recognised as non-divisible and non-rivalrous, but because a community recognises that its survival depends on its provision of the means of defending itself. Those who refuse to engage with their community in its defence are likely to be ejected from the community, locked up, or even killed – different societies have, at different times, had different means of persuading their people to fight in defence of the community, though by and large most people are ready to defend their society, recognising that the defeat of the society means harsh consequences for all its individual members. States have not confined themselves to the 'good' of 'defence'. Quite frequently the internal support-bargaining of states has caused them to attack other states. In this case, issues of excludability and non-rivalrousness do not arise in connection with the aggressor. Groups define what goods and services will be provided by the state, through support-bargaining.

Neoclassical economic theory defines 'public goods', though much of what governments provide is services. 'Goods' suggests physical things, which being in possession of one person cannot be in possession of another. Their physical nature makes them exclusive. So they will rarely be 'public' in accordance with the definition adopted. Hence, the use of the term 'public goods' largely pre-empts the distinction of the definition, between what is individually held and what is necessarily communally held. Use of the term 'public services' would make the definition much less apt to linking the phenomenon to the neoclassical model, since 'services' are easily understood as dispersed among many. It would call attention to the intrinsic communal aspect of many services and the inadequacy of the confinement of interest to individuals in neoclassical theory. Because of this natural 'shareability' of many services, as opposed to the natural 'excludability' of goods, they become readily matters of group identification and provision. The term 'public goods' suggests also a relatively easy assessment of how many or how much should be provided. But the provision of services is not so easily regulated. The economic definition of 'defence' as a 'public good' gives no indication of the volume of defence that is to be provided, or the expenditure that should be allocated to defence. That can only be determined by support-bargaining. 'Defence' in the context of a theory based on rational behaviour raises even further difficulties. Rational people might conclude that there was nothing to choose between one nation and another, and consequently there was nothing to gain by war, and much to lose, and consequently defence expenditure was in its entirety a waste of resources. 'Defence' is intrinsically a matter of communal prejudice. The idea of 'public goods' sacrifices the independence of the model, even sacrifices the model itself, in order to accommodate one of its anomalies.

The idea of 'rent-seeking' is similarly a contrivance of neoclassical theory to reconcile the observed disparity of actual economic practices with the behaviour required if the neoclassical model is to allocate resources optimally. It was seen in the previous chapter that guilds, regulated companies and chartered companies all sought reduction or elimination of alternatives to themselves in their trading through legislation and regulation. In neoclassical interpretation, this is 'rent-seeking' – contriving profit above what would be achieved in a free market through manipulation of the conditions of trading. 'Rent-seeking' is 'bad' in terms of neoclassical economic theory, since it distorts the allocation of resources away from the optimum that is achieved through the workings of the model. People will not, however, necessarily recognise the merits of the 'optimum' promised by the neoclassical model. There are probably few defenders now of the practices of guilds, regulated companies and chartered companies in constraint of trade, which were plainly consequent on the strong support-bargaining positions of those who derived benefit from the arrangements. But it is generally accepted that trade unions should be able to exercise some constraints on trade to protect the interests of their members. Taxi services are commonly licensed to control the numbers of participants vying for business in a certain area, so that taxi companies are able to extract an element of 'rent' from their clients. Considerations of order and public safety mean that licensing arrangements are commonly regarded as desirable. Patents are granted to protect inventors, raising their earnings above what could be acquired if their inventions were open to adoption by anyone. The arrangements that produce 'rents' are matters of communal support-bargaining. Whether they are 'good' or 'bad' depends on interests. What is adopted depends on support-bargaining positions. The implication is that the allocations brought about by an open money-bargaining system have to be modified to achieve communally acceptable trading arrangements. That is, a money-bargaining system requires regulation. The neoclassical model uses the definition of 'rent-seeking' to assimilate an anomaly into its framework, but the anomaly is more complex than the definition allows, being an outcome of a wider system of support-bargaining and money-bargaining.

Mokyr's conception of the role of the state as that defined by neoclassical economic theory exemplifies the way intellectual support-bargaining influences political support-bargaining. It makes clear how support assembled in a theory group can be deployed to influence the conduct of government. Mokyr assumes that neoclassical theory is in some way 'right', and consequently a state that wants to do the right thing must follow economic precepts. But it is easy to confuse general interest with factional interest. When large numbers of recognisably clever people in respected institutions of learning assert the validity of a certain theory, it can be difficult to resist the implementation of measures it justifies.

In the theory of support-bargaining and money-bargaining, the different theories are expressions of group support in pursuit of group interest. Neoclassical economic theory is the expression of individual interest. Socialist theory is an expression of group interest, providing a significantly different account of the role of government in money-bargaining. They exemplify the ongoing conflict of support-bargaining between the interests of the individual to do what he or she wants, and the interests of the group in ensuring that individuals conform to the communal interest. The 'role of the state' is determined through political, intellectual and social support-bargaining processes. The state is the epicentre of national support-bargaining processes, being vested through such processes with a bargaining position that makes it feasible to fulfil that role. The ascendant group determines what its role will be through the support-bargaining processes by which it becomes ascendant. Coleman's identified state objectives relating to social order, economic regulation, overseas trade and revenue may be seen as the outcome of this complex process in the period of which he writes.

Money-bargaining and social ascendancy

In a society based on land ownership deriving from conquest, as described in the previous chapter, political, social and economic interests are integrated through dependence on the landowner. Land control implies political control and, in large measure, economic control also. Few other than the landowner have any significant benefits to offer that would give them ascendant bargaining position. The potential and actual use of violence to keep the populace in order precludes any extensive use of bargaining over political issues. A landowning nobility supports the monarch and provides military services to the monarch, but expects to rule like a monarch in its own domains. In Britain violence became gradually less prominent as a means of social control and a support-bargaining process became more apparent. The easing of the grip of landowners opened the way to increased economic independence.

Money-bargaining gives scope for individuals to advance in wealth, and with wealth comes a degree of power and prestige. The simplest viability condition, revenue greater than costs, is also a profit condition, and by skilful development of bargaining position, or even just by good fortune, revenues of trade can greatly exceed the costs, making a businessman wealthy. The mediaeval wool trade centred in East Anglia and the West Country brought substantial wealth to farmers and merchants. Rich merchants and rich farmers could influence the behaviour of people in their vicinity. Their provision of employment and acts of philanthropy, such as construction of almshouses and churches, gave them communal support and communal protection against assaults from displaced or covetous overlords. Money-bargaining affects the struggle for social ascendancy.[7] New groups are formed with new interests. Strong money-bargaining positions are important to the formation of strong support-bargaining groups. Ascendant groups that lack the money to sustain the material interests of their supporters are likely to find their support eroding as people move to support of those who can sustain their everyday needs, or with even greater alacrity to those who can make them very comfortable.

While the 'new money' might conflict with the old, there was also scope for cooperation. Traditional landowners and the leaders of money-bargaining had interests in common, and were, in any case, not wholly distinct groups. Prosperous farmers mean that the rent revenues of landowners might rise. Landowners themselves might engage directly in the wool trade and other lucrative trades on their own account, making common cause with farmers and merchants in pursuit of privileges that would enhance the revenues and reduce the costs of their business. Endorsement by local landowning nobility of the activities of merchants would facilitate the work of the merchants. The most forthright and mutually advantageous endorsement comes with the marriage of the sons of the established nobility with the daughters of the rich merchants.

At a more humble level also the advance of farmers and merchants might benefit the landowning elite. Revenues accruing to ordinary people transmitted directly or indirectly through the money-bargaining network will alleviate poverty and reduce discontent, reducing the risk of uprisings against the ruling elite. A prosperous community is normally more amenable to government than an impoverished community. People are inclined to support those who give them their daily bread or a governing regime that makes possible the earning of their daily bread.

This kind of reciprocal accommodation links the support-bargaining and money-bargaining systems to the advantage of agents in both. A further link arises from the need of farmers and merchants, in common with landowners, for protection against violence and theft. The wealthy have a particular interest in the establishment of measures for the deterrence and punishment of crime, whether the perpetrators are the hungry poor or covetous nobility. The need for such measures, or at least the need for enforcement of measures established, is vividly apparent in the Paston letters written in the fifteenth century. The Paston family became wealthy mainly through the practice of law, and had acquired land and property. Their estates came under violent assault from the Dukes of Suffolk and Norfolk.[8] Wealthy families had a pressing interest in ensuring that part of their wealth was devoted to the maintenance of communal order.

'Rights' to land and other property

The problems of the Paston family arose largely from a dispute over the disposition of various properties in the will of Sir John Fastolf. Land and property are important because they are what people most readily fight over. As was seen in the previous chapter, 'property rights' are regarded by institutional economists as one of the most essential institutions for the operation of a system of economic exchange. Clearly, if the claims of people to own what they wish to sell are not recognised in their society, and if their ownership of what they buy is not recognised, then monetary exchange loses its efficacy.

The sense that land in particular, but also property in other forms, is to be defended by violence has been a major inhibition in the development of support-bargaining systems. For the operation of a formal support-bargaining system, a support convention is required by which support becomes a proxy for violence. The prospect is that with a support convention encompassing the support of all citizens there would be overwhelming support for depriving landowners and other property holders of their property. The fear of 'democracy' was, in large part, this fear of sequestration of private property in response to the demands of 'the mob'.[9] A full support convention was consequently unacceptable to the ascendant groups in European societies. In Britain, following the Civil War of the mid-seventeenth century, a support convention was increasingly acknowledged, but confined to those who owned land and substantial other property. With that arrangement, there was no prospect of extensive support for depriving property owners of their property.

Acceptance of individual ownership of property would be likely to emerge in conjunction with the recognition of individual identity independent of group identity. In violent times, the security of property would be tied up with the security of the group, just as individual security would be inseparable from the security of the group. If the group were overwhelmed by external violence, its individuals and its property would all be lost. In quieter times, with the recognition of a degree of individual freedom, or lighter imposition of group modes of thought and action, development of a sense of individual property ownership is also likely. Individuals and their kin might come to regard themselves as 'owning' a certain structure as their home, especially if built by themselves. They might similarly claim ownership of certain land on which they grew food, or at least ownership of the food they grew on the land. Given their own sense of ownership, they would be ready to recognise the ownership of others. Agricultural crops and livestock are easily stolen, so that a communal sense of 'yours' and 'mine' would be an important underpinning to any peaceable agrarian society with a significant sense of individual identity. People will fight to protect their vital interests: their families, and the homes, crops, livestock and other food supply on which their survival depended.[10] In a peaceable society these vital interests are likely to be protected by strong communal support. Early legal systems relate prominently to the protection of property.

Participation in the formal support-bargaining system in Britain, implying corresponding extension of the support convention, was opened to nearly all adult citizens in 1918 with the Representation of the People Act. The rise of companies has made land ownership much less important economically, socially and politically than it was in former times. There is extensive provision in law for the surrender, or compulsory sale, of private property for public purposes, but still a general respect for property has been maintained. Because property has been historically distributed through violence, the redistribution of property through a support-bargaining system is approached with caution. Land can be bought and sold, but not confiscated without compensation, as might be done in a violent society. Land ownership is, to some extent, 'frozen', like the borders of nation states, in accordance with outcomes of the latest bout of violence. Compulsory acquisition of land is permissible only where there is an immediate and clear public interest in the acquisition. The cost of land limits the amount of land that is released by money-bargaining from its frozen state. Rights of property are extended to the great range of goods that changes hands and changes ownership through money-bargaining.

There seems still a sense that 'property rights' are beyond the scope of support-bargaining; that the maintenance of the support convention still rests on the inviolability of land and other property. People still become combative when there are threats to their vital interests, including their property. Minimisation of violence in a society depends on the recognition of a 'property right' that limits the jurisdiction of the political support-bargaining process over property. While there are still groups that regard the distribution of land in Britain and the exceptional wealth that is still derived from ownership of large estates as an affront to principles of equality and social justice, there is little support for the expropriation of estates. There seems still the sense that you would, as General Ireton had it, 'take all by that'.

This understanding of the role of property in society is markedly different to the account of property rights provided by Douglass North. For North, 'Property rights are the rights individuals appropriate over their own labor and the goods and services they possess. Appropriation is a function of legal rules, organizational forms, enforcement, and norms of behaviour – that is, the institutional framework.'[11] The institutional framework makes it possible for individuals to 'appropriate' property rights. It also, as was seen in Chapter 4, reduces the impact of transaction costs – the costs of information and costs of enforcement of agreements. Nevertheless, the high transaction costs of 'political markets' result in inefficient property rights. Rulers will not enact efficient rules for fear of antagonising powerful constituents.[12] North's account depends on his understanding of 'institutions', which, as suggested in Chapter 4, are outcomes of support-bargaining. His account of the impact of transaction costs seems essentially based on an understanding that property rights should be established in accordance with requirements for economic efficiency. The pursuit of economic efficiency is thwarted by political processes. Like Mokyr, North takes economic theory as the determinant of what measures governments should enact. In social bargaining theory, as described above, the allocation of property is an integral part of the violent formation of a 'state' and political order. Being formed in this way, 'property rights' are matters of vital interest, so that it is difficult to establish a support convention that entirely displaces violence in society if property is thereby open to expropriation simply on the basis of majority support. Property rights retain a special status in full support-bargaining societies because of their associations with violence. Their acceptance has also made money-bargaining possible.

People fight for their rights, but everything else is subject to negotiation in the support-bargaining and money-bargaining system. The idea of 'rights' established beyond the scope of a national support-bargaining process, or beyond democratic process, has attracted the attention of many interest groups. An extensive array of 'human rights' has been adopted in a supra-national context, apparently beyond the jurisdiction of national parliaments. Law courts in Britain have frequently upheld human rights that are questioned in the national media as circumventing the jurisdiction of parliament. Human rights have ridden the same wave as 'divine right', 'natural rights' and 'property rights', born along as matters of such vital interest as to allow no dispute, as to be inalienable, as matters to be fought for, and not matters subject to negotiation in the normal processes of support-bargaining under a local support convention.

Enclosure of common land

The Pastons were at least rich enough to defend their property against those who would deprive them of it. Peasants faced with plans for enclosure of their common lands were not so well placed. E. P. Thompson, writing of the period 1790 to 1830, remarks of enclosures, 'Enclosure (when all the sophistications are allowed for) was a plain enough case of class robbery, played according to fair rules of property and law laid down by a parliament of property owners and lawyers.'[13] It was suggested above that property is what people fight for, but the peasants were not well placed to mount a violent defence. The property was held or used by communal right. In some cases the right to use the common land rested on occupation of a particular cottage, rather than as a personal right. Any defence of the common right required a high degree of organisation against a well-armed enemy, both in the physical sense and in a legal sense. The old hierarchies also ensured that each level above the lowest had some interest in maintaining the existing order. Small proprietors stood to gain legal title to a few acres from enclosure, and consequently did not feel the same antagonism to enclosure as those who stood to lose everything. Enclosure was also carried out irregularly. The commons of one village might be enclosed, while the commons of a neighbouring village might remain common for several decades more. Mustering and coordinating a large volume of support in such circumstances would have been a difficult undertaking. The communal interest could not, in this case, be established and financed. Even so, 'Enclosure-riots, the breaking of fences, threatening letters, arson, were more common than some agrarian historians suppose.'[14]

Resistance to enclosure was all the more difficult because it was part of a long-term redefinition of agrarian landholding. It was seen in the previous chapter that in the mid-seventeenth century resistance to enclosure was dwindling. The approach to land usage on the basis of common rights was losing its grip on society, particularly those parts of society, which were the parts that mattered in government, that wanted to pursue agricultural 'improvements'. As part of the long shifting of emphasis in social organisation from communal focus to more individual concern, the land itself was passing out of communal control and into the control of individuals. It is the change described above as a feature of the transition from a violent society to a more peaceful society. It was, as William Cobbett had it, all a matter of 'Scotch feelosofy.'[15] In the period 1790–1830 a wealthy and progressive ascendant group, its support bolstered by a well-supported theory group, was able to establish its interests in the formal support-bargaining system as 'for the best' and enclose land against the interests of a large but fragmented, uncoordinated and penniless group of peasants that was excluded from formal political support-bargaining.

Wealth and war

The wealthy were also in a position to finance one of the favourite pastimes of monarchs, that of making war. Violent societies develop ideas of honour and nobility associated with prowess in warfare. Leaders of such societies are expected to show their fitness through mastery of the art of war and outstanding conduct on the field of battle. The prospect is also of territorial acquisition and expanded revenues from taxation, pillage and, in some cases, ransom of captured enemies. Such heady prospects have largely to be paid for 'up front'. Equipping, transporting and maintaining armies is expensive, so there is an immediate requirement for finance. The wealth of merchants was an obvious source of finance. Merchants and traders were found ready to part with substantial sums of money in exchange for monopolistic rights to trade domestically or overseas. Such rights were regarded as within the gift of monarchs, by virtue of their or their ancestors' seizure of the domestic territory. As was seen in the previous chapter, guilds, regulated companies and chartered companies all involved payments to the crown for trading advantage.

Engagement in foreign wars was, in many cases, given added attraction by the relief it offered from pressures of domestic rule. Insecurity is the basis of support-bargaining and group formation. The greater the insecurity, the greater the cohesion of a threatened group. The rulers of societies consequently have an interest in cultivating external enemies as a means of cultivating loyalty to themselves. The stronger the external threat, the less likely internal insurrection. Inevitably such societies, with neighbours subject to the same dynamic, find themselves going to war in conformity with the scenarios they have created. Such wars require finance, and the courting of rich people with money to pay for favours or to lend at interest.

The impact of accelerated evolution of money-bargaining on support-bargaining

Employers, employees and communal provision

Over the eighteenth century the dominance of landowners was declining further in the face of the increasing influence of manufacturers and traders. Their wealth and their concerns over public policy gave the latter the means and motivation to engage in political support-bargaining. Lower down the social scale, peasant farmers were being eased out of their customary modes of livelihood by population growth, enclosures and the opportunities emerging as employees of the manufacturers and traders. The enclosure movement saw this change in a positive light: besides the agrarian advantages of enclosure, it freed labour for employment. Thompson notes that this was a specific objective of influential farmers and manufacturers.[16] The differences of interest between employers and employees were emerging as a major division of interest in the nation.

The acceleration in the evolution of the money-bargaining system in the eighteenth century and into the nineteenth century brought serious confrontations between these groups. Employers wanted workers to work as hard as possible for as long as possible, for the lowest possible pay. Employees and potential employees found themselves in a weak bargaining position, with many rivals to any individual seeking employment, obliging them to accept low pay and bad working conditions. The new industries led to rapid growth in concentrations of population and the emergence of congested and insanitary living conditions. Relief from such a situation, brought about by the rapid evolution of money-bargaining, could only be gained through communal action – that is, through the operation of the support-bargaining system. The congestion that was part of the trouble was also conducive to the remedy – people living close together in similar situations of discomfort readily form cohesive groups. The money-bargaining system could scarcely have sustained its more rapid rate of evolution if it had not been possible to alleviate the problems of employees through the support-bargaining system.

The differences of interest in the context of money-bargaining between employers and employees are differences over payments for service and conditions of service. But in the context of support-bargaining they are linked to the more fundamental conflict in human society between the individual and the group. Money-bargaining gives scope for individual initiative, but this is gained at some expense to the cohesiveness of the society. Individuals are able to distance themselves from their societies. They can behave in a manner at odds with the kind of behaviour that a group will normally approve. In support-bargaining, relationships of support between individual members of a group and the group itself are of prime concern. The linkage between money-bargaining and support-bargaining, tied up with the relationship between employers and employees, is of crucial importance to the harmony of societies. The conflicts in industry between employers and employees and the larger social conflict over freedom of the individual and the demands of the group have been a constant source of friction in Britain and around the world.

Urban congestion, resulting from an intensification of money-bargaining, facilitated group formation and a response to the adverse consequences of congestion. The money-bargaining system also brought remedies for the problems it created through its provision of public revenues. Increased money-bargaining meant increased tax revenues for government. These revenues could be directed to the improvement of conditions in urban areas, including the provision of clean water and more efficient drainage. They could also be directed to alleviation of difficulties encountered by people who lacked or lost employment, were paid very low wages, or who for some other reason lacked sufficient income to live in tolerable circumstances. Paradoxically, the individualism of money-bargaining made it possible to expand the communal support that could be provided, utilising central and local government budgets.

The provision was connected with the alleviation of tensions between employers and employees, individuals and society, the wealthy and the poor. It was instituted also in accordance with well-supported theoretical, moral or ideological principles concerning these divisions. Principles of equality, sharing and communal responsibility assembled support in parallel with the more direct pursuit of material provision. The evolution of the money-bargaining system required that the able and industrious should be rewarded. But at the same time it did not mean that the rewards of a flourishing money-bargaining system should be skewed too heavily towards the able and industrious. Those less endowed with the qualities and good fortune that bring success in money-bargaining might also be entitled to a share in the communal wealth. The existence of a flourishing money-bargaining system in which individuals could become wealthy owed much to the effective functioning of a support-bargaining system, and was consequently an achievement of society as a whole. Old ideas of the primacy of the group survived, even though the security situation no longer necessitated the tight communal solidarity of less settled times. Support-bargaining and money-bargaining evolve in tandem, but because of its violent associations support-bargaining has the front seat, where the steering is done.

The acceleration in the evolution of money-bargaining in Britain took place in a period of expanding population which was at least in part a consequence of the acceleration. It also changed the structure of society. Peasant farmers and cottage piece-workers, and in due course their children, became urban factory employees and railway workers. Even without universal suffrage in a formal support-bargaining system it was necessary for governments to take account of this new structure of employment and residence. The urban poor and disadvantaged were much more of a threat to social order and stability, local and national, than the old dispersed rural peasantry. E. P. Thompson notes that, 'In the years between 1780 and 1832 most English working people came to feel an identity of interests as between themselves, and as against their rulers and employers.'[17] Chartists were demanding representation of working men in parliament. Ideas appropriate to their interests were gaining support. Old traditions of compassion and care, long recognised in religious teaching as the foremost of human virtues, provided a natural foundation for new ideologies involving state care for the disadvantaged.[18] The poor laws originally introduced in the reign of Elizabeth I evolved, as money became available, into modern welfare provision.

The alleviation of poverty and prolongation of life consequent on the evolution of money-bargaining has far exceeded anything achieved through the exercise of private charity or the institutionalised charity of religious groups. Only when compassion is translated into bargaining position through organisation and assembly of support in a formal support-bargaining system, giving access to funds derived from money-bargaining agencies, does it have significant impact in the alleviation of poverty. Political compassion has different motivations to private compassion, but it is considerably more effective in achieving its purposes.

Impact of changes in money-bargaining on the state budget

The impact of the acceleration in the evolution of the money-bargaining system can be understood more broadly in the context of the changes it brought about in government budgets. Just as the growing significance of welfare provision can be seen in the evolution of budgetary allocations, so the importance of other forms of state engagement are reflected in budgetary provisions.

As was seen in Chapter 2, the agents of a money-bargaining system are all linked through their budgets. The state is most visibly engaged in the money-bargaining system through its operation of a money-budget. Its revenues and expenditures are, however, not governed by any monetary viability condition, as those of companies, but by the need to gain and retain support. Governments raise revenues through taxation in accordance with what people designate as acceptable through the support-bargaining system, and spend similarly in accordance with what is given support in the community. Budgetary expenditures represent, in broad terms, a response to identification of communal interests through support-bargaining, their relative importance and the return in terms of accommodation of communal interest per unit of expenditure.

This last constitutes an idea of 'value for money' in expenditure. In inversion, it is something like the unit cost of a provision. In some areas of public provision it is possible to establish unit costs of provision. The 'cost per student' of educational provision can be established, or the 'cost per applicant' of welfare administration. These measures give some indication of a price that would be charged if the provision were made through a company format. The 'prices' of public provision will generally be kept roughly in line, where possible, with the prices found acceptable in private provision. More broadly, the 'value for money' achieved in public provision has to be kept roughly in line with that of private provision, to forestall withdrawal of support on grounds of profligate spending. Allocations are reassessed on a continuous basis by reference to ongoing debate in society, conducted mainly through the media, as described in Chapter 9. Support-bargaining and money-bargaining systems interlink in government budgeting.

The acceleration in the evolution of the money-bargaining system consequently had major implications for government budgeting. The points of revenue collection by the state increased in number and the levels of revenue, both in absolute amounts and in their proportion to private transactions, became very much larger, with a corresponding expansion of the services provided by the state. To give an indication of the timing of change, the levels of revenues and expenditures involved, and their constituent parts, Table 6.1 shows the sources of revenue for central government through the period 1700 to 1950, while Table 6.2 shows the allocation of government expenditure for the same period.

In 1700 revenues from 'Customs and Excise' were around 60 per cent of total revenue, rising to around 65 per cent in 1750. By 1900 the share of Customs and Excise had fallen to less than 50 per cent and in 1950 it was estimated at 37 per cent. Other sources of revenue became more important, reflecting the growth and diversification of the money-bargaining system. Britain had also adopted a policy of 'free trade' in the 1840s, though as will be seen in Chapter 8, this policy had remarkably little impact on customs revenues. Income tax was introduced to finance the war against Napoleon. It is estimated that the taxes raised in 1802 constituted about 17 per cent of GDP. Half a century later the share was down to around 11 per cent and in 1900 it had fallen to about 8 per cent. There followed a long period of rising public expenditure, reaching its highest levels in the two world wars and not falling back to pre-war levels after either war. The financing of these increases in expenditure brought revenues in 1950 to around 36 per cent of GDP.

Expenditure allocations up to 1900 reflect the principal communal interest in defence. As shown in Table 6.2, defence spending constituted around 40 per cent of expenditure in 1700 and 1750, rising to nearly 60 per cent in 1802, during the

Table 6.1 Central government revenue from taxation and services, 1700–1950

£ million

	1700	% of total	1750	% of total	1802	% of total	1850	% of total	1900	% of total	1950	% of total
Customs and Excise	2.5	58.1	5.0	66.7	20.4	52.2	37.3	65.3	61.4	47.3	1,519.7	37.1
Stamps and Post Office	0.2	4.7	0.2	2.7	4.5	11.5	9.2	16.1	21.8	16.8	136.8	3.3
Property and income tax					5.8	14.8	5.6	9.8	18.8	14.5	1,553.1	37.9
Land and assessed taxes	1.4	32.6	2.2	29.3	4.6	11.8	4.5	7.9	2.5	1.9		
Profits tax											297.0	7.2
Telephone and telegraph									3.4	2.6	76.9	1.9
Death duties									18.5	14.2	189.6	4.6
Broadcast receiving licences											12.6	0.3
Motor vehicle licences											55.8	1.4
Total net income	4.3	100.0	7.5	100.0	39.1	100.0	57.1	100.0	129.9	100.0	4,098.0	100.0
GDP	n.a.		n.a.		232.0		523.3		1,642.9		11,391.0	
Revenue as % GDP	n.a.		n.a.		16.9		10.9		7.9		36.0	

Notes: 1700–1801 Great Britain; 1802–1980 UK; death duties included with Stamps up to 1869; GNP/GDP at factor cost; GNP for GB, 1801, 1851, 1901; GDP for UK, 1950; components are 'principal constituent items'; for further notes see Mitchell, 1988, pp. 577, 580, 586, and introductory text to Public Finance tables, pp. 570-4.

Source: Mitchell, B. R., 1988, *British Historical Statistics*, London: Cambridge University Press, Revenue: pp. 575–7, 581–4; GNP/GDP: pp. 822, 824.

Table 6.2 Central government current expenditure, 1700–1950

£ million

	1700	% total	1750	% total	1802	% total	1850	% total	1900	% total	1950	% total
Debt charges	1.3	40.6	3.2	44.4	19.9	30.4	28.5	51.4	23.2	16.1	499.7	14.2
Civil government	0.7	21.9	1.0	13.9	5.6	8.5	7.0	12.6	23.9	16.6	2069.6	58.6
of which:												
Education, art, science						0.1	0.4	0.7	12.2	8.5	241.7	6.8
Health, labour, insurance											685.7	19.4
Trade, industry, roads											150.6	4.3
Defence	1.3	40.6	3.0	41.7	37.4	57.1	15.1	27.2	69.6	48.4	740.7	21.0
Costs of collection					2.4	3.7	4.9	8.8	15.6	10.9	199.2	5.6
of which:												
Post Office, telegraphs, telephones					0.4	0.6	2.1	3.8	12.8	8.9	168.2	4.8
Net/gross public expenditure	3.2	100.0	7.2	100.0	65.5	100.0	55.5	100.0	143.7	100.0	3530.6	100.0

Notes: 1700–1801 net expenditure for Great Britain; 1802–1980 gross expenditure for Great Britain; 1802–1980 gross expenditure for UK: 'Education and broadcasting' in 1950; components are 'principal constituent items' to 1905 and 'main constituents' 1906–68; for further notes see Mitchell, 1988, p. 595, and introductory text to Public Finance tables, pp. 570–4.

Source: Mitchell, B. R., 1988, *British Historical Statistics*, London: Cambridge University Press, pp. 578–80; 587–95.

Napoleonic Wars. Much of the debt charge related to finance of war. With the outbreak of the Boer War in 1899 the government found itself obliged to allocate nearly half its expenditure to defence in 1900.

The first half of the twentieth century saw two world wars, the establishment of universal adult suffrage and major expansion in government education, health and welfare services. Universal suffrage meant that the communal interest to which the state would respond was expressed more formally and was wider in scope. It gave governments the incentive to assemble support through enhanced provision of social services. Defence expenditure rose steeply in the world wars, much of it financed by loans, but had fallen back to 21 per cent in 1950, in the uneasy peace of the Cold War. The fall in the proportion of expenditure going to defence is, in large part, a consequence of the rise in expenditure on social services. Expenditure on education rose in the latter half of the nineteenth century, reaching 8.5 per cent of total expenditure in 1900. Health expenditure increased sharply after the Second World War. The rise in these other expenditures also had the effect of diminishing the share of debt charges in government expenditure, in spite of the great increase in debt arising from the world wars.

Money-bargaining and military expenditure

One of the first obligations laid by people on their governments, whether installed by violence or by a formal support-bargaining process, is that of defending them against external attack. To do this, governments draw on whatever resources can be mustered. Since survival as a nation depends on successful repulse of external attack, people will normally be ready to make great sacrifices, in lives and in material wealth, to repel an enemy.

'Defence' is reckoned virtuous and worthy of support. Military expenditure is today classified in accordance with this virtuous purpose. Earlier times had a different idea of what was virtuous, and found nothing distasteful in the use of military expenditure to advance national interest, whether that involved attack or defence. As was seen in the previous chapter, violence was an important factor in the development of international trade. Much of British military expenditure was incurred in the advancement of British overseas trade. The accelerated evolution of money-bargaining meant a significant surge in the resources that could be assembled for war. Britain's position as the dominant European power after the Battle of Waterloo in 1815 involved heavy military and naval expenditures. Military expenditures remained high through the wars and Cold War of the twentieth century.

The acceleration in evolution also brought significant change in the kinds of resources that could be mustered. The technology and corporate formats of the money-bargaining system had applications in defence. Good-quality and low-cost iron increased the output and effectiveness of weaponry, and provided also protection against the weaponry of the enemy. Iron-clad and steam-powered ships were much more formidable instruments of war than wooden sailing ships. Railways transformed the conduct of war by making possible much more rapid troop movements over long distances. Arms industries raced with their potential enemies to develop the best weaponry. Those with the best military technology often succumbed to the temptation to use it.

The technological crossover was not all from the private sector to the state. Much government military expenditure was devoted to research and development of new technology. A major technological evolutionary stream is concerned with military requirements. British government dock yards were innovators in marine engineering. In ship construction, in particular, technology passed from public sector to private sector, as well as the other way. Links were developed between government and companies engaged in research on military technology.

State services in support of money-bargaining

While state revenues have historically been spent in large part for military purposes, the accelerated evolution of the money-bargaining system gave rise to extensive requirements for communal expenditures in direct support of money-bargaining. It was recognised that the potential of money-bargaining would not be realised unless certain essential facilities and services were provided by the state. And with such essentials, the state could expect returns in the form of expanding revenues.

One of the first essentials of a money-bargaining system is transport. As was seen in the previous chapter, transport systems extend bargaining sets and make it easier to format viable companies. Development of transport systems was essential to the acceleration in the evolution of the money-bargaining system in Britain. Yet there are substantial obstacles in the way of the creation of transport systems by individual agents. The most important is the requirement for land. Transport infrastructure requires land, and land with tight specifications. Acquiring land in the required sequence for a particular route from different landowners was potentially difficult. Landowners would naturally be hesitant over release of any part of the land from which they derived their rents and status. Some might be ready to sell, but others might be reluctant. Some might feign reluctance to strengthen their bargaining position. The owner of the last outstanding 100 yards might find his land worth a large sum. Landowners could make money by selling land for transport infrastructure, but they could also prevent the construction of canals or railways across their land. The Marquess of Stafford initially refused to release land for the construction of the Liverpool–Manchester railway. Acquisition of land for transport infrastructure required multi-party concordance and, in some cases, a degree of compulsion to prevent any particular 'stand-out' from impeding the advance of communally important developments or receiving disproportionately high monetary returns.

Up to the mid-nineteenth century the incorporation of any company, as was seen in Chapter 5, required an Act of Parliament. Through these Acts of Parliament the state became involved in the acquisition of land for canals and railways. The legislation specified the route of the canal or line. Negotiations for the acquisition of land could be conducted in conjunction with the preparation of the Act. Compensation could be agreed with those potentially disadvantaged. But an Act, once passed, gave authority for the compulsory purchase of the necessary land. Since duplication of lines would be regarded as contrary to any public interest, a railway company gained a monopoly of its assigned route. In recognition of the advantages of this, regulations and restrictions were commonly imposed on railway companies.[19] Through these procedures the Marquess of Stafford was reconciled to the Liverpool–Manchester railway, and became a shareholder.

Yet more state engagement was contemplated. The Railways Act of 1844 set up an inspectorate to enforce safety standards, imposed conditions on prices of tickets and imposed certain scheduling requirements. Perhaps more remarkably, given the prevailing ideological tenets of the time, it included provision for the public acquisition of all the railway companies when their charters expired in the 1860s.[20] The railways were already seen as being of such communal importance that there was a case for communal ownership. The provision was not taken up. It was more than a hundred years, in 1946, before the railways were taken into public ownership. Railway services were returned to private ownership in 1993, with heavy regulation designed mainly to protect against abuse of the potentially strong bargaining positions attendant on the grant of fixed-term monopolies. The advantages of monopolies for the provision of transport services make it plain that a 'free market', implying regulation by competition, is not feasible. There is, then, an extensive role for the state, either as regulator or as owner and operator.

The development of road infrastructure was similarly facilitated by the state. In the eighteenth and nineteenth centuries Turnpike Acts were passed giving private companies the right to place barriers across roads and exact tolls from travellers, in exchange for their maintenance of the roads. The acts brought about a major expansion of travel, both for business and social purposes. Journey times between major towns were markedly reduced. All-season travel became possible on many roads that had previously been impassable in winter. The railways spoiled the format of many of the turnpike companies and they largely disappeared in the latter half of the nineteenth century. Responsibility for the maintenance of roads passed to local authorities. Costs of the maintenance of roads had henceforth to be included in government budgets. By 1900 current and capital expenditure on highways, bridges and harbours by central and local government had risen to £23.1 million out of £265.1 million, a share of 8.7 per cent.[21]

The importance of education in the shaping of attitudes and consequent demands for provision of education in various forms was noted in the previous chapter. As well as shaping attitudes, education develops capacity to deal with information and ideas. Definition of social and political situations, and hence the interests arising from them, requires information and the ability to interpret it. People without education are invariably obliged to accept what they are told, and they are told mostly what is advantageous to the interests of the teller. The uneducated are doomed to weak bargaining positions. Those in the nineteenth century who aspired to greater participation in the formal support-bargaining process than was offered to them necessarily set high priority on the acquisition of education. The support-bargaining system responded to burgeoning interest in state provision of educational services from people who were in no position to finance their own education.

But education is also important to the format and functioning of companies. Potential employees of companies, as well as potential employees of the state, would have recognised that jobs, particularly the best jobs, went to the qualified. Company formats were increasingly generating requirements for well-educated employees. It was an understanding of its implications for commerce, as well as its importance to political change, that brought significant expansion of state provision for education in the later nineteenth century. Education Acts in 1870 and 1880 made primary education compulsory, with elementary education provided free under the 1891 Education Act. British investment in education fell short of the provision being made in other countries. As noted in the previous chapter, it has been argued that the inadequacies of the education system in Britain led to weaker evolution in the British economy in the late nineteenth and early twentieth century than was occurring elsewhere. In 1850, as shown in Table 6.2, only 0.7 per cent of government spending was on 'Education, art and science', but by 1900 the proportion had risen to 8.5 per cent. The 1918 Education Act raised the school leaving age to 14 years. The Education Act of 1944 reorganised the school system and raised the school leaving age to 15. By 1950, in the aftermath of the Second World War, with high demand for budgetary funds from the new National Health Service, education and broadcasting received 6.8 per cent of expenditure.

Government provision of education services posed similar difficulties for neoclassical economists as the provision of 'defence'. Education did not, however, conform to the idea of a 'public good'. It could easily be provided on an exclusive basis, and providing to one person would potentially reduce the supply to others. The solution was another definition – the 'merit good'. A merit good is a good, or a service, that has economic advantages for a nation beyond those accruing to an individual who pays for education. It was argued that individuals left to themselves will spend less on education than is necessary to gain the full social value of education, so there is justification for state expenditures on education. In that way, state provision of education is reconciled with the neoclassical model, at least to the satisfaction of the theory group. Resources are allocated to greatest effect. In the case of a 'merit good', 'objectivity' derives from the identification of the economic benefit of education to the community.[22] As noted above, education is necessary to underpin the performance of companies in a money-bargaining system. There is no disputing the 'merit' of education as contributory to economic advance. But the justification for provision of education with finance by the state does not rest entirely or even principally on deficiencies of individual expenditures in the realisation of economic benefits. Education, as noted above, is of much more fundamental and wide-ranging importance. The motivations associated with government provision of education are readily understood in terms of support-bargaining. A communal interest was defined and support assembled for provision by government of educational services. Support-bargaining brought about government budgetary expenditures on education and, in doing so, profoundly affected both support-bargaining and money-bargaining systems. Education is a point at which support-bargaining and money-bargaining systems interlink with important consequences for the evolution of economies.

An extensive evolution of law was required to promote and regulate the evolution of the money-bargaining system. The neoclassical model of an economy implies a wholly transparent, self-correcting system that has only to be left alone to generate 'optimal' social benefit. But a bargaining system offers great scope for development of bargaining position through misrepresentation, elimination of competition, exploitation of ignorance and exploitation of weakness. Almost all the activities of companies were found to require some element of regulation so customers could buy with an assurance of getting what they paid for without undue risk to their health, a company could be assured of getting paid for what it sold, employees received their due rewards in conditions compatible with their health and safety, the general public were not unduly inconvenienced by the side effects of making and selling and shareholders received their due returns. Regulation was also found necessary to moderate collective bargaining by workers in trade unions. Regulations were often introduced in response to movements in public support in reaction to breaches of what is regarded in common theory as fair practice. They were evolutionary changes consequent upon unsatisfactory situations. Without this protection of the various agents of the money-bargaining system through regulation it is doubtful whether the money-bargaining system could have maintained the evolutionary pace it established early in the nineteenth century. Agents of the system had to be reassured with regard to its proper functioning. This did not, of course, inhibit too much the arguments of the interested for a *laissez faire* approach to the money-bargaining system. The cult of the rational did not concern itself with the misbehaviour of the irrationally acquisitive. Their theory promised, in any case, to enhance the freedom of individuals to acquire.

Evolution of the support-bargaining system in tandem with the evolution of money-bargaining

The accelerated evolution of the money-bargaining system raised many new issues and interests. As noted above, relations between employers and employees, and more generally between individuals and the community, always contentious, became yet more fraught. As it stood in the early eighteenth century, the support-bargaining system was ill-equipped to deal with the new interests. Acceleration in the evolution of the support-bargaining system was required to cope with the new and rapidly changing situations. The back seat of the tandem forced the front seat to pedal harder and steer straighter.

Opinions differ as to how close British society came to breakdown into violence in the nineteenth century. Contemporaries certainly feared violent insurrection, such as occurred elsewhere in Europe. The historic divisions in society seemed to have widened and taken on new forms. Both the established ruling class and the emerging new groups seemed too rigid to accommodate one another under a support convention. Money did not seem sufficient, and certainly not available in the right hands, to narrow the divisions enough to offset the threat to social order. The hands that held the money, which were the hands that held the property, seemed determined to hang on to it, along with their privileges as property owners. Sections of the working class seemed equally determined to take both. The quotation from Thompson above, at note 17 ('In the years ... rulers and employers'), marks the fissure in British society.

Judgement is complicated by the need for support-bargainers, on occasion, to make clear the association of support with violence in order to give weight to their expressions of support. Even in a full support-bargaining society there is always the possibility that the government will 'bring in the army' to suppress civil unrest. Those who seek radical change may find that dramatic demonstrations of numbers and violent potential are sufficient to gain concessions that take them acceptably close to their objectives, without the extreme rigour of actual violence. A certain amount of 'theatre' is an essential part of support-bargaining. Those whose support was reckoned of no account because it lacked the backing of land and property, who were also those who suffered most from the accelerated evolution of money-bargaining, had no recourse except rancorous demonstrations. In retrospect, the support-bargaining system may be judged to have been just sufficiently flexible and accommodating to make the evolutionary changes necessary. Informal pressure groups played a major role in persuading the landowning elite that occupied most parliamentary seats, including virtually all the seats in the House of Lords, to respond to the issues. Their assembly of support in the society and in its political institutions made possible the passage of legislation that gave workers some alleviation of the hardships of their employment. More importantly, they also achieved reform of the formal support-bargaining system itself, making it possible for the less exalted and less propertied to participate.[23]

Even so, it was not until 1918 that anything like universal suffrage was achieved, and a full support-bargaining society established. The Representation of the People Act marks the culmination of a century of intensive evolution of the British support-bargaining system in response to the onset of accelerated evolution in the money-bargaining system and the subsequent maintenance of a higher rate of evolution. It might be seen also as the culmination of a long period of evolution from the dominance of landowners and the violent repression of common sentiment to the institution of a system in which the support of all is recognised as relevant to the conduct of communal affairs. Even then, the value of the support of ordinary people was only recognised after they had demonstrated their capacity for violence in defence of what they regarded as their land in the First World War.

This evolution of the formal support-bargaining system to a state of near universal adult participation was accompanied by a further evolution that was even more directly related to the accelerated evolution of the money-bargaining system.

Political parties, in the form of Whigs and Tories, had long dominated the British parliament. Elections were fought on party lines. But becoming a member of parliament seems to have been rather like joining a gentleman's club of the more rowdy type. If you were the right sort, with the right money, you could 'put up'. Spending was the key to success, so someone ready to spend was likely to be welcome as a candidate for one or other party, and likely to be elected. The character of elections changed around the turn of the twentieth century when trade unions found that the engagement of their members in the money-bargaining system generated sufficient revenues in membership dues to finance candidates in parliamentary elections. Union funds could be used for political purposes. The growth of money-bargaining and the organisation of working men in trade unions made it possible for men from the working class to enter parliament. The trade unions formed and funded the Labour Party, which subsequently became one of two major support-bargaining agencies vying for ascendancy in the formal British support-bargaining system. The evolution of money-bargaining has made it possible for both Labour and Tory parties to attract substantial revenues to party budgets for the finance of electoral campaigns. In this way also the evolution of the money-bargaining system made possible the radical evolution of the support-bargaining system.

Further aspects of state engagement with money-bargaining

As has been seen, overseas trade constituted a vital element in the format of many companies. Here also the evolution of the money-bargaining system depended heavily on the support-bargaining system. To secure advantage in overseas trade, government diplomacy was necessary to open doors and obtain 'concessions' to access foreign bargaining sets. The evolution of foreign trade in a context of political and intellectual support-bargaining is considered further in Chapter 8.

It was seen in Chapter 2 that money is an outcome of support-bargaining. Control over the supply of money, crucial to the maintenance of support for a currency, becomes a responsibility of the state. The supply of money is determined to a considerable degree by the provision of credit from financial organisations. Hence maintenance of support for a currency involves maintenance of confidence in the financial system that extends credit. The linkages between money-bargaining and support-bargaining arising from provision of credit are considered in the following chapter.

Notes

1 Coleman, D. C., 1977, *The Economy of England 1450–1750*, Oxford: Oxford University Press, pp. 173–4.
2 On the emergence of the support convention, see Spread, Patrick, 2008, *Support-Bargaining: The Mechanics of Democracy Revealed*, Sussex: Book Guild, Chapter 13, The Emergence of Bargaining Societies, Part 4, Emergence of the Support Convention, pp. 386–90.

3 See Spread, Patrick, 2013, *Support-Bargaining, Economics and Society: A Social Species*, Abingdon and New York: Routledge, Chapter 8, Common Theory and Personification. See also, Spread, Patrick, 2004, *Getting It Right: Economics and the Security of Support*, Sussex: Book Guild, pp. 177–81, 183–4.
4 On theory formation, see Spread, 2008, Chapter 10, Intellectual Support-Bargaining.
5 Mokyr, Joel, 2011, *The Enlightened Economy: Britain and the Industrial Revolution 1700–1850*, London: Penguin.
6 Mokyr, 2011, pp. 392–3.
7 See Spread, 2013, pp. 64–7.
8 Gairdner, James (ed.), 1983, *The Paston Letters*, Gloucester: Sutton.
9 See Thompson, E. P., 1991, *The Making of the English Working Class*, London: Penguin, pp. 26–7.
10 On vital interests and the support convention, see Spread, 2013, pp. 39–40, 70.
11 North, Douglass C., 1990, *Institutions, Institutional Change and Economic Performance*, Cambridge and New York: Cambridge University Press, p. 33.
12 North, 1990, pp. 47, 51–2.
13 Thompson, 1991, pp. 237–8.
14 Thompson, 1991, p. 241.
15 Thompson, 1991, pp. 237–44.
16 Thompson, 1991, pp. 243–4.
17 Thompson, 1991, p. 11.
18 Cf. Thompson, 1991, p. 213. See also Spread, 2008, pp. 309–10.
19 Mathias, 2001, pp. 106–7.
20 Mathias, 2001, p. 264.
21 www.ukpublicspending.co.uk. Accessed 27 March 2014.
22 On 'public goods' and 'merit goods', see also Spread, 2004, pp. 23–6.
23 On the emergence of the bargaining society in Britain in the nineteenth century, see Spread, 2008, pp. 384–6, and Spread, 2013, pp. 59–67.

7 Support-bargaining, credit and confidence

Money-bargaining necessarily involves money, so the evolution of money-bargaining is tied up with the ways in which money is used and provided. What is conceived as a means to an end – the facilitation of exchange of goods and services – becomes a major influence on the way trade is conducted. As was seen in Chapter 2, the way money is provided and the quantities that are available can enhance or inhibit the expansion of money-bargaining systems. The provision of money and various services associated with the provision of money provide a great range of opportunities for the format of companies, giving rise to a financial services sector which is essential to the activities of all other sectors of money-bargaining. Financial services companies make possible the functioning and growth of extensive money-bargaining systems. When faults or failures occur among these companies the effects are felt across entire bargaining networks.

The main category of financial services is concerned with the reconciliation of disparities in time between different transactions. People are paid for work in one period, but do not want to expend that money at the same time as they receive it. People want homes, but it can take a lifetime to save enough money to buy one. People want pensions when they retire. Companies want capital to set up their format, in expectation of revenues at a later date. Financial services are largely directed at accommodating these time disparities.

The time disparities introduce risks and uncertainties. There is always the prospect that investments will fail to realise expected returns and borrowers will default on loan repayments. Situations change over time, and the situation which made a loan and a promise of repayment good in prospect may so change that repayments are not made. Because of the time disparities and the associated uncertainties, financial systems are even more dependent for their operation on support-bargaining than the ordinary exchange of goods and services. 'Confidence' must be sustained – the confidence that risks and uncertainties are manageable.

'Uncertainty' is intellectual insecurity, and just as the search for support is triggered by physical or psychological insecurity, so intellectual insecurity also triggers a search for reassuring support.[1] This is partly manifest in the development of theories about how economies and financial systems work. People get a sense of security when theories and ideas about the nature and conduct of financial affairs are widely supported among 'those who know'. Academia provides neoclassical economic theory as the basic understanding of how economies function, and derives from it theories related more specifically to financial systems.[2] But the need for support is manifest as much in the establishment of institutions and organisations as dependable. The companies and institutions involved in the provision of financial services try to gain recognition as rocks of reliability. Central banks are designed and run so as to promote in the public mind the impression of complete understanding and security. Commercial banks similarly present themselves as dependable depositories for savers. Theory is absorbed into a 'mystique' of banking and bankers, providing the reassurance necessary to the maintenance of confidence. Support is assembled around intellectual abstractions taken up by august institutions to dispel the fear of risk and uncertainty.

Yet this is not sufficient for the maintenance of confidence. The importance of confidence and the generation of confidence through support-bargaining mean that national support-bargaining systems are essential to the maintenance of confidence. Confidence in financial systems depends on people's understanding that the systems have the backing of the state. The state owns or controls the central bank; through the central bank, the state ensures the reliability of commercial banks. The state may guarantee to depositors some part of the deposits made with commercial banks. Communal support, through the state, is the essential underpinning of confidence in financial systems. Support-bargaining sustains the financial systems that make extensive money-bargaining possible.

In Chapter 2 it was shown how money is dependent for its function and value on support-bargaining. The 'intellectual support-bargaining' over the valuation of money, involving such men as Thomas Mun and Henry Thornton, was discussed. This chapter is concerned with the function of financial systems in accommodating time disparities and the way support-bargaining societies have evolved institutions and organisations intended to sustain public confidence that the risks and uncertainties inseparable from time disparities can be managed. The global financial crisis originating in provision of sub-prime mortgages in the USA, beginning in 2007, illustrates the importance of confidence and the way it can be generated by artifice. The chapter also reviews John Maynard Keynes's theory regarding the dynamics of savings and investment from the perspective of support-bargaining and money-bargaining.

Money supply and the Bank of England

Money itself is in part a means of accommodating time disparities. As described in Chapter 2, it displaces the communal support which sustains obligations in a gift economy. Money is a conveniently visible and tangible token of a communal credit.

An alternative, if everyone could read and write, and there were paper to write on, would be the use of IOUs. A farmer receiving fish might give the fisherman an IOU redeemable when the farmer's maize crop was harvested. The fisherman might pass the IOU to someone who had vegetables immediately available. That seller could then present the IOU later for maize from the farmer. But where people cannot read or write, and there is no paper, an acceptable common coinage resolves the time disparities. And even when they can, money has proved itself an effective common bargaining counter.

Money functions as a multi-agent IOU – a 'society owes you' – dependent for its efficacy on its wide recognition within a society. It is the creation of a support-bargaining process, in that all members of society see it as advantageous to the interests of the society if all support the valuation of the currency tokens. The interest, in addition to the other qualities of coins relevant to exchange, described in Chapter 2, lies in the convenience of coins as a means of tiding over the time lapses between disposing of something and acquiring something else. In monetary economic theory money is conceived as a 'medium of exchange' and a 'store of value', with a 'transactions motive' for holding money.[3] In the neoclassical model money has no essential role. In the strict Arrow–Debreu formulation, as was seen in Chapter 3, it has no role at all, since all transactions take place simultaneously.

Money only tides over time gaps if its value is sustained in the community using it. Maintenance of support for a currency has been a major preoccupation for most societies using money – hence the ongoing debates over value discussed in Chapter 2. The more 'monetised' a society is, the greater its dependence on money and the greater the concern over its continued value. A 'loss of confidence' in a currency means that it cannot fulfil its primary role in accommodating the time shifts between selling and buying. If people lack confidence that money they acquire at one point in time will have a similar value in exchange when they come to spend it later, they will not accept the money in the first place. Loss of confidence in a currency implies the breakdown of monetary exchange and consequently the breakdown of a major part of the business of monetised societies.

While the value of a currency is a communal matter, it was not, in Britain, a matter that society was ready to pass fully into the hands of its government, or to the state. People have not easily trusted the guardianship of their currencies to their rulers, knowing that their rulers do not necessarily have at heart the interests of their people, and knowing also that they are perennially short of the money necessary to fulfil their aspirations. Recognising gold and silver in the form of bullion or coin as money meant that governments were, to some extent, relieved of responsibility for the supply of money. Money could be coined only in so far as there was gold or silver available to mint. The international recognition of the value of gold and silver meant also that whatever a single government might do, gold and silver, and the currencies minted from them, would retain their value.

In Britain the national administration of money was allowed to pass into the hands of a joint-stock company, though a rather special joint-stock company that called itself the Bank of England, since it was set up principally to meet the requirements of government for loan finance. The name and the link to government finance meant that it was easily identified with government. It was set up in 1694. Besides its primary role as lender to government, it made loans to private clients, took deposits and issued banknotes for use in London, backed by its holdings of bullion. Its personnel reinforced the government connection. Its early directors were predominantly members of the ruling Whig Party, as were many of its shareholders. Its pre-eminence in the administration of money was established with the grant by parliament of various privileges when it succeeded in raising a substantial sum of money to finance the war against France.[4] The Bank of England came to be regarded, if not as a government institution, then as an institution that could depend on the support of government. It was a joint-stock company with a unique format. Its basic business was with government, suggesting that the business was secure while government was secure. When the Tories tried to establish the South Sea Company as a rival, with similar techniques, the result was a fiasco. As was seen in Chapter 5, confidence at first rose high, on account of the presumed association with government, but then collapsed. With regard to the maintenance of confidence, competition could be counterproductive. What was needed was support, and support in the highest ranks of government. As government credit requirements expanded in the course of the nineteenth century, the role of the Bank of England expanded and it became progressively more closely associated with government while maintaining sufficient autonomy to ensure that politicians could not dictate its administration of money.

The Bank of England issued banknotes for use only in London up to 1826, when its note issue was extended beyond London. Outside London, country banks issued banknotes for local use. In 1708–9 legislation was passed restricting the size of banks, other than the Bank of England, that could issue banknotes to a maximum of six partners, all personally liable to the full extent of their wealth for the debts of their banks.[5] The first country bank was set up in 1716, but they did not become common until after 1760.[6] The restriction on partners meant that the country banks were very small. They issued notes with the backing of their own holdings of coins, establishing links with London banks as back-up in case their own reserves of coin were exhausted. London banks depended in turn on the coin reserves of the Bank of England.[7] Such private note issues depended on local confidence that the issuer would always honour the commitment. The risk was that any small question over the capacity of the issuer to honour its commitments would dispel confidence in the issuer and cause a rush to cash in the notes for coin. The issuer would seek supplementary coin from London. If that was not forthcoming, there would be no option but to close. Country banks were severely affected by the financial crises of 1793 and 1825. In 1826, in the wake of the 1825 crisis, joint-stock banks, in addition to the Bank of England, were permitted, to the dismay of many established bankers.[8] The Bank Charter Act of 1844 made the Bank of England the sole issuer of notes, except for country banks that already issued notes. It also separated the issue of notes from general banking business, making the Bank of England de facto a public institution and agent of the state.[9] The Bank of England was accorded a full monopoly of note issue in 1921.

The format of joint-stock banks differed from that of partnerships in other ways, besides the arrangements for finance. They were larger and could spread risk more widely. They could accept bills of exchange that were of more dubious quality than those acceptable to the partnerships. Part of their profits derived from the difference between the high interest rates they could get on the bills of exchange they accepted in the provinces and the low interest rates they were charged on funds from London banks, which treated them as first-class risks. Mathias notes that the new bankers brought to banking the aggression and high-volume/low-margin techniques of the new industrialists. Acts of 1858 and 1862 gave investors in joint-stock banks limited liability, inducing further rapid expansion in their operations.[10] The new joint-stock banks brought a new sort of format to the provision of financial services.

It was in the course of pragmatic evolution, the movement from actual situation to situation, more than through any theoretical evolutionary process generating explicit design, that the Bank of England assumed responsibility for the general maintenance of confidence in the financial system and, in particular, for the assurance of liquidity in the system. As was seen in Chapter 2, the outbreak of war with France in 1793 brought about a serious loss of confidence in the country banks. They sought to draw coin from their correspondent London banks, which turned to the Bank of England for accommodation. Many country banks failed to get the accommodation they needed and the partners in them lost their fortunes. Banknotes issued by the failed country banks became worthless. Traders became wary of the banknotes issued by other country banks, which reduced their issue of banknotes to protect their reserves. As a commercial bank, answerable to its stockholders, the Bank of England might similarly have reduced its note issue to protect its reserves against possible loss of confidence in its notes. The whole system would then have been short of viable banknotes and a sharp decline in economic activity would have been inevitable. The Bank of England opted instead to increase its note issue to accommodate requirements. Its notes still retained the confidence of users, on the understanding that the Bank, though private, was so closely associated with government as to guarantee the lasting value of its notes. Confidence in the system recovered.[11] The Bank of England accepted responsibility for the stability of the financial system when the situation gave it little alternative. It found itself obliged to learn the same lesson again in 1825.[12]

Outflows of gold associated with the Napoleonic War and fears of a French invasion prompted the British government in 1797 to suspend the convertibility of sterling into gold. In the aftermath of this crisis Henry Thornton subjected the British financial system to systematic analysis in *An Enquiry into the Nature and Effects of the Paper Credit of Great Britain*.[13] This work constituted an important development in the evolution of theory relating to the management of credit. It confirmed the important role of the Bank of England in increasing its note issue when the country banks were contracting theirs, as it had done in 1793. Thornton also made clear in formal terms how the supply of money influenced the price of goods and the balance of overseas trade.[14] His assessment advanced the responsibility of the Bank of England for the general health of the banking system and established principles for control of the money supply. The *Enquiry* marked a further important step in the advancement of the role of the state in financial administration, through the agency of the Bank of England. The Bank Charter Act of 1844, as noted above, confirmed the predominant role of the Bank of England.

The assumption of responsibility for national liquidity by the Bank of England in 1793 was a response to a crisis situation brought on by a loss of confidence relating to the declaration of war with France and the prospects for trade. Time disparities are always a source of uncertainty and, in a war situation, the uncertainties are heightened; the maintenance of confidence becomes even more difficult than in peacetime. The evolutionary process quite commonly moves forward decisively in response to crisis situations, these being the most pressing situations, which demand immediate action. People are most ready to get together and support change when they can all see easily that an existing situation is unsustainable. A crisis focuses minds on the very apparent shortcomings of an existing situation.

There were, however, longer-term evolutionary pressures bearing on the financial system during the eighteenth and nineteenth centuries. The accelerated evolution of the economy meant increased needs of industry for credit and other financial provision. Acceleration in the evolution of the financial system was required if it was to keep pace. The industrial start-ups of the later eighteenth century were mainly self-financed, or were financed by mortgages of factory buildings to wealthy local people, or derived finance from personal acquaintances of the proprietors.[15] T. S. Ashton comments in his 1948 study of *The Industrial Revolution*, that, 'In 1760 there was nothing that could justly be called a capital market. Lending was still largely a local and personal matter.'[16] But there were sharp limits to the levels of investment that could be undertaken with these sources of finance. Increasing requirements for fixed investment to incorporate technological innovations into company formats meant increasing requirements for more substantial capital finance, both for working capital and fixed capital, involving increasing time delays between provision and repayment. The larger investments meant larger companies and more sophisticated managerial and staff structures. Ashton writes, 'By 1830 the volume of investable funds had grown beyond measure. Banks, and other institutions, served as pools from which capital, brought by innumerable streams, flowed to industries at home and abroad.'[17] In this situation, more agile and innovative financial services organisations were required, and the problems of maintaining confidence in their reliability became more acute, requiring, in turn, increased recognition that the state had a role in ensuring the reliability of the system. The state could not eliminate all risk, since to do so would be to leave financial organisations free to lend on ventures of the highest risk without risk to themselves. In any case, the state did not have the funds, even with its authority over taxes, to make credible guarantees on extensive credit provision. The requirement was for a state that provided sufficient sense of security in the system to maintain confidence in its general functioning, but left organisations within the system to determine what risks they would take, in the knowledge that they would suffer the consequences if their investments failed.

Budgets, credit and confidence

With money and a money-bargaining system established, all the agents involved operate money budgets. The main function of these budgets is to reconcile the time disparities between revenues and expenditures. The main services of the financial services sector are the provision of credit, making possible expenditures in advance of income, and the provision of savings facilities, making it possible to set aside money for future use. These services typically involve also the translation of 'lump sums' into recurrent payments, or the accumulation of recurrent payments into lump sums. Lump sums in credit or savings produce regular payments in return. Regular savings produce a terminal lump sum. The reconciliation of time disparities is paid for through rates of interest. Borrowers pay interest to lenders, while savers receive interest from those who accept their savings. The rate of interest will take account of the risk involved in parting with money over a time period. Use of money at low risk comes cheaper than use of money at high risk. Because the rate of interest is an indicator of risk, a high interest rate offered to attract savers may deter them, if they conclude that the high rate implies unacceptably high risk.

The situation and, hence, the bargaining position of a borrower changes with the receipt of a loan. On the one hand, before receipt of the loan, the borrower needs money, and may need it urgently. There are, moreover, likely to be many in the same position, in need of funding. The potential lender, on the other hand, holds money and is likely to have many options as to where he lends it, though he too is likely to have competitors keen to make loans. The lender will normally be perceived as having a stronger bargaining position than the borrower. Once the loan is agreed, the borrower has money and the lender is dependent on the borrower for repayment. Loans are set up so that, as far as can be established, the borrower has a strong interest in repayment of the loan in accordance with whatever schedule is agreed. He will normally have provided collateral which is forfeit if he breaks the loan agreement. If his default is publicised, he is likely to have difficulty in getting further credit from other sources. Nevertheless, the penalties for default considered purely in relation to the agreement between the borrower and lender may still incline the former to default rather than, in an awkward situation, exert maximum effort to maintain repayments. The borrower is in a stronger bargaining position relative to the lender than before the loan was provided. The lender needs supplementary provisions to increase the likelihood that his lending will be repaid in full with due interest. To provide this, the support-bargaining system has established a range of legislation relating to the enforcement of loan agreements and the collection of debt. Without these communal provisions regarding the conduct of credit agreements, this major element of money-bargaining systems would hardly be viable. It could occur only on a much smaller scale. Private enforcement of credit agreements, still sometimes seen as necessary at the very high-risk end of the market, tends to be crude and increases the potential for violence in society. Credit provision depends on the existence of regulation and enforcement through a support-bargaining system.

Enforcement of legislation on credit agreements has always been controversial. Public sympathies are easily engaged through association of lenders with 'the rich' and borrowers with 'the poor', so that enforcement of credit agreements can be presented as a facet of the exploitation of the poor by the rich. Novelists such as Charles Dickens easily arouse the sympathies of their readers for debtors. Dear *Little Dorrit* was born in the Marshalsea, one of the several real debtors gaols in nineteenth-century London, where her father was incarcerated for debt. The Marshalsea closed in 1842. Antipathy to lenders is apparent also in the mediaeval Christian condemnation of usury and the still-existing Muslim interdiction on usury. The British government has historically set legal limits on the rates of interest that could be charged. Under the Usury Laws, the maximum interest chargeable on commercial loans from 1700 to 1714 was 6 per cent, and from 1714 to 1832 5 per cent.[18] In the late seventeenth century John Locke opposed a suggestion that the legal limit should be reduced to 4 per cent to match that in Holland, on the grounds that there was a natural rate of interest, and any deviation from the natural rate would be damaging.[19] The legal limits were widely evaded through the imposition of other charges on borrowers, so that any constriction of lending was not severe.[20] The Muslim ban on the charging of interest is similarly evaded. There are now advocates of a ceiling on interest rates for 'pay-day' and similar very short-term high interest loans.

The provision of credit has, nevertheless, been essential to the evolution of the money-bargaining system in Britain, and penalties for default have been maintained at sufficiently uncomfortable levels as to sustain the profitability of provision of credit. Treatment of debtors has changed radically. Various methods have been adopted to resolve problems of debt collection without the necessity of incarcerating defaulters. Support-bargaining has provided extensive legislation and regulation to ensure that credit provision is feasible, but it also limits the ways in which loan agreements can be enforced.

The engagement of the formal support-bargaining system in the administration of credit facilities is essentially a means of maintaining confidence in the efficacy of a credit system. Without legislative backing for loan agreements, lenders would lack confidence that their outlays would be recoverable. The increasing capital requirements attendant on the accelerated evolution of the money-bargaining system referred to at the end of the last section had to be met within tolerable limits of risk. With non-existent or weak legislative backing, credit provision tends to be confined to persons known and trusted by the lender. Banking has become a mass-market service, but in its early days it was confined and personal. Mokyr comments:

> Yet throughout their history, most British banks remained conservative in their lending practices, confining themselves to discounting commercial paper and lending mostly to familiar customers. Such inside lending has sometimes been condemned as discriminatory and cronyist, but modern financial economics indicates that it is primarily a tool to overcome asymmetric

information, that is, the basic fact that the borrower knows things about himself that the lender does not, and therefore makes the lender reluctant to engage in the transaction in the first place. Many decades later, at the end of the nineteenth century, the dependence on people of known reputation was still an important tool in capital markets.[21]

Lending to known people reduces uncertainty and increases confidence that loans will be repaid. The lender knows that his money-bargaining advantage over the borrower is lost once the loan is agreed. But a known customer is assumed to recognise the same code of conduct as the lender. The known customer will suffer loss of support in the local community as a penalty for default. The enforcement of the 'gift economy' is used to bolster other penalties for default. The immediate sanctions of a social group are employed as substitute for or as a means of forestalling any necessity to resort to the more complex, uncertain and costly enforcement of the society as a whole through procedures established by support-bargaining. The availability of capital was not such a problem for bankers in the nineteenth century as the identification of suitable trustworthy recipients of loans: 'the problem of the banker was not to find money but names with sufficient standing to entrust it to'.[22]

The banking system nevertheless responded in other ways to expand credit without excessive risk. It began to evaluate more systematically the credit-worthiness of borrowers. 'Instead of the guess, shrewd or ill-founded, as to the credit-worthiness of the borrower, there was, for part of the field, the published List [i.e. the Stock Exchange List. The Stock Exchange was founded in 1773] as a guide. Capital was becoming impersonal – "blind", as some say – and highly mobile.'[23] The larger banks established following the provision for joint-stock banks in 1826 had greater capacity for loan evaluation.

Mokyr notes in the quotation above that modern financial economics explains discrimination between borrowers by lenders in terms of 'asymmetric information'. Neoclassical economists have no understanding of confidence, trust, budgets or support-bargaining, and consequently have difficulty in understanding why it is that bankers define the bargaining sets in which they are prepared to lend in a way that excludes those who present high risk of default. The best they can do to reconcile observed practice with the neoclassical model is to account it a consequence of 'asymmetric information'. This sacrifices the assumption in the model of 'perfect information', but permits something like rational assimilation of the lending practices of bankers. As with 'public goods' and 'merit goods', discussed in the previous chapter, neoclassical economists select a particular feature of the transaction and use that feature to reconcile the phenomenon with the model. Outside the neoclassical theory group, it is a matter of common sense to lend to people you trust, and not lend to the untrustworthy. Only within the neoclassical theory group, where the normal circumstance is taken to be 'perfect information', does it appear remarkable that people know more about themselves and their business than others. Here again, the theory developed by neoclassical economists gives poor guidance with regard to the issues of concern to economic historians.

While private people take loans for various purposes, they also deposit large sums of money with banks. These deposits can be seen as loans to the banks, recoverable on demand, with some banks paying interest on sight deposit accounts. More commonly they are conceived in terms of provision by banks of a service of safe-keeping from the time of deposit to the time of requirement, with services relating to the administration of receipts and payments, for which banks may charge a fee. Whatever the understanding, depositors need to have confidence that their bank will be able to return the deposited money when it is required. The country banks that grew up in Britain in the eighteenth century became deposit bankers on the back of their role in the issue of notes. Users of their notes developed enough confidence in them to entrust them with their money on deposit. The development of deposit banking made available money for investment in the economy.[24] The country banks were substantially diversified, so that the confidence placed in them did not rest entirely on their role as bankers.[25] Country bankers might be engaged as millers and corn merchants, as hosiers, or as partners in mines.[26] In times of crisis, failure rates of country banks could be high. In the crisis of 1825 80 country banks failed, with knock-on effects on the London banks most closely involved with them. Many more would probably have failed if the Bank of England had not, after much persuasion, expanded its note issue. In the twentieth century some countries, beginning with the USA in 1934, introduced deposit insurance schemes which provide government guarantees for deposits to a certain amount. In Britain most deposits are currently (2015) guaranteed by the state up to £85,000, though the guarantee reduces to £75,000 on 31 December 2015. Communal support, expressed through the state, has been used to maintain high levels of confidence, hence high levels of deposits, and hence high levels of funding for investment.

Home-buyers' time shift

The largest time shift of revenue and expenditure for most families involves the acquisition of a home. As noted above, people need a house to live in, but it can take a lifetime to save enough money to buy one. The alternative is to borrow the funds immediately, buy the house and pay off a mortgage over a lifetime, or at least a long period. In Britain and in many other countries this has been one of the most popular and most rewarding household investments. Because of its popularity, and because of the support that can consequently be derived from promoting it, house purchase has been encouraged by governments. In Britain governments commonly make credit conditions much easier than would otherwise be possible, particularly with regard to deposit requirements. House buyers in the late twentieth and early twenty-first centuries could borrow all or nearly all the cost of a house. For many years they could claim tax relief on mortgage interest. The relaxed conditions meant that 'ordinary people', if not 'poor people', could own their own homes. Under Margaret Thatcher, Prime Minister of the United Kingdom from 1979 to 1990, home ownership was associated with democracy and free enterprise. Ordinary people would become owners of land

and property. Council houses were sold to promote private home owning as an appropriate aspiration for ordinary people in a capitalist democracy. The expanding supply of money for house purchase resulted in substantial increases in house prices, well above the general rate of inflation. House purchase was not just the acquisition of somewhere to live, but acquisition of an appreciating asset that could serve later as a source of budget revenue to cover the requirements of old age.

The confidence generated by government support for mortgage lending led to the sub-prime mortgage crisis that engulfed the USA and Europe from 2007. Gretchen Morgenson and Joshua Rosner describe in *Reckless Endangerment* how Fannie Mae, the US government-sponsored housing finance agency, convinced President Clinton in the 1990s that it could extend home ownership to poor families in the USA through new techniques of lending. The chief executive of Fannie Mae assembled support for his campaign within the Clinton administration and across Congress by lobbying, the provision of financial support to influential people and other favours. Fannie Mae's involvement in provision of home finance was largely through the purchase of bundles of sub-prime mortgages from mortgage companies that dealt directly with borrowers. This made available additional funds to the mortgage companies for further lending. Initially, the main sub-prime lender was Countrywide Financial, whose chief executive had personal links with the chief executive of Fannie Mae.[27] As the profitability of sub-prime lending became apparent, other companies took up the business. The ratings agencies boosted confidence immeasurably by giving triple-A credit status to Fannie Mae securities, largely based on perception of Fannie Mae as a government-sponsored agency.[28] They came to be regarded as almost equivalent to government debt. The US Treasury ceased issue of 30-year bonds in 2001, leaving Fannie Mae and Freddie Mac securities as the leading options for securities of this maturity.[29] The 30-year Treasury bond was, however, reintroduced in 2006.

Yet the new lending techniques involved the provision of mortgages to borrowers who lacked the levels of income necessary for repayment. The mortgage lenders found it unnecessary to concern themselves greatly with the quality of their lending, since they immediately removed the loans from their accounts by packing them up together and selling them to Fannie Mae and other investors. The process met the political commitment of Fannie Mae to make housing finance available to the poor, and seemed, by virtue of the credit ratings, to do so in a secure and financially respectable manner. In 2000 debt issued by Fannie Mae and Freddie Mac stood at $1.4 trillion and was assessed as likely to double by 2005.[30] The less public interest of Fannie Mae lay in meeting income targets that would trigger large bonus payments to the board and top executives. Accounts were illegally adjusted to make it appear that the income targets were met. The appraisal of each mortgage became superficial in the rush to assemble the necessary volumes for packaging into securities.[31] Computerised assessments were made to speed the process. In many cases applications to Countrywide Financial for mortgages were adjusted by the company to ensure they met criteria for approval.

This practice became widespread in companies providing sub-prime mortgages when Wall Street banks became heavily engaged in the sale of mortgage-based securities in the first decade of the new century.[32] In this phase, collateralised debt obligations (CDOs) were reinvented, toxic packages of toxic loans that had failed to sell in plain security packages. In 2006, $521 billion of these securities were sold. Wall Street banks were fully aware of the risks attaching to the loan packages they were selling, even if the ratings agencies were not, but chose to ignore them in the interests of profitability. Their awareness is apparent from their parallel sale of securities that depended for their return on falls in the value of securities based on sub-prime home loans, a practice initiated by Goldman Sachs.[33] 'While nobody mistook Wall Street banks for charity organizations, the degree to which these firms embraced and facilitated corrupt mortgage lending was stunning.'[34]

The neglect of the debt to income ratio as a criterion for identification of appropriate borrowers might be seen as a generous concession to facilitate lending to low-income borrowers, consistent with the charitable principles under which the loan programme was promoted. The poor were accommodated also through very low or zero deposit requirements. In some cases, loans were available that covered more than the cost of the house to be acquired. Immediate interest rates also appeared very attractive. The catch was, however, that once signatures had been appended, the terms were hard. The low initial interest rates rapidly escalated to very high interest rates. The idea that borrowers could escape the higher interest rates by refinancing on more favourable terms, with their houses at higher valuations, proved mistaken. People found themselves locked into payments that took very large proportions of their disposable incomes. Morgenson and Rosner comment that, in many cases, 'These borrowers may not have known it, but they were trapped in high-cost and murderous loans. It was only a matter of time before they defaulted.'[35]

Political and regulatory agencies were won over by the high-principled advocacy by Fannie Mae of home ownership for the poor, and the ideological predisposition to let 'markets' dictate the development of mortgage lending. The high principles assembled support in the White House, in Congress, in social-housing organisations and across the country. Fannie Mae and Freddie Mac were hailed as bringers of a new era to housing finance and social liberation. Advocates of social housing made their views known to Congress, at the behest of Fannie Mae, whenever any threat appeared to the continued privileges enjoyed by Fannie Mae under its government sponsorship. Confidence in the programme rested heavily on the perception that Fannie Mae and its sister company Freddie Mac had the support of government. The White House, Congress, government departments, the Federal Reserve Bank, other regulatory institutions, ratings agencies and financial services companies all became convinced that a new and rich vein of credit provision had been revealed.

The faith in 'markets' included a predisposition to accept that bank lending had been over-regulated in the past. Conservative credit conditions had deprived great numbers of deserving Americans from realising the 'American dream' of home ownership. Alan Greenspan, admired chairman of the Federal Reserve Bank, accepted that new techniques for appraising mortgage loans rendered the old regulatory regime out of date, and approved the relaxation of capital reserve requirements for financial institutions. Mortgage securities issued by Fannie Mae, Freddie Mac and other government-sponsored enterprises required only a capital reserve backing of 20 per cent of their value, giving banks a strong incentive to buy such securities.[36] The Federal Reserve Bank judged that the bankers knew what they were doing and accepted that 'the market' should be permitted to dictate the course of events, with lesser regulation by the monetary authorities.[37] Voices within the Federal Reserve nevertheless questioned the role of the non-free-market players – Freddie Mac and Fannie Mae. Greenspan himself noted the risks of over-confidence with regard to the securities issued by government-sponsored enterprises.[38] Various technical reports questioning the soundness of the new lending practices and the companies engaged in them were successfully discredited by proponents of the expansion of mortgage lending, led by Fannie Mae.

If regulators had studied economic history instead of neoclassical economics, they might have been alerted to potential trouble by the similarity of the techniques used by Fannie Mae to promote the sub-prime mortgage business to the techniques used by the promoters of the South Sea Company in Britain in the early eighteenth century. In both cases the promoters were at pains to establish the close connection between their enterprises and their governments, both as matters of principle and as matters of profit. The South Sea Company undertook to provide loans to government on more favourable terms than the Bank of England. Fannie Mae promised expansion of home ownership among the poor, and ensured that its virtuous ambitions were known and supported in Congress. Both the South Sea Company and Fannie Mae recognised that their success depended on the confidence of investors that their investments were backed by governments. The South Sea Company hyped its trading prospects and gave its shares inflated value. Fannie Mae exaggerated the security of the mortgages on which its income was based. Even after such a long time interval, and with such enormous differences of context, the basic technique of cultivation of at least the semblance of government guarantees was common to both initiatives because support-bargaining, and the major support-bargaining agencies, are essential to the propagation of confidence.

The outcomes were also similar. In the case of the South Sea Company, it became apparent that its prospects had been grossly overrated. Questions over the credibility of its claims suddenly emerged more audibly above the propaganda of its promoters, and people disposed of their shares in panic. The value of shares in the company fell precipitously until it was bailed out by the government, nervous of the damage a complete collapse might entail. In the case of Fannie Mae, it became increasingly apparent that securities based on sub-prime mortgages were not what they were touted to be, and the company was not what it was supposed to be. Fannie Mae and Freddie Mac were both taken over by the US government in September 2008. By that time sub-prime mortgage-linked securities were prominent in the assets of many financial services companies. Lehman Brothers, the largest packager on Wall Street of residential mortgage loans sold to investors, was allowed to fail. Other banks and financial service companies were bailed out

214   *The Evolution of Economies*

by the government. Overseas banks that held the toxic securities found their assets suddenly depleted. In the United Kingdom a contraction of inter-bank lending brought queues of depositors to the doors of Northern Rock in 2007. In the following year it was taken over by the government. In 2008 also the government rescued the Royal Bank of Scotland, Lloyds TSB and other financial services companies. The British government found itself the financier of last resort, just as the Bank of England had found itself responsible for the liquidity of the financial system in 1793, because the alternative was extensive collapse of the financial system.

Confidence and over-confidence

Confidence is essential for the undertaking of transactions that involve time shifts and the uncertainties attendant on the passage of time. The situations of borrower and lender change significantly with the signing of a loan; situations more generally can change in the time between loan and repayment. The changes in situation can produce changes in the interests of the agents involved. Earlier commitments may be regretted and means sought of evading them. Because of the high risks of default, personal relationships and familiarity have been important to the maintenance of lending for private and commercial purposes. Nevertheless, the maintenance of accelerated rates of evolution in money-bargaining required high levels of savings and extensive provision of credit to businesses. States established central institutions for the administration of financial systems, implying state backing for their commitments, and these institutions enfolded an idea of state concern for the financial services organisations they administered. State backing of financial services provision increased confidence in financial systems. The community, through the support-bargaining system, regulated and administered the financial services sector to enhance public confidence in the security of credit. Wherever there is uncertainty, the formation of groups through support-bargaining is the common means of establishing the confidence necessary for action. Governments can generate confidence because they are recognised as voicing and implementing the outcomes of national support-bargaining. The size of national government budgets and the potential call of governments on tax payments give their backing material credibility. Support-bargaining gives governments the will to back financial service provision; their own financial position makes their support credible.

In some circumstances the support-bargaining process can lead to over-confidence and a short-term inflation in the value, price or importance of whatever a group has focused its support upon. 'Manias', 'euphoria' and 'the herd instinct' are manifestations of the over-confidence that can arise from support-bargaining.[39] Confined groups become convinced that their valuations and assessments of trends are incontrovertible. In the course of time, as performance becomes apparent, the assessments are recognised as mistaken. There is then likely to be a rapid collapse in the valuations that have been built inside the group. Valuations that rest on group support and little more can be nullified by the withdrawal of group support.

While the build-up of support is often slow, the withdrawal of support can occur with the rapidity of panic.

The build-up to the sub-prime crisis in the USA suggests some of the conditions in which over-confidence can be generated. There needs to be universal, or near universal, assent to the central group proposition of what is valuable. Theoretic assurance plays a large part in this. The support attaching to neoclassical economic theory and the implications of the theory for financial transactions and the valuation of assets gave financiers and others confidence that they had the right approach. Relatively few fully understood the theory, so it was essentially faith in 'the experts' or 'those who know' or in the output of learned institutions.

Such belief gives different institutions the same convictions, so it appears that several admired institutions have all independently made their assessments and the valuations they provide are consequently likely to be realistic. The impression of security is accentuated when the institutions concerned are understood to include some with responsibility for oversight or regulation of others, or with responsibilities under the 'checks and balances' of a democracy. Institutions with these oversight and regulatory responsibilities are set up precisely to impede the development of potentially damaging ideas in one or some of them. In the USA all the institutions concerned with the regulation or provision of financial services seemed to agree on the virtues of relaxing credit conditions so that the poor could acquire houses, and supported the pioneer work of Fannie Mae and Freddie Mac in developing sub-prime mortgage provision. The apparent unanimity of support was sustained by success in discrediting technical analysis carried out in oversight institutions that challenged received opinion.

The proponents of sub-prime mortgages were able to assemble support for their activities by enveloping them in high principles. High principles and charitable purposes assemble support and repel criticism. 'Virtue' is an effective cover because it assembles extensive and largely undiscriminating support. People have difficulties in evaluating the intricacies of financial securities and other complex matters, but virtue is an easy 'yes'. Critics alienate themselves from the consensus on virtue in their societies. Such support was used to blanket conduct that, exposed to view, would be regarded as immoral. Existing concerns over the provision of housing for poor people meant that an agency coming up with a credible 'solution' readily attracted support. The government was particularly susceptible to pleas that it should back what seemed unambiguously a 'good cause', promising electoral support from a significant segment of the community. Concerns over housing, and relaxation of credit conditions for housing, led to financial crises in Ireland and Spain at the same time.

There were also cruder means of gaining the semblance of support: prominent people were paid or given favours in return for expressions of support for the group cause. Very often these favours cemented personal friendships or arose from interlocking representation on boards. The 'individualism' of money, as described in Chapter 2, can be used to subvert what should be a matter of support-bargaining. The 'insiders', both institutional and individual, were protected from external criticism by the legal and technical complexity of financial services.

Too few insiders with the necessary expertise and information were prepared to risk their positions within the group by making known their concerns. 'Whistleblowers', while lauded in public, are invariably isolated and rejected by the organisations they call to account. Few 'outsiders' were in a position, and at the same time sufficiently courageous, to challenge the positions of the insiders. Aspirations to acquire and retain the support of associates, and fears of losing support, cause people to subordinate the judgements they might make as members of a wider community to those appropriate to their immediate organisational or institutional position.

At the core of the 'inside' is the central bank. At the centre of financial crises are central banks. Using whatever theory is available to them, and whatever advice is available to them, they have to work out who is right and what is right with regard to the interests of the economies dependent on the financial systems they oversee. They are, if nothing else, aware of the importance of confidence to the stability of financial service companies and the financial system as a whole. Their public pronouncements are invariably crafted to suggest infinite wisdom and infinite assurance in the well-being of the systems for which they are responsible. Alan Greenspan presented himself as a parody of the patrician central banker when he said, 'I guess I should warn you, if I turn out to be particularly clear, you've probably misunderstood what I've said.' The comment references a long history of enigmatic circumlocution from the guardians of financial systems. Yet without an understanding of support-bargaining and money-bargaining it is impossible to understand how financial systems work and the nature of the 'confidence' that is so important to them. Central bankers could not be clear, even if they wanted to be. The lack of understanding over the nature of 'confidence' means that there is a predisposition to explain away adverse trends and gloss over malpractices to 'maintain confidence'. When the fundamental 'understanding' of the system is that provided by neoclassical economic theory and its 'markets', warning signs of danger will almost inevitably be missed. They imply that security lies in inaction. In the USA, faith in 'markets' was dramatically overtaken by the reality of failures of major bargaining agencies in financial services and contraction of the money-bargaining system. In both Britain and the USA governments found themselves thrust into positions of 'financiers of last resort'.

The time shifts of expenditures and revenues involved in home buying are long and the sums involved are large relative to most household expenditures. The psychological importance of a home and the historical status attaching to home ownership further raise the significance of credit provision for home ownership. House purchase becomes a matter of political as well as material importance. The money-bargaining system becomes more than usually entwined with the support-bargaining system. The latter is used to raise the confidence of lenders in the security of housing loans. But the promotion of confidence may become of such importance that people lose the inclination to investigate the realities of situations. When it is suggested that something is wrong, the maintenance of confidence may take on even greater importance as the means of protecting current positions, with redoubled efforts to suppress evidence suggesting that current positions are ill-founded. In the end, confidence evaporates as the realities become apparent to all and assets that seemed secure suddenly become worthless.

Employment, borrowing and business cycles

With confidence in the provision of credit resting, in large measure, on guarantees, explicit or assumed, of government, there tends to be high confidence in lending to government itself. Governments can generally borrow at lower interest rates than other agents. Credit is inherently attractive to governments since it offers the prospect of assembling support through expenditures without any need to sacrifice current support through the levy of taxes. While repayments are going to be necessary in the future, the prospect is that a new government will bear the odium of raising the necessary tax revenues. The consequence is a tendency for all states to accumulate debt, with each new government obliged to raise taxes not just to finance its current expenditure, but to service the debt incurred by previous governments. The 'technicians' in state treasuries and ministries of finance may have to restrain spendthrift politicians to prevent government debt rising to unmanageable levels. The technicians will try, generally, to restrict borrowing to levels that generate no increase in levels of debt relative to gross domestic product (GDP) – that is, borrowing can rise in step with the growth of GDP, assuming levels of debt as they stand are manageable and not so low as to suggest missed opportunities. As with other agents, there are also requirements for short-term borrowing, to bridge the gap between 'pay days', when tax revenues come in, and the ongoing expenditure obligations of government.

Budgets give governments great scope for bestowing favours on selected groups within their societies. Individual politicians want their own electoral prospects advanced through the funding of projects in their constituencies, whether roads, schools, hospitals or other facilities that attract the support of constituents. Government support in critical marginal constituencies may be raised by expenditures on local facilities. Governments can gallop to the rescue with special financial allocations when issues arise concerning crime, health services, child welfare and other matters that commonly produce strong reactions within societies. In Britain in the 1950s and 1960s it was more or less routine for a government to produce an 'electioneering budget' just before a general election. The priority given to the assembly of support means that debt is often incurred to finance this sort of provision. Sharper criticism of measures designed most obviously to raise support in elections at the expense of the more fundamental effectiveness of government budgets has, to some extent, curbed the practice.

One of the major debates over economic management has concerned the extent to which a government can and should be held responsible for the overall performance of its national economy. When government budgetary expenditure is equivalent to 40 per cent or more of GDP, with corresponding levels of revenue from taxation, government decisions clearly have an important impact on the performance of an economy. The issue of employment has been at the centre of debate. Government expenditure affects levels of employment, and it may be desirable that governments combat unemployment by borrowing to increase their expenditure. Borrowing can finance additional expenditure without the necessity of raising additional revenue, so that there is a net 'stimulus' to the economy. It is assumed that the government borrowing has little or no effect on finance available to private investors. Such additional expenditure offers at least the theoretical prospect of being self-financing, with the borrowing repaid from the increased revenues arising from the more rapid growth generated by the expenditure. The sensitivity of political support to unemployment rates gives governments a predisposition to borrow and spend to lift employment.

As has been seen, the dominant theory guiding economic management has been the neoclassical marginal model, or the 'free-market' model. The model involves a self-adjusting mechanism that moves an economy to equilibrium at full employment and maximum output. This concept meant that unemployment, except as a mere matter of transition, was difficult to explain. To deal with the manifest occurrence of unemployment in actual economies, a related study of 'business cycles' was developed. Knut Wicksell, the main theorist of business cycles in the early twentieth century, explained the cyclical movements in industrial output and employment in terms of deviations of interest rates from a 'natural' rate of interest that rendered savings equal to investment. A period of over-investment stimulated by low interest rates would be followed by a period of under-investment as interest rates rose. An 'Austrian' theory of business cycles was derived from Wicksell's theory, arguing that credit expansion was the primary factor behind the movements in rates of interest, and consequently behind the business cycle. A 'Stockholm School' also based its theory on that of Wicksell, but argued that unexpected changes in prices caused planned savings to diverge from planned investment and gave rise to cyclical movement in output.[40] There were, thus, contrasting 'monetary' and 'real' theories of business cycles, echoing the monetarist and trade-based theories of exchange rates and money supply. After the First World War the question of government response to unemployment was approached through the theory of business cycles.

In Wicksell and his followers the role of 'confidence' is subsumed in ideas regarding expected returns on investment. In Britain Alfred Marshall's theory of business cycles centred directly on the role of 'confidence'. Referring to the depression stage of the business cycle, he and M. P. Marshall wrote: 'The chief cause of the evil is want of confidence.'[41] As was suggested above, without an understanding of support-bargaining, it is difficult to understand the workings of 'confidence'. But with the understanding, it can be seen that ideas and actions of groups deriving from an established trend will carry the trend further, until dissenters gain ascendancy and tip the balance the other way, so that the trend reverses. Business cycles are, then, a natural consequence of the operation of support-bargaining in business communities. The risks and uncertainties inseparable from business investment are resolved by support-bargaining, but the resolution lasts only so long as the group maintains its resolve. The accentuation of trends in one direction will change the situation, until it is seen increasingly that the trends are unlikely to be prolonged much longer. Individuals will change their assessments, and the reassessments of the few, given the changing situation, are likely to be taken up by the many, so that the original commitment is reversed.

Interest in business cycles was particularly strong in the USA because, although Britain after 1860 had been relatively free from financial crises, the USA had experienced several crises.[42] Business cycle theory came to be seen as a distinct branch of economics. Debate centred on whether business cycles arose from monetary factors or factors relating to non-financial business behaviour, reflecting the views of the 'Austrian' and 'Stockholm' theory groups. The 1921 President's Conference on Unemployment, chaired by Herbert Hoover, then Secretary for Commerce, produced proposals for counter-cyclical expenditure by government on public works. As President, it fell to Hoover to lead the government response to the Stock Exchange crash of 1929. In keeping with the earlier proposal, his response was to increase spending. By 1930, however, with unemployment still rising, it was concluded that the rate of public expenditure could not be sustained. The commitment to spend rested on the assumption that spending would be on projects that were justified in terms of their economic returns, and such projects could not be identified. Doubts arose also about the effectiveness of the spending. It might not have the anticipated 'multiplier' effects if the borrowing necessary for it raised interest rates and choked off private investment. There were concerns also that anxieties over the stability of public finances with further borrowing might adversely affect business confidence. The public works policy was dropped.[43]

When Franklin Roosevelt became President in 1933 he instituted the range of initiatives known as the 'New Deal'. The programme was influenced by Irving Fisher, who doubted whether there was any such thing as a business cycle, but recognised fluctuations in price levels.[44] The thinking behind the New Deal was that a rise in prices would reduce the real value of debts, relieving both investors and government of their burdens of debt servicing. The New Deal involved monetary expansion and public works specifically aimed at promoting inflation. The government budget deficit was allowed to rise sharply and remained high through the 1930s. The New Deal had its counterpart in Sweden, where home-grown theory was readily available.[45]

The 1929 Stock Market crash in the USA followed a period of rapid economic growth and heavy speculation on the price of stocks. In Britain, by contrast, the 1920s was a period of slow growth, with unemployment remaining above 10 per cent. The decision to restore sterling to its pre-war gold standard, implemented in 1925, was an important factor in the sluggish performance. The unit costs of all companies, in terms of foreign currencies, rose and made many formats unviable. John Maynard Keynes opposed the return to the gold standard, insisting that the stability of business, prices and employment was more important than a 'barbarous relic'.[46] It was a replay of the Malynes versus Misselden and Mun dispute of the early seventeenth century. Britain was forced, once again, to abandon the gold standard in 1931 in the Depression brought on by the collapse of stock markets in 1929. The pound depreciated against the US dollar by nearly 30 per cent.

Keynes versus money-bargaining

Keynes formulated his own response to the unemployment of the 1920s and early 1930s in *The General Theory of Employment, Interest and Money*, one of the most influential books on economics ever published.[47] While it can be said that it was written in response to the real economic problems of the 1920s and early 1930s, it was presented in strictly academic terms as a critique and displacement of 'classical' economic theory as presented in Pigou's *The Theory of Unemployment*[48] and earlier works of Jean-Baptiste Say (1767–1832), David Ricardo (1772–1823) and John Stuart Mill (1806–1873). Keynes's understanding of 'classical economists' includes David Ricardo, James Mill and their predecessors, and also, as a personal idiosyncrasy, those later followers of Ricardo who 'adopted and perfected' Ricardian economics, such as J. S. Mill, Marshall, Edgeworth and Professor Pigou.[49] To a remarkable degree, *The General Theory* set the agenda for macroeconomic debate from the time of its publication.

Keynes sums up 'classical theory' as depending on three assumptions:[50]

1   that the real wage is equal to the marginal disutility of the existing employment;
2   that there is no such thing as involuntary unemployment in the strict sense;
3   that supply creates its own demand in the sense that the aggregate demand price is equal to the aggregate supply price for all levels of output and employment.[51]

The implication of these assumptions is that an economy will always settle into equilibrium at full employment. Any fall from full employment will automatically bring about a reduction in wages, leading to an increased demand for labour and the restoration of equilibrium at full employment. The interest rate, the 'price of credit', will balance savings and investment. The unemployment in Britain in the 1920s and 1930s was difficult to explain with this 'classical' theory.

Keynes argued that the assumptions were invalid. While equilibrium would come about, it would not necessarily be an equilibrium at full employment because the economy did not function in the manner portrayed by classical theory. In particular, the rate of interest would not balance savings and investment. In spite of assumption 3 of classical theory, demand could fall short of what was necessary to generate full employment. Keynes's idea of the 'marginal propensity to consume' suggested that as incomes rose a decreasing proportion would be spent on consumption. The greater the income, the smaller the proportion of additional income that would be spent on consumption and the greater the proportion that would be saved. Conversely, falling income would mean a higher proportion of consumption expenditure, and a smaller proportion of saving. The dependence of saving on the level of income meant that savings would not be increased by a rise in interest rates. If the rate of interest rose, investment would fall and income would fall. If income fell, the level of savings would fall more than proportionately. The fall in savings due to the income effect would offset any increase in savings that might be prompted by the rise in interest rates.

Equilibrium would only be achieved when incomes fell to a level at which savings were equal to investment. This would be likely to occur at a level of activity that did not give full employment.[52] Though workers might try to adjust their wage requirements to gain employment, as classical theory suggested they would, there would remain a certain involuntary unemployment not possible in classical theory. This adjustment of savings to investment via incomes marked a major break with classical theory.

A further important break concerned the establishment of the rate of interest. In classical theory the demand for investment funds and the supply of savings would determine the interest rate. Without this simple mechanism, interest rates had to be determined in some other way. Keynes conceived 'liquidity preference' and the quantity of money as the determinants of the interest rate. People like to hold funds readily available, rather than accessible only after a period. The cost of this liquidity preference is the foregoing of interest on savings. Keynes distinguishes between liquid and illiquid funds by reference to interest paid on them. Liquid funds earn little or no interest, while savings earn interest. The more people prefer to hold their money in liquid form, the less money will be placed in interest-bearing bonds. The distinction, in practical terms, is between holding funds in cash or bank deposits and holding bonds.[53] For any given quantity of money, the level of liquidity preference would determine the rate of interest. If the supply of money was increased, interest rates would tend to fall and people's liquidity preference would be likely to increase, since they would be foregoing less interest by having high liquidity. If liquidity preference increased for some other reason, the reduction in sums available to interest-bearing bonds would be likely to bring about a rise in interest rates.[54]

The rate of interest influences the level of investment through the 'marginal efficiency of capital'. The marginal efficiency of capital is the expected rate of return on capital, or the rate of discount which when applied to expected annual returns from an investment makes their present value equal to the supply price of the investment asset.[55] The inducement to invest is the excess of the marginal efficiency of capital over the prevailing rate of interest. In equilibrium, the marginal efficiency of capital will be equal to the prevailing rate of interest. The effects of investment are transmitted through the economy in accordance with an investment 'multiplier'. An investment expenditure will produce aggregate income that is a multiple of the original investment.[56] While the difference between the prevailing rate of interest and the marginal efficiency of capital constitutes the incentive to invest, the actual level of investment is defined by Keynes as the counterpart to savings. Savings are the residual of income after consumption expenditure. Investment is the residual of output after consumption. If the value of output is equal to income, savings must be equal to investment.[57]

Keynes recognises that the rate of interest might be understood as determined by the marginal efficiency of capital. But he argues that this involves a circular argument because, 'the "marginal efficiency of capital" partly depends on the scale of current investment, and we must already know the rate of interest before we can calculate what this scale will be'.[58] According to Keynes, this circularity stalled an earlier attempt by Alfred Marshall to develop a theory of interest rates based on the marginal efficiency of capital. Keynes developed the idea of 'liquidity preference' in order to escape the circularity. It leads to his conclusion that interest payments are 'the reward for not hoarding' rather than a reward for not spending. The 'propensity to hoard' is 'substantially the same thing' as liquidity preference.[59]

Keynes notes that, for the most part, economies are not highly unstable, but fluctuate around a norm that provides less than full employment: 'the economic system ... is not violently unstable. Indeed it seems capable of remaining in a chronic condition of sub-normal activity for a considerable period without any marked tendency either towards recovery or towards complete collapse'[60] As far as employment is concerned, 'we oscillate ... round an intermediate position appreciably below full employment and appreciably above the minimum employment a decline below which would endanger life'.[61] He argues that the four factors, the 'marginal propensity to consume', 'liquidity preference', the 'marginal efficiency of capital' and the 'multiplier', together with the psychological and other assumptions behind them, are consistent with such outcomes, and his model is consequently likely to be a good representation of the behaviour of economies.

These normal propensities of economies imply for Keynes the need for radical change in government engagement in an economy. In *The General Theory* he advocates substantial government intervention to control and direct interest rates and investment:

> In conditions of *laissez-faire* the avoidance of wide fluctuations in employment may, therefore, prove impossible without a far-reaching change in the psychology of investment markets such as there is no reason to expect. I conclude that the duty of ordering the current volume of investment cannot safely be left in private hands.[62]

In his 'Concluding Notes' Keynes identifies the failure to provide full employment and the arbitrary and inequitable distribution of wealth and incomes as the two outstanding faults of society. To remedy them, he advocates extensive government intervention: 'I conceive, therefore, that a somewhat comprehensive socialisation of investment will prove the only means of securing an approximation to full employment.'[63] This involves eliminating the scarcity value of capital through setting interest rates very low and expanding communal saving through the state. The prevalent idea that high rates of tax on the wealthy stop them saving, and hence impede investment, is displaced by the idea that high rates of taxation will transfer income to poorer people and promote consumption, and in that way increase the inducement to invest. It is, therefore, economically desirable to impose high rates of taxation on the wealthy. The process would involve the gradual 'euthanasia of the rentier, of the functionless investor'.[64]

In earlier work Keynes supported schemes of 'national development' to raise the level of public investment, to be financed by government borrowing. In the 1920s the Treasury had already opposed such schemes, arguing that any government borrowing to finance public investment would reduce the finance available for private sector investment. Hence there would be no increase in aggregate demand. The argument can be seen as part of the ongoing efforts of 'technicians' to restrain the borrowing and spending of profligate politicians. Keynes argued in response that much saving was not used productively but was 'hoarded' in bank deposits. Government borrowing could draw on this element of saving, and would consequently have no effect on private investment.[65]

In *The General Theory*, the case for government borrowing to increase public expenditure to secure full employment is not argued extensively. It is presented in an apparently light-hearted, though provocative, manner in just three short pages. Keynes suggests,

> Pyramid-building, earthquakes, even wars may serve to increase wealth, if the education of our statesmen on the principles of the classical economics stands in the way of anything better ... If the Treasury were to fill old bottles with banknotes, bury them at suitable depths in disused coal mines which are then filled up to the surface with town rubbish, and leave it to private enterprise on well tried principles of *laissez-faire* to dig the notes up again ... there need be no more unemployment.[66]

Keynes, of course, knew well that public spending was already being extensively used to raise aggregate demand and combat unemployment to offset fluctuations due to the cyclical nature of trade. In his 'Notes on the Trade Cycle', one of the 'Short Notes Suggested by the General Theory' in Book VI of *The General Theory*, he attributes the cycle mainly to changes in the marginal efficiency of capital. The marginal efficiency of capital, as has been seen, depends on expectations. Hence it depends on people's outlook or confidence. Keynes lapses into plain English to explain his position: 'It is the return of confidence, to speak in ordinary language, which is so insusceptible to control in an economy of individualistic capitalism.'[67] The fluctuations in confidence mean that: 'with markets organised and influenced as they are at present, the market estimation of the marginal efficiency of capital may suffer such enormously wide fluctuations that it cannot be sufficiently offset by corresponding fluctuations in the rate of interest'.[68] The marginal efficiency of capital boils down to questions of confidence, and Keynes recommends 'socialised' investment to eliminate the fluctuations in investment arising from the volatility of confidence and maintain demand at the level necessary to full employment. More than that, Keynes justifies his recommendations for a much wider role for government in the direct organisation of investment by reference to government capacity for discerning what is good investment. He writes that the state, 'is in a position to calculate the marginal efficiency of capital-goods on long views and on the basis of the general social advantage'.[69] Not all will agree that governments have such capacity. The marginal efficiency of public capital is more likely to be high because it is the nature of politicians to be optimistic. The professional optimism, and the absence of risk to their own personal finances, means that politicians are unlikely to be the best investors. No doubt Keynes envisaged that technocratic civil servants would calculate the returns without either optimism or pessimism and direct the investment on behalf of their political masters.

Keynes in the new perspective

The theory of support-bargaining and money-bargaining provides a new perspective on Keynes's theories. It has already been seen that the theory provides a quite different account of the functioning of an economy from that of neoclassical or marginal theory. Keynes attacks his version of 'classical' theory, but by including Alfred Marshall as a 'classical' theorist he retains all the theory, perhaps better known as neoclassical theory, developed in the late nineteenth and early twentieth centuries, offering a refined and mathematical marginal analysis. He sustains the notion that economies are self-stabilising, while introducing a mechanism whereby the stabilisation is likely to occur at levels of demand and output below what is necessary for full employment. Deal with the shortfall in demand, it seems, and the system will be restored to equilibrium at full employment.

In the understanding of money-bargaining, the system does not stabilise. All the agents of a money-bargaining system want something, whether employment, goods and services, or sales of goods and services, and will adjust their demands to get the best deal they can. All individual agents will try to engage in transactions that give them money revenues, creating some tendency to full employment. The process will bring prices broadly in line with costs of production, and wages broadly in line with the contributions of their recipients to the value of output. All these suggest movement towards full engagement of the agents of a money-bargaining system. But product innovation, technology, imperfect information, the variety of formats, locational formats, failure of formats, time constraints, combinations, mergers and takeovers, notions of fairness, government engagement – in short, the operation of a bargaining system – mean that there will be no equilibrium and no necessary full employment. Rather, the process will create situations continuously in flux – the evolutionary process described in previous chapters. Keynes seeks to sustain the concept of equilibrium in an economic process that is evolutionary.

Keynes sets the scene to accommodate his theory. He allocates much space in *The General Theory* to the definition of terms. As noted in Chapter 4 and, earlier, in *Support-Bargaining, Economics and Society*, this is a standard academic practice, designed to eliminate the vagueness of 'concepts' and remove uncertainties relating to semantic usage.[70] It is an essential preliminary to mathematical procedures. Definitions are also essential to a system of national accounts. It has the effect, however, of establishing a framework within which a theory can be confirmed as valid because the phenomena at issue have been defined by reference to the theory. Keynes is not defining how things actually *are* but how his theory requires them to be. Then treating the definitions as how things *are* he demonstrates that his theory is entirely consistent with the reality. The definition of 'involuntary unemployment' is essential to the existence of sustained unemployment when savings are equal to investment at a low level of economic activity. The concept of involuntary unemployment is not part of classical theory, but is an innovation of Keynes.[71] It is clearly defined in such a way as to give it the role that Keynes's theory requires:

> *Men are involuntarily unemployed if, in the event of a small rise in the price of wage-goods relatively to the money-wage, both the aggregate supply of labour willing to work for the current money-wage and the aggregate demand for it at that wage would be greater than the existing volume of employment.*[72]

Defined in this way, it is no more than a theoretical convenience, inaccessible to empirical observation. The concept of the rate of interest as 'the reward for not hoarding' is similarly convenient to the theory. Keynes is able to follow just those trains of cause and effect set up through his definitions that demonstrate how his theory is fulfilled. Whether they hold in an actual economy is a different matter. The function of definition is particularly apparent in Keynes, since he changes his definitions of income, savings and investment from his *Treatise on Money* to *The General Theory* in accordance with desired implications for savings and investment. The definitions of savings and investment in the *Treatise* make it possible for savings to be different from investment, but in *The General Theory* the definitions make them necessarily equal.[73]

The definitions have also the effect of selecting certain aspects of a situation as of predominant importance, while other phenomena are diminished to the point of irrelevance. Technology in particular is diminished by this means – the important interactions take place 'in a given state of technique'.[74] In effect, 'investment' is defined in such a way as to preclude any considerations relating to technology. But investment is the embodiment of technology and technological innovation. It is scarcely coherent to write about investment without considering the role of technology, especially when the main concern is the effects of investment on employment. Technological innovation has had major impacts on employment, both positive and negative. As was seen in Chapter 5, technology and company format are the driving force behind the evolution of economies. Technology all but disappears from Keynes's analysis, since it is not favoured with definition, does not feature in his concept of 'investment' and does not become part of a chain of cause and effect. The definitions are like secure stepping stones in a pond. Anyone skipping across the stones inevitably arrives at Keynes's appointed place.

It was seen in an earlier section of this chapter that 'confidence' plays a large part in the performance of financial services organisations. Keynes also emphasises the importance of confidence. He notes:

> The *state of confidence*, as they term it, is a matter to which practical men always pay the closest and most anxious attention. But economists have not analysed it carefully and have been content, as a rule, to discuss it in general terms.[75]

As has been seen, Keynes's idea of confidence is subsumed into what seems, at first acquaintance, to be a technical measure, the 'marginal efficiency of capital'. Keynes emphasises that assessment of capital returns is necessarily done on the basis of very limited knowledge. Because of this limitation, people resort to a conventional assumption that existing trends will be maintained. In markets for investment funds assessments may be very precarious:

> A conventional valuation which is established as the outcome of the mass psychology of a large number of ignorant individuals is liable to change violently as a result of a sudden fluctuation of opinion due to factors which do not really make much difference to the prospective yield.[76]

It was suggested earlier in this chapter that confidence is a matter of support. People feel confident when they are in a group that has reached accord on the issues confronting them. Without any distinctive theory of the creation of confidence, Keynes is obliged to subsume ideas of confidence in the marginal efficiency of capital. 'Confidence' is expressed in a discount rate. He specifically rules out any idea that the marginal efficiency of capital and the state of confidence are separate factors influencing the rate of investment, though in places he distinguishes between technical factors and confidence factors in determination of the marginal efficiency of capital.[77] He also, as noted above, recognises that the marginal efficiency of capital may suffer such 'enormously wide fluctuations' as a consequence of changing levels of confidence that levels of interest rates have little or no effect on the incentive to invest – in other words, confidence is the paramount factor in determining levels of economic activity. With the theory of support-bargaining, there is a basis for distinguishing the effects of confidence, and the effects of group formation, or the herd instinct, from the more analytical considerations that also form part of the assessment of a marginal efficiency of capital. Business analysts will quite commonly express estimates of returns on investment in terms of an 'optimistic' scenario and a 'pessimistic' scenario, thus separating, to some degree, the technicalities from the psychology. The analysts will express their assessment of an investment proposal in terms of a rate of return, and businessmen will take note. But many businessmen will make their decisions on the basis of their own assessment of the likelihood that the proposal will enhance the format of their company, making it more secure in fulfilment of the viability condition, and beyond that generating high profit. In this context the confidence or lack of it among businessmen will be expressed, along with their experience of the way their company format works and the threats arising from the formats of others. Businessmen may be read by economists as investing in accordance with assessments of the marginal efficiency of capital, but their investment decisions may be based pragmatically on assessments of the viability of formats.

The importance of confidence in determination of the marginal efficiency of capital means that the effects of changes in interest rates on investment will not be straightforward. In Keynes's theory, a rise in interest rates may give an immediate stimulus to savings, but that effect will at some point be overtaken by the income effect – the rise in interest rates will reduce investment, which will reduce incomes, which will reduce savings more than proportionately. But in his note on business cycles, as summarised above, Keynes recognises that businessmen may not react in this way. People interpret situations in different ways when they are confident and when they lack confidence. If the rise in interest rates arises from a surge in confidence among businessmen, they may still see the marginal efficiency of capital as attractive, and maintain or increase their investment. The marginal efficiency of capital appears as a technical measure and secure in its function, but its psychology, its dependence on confidence, means it will not perform the theoretical role required of it. As the Marshalls imply, confidence itself is the critical factor. The marginal efficiency of capital is a slippery stepping stone. Keynes's insistence that the marginal efficiency of capital and the state of confidence are not separable with regard to their influence on investment suggests that he was aware of the difficulties for his theory in a distinction between technical and psychological factors.

It was suggested at the start of this chapter that money, budgets and financial services in general are essentially concerned with time shifting between revenues and outlays. Keynes's definitions are often ambiguous with regard to time. The marginal efficiency of capital involves assessment of future returns. Liquidity preference arises from considerations of temporal requirements for funds. But the crucial effects of a rise in interest rates on investment, incomes and savings are not given any clear time dimension. A distinction is made between changes in investment that are foreseen, so that consumption industries have a ready response, and unforeseen changes. In the former case time is not accounted a considerable factor. In the latter case Keynes acknowledges that time delay is important in certain contexts, in particular in relation to trade cycles, but suggests that it does not affect the significance of the theory of the multiplier.[78] The issue of the significance of time is, in effect, downplayed, if not brushed aside. A new equilibrium could take years to emerge, and there is no account of the relationships between savings and investment in the intervening time. A change in the rate of interest is likely to affect savings directly before it affects incomes. In a system of cyclical trade, the crossover point where the income effect exceeds the direct effects of interest rates on savings might occur quickly or not at all. In an evolutionary context, there are probabilities and possibilities, but no necessary outcomes. Each emergent situation is the basis for decisions that create a new situation. The effects of a change in interest rates, and their timing, would, furthermore, depend on the situation which prompted the change in interest rates. Liquidity preferences and changes in the quantity of money are, as has been seen, the immediate determinants of interest rates in Keynes's theory. Keynes introduces a time factor when it is convenient, but skimps on the significance of time when it is not. The neglect runs through neoclassical theory, reaching its absurd apogee, as was seen in Chapter 3, in the instantaneous occurrence of all transactions in the Arrow–Debreu model. People employ money, budgets, savings and investments to deal with time as a central factor in their lives. Any train of cause

Savings and investment

The relationship between savings and investment and the way they adjust to each other are central to Keynes's theory. As has been seen, in Keynes's theory, savings adjust to investment through the changes in income induced by changes in investment. For this adjustment to function smoothly, savings have to be understood as the residual of income after consumption requirements have been met.

Keynes takes this definition of savings to be common understanding, at least among economists: 'So far as I know, everyone is agreed that *saving* means the excess of income over expenditure on consumption,' adding later that, 'It would certainly be very inconvenient and misleading not to mean this.'[79] People do not so much choose to save as choose to consume, and what they do not spend on consumption is saving. For Keynes, issues surrounding the balance of savings and investment are best understood by treating saving as residual: 'Clearness of mind on this matter is best reached, perhaps, by thinking in terms of decisions to consume (or to refrain from consuming) rather than of decisions to save.' To end his chapter on 'The Definition of Income' he writes: 'the conception of the *propensity to consume* will, in what follows, take the place of the propensity or disposition to save'.[80] Even when Keynes lists motivations for what is obviously 'saving', it is in the context of subjective factors relating to the propensity to consume. He classifies them as motives to 'refrain from spending'.[81] When a company retains income, Keynes recognises that the motive is investment or other interests of the company, but still they are motives that, 'favour the withholding of a part of income from consumption'.[82] For his theoretical mechanism to function, savings have to be residual income after consumption, and he argues at length the case for recognising savings in this way.

In support-bargaining and money-bargaining 'situation' is the determinant of interests and requirements. Decisions are made by reference to situation. This extends to decisions on savings. The requirements of situation will be effected through budget management. Related to their assessment of situation, people will budget in such a way as to keep certain sums of money immediately available, certain sums accessible in the short term and other sums accessible only after the elapse of considerable time. An 'emergency fund' will be immediately available. Savings for a holiday will be set aside so as to be available when holiday costs become due. People burdened with high rental charges for accommodation may save over a few years to accumulate the deposit needed to purchase a house. Long-term saving may be used to cover future necessities, such as pensions, when there are no budget revenues from employment, but a continuing requirement for consumption expenditure. Some saving will be made principally with a view to the returns it provides, and is likely to be referred to as 'investment'. It is 'financial investment' rather than 'fixed investment', but has much of the purpose of fixed investment, in that it will generate future returns. Much saving is done through regular payments into savings funds, translating regular outlays into future lump sums or future income streams. Saving forms an essential part of the budgetary process whereby time disparities between revenues and expenditures are reconciled. Lacking any concept of personal budgeting or budget management, Keynes's 'classical' theory cannot recognise the central importance of saving.

A certain level of saving is as desirable in most situations as a certain level of consumption, so it seems inappropriate to treat savings entirely as residual. In any listing of priorities for budgetary outlays, items of consumption will be mingled with savings. Some items of food, clothing and shelter will be given the highest priority, but other items will come below the requirement for pension saving and holiday saving. There are savings that are specifically provided for in most household budgets. There may be, in the outcome, a budget surplus, as a result of lower outlays than budgeted or higher revenues. This may be regarded as 'residual', and constitutes savings if the only two categories are 'consumption' and 'savings'. It is easily understood as 'unbudgeted savings'. But a budget surplus clearly has different implications in terms of both relationship to situation and budget management from budgeted savings. A budget deficit is the negative counterpart to a budget surplus and has implications that mean it would not normally be classified as 'negative savings'. The classifications 'budget surplus' and 'budget deficit' are not available in 'classical' theory because there is no concept of personal budgeting. The essential saving is a matter of situation-related selection; a matter of conscious volition and a matter of budget provision.

Because saving is situation related, and savings are made to meet various different situations, there is a corresponding variety of savings options for individuals and companies. If 'savings' were all the same, as implied when they are merely a residual of income after consumption, there would be no need for all the different savings options. Financial services companies format for the provision of savings options that fall into the bargaining sets of savers – that is, meet the situation-related requirements of savers.

The savings made by budget provision are unlikely to be equal to the investment that businessmen find appropriate by reference to their business situations. What people want to save, plus what they are obliged by law to save (see below), are unlikely to be equal to what businessmen think it wise to invest, moderated in accordance with what bankers are prepared to finance. Savings become equal to investment only when savings are defined wholly as the residual of income after consumption. Keynes's dynamic of savings adjusting to equal investment through changes in income is then conceivable. Keynes's treatment of savings as entirely residual is, as he recognises, convenient to his theory regarding the effects on employment of balance between savings and investment at different levels of output, but it does not well represent the dynamics of saving. The faithful representation of observed phenomena is subordinated to the requirements of a model. Categorisation in terms of budgetary outlays, based on the situation-related motivation of money-bargaining theory, makes it possible to discern the different forms of saving and their different implications for the functioning of economies.

The bulk of savings will be budgeted savings, since most people will spend all or nearly all the funds available after provision has been made for identified future requirements. A substantial part of budgeted savings will be aimed at provision for pensions, and hence will be locked up for long periods. The importance of pension funds gives the financial services companies that handle them considerable influence in the allocation of investment finance.

In money-bargaining savers and investors base their decisions on different situation references, whereas in the Keynesian dynamic savings and investment are elements of an integrated model generating equilibrium at different levels of output. In Keynes's system, savings are brought into balance with investment through changes in incomes. In money-bargaining budgeted savings and investment evolve from situation to situation, with no necessary match between the two. Investors assessing the situation in such a way as to indicate that investment is unlikely to produce returns, or finding that loan finance is difficult to acquire, will restrict their investment and slow the rate of growth of incomes and output. Companies will take steps to reduce their unit costs and keep prices down. Those wanting employment are likely to reduce their requirements for remuneration in order to retain or gain employment. But if such adjustments do not take place, or if they take too long, unemployment will arise.

The Keynesian equilibrium of savings and investment achieved through changes in incomes is commonly presented as a matter of 'planned savings' adjusting to investment, so that 'actual savings' are equal to actual investment.[83] In *The General Theory*, however, it is only consumption that is a matter of volition. Savings are a consequence of not consuming. The propensity to consume dictates savings. In money-bargaining, savings are unambiguously planned, or budgeted, but planned by reference to situation and, consequently, unlikely to match requirements for investment funds. As has been seen, Keynes also accounts investment as the residual of output after consumption, but he provides also the mechanism of the marginal efficiency of capital as the motivation for investment. Equilibrium is more readily understood if savings and investment do not both have independent motivations. The one can then adjust to the other.

National income accounts follow the Keynesian concept of savings as wholly a residual of income after consumption. This approach is partly a consequence of the practical difficulties in assembling direct data on savings. The accounts consequently do not directly record a category 'savings'. In the accounts, savings are equal to investment as a matter of definitional and mathematical necessity.[84] The accounts do not reflect the motivational dynamics of savings. The tail wags the dog if the behaviour of an economy is understood only by reference to its accounts. This 'confirmation by accounts' is an aspect of 'confirmation by definition' and the general confirmation of theory by the selection it gives rise to.

Keynes's 'marginal propensity to consume' is clearly situation related. When people are sufficiently fed and clothed, they may well choose not to increase their expenditure on food and clothes in the same ratio as their income increases. However, in many situations they may choose to consume a higher proportion of incremental income. It was suggested above that most people spend all their remaining income on consumption after providing for identified future requirements. Rather than savings being a residual after consumption, some consumption is residual after savings. This refers to the majority of people whose consumption is restricted by low or moderate incomes, which nevertheless enable them to make essential savings. When their incomes rise, they are very likely to spend a large proportion of the increment on consumption. Conversely, when their incomes fall, consumption may fall by a larger proportion than savings. The income effect envisaged by Keynes, in which consumption is maintained as income falls, to the detriment of the proportion of income going to savings, is likely to apply only to those with the lowest incomes. Defining savings as a residual after consumption leads to an assumption that people generally will give consumption priority in their spending decisions.

There can also be a cyclical influence on the marginal propensity to consume. Keynes associates increases in income with increases in employment, and because the propensity to consume falls as income increases, he holds also that the propensity to consume will fall as employment increases.[85] But high levels of employment imply strong bargaining positions for employees, potentially giving them the confidence to spend on consumption. If a nation is in a buoyant mood, and there is little risk of unemployment, and budgets look healthy, people may splash out on high-value consumption, such as fitted kitchens and new cars. In the upswings of trade cycles, when employment is high, there is commonly a fall in savings ratios. People feel so confident that they draw on their savings for purposes of consumption. The critical determinant of consumption and saving is situation, understood in both a physical and conceptual sense. The understanding of situation is affected by individual and communal confidence. Keynes stresses the importance of confidence, but confines it entirely to its role in determining the marginal efficiency of capital.

In many countries the state requires individuals to save in order to provide for the time when they are unable to earn. 'National provident funds' in various forms are used around the world, requiring people to set aside part of their incomes for the later provision of pensions. In effect, society, through the state, takes over from individuals the responsibility for assessment of situation and determination of the savings that ought to be made. All individual assessments of situation are influenced by support-bargaining. People tend to understand their situation in terms of what their associates approve, and will buy goods and services that match with what they take to be their own assessment of situation, but which is, in effect, a situation defined with substantial input from others. The social pressures tend to reinforce individual inclinations to spend on consumption, so that people may fail to take appropriate stock of their situation and how it is likely to develop in the future. They may fail to recognise the implications of old age. Most societies protect people from such failures. The motivation of society, of course, is more the avoidance of a future situation in which it is obliged, on grounds of its own humanitarian commitments, to finance people who should have accumulated their own savings to finance their old age. Budgeted savings include those savings which people themselves regard as necessary and the savings made obligatory by the state, though the administrative arrangements usually mean that the obligatory savings are made as deductions at source from income, without ever appearing as revenue in personal budgets.

Budgeted savings, volitional and obligatory, are unlikely to match the requirements for funds for business investment. Furthermore, budgeted savings are likely to be more stable than investment requirements. Much budgetary saving is done on a regular basis. People generally contribute to pension funds on a regular basis. Investment, by contrast, tends to be volatile, or at least cyclical. Financial services companies format in such a way as to accommodate these disparities. They accept savings in interest-bearing funds for varying periods at varying interest rates, mainly related to the term of the deposit. They are ready to accept deposits at any time and almost without limit. Their lending is dictated principally by the demand for credit, dictated, in turn, by levels of confidence of businessmen and consumers in the prospects for the economy. Banks provide credit at various interest rates based on assessed risk. Some financial services companies will utilise large sums for speculation on movements in exchange rates, interest rates and stock valuations. Financial services companies take up the options open to them to get the best returns, subject to conformity with regulatory requirements. But their main business, or at least their central role in the functioning of a money-bargaining system, lies in the provision of credit and the attraction of savings and 'ready money' deposits aligned in volume, time profile and risk with the credit they provide.

Liquidity preference, money and interest rates

Keynes introduces 'liquidity preference' as a primary determinant of interest rates. 'Liquidity preference' involves withholding money from interest-bearing funds, meaning that less money goes into such funds than would be the case without 'liquidity preference'. Hence 'liquidity preference' influences interest rates. Since savings are defined by Keynes as the residual after consumption, money held in liquid form still constitutes savings.

But Keynes's idea of 'liquidity preference' is perhaps most remarkable for its introduction of the ideas of money and exchange into 'classical' economic theory. As was seen above, in the 'classical' model money has no essential role.[86] Keynes develops his ideas in accordance with the classical idea, using 'wage-units' as the unit of account. But immediately after his exposition of liquidity preference he remarks, 'We have now introduced money into our causal nexus for the first time.'[87] One of the reasons why people have a liquidity preference is from a 'transactions-motive, i.e. the need of cash for the current transaction of personal and business exchanges'.[88] Not only is money introduced, but, along with it, the notion of exchange. The economy is no longer conceived purely in terms of the allocation of resources, but also in terms of monetary exchange. In other words, it becomes a money-bargaining system.

From the point of view of money-bargaining, however, the analysis is back to front. Keynes postulates an abstract model of resource allocation rendered more realistic by 'liquidity preference' arising from a transactions/exchange motive. But, in terms of money-bargaining, exchange is the fundamental of the system, and money is the bargaining counter by which exchange is facilitated. Money is the basic bargaining counter; whatever else happens is supplementary to this basic function. Economies in all their complexity have grown up around the use of money in exchange, not the other way round. Financial services related to savings and investment are an evolutionary growth of monetary exchange. Financial services companies format for the provision of savings and investment services, formulating their 'products' in accordance with the situations of those whom they recognise as potential clients. Investment on a substantial scale only becomes possible when there is money and money-bargaining, and the supplementary financial services to deal with savings and investment.

Keynes argues that liquidity preference and the quantity of money are the determinants of interest rates. As noted above, however, he introduces the idea of liquidity preference as a determinant of interest rates to escape what he regards as circularity arising if the marginal efficiency of capital is regarded as a determinant of interest rates. The marginal efficiency of capital depends partly on the scale of current investment and, hence, on the existing rate of interest, so Keynes rejects it as a determinant of interest rates, since that would imply it was at least in part a determinant of itself. The marginal efficiency of capital is, however, also determined by levels of confidence. A high marginal efficiency of capital deriving from high confidence will generate a high requirement for investible funds and will influence prevailing rates of interest. Again, as noted in connection with the effects of interest rates on investment and incomes, Keynes's insistence on the inseparability of confidence from the marginal efficiency of capital in the determination of investment suggests some awareness of the implications of a distinction between the technical and psychological elements of the marginal efficiency of capital. If confidence is an independent influence on the level of investment, then it is also a determinant of interest rates.

The designation of liquidity preference as a determinant of interest rates implies that people are reluctant to part with their money and have to be paid interest to induce them to do so. Certainly, interest constitutes an important inducement to save and to commit savings to interest-bearing funds. Keynes's approach, however, diminishes the significance of the positive motivation to save. Keynes builds 'liquidity preference' as a focus of attention over several pages, analysing the reasons why people might prefer liquidity.[89] 'Liquidity preference' becomes the focal motivation, while other savings are just a consequence of not consuming. This drains the motivation from saving. The role of saving in the economy is diminished, just as the role of technology is diminished by Keynes's treatment of investment. Yet people have strong motivations for saving. It is integral to the time shifts involved in budget management. One implication of this is that interest rates are partly determined by the strength of the motivation to save. A low motivation to save will result in high interest rates, as financial service companies bid for funds required by their clients for investment purposes. But strong motivations to save will mean that interest rates can be much lower.

The bargaining positions of financial services companies become stronger the stronger the motivations to save. Low interest rates payable on savings will permit financial services companies to offer low interest rates to their investor clients, and many more clients will find their company formats viable at the interest rates payable.

Motivations to save involve also dispositions to retain funds for different periods. As has been seen, some situations generate motives to lock savings away for years, or even, as in the case of pension saving, for decades. Financial services companies seeking to lend for purposes of long-term investment will find long-term savings better suited to their lending than short-term savings, and will pay higher interest rates for them. The level of interest rates in general will be determined by the levels of acceptance or rejection of the rates on offer from financial services companies to savers and investors.

Motivations to save include also the prospect of receiving income, earmarked for no specific purpose beyond that of providing future budget revenues. This is the saving referred to above as being likely to be described as 'investment'. The level of this saving will clearly be influenced by, and will influence, the level of interest rates. This motivation towards returns is apparent in 'speculation', a term generally applied to purchase of assets with a view to short-term increases in their prices, normally involving substantial risk. When asset prices move under a 'herd instinct', opportunities for profit naturally arise from anticipation of the moment when the herd changes direction. It was seen above that some financial services companies engage extensively in speculation. Keynes identifies the 'speculative motive' as one of the general motives for liquidity preference, and an important influence on interest rates.[90] Funds used in short-term speculation would certainly not be regarded as 'savings' in the ordinary sense of the term. They are more like the outlays of gamblers. In the explanation of movements in interest rates they do not seem a satisfactory substitute for the savings that are invested longer term in financial securities of various kinds. Keynes acknowledges that it is difficult to identify the influence of the speculative motive on liquidity preference, given the other factors involved. The influence on interest rates assumes that, in the absence of opportunities for speculation, they would be assigned to interest-bearing funds. They are, with that characteristic, in the same category as consumption. If money is not spent on consumption, it may be put in interest-bearing funds; consequently, consumption may be regarded as a major influence on interest rates. The alternatives always affect bargaining positions. In contrast, motivations to save and consequent levels of saving have a direct influence on interest rates. Keynes's theory of liquidity preference gives rise to neglect of important direct influences on interest rates.

Keynes's treatment of interest rates assumes, in accordance with 'classical' theory, that there is a seamless translation of savings into investment. It happens with the automaticity of neoclassical markets. The activities of what is now a huge global financial services industry, and what was in Keynes's time a very substantial industry, are thus set aside. The basic format for a financial services company involves the provision of investment funds and the attraction of deposits.

Financial services companies employ a range of expertise, including expertise relating to data processing, design of financial 'products', assessment of risk with very large sums of money, monitoring of financial transactions, conformity to extensive regulations and coordination of different functions. They 'mark up' the cost of their inputs, or at least the rate of interest paid to depositors, to give a 'price' to borrowers, the rate of interest required from borrowers, and adjust that price in accordance with the risks involved and the alternatives open to the borrowers. The 'mark-up' on the rate of interest to savers constitutes the spread of interest rates between saving and borrowing rates. Current interest rates (mid-2015) in the UK are at an historic low point, with the central bank reference rate at 0.5 per cent and the yield on government ten-year bonds just over 2 per cent. Savers in the UK are paid about 2 per cent on a two-year fixed rate deposit. People can borrow money for house purchase, with the house as security on the debt, at around 5 per cent. The rate on personal bank loans is around 4 per cent. In effect, savers and borrowers buy services related to savings and loans from financial services companies. Financial services companies have many different formats, involving different 'products', different depositors and different time periods of lending. But the format idea is the same as for other companies. A rate of interest is the 'unit cost' of money, so that a substantial part of their overall unit cost is the rate of interest on savings, while the 'price' of their output is the rate of interest charged to borrowers. Money-bargaining companies formatted for the provision of financial services operate profitably in provision of credit based on the situations of businessmen and the attraction of deposits contingent on the situations of savers.

The formats of financial services companies have important impacts on the conduct of financial affairs. It was seen above that the introduction of joint-stock banks in Britain following the financial crisis of 1825 affected the availability and price of credit. The introduction of limited liability further expanded their scope. Since then, formats have immeasurably increased in variety and complexity. Most recently, computer technology has greatly facilitated the processing, monitoring and communication of data and radically changed the formats of financial services companies. The formats of financial services companies have affected the forms taken by money. Metallic coins were supplemented by paper notes, and by entries in the ledgers of financial services companies. Their formats allowed financial services companies to transfer money between themselves on the instructions of the owners of the money they held on account. Digital technology has further changed the forms in which money is used.

Keynes's treatment of savings as the residual of income after consumption and his emphasis on 'liquidity preference' do not provide a satisfactory account of the dynamics of saving and the determination of interest rates. They both derive from the attempt to modify 'classical' theory while retaining as much of it as possible. With the notion of 'liquidity preference', however, Keynes touches on one of the most profound misconceptions of his 'classical' theory. Keynes 'discovers' money and exchange, and the reality of money-bargaining, when he escapes the 'classical' model and finds 'liquidity preference'. Money and exchange are the basis of economic systems, not the rational motivations and marginal calculations that supposedly give rise to equilibrium and the optimal allocation of resources.

Investment and money supply

These misconceptions of neoclassical and Keynesian theory may have led to a general misunderstanding among economists of the functioning of the monetary system and the role of the financial services industry. The role of the industry has been understood as a matter of intermediation between savings and investment, with commercial banks permitted to supplement savings by lending more than the savings they hold, subject to maintenance of certain ratios relating to liquidity and equity finance. According to the Bank of England, such arrangements are commonly described in textbooks, but do not reflect accurately the functioning of the monetary system.[91]

Instead, the Bank describes a system in which commercial banks create deposits through their provision of credit. Deposits are destroyed by the reverse process, the repayment of credit. In creating deposits the commercial banks create money, so that a variation in money supply is the net outcome of the provision and repayment of credit in any period. Rather than savings being the source of investment funds, the sequence of activity runs the other way: provision of credit for investment expands deposits and money supply.

Commercial banks are not constrained in their provision of credit by considerations of the ratio of their lending to their reserves at the Bank of England. Rather, reserves are expanded as deposits increase as a necessary part of the conduct of their business. Commercial bank reserves are not entirely 'reserves' in the sense of being held to meet contingencies, but working deposits that are shifted from bank to bank as payments in accordance with transactions of their depositors. The Bank of England provides reserves 'on demand' in normal times for commercial banks in return for other assets.[92] Commercial banks must, nevertheless, observe certain liquidity requirements laid down by the central bank.

A bank will not necessarily retain the deposits it creates in providing credit. It must then attract deposits from other consumers in order to protect the level of its reserves and meet obligations to other banks. Inability to attract deposits would imply incapacity to pay for them at prevailing interest rates. A bank may also sustain its lending by attracting non-deposit liabilities to maintain the balance of assets and liabilities. A prudential regulatory framework established by the central bank imposes constraints on the structure of banks' liabilities in relation to their lending and other assumption of risk.

The main influence of the Bank of England on the financial system is exercised through its setting the interest rate on commercial bank reserves. This rate influences the rates charged by banks for credit and paid on deposits. Hence it influences the demand for credit.

This account of the functioning of the monetary system is consistent with the theoretical account provided above of savings and investment in a money-bargaining system. Investment is not directly dependent on savings, but is determined by the situation-related requirements of borrowers and the assessments by banks of the viability of proposals at the rates of interest they can offer. Savings are determined by the needs of consumers to set aside current revenues for future expenditures, based on assessments of their circumstances. A time profile of savings is established by reference to the different purposes of savings and the interest rates offered on different term deposits. Requirements for 'ready money' are held in sight deposits, often without interest. The two are connected, in reverse, by competition among banks for the deposits created by the provision of credit. While the sequence of activities runs from credit provision or credit repayment to savings, the obligations of banks to match liabilities to assets means that there are constraints on the provision of credit by any bank related to its deposit and non-deposit liabilities. The 'sequencing' may be better understood in terms of accommodation of credit, deposits and non-deposit liabilities in the balance sheets of banks, and within that the accommodation of savings of various types and investment of various types.

The large sums saved for the provision of pensions go mostly to specialist financial organisations. These constitute a simple intermediation process of savings to investment, since they invest the funds they receive directly, and cannot create money as commercial banks do. The process of quantitative easing introduced in the United Kingdom to expand money supply when interest rates could be reduced no further and investment was still sluggish is, as described by the Bank of England, an intervention in this direct intermediation that has the effect of expanding money supply.[93]

The role of government

'Classical' theory is microeconomic theory dealing entirely with private economic activity as a process of optimal resource allocation. There is no role for government. Extended to the macroeconomic sphere, it provides the justification for policies of *laissez faire*. It suggests that resources will be optimally allocated when governments refrain from engagement. Keynes makes extensive reference to the engagement of governments in economic affairs, but government intervention takes place outside the main theoretical context of Keynes's analysis. The analysis of the effects of interest rates on income and savings assumes that the macroeconomy is an aggregate of private economic transactions as represented in the model. No account is taken of the difficulties of extending microeconomic theory to the macroeconomic sphere, as discussed in Chapter 3.

On the basis of his analysis of the movement of economies to equilibrium at less than full employment, Keynes makes recommendations for the engagement of government in economic affairs. As noted above, his main recommendation is that governments take over responsibility for investment, ensuring that it is sufficient to stabilise an economy at full employment. Communal savings are to be used, involving high rates of taxation, to finance the investment. In effect, Keynes concludes that the private 'classical' economy does not work in the national interest, and needs to be replaced by state initiatives. His prescription arises, however, from the misunderstanding of economic processes embedded in 'classical' theory.

In Keynes's 'classical' system an economy is conceived in terms of supply and demand for homogeneous factors of production, consumer goods and investment goods adjusting to equilibrium through price changes dictated by marginal choices. What happens is largely automatic, given the rationality of the individuals concerned. 'Firms' expand production until marginal revenues are equal to marginal costs. Because all elements are small in relation to the aggregates, prices are determined independently of any particular 'firm'. The system makes 'investment' a matter of small homogeneous units falling into place in accordance with the marginal efficiency of capital, understood largely in a technical sense. In such aggregated and abstract form, 'investment' is part of the clockwork of the classical system. With that understanding, it is easy to conceive that governments might take over the investment functions of 'firms'. They might fulfil them better because, according to Keynes, governments are better placed than private investors to make sound assessments of the long-term marginal efficiency of capital. They might also fulfil them better because they would not duplicate investment and thus waste money.

For Keynes, the 'entrepreneur' represents the function of the firm, but the entrepreneur is no more than a personification of the process by which classical firms operate.[94] While classical theory emphasises the similarity of economic transactions and, hence, classical theorists are content to deal with undifferentiated aggregates, the process of selection by reference to situation in money-bargaining differentiates transactions. Though there are similarities of situation, none are the same. The investment that is part of the format of a company targeting buyers' bargaining sets is consequently also diverse. Companies are the leading bargaining agencies of money-bargaining systems and have the central role in determining what investment will generate returns, or will contribute to viable formats. Successful companies differentiate themselves from others in order to build bargaining position and viable format. Capital investment is an important element in the differentiation, particularly because it involves introduction of technology. The ingenuity of many private businessmen and their acceptance of risk to their own money are necessary to effective investment. It is immediately apparent that government is no substitute for companies, except at the sort of cost incurred by the Soviet Union.[95] The civil servants who Keynes seems to suggest might control investment might be good economists and might be good at discounting cash flows, but they could not conceivably perform the functions of companies. The costs of duplication and business failures are offset by the growth generated by many independent investment decisions. The evolutionary process involves failure as well as success; the successes generate the evolutionary advance.

The pursuit of viable format tends to produce companies of large size, since scale of production is an important determinant of unit costs. The largest companies in an industry tend to have the lowest unit costs and set the pace with regard to pricing in the industry. They make the large investments that are important to the evolution of economies. They often have the capacity to finance technological research while maintaining unit costs within the confines of a viable format. Consequently they often introduce the most advanced technology. It was seen in Chapter 3 that companies are quite commonly of such size as to give them an important influence on the movement of macroeconomic aggregates. Far from being so small as to be 'invisible' in the workings of markets, as in classical theory, companies can have major impacts on particular markets and on the growth of economies. As was seen, Alfred Chandler's study of industrial development identified the impact of large companies on economic growth:

> But in the history just told the modern industrial enterprise played a central role in creating the most technologically advanced, fastest growing industries of their day ... Therefore the enterprises whose collective histories have been reviewed here provided an underlying dynamic in the development of modern industrial capitalism.[96]

It is scarcely conceivable that governments would be able to take over the investment role to bring demand up to the level required for full employment when such large and complex investments play so great a role in the growth of economies. That Keynes could conceive it so is a measure of the distance between his theory group and the realities of economic evolution.

Keynes's analysis indicates that the classical expectation of automatic full employment in an economy will not come about because savings adjust to investment through changes in incomes rather than directly through interest rates. Equilibrium may come about at lower incomes than those required for full employment. The remedy is then to boost demand and lift incomes, so that equilibrium is achieved at full employment. Keynes accordingly advocates that governments should borrow money and spend to make good the demand deficiency. Government is conceived, in this case, as an external agency that can rescue an economy from ill effects arising from processes not taken into account in the classical model.

But money-bargaining involves an entirely different dynamic, so that Keynes's justification for government spending loses application. Failure to achieve full employment cannot be attributed to any mechanistic failure. Full employment is not a necessary outcome of an evolutionary money-bargaining system. Something more than a deficiency of demand is involved in underemployment. The attainment of full employment requires the successful format of many companies and the establishment of conditions in which this can be achieved.

The role of government is then the effective performance of the integral part it plays in the evolution of money-bargaining systems. Governments must provide the communal amenities and regulations necessary for the functioning of money-bargaining systems. Provision has to evolve to accommodate emerging situations and create opportunities for successful format of companies. Government budgets have to be managed in such a way as to ensure provision of these amenities as they are needed. Stable and strong public finances are an essential part of the evolution of a money-bargaining system. Governments are also responsible for regulation of money-bargaining to facilitate its expansion and protect against adverse communal consequences of private initiative. Governments must ensure regulation of money supply in accordance with the requirements of traders. They must also regulate the provision of financial services in such a way as to meet requirements for credit and maintain confidence in the financial system. Governments of countries engaged extensively in international trade must also establish regulations governing trade and the setting of exchange rates. Government is an integral part of the evolution of a money-bargaining system set in the broader context of a support-bargaining system. What a government does is contingent on what it already does, the changing situation in which it operates and the support it receives.

The sensitivity of support to levels of unemployment gives governments an incentive to use their capacity to borrow and make budgetary expenditures to boost employment. The cyclical movement in money-bargaining, irregular as it is, results in frequent calls on governments to spend for the reduction of unemployment. Business cycles, however, are a consequence of the tendency of businessmen to act on tides of group opinion, affecting bargaining positions in the money-bargaining system. In the upswing growth is strong and high levels of sales are relatively easy to maintain. Control of unit costs becomes weaker. In the downturn weaknesses of format become apparent and it is necessary to focus attention on reductions in unit costs and adjustments of format. Government deficit-financed expenditure potentially so strengthens the bargaining positions of companies that they find themselves under no obligation to protect the viability of their formats by reducing unit costs and restoring sales through their own ingenuity. Unit costs are likely to increase, and with them prices. These effects are likely to be particularly significant in those industries that do not compete with imported goods. In industries with a high level of competing imports, the stimulus to demand is likely to stimulate imports as much as, or more than, domestic production. With no corresponding stimulus to export demand, the balance of trade is likely to deteriorate. The British economy hobbled along in the 1960s and 1970s with 'Keynesian' government expenditures to raise employment, apparently relieving industry of the necessity of dealing with the constant escalation of costs due to trade union bargaining strength, and inducing recurrent balance of payments crises.[97] More generally, periods of deficit-financed expenditure designed to reduce unemployment, without offsetting budgetary surpluses in times of high employment, have led to the accumulation of high levels of debt in many nations. Governments do what they are supported to do, but that will often cause them to take actions that are damaging to the evolution of a money-bargaining system, especially when the return in support is immediate, while the damage emerges in the longer term.

As was seen above, Keynes suggests that the promotion of employment might be achieved through the building of pyramids if the predispositions of statesmen precluded any other approach. The suggestion may be light-hearted, but apparent lightness of heart often veils a degree of confusion. Keynes appears to base his argument for deficit financing of employment creation on economic grounds – for the involuntarily unemployed, labour may have positive marginal utility rather than disutility.[98] For this reason, building of pyramids might increase national wealth. Even burying banknotes and leaving private companies to dig up the notes might be used to increase national wealth.

But such measures are predicated also on political advantages: 'It would, indeed, be more sensible to build houses and the like; but if there are political and practical difficulties in the way of doing this, the above would be better than nothing.'[99] It is odd that 'political and practical difficulties' are regarded as potentially standing in the way of building houses rather than constructing pyramids or burying banknotes, but if that were the case, there would be political advantage in building pyramids or burying banknotes instead. Keynes confuses economic and political rationales in an attempt to justify what might be regarded as absurd.

There is a deeper confusion of economic and political rationales in Keynes's theory. The concern for full employment, which is the basis of the theory, is apparently a matter of resource allocation and 'increasing national wealth'. No other motivation or justification is required in the 'classical' understanding. The economic system functions independently of any political system. But, if an economy fails to generate full employment, it is a matter of political motivation and judgement whether government budgetary expenditures should be incurred for the restoration of full employment. That is, it is a matter of support-bargaining. In the Depression of the 1930s, the need for increased employment would scarcely be queried. But it has to be recognised that the paramount interests and motivations related to the maintenance of support. If there is support to be had from simply increasing employment, then any measures, including the construction of pyramids, will suffice. From a purely technical economic standpoint, full employment is no more desirable than full use of land.

In the context of a support-bargaining system, further considerations become apparent. Governments will lose support if they engage in apparently useless projects such as the construction of pyramids or burying banknotes. Yet, at the same time, people may well tolerate the construction of houses, ports or roads, whose justification is, in part, the creation of employment. The projects may not top the list of priorities for immediate government investment on the basis of their longer-term economic impact, but they are likely to be seen as useful because, in addition to their immediate short-term and short-lived stimulus to employment, they also provide some longer-term economic benefits.

It is conceivable that in some societies the building of pyramids will be seen as essential to national well-being. In those societies, if such construction is recognised as a matter for government engagement, governments will raise support by construction of such buildings. Those who wish to see evolution of a money-bargaining system will, however, point out that the benefits of such edifices accrue only in an afterlife. In this life they do little to extend money-bargaining systems. The employment required to build them lasts only over the construction phase. The incomes paid for construction will provide some stimulus to local business, but are similarly short-lived. Pyramids once built do not generate sales, as would construction of a port; they do not create opportunities for the format of companies, as does infrastructure. As far as money-bargaining is concerned, they generate no evolutionary impulse. It is, of course, possible to construct ports and roads that have no evolutionary impulse. Ports without ships and roads without traffic are no better than pyramids. If a money-bargaining system is to evolve, the government has to ensure that a substantial part of its budget is expended on projects that promote the evolution of the money-bargaining system.

Keynes and intellectual support-bargaining

Keynes makes clear in his preface that *The General Theory* is addressed to economists.[100] He conceives knowledge and theory-making in terms of an intellectually elite theory group endowed with special skills in reason and mathematics applying itself to the identification of an absolute truth. He uses the technical language of an intellectual elite, with only the occasional 'lapse' into ordinary language. The definitions and high confinement of the theory have been acceptable to economists since neoclassical economics accepts similar limitations. The views of those who are not trained in the techniques of neoclassical economic analysis, such as businessmen, consumers and workers, even though they engage on a daily basis in economic activity, are of little or no account. People in these categories might regard technology as a crucial factor in the performance of an economy, but to mainstream economists, because of the model around which they focus their debate, it is acceptable that it should be put to one side.

As was seen in Chapter 3, Backhouse attributes the success of Keynes's theory to its establishment of a simple but effective theoretical framework for macroeconomic research. In particular, it created a framework for mathematical treatments of macroeconomic issues.[101] Keynes was an acknowledged leader of the mainstream economic theory group, based in Cambridge University – another of the oracular institutions of neoclassical theory. Loan finance had already been used by governments to finance public expenditure, with a rationale derived from theories of the business cycle. Keynes was concerned to reconcile such expenditures with the ideas of his own theory group. It was part of the competition inseparable from intellectual support-bargaining. Backhouse notes that younger economists were enthusiastic about it, while older economists thought much of his treatment oversimplified the issues. Young people tend to have the greater prowess in mathematics, while older people may have greater conceptual understanding and range. But the future lies inevitably with the young, so Keynesian economics developed the highest possible prominence in the years after the Second World War. It played a major part in the extension of mathematical treatments of economic issues, a trend that has subsequently intensified.

Perhaps few students will agree that it is 'simple', as Backhouse suggests, though it was propagated in simplified form, or at least in clarified form. The abstruse nature of Keynesian theory helped to isolate economics from the scrutiny of those outside the theory group. It gave economists an enviable gravitas and exclusivity, and hence a strong bargaining position as global purveyors of enlightenment. But intricacy and ambiguity are invariably indicators that preconceptions, the paradigm, are incapable of straightforward accommodation of the phenomena they are supposed to make comprehensible. The phenomena are 'welded' into conformity with the paradigm by subtle selection and attribution of features, including tendentious definition. When the preconceptions are sound, the phenomena fall easily into place. The patterns, or symmetry, give a sense of understanding. Keynes was an ingenious 'welder', but he worked on the wrong paradigm.

In terms of intellectual support-bargaining, it was an unfortunate evolution of mistaken foundations. Although Keynes advocated a 'socialisation' of investment, that part of *The General Theory* was largely overlooked. Instead, emphasis was placed on his endorsement of the more general applicability of classical theory, subject to injections of government investment to make good 'demand deficiencies'.[102] It sustained the illusion of a largely self-adjusting system in which individuals would benefit society by pursuing their own self-interest without 'government interference'. Given the propensity of governments to borrow and spend, the theory provided welcome theoretical support for what was anyway their inclination. With such harmony of interest and theory, it was never necessary to know the precise relationship of 'savings' – that is to say, 'non-consumption' – to investment, or the level of 'involuntary unemployment'. As a residual in the national accounts, 'savings' was anyway a doubtful quantity, being necessarily a mixture of different categories of savings, and perhaps including some items not well classified as 'savings'. 'Involuntary unemployment' was a hypothetical state, indistinguishable from any other sort of unemployment. Unemployment of itself could be taken as justifying a 'Keynesian stimulus'. The escalation of national debts in the latter half of the twentieth century and into the twenty-first century is attributable in large measure to the theoretical justification given by Keynes for the spending propensities of governments. Keynes recognises in his preface that the divergence of opinion among economists over the causes of the post-1929 Depression, 'have for the time being almost destroyed the practical influence of economic theory, and will, until they are resolved, continue to do so'.[103] The failure of classical economics to explain the Depression seemed to threaten the continued prestige of the profession. Keynes lifted the threat. It might be said that he resurrected the mainstream economists' theory group, though it was done at some cost to the proper understanding of economies.[104]

Hub of the wheel

As was seen in the opening paragraph of this chapter, financial services play a central role in an economy, affecting all industries. They are the hub that provides money and credit to the wheel of industry. If banks fail, their clients may fail. If the whole financial services system fails, the whole economy contracts. Because it has such a central role, it can seem appropriate that financial services are provided on a communal basis – that is, by the state. But the idiosyncrasies of politics and the drawbacks of bureaucracy make it doubtful whether the security of a financial services system would be enhanced by placing it entirely in the hands of the state. Furthermore, there is a need for vigour and innovation in the provision of financial services which is more likely to arise from competitive format of financial organisations.

Much of the evolution of financial systems has been the evolution of working compromise between the security and social responsibility that can be provided by state backing and the vigour and initiative that derives from competition. The state provides extensive regulation of the conduct of private providers of financial services, implying at least some protection of those involved against deception, fraud and evasion of obligations undertaken. People can provide and make use of financial services with some basic confidence that the deals they make will be fulfilled according to their expectations. The state also establishes an institutional basis for regulation of financial services provision, in the form of a central bank, with powers also to help financial services companies out of difficulties that might be deemed a threat to the system as a whole. These arrangements sustain confidence under which private financial organisations can operate. Public and private accommodation in the evolution of conditions under which private organisations provide extensive credit has been essential to the maintenance of the high rates of evolution of money-bargaining systems.

The risks have always been that, on the one hand, lack of sufficient government backing will so reduce confidence in financial organisations that companies will be starved of credit and, on the other hand, the idea that lending is so extensively guaranteed by the resources of government and its taxpayers that credit risks are minimal, leading to assumption of excessive risk. The volatility of understanding within the communities involved in provision and use of financial services, arising from the internal support-bargaining of those groups, means that the balance is always difficult to maintain. Central bankers try to ensure that the organisations they oversee run in the narrow channel between confidence and over-confidence, initiative and prudence. From time to time, they break out of this channel, with damaging consequences. Governments hold the line partly by leaving obscure the precise nature and degree of the backing they provide, so that financial communities gain confidence from the idea that some backing is provided, but at the same time act prudently for fear of finding that the supposed backing does not stretch as far as they had hoped. Central bank governors are required to express the ambivalence of the state with assurances of support that leave obscure the precise limits of that support. In the global financial crisis that emerged in 2007 governments found themselves obliged to meet the requirements of financial organisations for 'last resort' finance to a far greater degree than had ever been anticipated, such was the central importance of financial systems to the rest of their economies. The support-bargaining process provided a necessary way out of failures in the provision of financial services.

Government itself plays a major part as 'hub of the wheel' not only because of its role in maintaining confidence in financial systems and its indirect responsibility for their administration, but also because of its role in the provision of the communal amenities and services that make possible the working of a large money-bargaining system. This responsibility is evident in the large budgets of governments, controlled indirectly through support-bargaining systems. The size of government budgets, in relation to other money-bargaining organisations, and the actual and potential access of governments to tax revenues, make meaningful the backing that governments can give to financial systems. The large size of government engagement in money-bargaining means also that the credit requirements of governments, long and short term, are of significant size in relation to total credit provision and influence the evolution of the financial system.

While they play a major role in money-bargaining systems, the primary role of governments as support-bargaining agents means that their budgets are always principally directed by reference to the accumulation of support. The short-term interests of politics can be detrimental to the long-term health of a money-bargaining system. This is most particularly apparent in the accumulation of debt. Accumulation of debt faster than the rate of growth will increasingly impede the capacity of a government to provide other services and amenities through budgetary expenditure, since an increasing proportion of expenditure has to go on debt servicing. People are more likely to avoid and evade taxes if they think their money is not well spent. Any erosion of confidence in a government's financial management raises the risk of loss of confidence also in in the backing it provides to financial services. If the hub of the wheel is seen to be weak, the whole wheel may turn more erratically.

Notes

1 Spread, Patrick, 2012, 'The Evolution of Economic Theory: And some Implications for Financial Risk Management', *Real World Economics Review*, No. 61, 26 September, pp. 125–35.
2 Spread, Patrick, 2013, *Support-Bargaining, Economics and Society: A Social Species*, Abingdon and New York: Routledge, pp. 193–4.
3 See, for example, Begg, David, Fischer, Stanley and Dornbusch, Rudiger, 1984, *Economics*, British edition, Maidenhead: McGraw-Hill (UK), pp. 500, 522.
4 Mokyr, Joel, 2011, *The Enlightened Economy: Britain and the Industrial Revolution 1700–1850*, London: Penguin, p. 225.
5 Backhouse, Roger E., 1993, *Economists and the Economy: The Evolution of Economic Ideas*, 2nd edition, New Brunswick, NJ: Transaction, p. 122.
6 Ashton, T. S., 1968/1948, *The Industrial Revolution 1760–1830*, Oxford: Oxford University Press, pp. 82–3.
7 Backhouse, 1993, p. 122.
8 Mathias, Peter, 2001, *The First Industrial Nation: The Economic History of Britain 1700–1914*, Abingdon and New York: Routledge, pp. 321–2.
9 Mokyr, 2011, p. 227.
10 Mathias, 2001, pp. 322–3.
11 Backhouse, 1993, pp. 122–3.
12 Mathias, 2001, p. 324.
13 Thornton, Henry, 1802, *An Enquiry into the Nature and Effects of the Paper Credit of Great Britain*, London: J. Hatchard.
14 Backhouse, 1993, pp. 126–30.
15 Ashton, 1968/1948, pp. 76–9.

16 Ashton, 1968/1948, p. 87.
17 Ashton, 1968/1948, p. 87.
18 Mathias, 2001, p. 44.
19 Backhouse, 1993, p. 200.
20 Mokyr, 2011, pp. 397–8.
21 Mokyr, 2011, p. 224.
22 Chapman, S. D., 1979, 'Financial Restraints on the Growth of Firms in the Cotton Industry, 1790–1850', *Economic History Review*, Vol. 32, No. 1, pp. 50–69, p. 60. Quoted by Mokyr, 2011, p. 220.
23 Ashton, 1968/1948, p. 87.
24 Mathias, 2001, pp. 153–4.
25 Mokyr, 2011, p. 386.
26 Mathias, 2001, p. 152.
27 Morgenson, Gretchen and Rosner, Joshua, 2012, *Reckless Endangerment*, New York: St Martin's Griffin, pp. 11, 185.
28 Morgenson and Rosner, 2012, pp. 151–2, 158–9.
29 Morgenson and Rosner, 2012, pp. 138, 159.
30 Morgenson and Rosner, 2012, p. 165.
31 Morgenson and Rosner, 2012, p. 143.
32 Morgenson and Rosner, 2012, pp. 283–4.
33 Morgenson and Rosner, 2012, p. 282.
34 Morgenson and Rosner, 2012, p. 274.
35 Morgenson and Rosner, 2012, p. 285.
36 Morgenson and Rosner, 2012, pp. 135, 143.
37 Morgenson and Rosner, 2012, pp. 110–11, 124–33.
38 Morgenson and Rosner, 2012, pp. 175–6, 179, 252–3.
39 Spread, 2012, p. 132.
40 Backhouse, Roger E., 2002, *The Penguin History of Economics*, London: Penguin, pp. 211–19.
41 Marshall, A. and Marshall, M. P., 1994, *The Economics of Industry*, Bristol: Thoemmes Press, pp. 154–5. Quoted by Backhouse, 2002, p. 220.
42 Backhouse, 2002, p. 216.
43 Backhouse, 1993, pp. 175–6.
44 Backhouse, 2002, pp. 224–5.
45 Backhouse, 1993, pp. 177–8.
46 Backhouse, 2002, pp. 222–3.
47 Keynes, John Maynard, 1961, *The General Theory of Employment, Interest and Money*, London: Macmillan, New York: St Martin's Press. First published 1936.
48 Pigou, A. C., 1933, *The Theory of Unemployment*, London: Macmillan.
49 Keynes, 1961, p. 3, fn. 1.
50 For further comment by Keynes on classical theory, see Keynes, 1961, pp. 175–85.
51 Keynes, 1961, pp. 21–2.
52 Keynes, 1961, pp. 110–11, 184.
53 Keynes, 1961, p. 168.
54 Keynes, 1961, pp. 166–8.
55 Keynes, 1961, p. 135.
56 Keynes, 1961, p. 115.
57 Keynes, 1961, p. 61.
58 Keynes, 1961, p.184.
59 Keynes, 1961, pp. 174, 182.
60 Keynes, 1961, p. 249.
61 Keynes, 1961, p. 254.
62 Keynes, 1961, p. 320; see also pp. 221, 324–5.
63 Keynes, 1961, p. 378.

64 Keynes, 1961, pp. 372–81, p. 376.
65 Backhouse, 1993, p. 178.
66 Keynes, 1961, p. 129.
67 Keynes, 1961, p. 317.
68 Keynes, 1961, p. 320.
69 Keynes, 1961, p. 164.
70 Spread, 2013, pp. 154–6. For discussion of the propensity to select and define by reference to preconceptions, see Spread, Patrick, 2008, *Support-Bargaining: The Mechanics of Democracy Revealed*, Sussex: Book Guild, Chapter 11, Frames and Echoes.
71 Keynes, 1961, pp. 15–17, 21.
72 Keynes, 1961, p. 15. Original emphasis.
73 Keynes, 1961, pp. 60–1, 74, 77–9. See also Backhouse, 2002, p. 223.
74 Keynes, 1961, pp. 23, 24, 28, 245.
75 Keynes, 1961, pp. 148–9. Original emphasis.
76 Keynes, 1961, p. 154.
77 Keynes, 1961, pp. 147, 149.
78 Keynes, 1961, pp. 122–5.
79 Keynes, 1961, pp. 61, 74. Original emphasis.
80 Keynes, 1961, pp. 64–5. Original emphasis.
81 Keynes, 1961, p. 107.
82 Keynes, 1961, pp. 108–9.
83 See, for example, Begg *et al.*, 1984, pp. 447, 470.
84 See Keynes, 1961, p. 63.
85 Keynes, 1961, p. 120.
86 Cf. Keynes's comments on the role of money in classical theory, at Keynes, 1961, pp. 19–20.
87 Keynes, 1961, p. 173.
88 Keynes, 1961, p. 170.
89 Keynes, 1961, pp. 194–209.
90 Keynes, 1961, pp. 196–9.
91 McLeay, Michael, Radia, Amar and Thomas, Ryland, 2014a, 'Money in the Modern Economy: An Introduction', *Bank of England Quarterly Review,* March 2014, pp. 4–13; McLeay, Michael, Radia, Amar and Thomas, Ryland, 2014b, 'Money Creation in the Modern Economy', *Bank of England Quarterly Review,* March 2014, pp. 14–27.
92 McLeay *et al.*, 2014b, p. 16.
93 McLeay *et al.*, 2014b, pp. 21–5.
94 See, for example, Keynes, 1961, pp. 52–3, concerning the entrepreneur and the definition of income.
95 Cf. Spread, Patrick, 2004, *Getting It Right: Economics and the Security of Support*, Sussex: Book Guild, pp. 106–8.
96 Chandler, Alfred, 1990, *Scale and Scope: The Dynamics of Industrial Capitalism*, Cambridge, MA, and London: Belknap Press, p. 593.
97 See Spread, 2008, pp. 132–5.
98 Keynes, 1961, p. 128.
99 Keynes, 1961, p. 129.
100 Keynes, 1961, p. v.
101 Backhouse, 1993, p. 182.
102 Keynes, 1961, pp. 378–81.
103 Keynes, 1961, p. vi.
104 Thanks to Joe Pimbley of Maxwell Consulting, New York, for advice on monetary and sub-prime mortgage issues in this chapter. See also Pimbley, Joseph M. and McDevitt, Laurel, 2014, *Banking on Failure: Fixing the Fiasco of Junk Banks, Government Bailouts and Fiat Money*, New York: Maxwell Consulting.

8 The evolution of foreign trade

The defining feature of foreign trade is that it is trade between nations, or trade between different formal support-bargaining societies. Nations have been, for the most part, established by violence, or threats of violence, with their borders secured by armed force. Within the borders, order is initially maintained through armed force or the threat of it, but this increasingly gives way to the adoption of a support convention and the establishment of formal support-bargaining systems. The courses taken by nations are determined by their internal support-bargaining. Any differences between domestic and foreign trade must relate to the differences that arise from separation into distinct support-bargaining jurisdictions.

The interests taken into consideration in the formulation of national regulations regarding foreign trade are those of the various groups within a nation state. Regulations have to accommodate the interests of 'our people', 'our industry', 'our trade', 'our employment', rather than any wider interests. If the interests of other nations are taken into consideration, it is only by reference to their likely impact on domestic interests. If foreigners, especially well-armed foreigners, are likely to take offence at some regulatory measure, then the measure may be modified or dropped, implying that the risk of damage to domestic interests from foreign response is deemed too high a cost to pay for the measure. If foreigners are likely to retaliate against regulations that constrain trade by introducing similar measures of their own, then that will diminish the advantages of measures constraining trade. Each national support-bargaining system can regulate only its own side of transactions.

Internal support-bargaining produces regulations relating to domestic trade, as well as regulations relating to foreign trade. Contract laws, conditions of employment, environmental impact and many other aspects of trade are regulated through internal support-bargaining systems. All nations consequently have different internal regulations which their companies must follow. Because of the differences in regulations established by the different support-bargaining systems, foreign trade is inherently 'unfair'.[1] Companies can take measures to save on unit costs in one country that are not permitted in another.

Foreign trade was commonly seen, up to the nineteenth century, as a process of competition between nations for a fixed volume of business, or a volume of business that could only be increased by opening up new territories. Each nation carved out as big a share as it could of the available trading opportunities. As was seen in Chapter 5 in the context of the operations of chartered companies, competition involved a large measure of violent competition. British foreign trade was conceived in the eighteenth century as necessarily advanced through armed force. Occupation of a territory by armed force implied that its trade was largely secured to the occupying state. Trade treaties were negotiated on the assumption that the parties would use armed force to make good their commitments. Colonies brought the conduct of the affairs of the colonial people and territory under the jurisdiction of the support-bargaining system of the coloniser. British colonies were understood as opportunities for British companies to trade profitably under the protection of British armed force. The British East India Company combined the functions of trading, military coercion and government administration in a single organisation. Foreign traders were often forcibly excluded from trade with British colonies. The French and Dutch had to be kept out of British colonies, and they kept British traders out of their territories. Tea, sugar, spices, cotton, tobacco and many other exotic products were exported profitably to Britain from territories and along shipping routes secured by the East India Company, the British navy and the military.

Both the securing of territory and the regulations were designed to establish exclusivity of trade. In terms of bargaining theory, they were designed to establish strong bargaining positions for British companies. One of the major determinants of money-bargaining position is the availability of alternatives. Eliminate alternative sources of the same or similar products, and company format becomes easier and potentially more profitable. Using force to eliminate alternatives was an obvious expedient in a violent world, particularly for a nation with preponderant violent capacity. Regulations marked the positions which would be maintained by armed force.

Those European states that acquired colonies were able to establish regulations affecting the interests of the inhabitants of the colonies without taking into account to any great degree the interests of the colonials. The conduct of trade with the colonies was regulated in accordance with the interests of the domestic groups most strongly engaged with the domestic support-bargaining systems. In the case of Britain, this gave rise to severe restrictions on the economic evolution of the colonies. The restrictions were most strongly felt and resented in the settler colonies of North America. Production of steel, refining of iron and manufacture of finished products from iron were prohibited in the North American colonies in 1750.[2] The Navigation Acts restricted carriage of the trade of colonies to British ships. The exclusion of North American colonials from the British support-bargaining that obstructed the evolution of their economy fed an evolutionary stream that led to war and independence.

The violence associated with the conduct of international trade gradually diminished in the nineteenth century as the influence of that 'body of distinct economic theories' referred to by D. C. Coleman, mentioned in Chapter 6, was felt.

Trade, however, remained connected with the imperial territories of European powers. Rivalries over empires and trade played a part in the two world wars of the twentieth century. After the Second World War the General Agreement on Tariffs and Trade (GATT) was established to provide a regulatory basis for the conduct of international trade. GATT was based on the global support for the idea of 'free trade' accumulated largely on the basis of the theory of 'comparative advantage' propounded by David Ricardo, though 'escape' clauses were included. The period also saw the establishment of various international organisations designed to reduce international violence and facilitate the global development of economies and trade, forming, in effect, embryonic institutions for global support-bargaining.

The general confinement of support-bargaining systems to nation states is critical not only with regard to the conduct of foreign trade, but also in the formulation of the money budgets of trading nations. As was seen in Chapter 6, a government plays a major role in the money-bargaining of a state through its budget. Revenues for government budgets in Britain and many other states were very largely derived from tariffs on foreign trade. In the period 1700 to 1880 British governments derived in most years between 60 and 70 per cent of their annual revenues from Customs and Excise duties.[3] Tariffs on imports could be levied apparently without diminishing the incomes of any domestic group, and consequently without any loss of support for the government. Import duties fell on foreigners. If anything, the duties seemed advantageous to domestic interest groups, since they made foreign goods more expensive, and consequently enhanced the bargaining positions of domestic producers and employees. Import tariffs had also the important advantage of being generally easier to collect than inland taxes. High import tariffs were introduced in England in the late seventeenth century to finance the wars with France that lasted through to 1713. They were retained because they raised revenues for government and because influential groups benefited from them.

Smugglers were also beneficiaries. Popular opinion seems, in this instance, to have favoured free trade, regarding the high tariffs as unwarranted protection of the undeserving or unjustifiable exactions of spendthrift governments. Smuggling was a large-scale business. The smugglers followed the same practice as the 'legitimate' foreign traders in protecting their trade with armed force. Whole communities were involved, though for some this meant only looking the other way. It was said that a bale of wool could be moved all across Whitby by secret passages without ever going out of doors. The Commissioner of Customs for Scotland, Adam Smith, wrote to a friend in 1780 that on taking up office in 1778 he had examined the list of prohibited goods and found:

> to my great astonishment, that I had scarce a stock, a cravat, a pair of ruffles, or a pocket handkerchief which was not prohibited to be worn or used in Great Britain. I wished to set an example and burnt them all. I will not advise you to examine either your own or Mrs Edens apparel or household furniture, least you be brought into a scrape of the same kind.[4]

He concludes that, 'The sole effect of a prohibition is to hinder the revenue from profiting by the importation'. According to Peter Mathias, government requirements for revenue were the major impediment to the introduction of freer trade in the eighteenth and into the nineteenth centuries.[5] The growth in British foreign trade took place under conditions of substantial protection, diluted by smuggling, up to the mid-nineteenth century. One fortunate side-effect was that the British were too good at smuggling to succumb to Napoleon's embargo on trade.

Evolutionary acceleration and free trade

The success of the cotton format, in particular, set British businessmen and politicians thinking about the role of foreign trade in the nation's advancing prosperity. The format depended heavily on imports of raw materials and export of finished goods. Import of cheap raw materials with low duties enhanced the viability of the format. Exports provided the sales necessary to the use of the machinery that permitted a high volume of production at low unit cost. The lesson was easily learned: high-volume low unit cost production with export sales, coupled with imports of cheap raw materials, was a profitable arrangement that might be applied in other industries. The production of iron machinery was, at the same time, permitting investment in the production of a growing variety of manufactured goods that could be sold overseas. Trade on a selective basis appeared very profitable. Furthermore, if there was to be growth in exports, it was necessary that people overseas should have the money to buy. If they were given access to the British market for their raw materials in particular, and possibly whatever else they could produce, their earnings would potentially be spent with British companies, the world's leading manufacturers. In such circumstances, it might even be worth sacrificing some less profitable lines of business in order to take advantage of the expansion of the strong. The debate over trade in Britain reflected the potential for winners and losers in companies and industries.[6] Which was which was a matter of dispute.

There were clear winners in shipbuilding and shipping services. To the formats of cotton, iron and railways critical to the accelerated evolution of the British economy must be added, in this context of foreign trade, the two closely related formats of shipbuilding and shipping services. The two together did for international trade what the railways did for domestic trade. They expanded international bargaining sets, so that producers around the world, as well as in Britain, could format on the basis of international sales.

The value of shipping tonnages built and registered in Britain and built in Britain from 1815 to 1908, and the net value of shipping services for the same period, are shown in Table 8.1.

The value of ships constructed grew rapidly from the mid-1820s. This early expansion was followed from around mid-century by yet faster growth in output, including significant growth in the value of British-built ships registered overseas. The annual average value of tonnage produced in the period 1825–34 was £2 million. This had expanded to £17.9 million by 1875–84. Phyllis Deane and W. A. Cole

Table 8.1 Value of shipping tonnage built in Britain and net shipping services

£ million, annual averages

	Value of tonnage built and registered in UK	% change	Value of tonnage built in UK	% change	Implied value of British-built ships registered overseas	% change	Net shipping earnings from the rest of the world	% change
1815–24	1.9		2.0		0.1		9.7	
1820–9	1.7	−10.5	1.8	−10.0	0.1	0.0	9.3	−4.1
1825–34	1.9	11.8	2.0	11.1	0.1	0.0	9.9	6.5
1830–9	2.1	10.5	2.2	10.0	0.1	0.0	11.2	13.1
1835–47	2.5	19.0	2.6	18.2	0.1	0.0	12.9	15.2
1840–9	2.5	0.0	2.7	3.8	0.2	100.0	14.6	13.2
1845–54	3.2	28.0	3.5	29.6	0.3	50.0	16.5	13.0
1850–9	4.7	46.9	5.2	48.6	0.5	66.7	20.6	24.8
1855–64	6.8	44.7	7.9	51.9	1.1	120.0	28.6	38.8
1860–9	8.8	29.4	9.9	25.3	1.1	0.0	37.5	31.1
1865–74	11.6	31.8	14.6	47.5	3.0	172.7	46.6	24.3
1870–9	13.0	12.1	16.3	11.6	3.3	10.0	51.1	9.7
1875–84	14.9	14.6	17.9	9.8	3.0	−9.1	56.6	10.8
1880–9	13.8	−7.4	17.1	−4.5	3.3	10.0	58.7	3.7
1885–94	11.6	−15.9	14.5	−15.2	2.9	−12.1	57.3	−2.4
1890–9	12.4	6.9	16.0	10.3	3.6	24.1	59.1	3.1
1895–1904	14.0	12.9	18.7	16.9	4.7	30.6	64.1	8.5
1900–8	16.7	19.3	22.6	20.9	5.9	25.5	75.7	18.1

Notes: For sources used by Deane and Cole and the derivation of estimates, see notes to their table on p. 234 and text on p. 235; implied value of British-built ships registered overseas and % changes added.

Source: Deane, Phyllis and Cole, W. A., 1962, *British Economic Growth, 1688–1959*, Cambridge: Cambridge University Press, p. 234.

estimate that ship construction accounted for little more than 0.5 per cent of national income at the start of the nineteenth century, but by the 1860s it was probably more than 1 per cent of national income. At its peak in 1875–84 ship construction is estimated to have accounted for 1.6 per cent of national income. Seventeen per cent of this construction was for foreign owners. The surge in output in the 1840s involved increasing construction of iron ships. Construction of steamships overtook construction of sailing ships in the 1870s.[7] Construction in Britain was spurred on by technological innovations such as the multiple expansion engine and the steam turbine engine.[8]

The development of shipping services was perhaps even more remarkable. Growth rates were high, albeit lower than those for the value of ship construction. But the absolute value of net shipping services was significantly higher. In the peak period of shipbuilding, 1875–84, net average annual shipping earnings were more than three times the value of ships built, and they grew further in subsequent decades. It is estimated that net shipping earnings constituted about 4 or 5 per cent of national income in most of the 50 years from 1860, and more than 5 per cent in the period 1875–84.[9] Britain built the greatest proportion of the ships and provided the greatest part of the shipping services that were both instrumental and necessary to the major expansion of world trade that occurred from the mid-nineteenth century on. The scope of British provision of shipping services gave extensive opportunities for picking up return inbound freight, in addition to outbound freight, thus reducing unit costs of freight and increasing the chances of establishing profitable formats.

This dominance of British shipbuilding and provision of shipping services owed something, perhaps a lot, to the Navigation Acts. British shipbuilders and providers of shipping services built up contacts, expertise and volume of business through the near-monopoly accorded to them by the Navigation Acts for the carriage of British trade. With the exclusion of rivals, British companies developed strong bargaining positions in the provision of shipping. As British trade grew, it became more and more difficult for other providers of shipping services to establish and maintain viable formats without a good share of the trade into and out of British ports.

Adam Smith, in spite of his general advocacy of free trade, approved the Navigation Acts on strategic grounds. Smith gives the provisions of the Navigation Acts roughly as follows: 1) exclusion of non-British ships from trade with British colonies and British coastal trade; 2) prohibition of the import into Britain of many articles on non-British ships, except ships belonging to the country of origin of the articles. Articles imported on ships of the country of origin were subject to a double aliens duty; 3) prohibition on import of any products other than directly from their country of origin; 4) double aliens duty on salt fish and other sea products not caught by British ships. Smith notes that the provisions were aimed directly at combating the success of the Dutch in British colonial and other trade. When the first Navigation Act was passed under the Commonwealth in 1651 the Netherlands was the centre of a flourishing entrepôt trade in goods from outside Europe destined for European ports. Provision 3 restricted this trade.

The main fishermen in the North Sea were Dutch – hence provision 4.[10] The 1651 Act was declared void at the Restoration and replaced by Acts of 1660 and 1663. Smith notes that the restriction on import of goods on non-British ships would have the effect of curtailing exports of British goods on non-British ships, since foreign vessels wishing to export British goods would incur the costs of coming into British ports unladen. Smith argues that, even though Britain was not actually at war with the Dutch when the Navigation Acts were passed, there was a state of extreme animosity between them and, since security was necessarily the primary concern of any nation, the protection of British ships and seamen through the Acts was justified.

The German economist Frederick List, publishing in 1841, suggested that Smith's defence of the Navigation Acts on strategic grounds was merely expedient. It relieved Smith of the necessity of recognising that the Navigation Acts, plainly restrictive of trade, had been beneficial to the development of Britain's trade.[11] List argues that Britain's protective trade policies, including the Navigation Acts, built Britain's 'productive power'. In terms of bargaining theory, they provided opportunities for the format of companies and the evolution of strong company bargaining positions. The Navigation Acts were repealed in 1849, by which time competition from the Dutch was no longer a significant problem, though a new challenge had emerged from the USA. As is apparent from the data in Table 8.1, at the time of repeal Britain was entering its strongest phase of expansion in shipbuilding and had experienced two decades of rapid growth in the provision of shipping services.

The emerging concept of Britain as the exporter of manufactured goods and an importer of raw materials and the recognition that it might be advantageous to sacrifice some industries to foreigners in order to benefit others are most apparent in the controversy over the Corn Laws. Corn was the key commodity of the time, its price being, in large measure, a determinant of whether poor people could feed themselves adequately. The controversy was no doubt sharpened yet further because it brought into prominence that process identified in Chapter 5 as central to the evolutionary experience of the British economy: the transition from an economic and socio-political order based on land ownership to one based on companies. An Anti-Corn Law League was formed in 1839 in Manchester, led by Richard Cobden and John Bright, to campaign for the repeal of the Corn Laws. These laws kept the price of corn high by controls on the import of corn for the protection of landowners and farmers. Repeal of the Corn Laws promised lower prices of bread and other foods. The cash released by lower food prices might be spent on manufactured goods. But since wages were widely regarded as tied to the cost of food, there was also the prospect that a fall in the cost of food would be used to justify a reduction in nominal wages. The prospect of lower food prices was attractive to workers, though the associated prospect of a reduction in wages meant support from the working class was less than wholehearted. Agricultural labourers were also threatened with a decline in their employment and incomes as domestic corn production contracted. The attractions to manufacturers are apparent. Landowners heartily opposed the repeal.

The situation that precipitated evolution to free trade and the repeal of the Corn Laws was the trade depression of the late 1830s and early 1840s, the worst of the century. This focused the attention of politicians, businessmen, voters and workers, increasing their readiness to take risks on the outcome of free trade. Robert Peel was returned with a secure majority in parliament in 1841, with the 1840 report of a parliamentary Committee on Import Duties – firmly advocating a move to free trade – ready to hand. The budget of 1842 lowered the sliding scale of corn duties, along with other reductions in duties. The same budget also reintroduced income tax to compensate for the expected losses of revenue from reductions in tariffs. An immediate recovery in trade was easily attributed to the introduction of freer trade, so that it was possible to make further reductions in duties in the budget of 1845. The fortunes of landowners were further eroded with the abolition or reduction of duties on cattle, meat, fish and dairy products. In 1846, with vociferous campaigning by the Anti-Corn Law League, coupled with horrific agricultural failure in Ireland, the Corn Laws were repealed.[12] Keith Robbins, in his biography of John Bright, records that, 'In Rochdale, the victory was presented as one for the commercial and industrial classes against the great proprietors of the soil.'[13] The trade legislation of the 1840s retained some tariffs for strategic and other reasons, but was the main factor in the reduction of the average tariff level between 1820 and 1850 from about 60 per cent to about 20 per cent.[14] The new income tax was a successful response to the potential revenue losses arising from tariff reductions. More than that, it changed the basis of government finance. One evolutionary stream ran into another.

The outcomes of the free-trade legislation were not entirely as anticipated. The price of corn, the main focus of interest for those opposed to the Corn Laws, did not fall until much later in the century – around 1870. Prices of food in general did not fall. In some respects, however, free trade spectacularly fulfilled its promises. It gave overseas business people opportunities to format companies on the basis of sales to Britain. Prices of imported goods rose under the formats adopted, but the proceeds of sales swelled the budgets of overseas businessmen and employees. A considerable part of their new expenditure was, as had been foreseen, spent on British goods.[15] New opportunities arose for British companies, and exports expanded rapidly. Britain's foreign trade as a proportion of national income increased significantly. Around the start of the nineteenth century domestic exports were around 14 per cent of national income, and imports around 16 per cent. The export proportion probably declined slightly in the period to 1840, while the import proportion remained roughly the same. By the 1870s, however, domestic exports had increased to about 22 per cent of national income, while imports increased to 33 per cent.[16] Perhaps most unexpectedly, the revenues to government from customs duties scarcely fell. The great expansion of imports maintained customs revenues very close to their earlier levels, even at the lower tariff rates.[17]

While import prices rose, export prices decreased markedly relative to import prices. The terms of trade deteriorated significantly from 1800 to 1860. The relative fall can, however, be attributed in part to the effective formatting of

256 *The Evolution of Economies*

British companies. Controlling unit costs by innovation and scale, they were able to offer low prices to overseas buyers, and expand the volume of their sales. It was seen in Chapter 5 that the cotton format involved substantial reductions in prices throughout the nineteenth century. The effects of continued technological advances were supplemented in the period 1850–60 by a steep fall in the price of raw cotton. Mathias remarks that, 'the terms of trade by itself does not tell very much about the determinants of growth and profitability in the cotton industry, or in the economy as a whole'.[18] The idea of company format explains the growth of both cotton industry and economy with a deterioration in the terms of trade.

While the rise in imports and the fall in the relative price of exports produced substantial deficits in overseas commodity trade, the earnings from shipping and other services produced a substantial surplus on the current account of the balance of payments. Table 8.2 gives a summary of movements in the balance of payments for the nineteenth century.

The great involvement of British companies in the provision of shipping services gave British businessmen opportunities for the provision of other services related to overseas trade, such as insurance and banking. Merchants could arrange shipping services in Leadenhall Street and Gracechurch Street in the City of London, and arrange banking and insurance round the corner in Lombard Street and Cornhill.[19] The Navigation Acts thus stimulated the provision of services outside the specific confines of shipping that facilitated the profitable

Table 8.2 Summary balance of payments, 1816–1913

£ million

Years	Net imports	Exports of UK products	Balance of commodity trade	Net income from services	Net income from interest and dividends	Balance on current account	Accumulating balance of capital abroad
1816–20	49.3	40.3	−9.0	14.5	1.7	7.2	46
1826–30	48.7	35.9	−12.8	10.6	4.6	2.6	111
1836–40	73.8	49.8	−24.0	18.6	8.0	2.6	156
1846–50	87.7	60.9	−26.8	22.0	9.5	4.7	209
1856–60	158	124.2	−33.8	43.5	16.5	26.2	380
1866–70	246	187.8	−58.2	67.9	30.8	40.5	692
1876–80	325.9	201.4	−124.5	93.0	56.3	24.9	1189
1886–90	327.4	236.3	−91.1	94.6	84.2	87.6	1935
1896–1900	413.3	252.7	−160.6	100.7	100.2	40.3	2397
1906–10	539.6	397.5	−142.1	136.5	151.4	145.8	3371
1911–13	623.2	488.9	−134.3	152.6	187.9	206.1	3990

Notes: Annual averages for five-year periods; last column is accumulated total at end of period; bullion transfers and ship sales not included.

Source: Abbreviated from Mathias, Peter, 2001, *The First Industrial Nation: An Economic History of Britain, 1700–1914*, Abingdon and New York: Routledge, p. 279. Original source: Imlah, A. H., 1958, *Economic Elements in the Pax Britannica: Studies in British Foreign Trade in the Nineteenth Century*, Cambridge, MA: Harvard University Press, pp. 37–8, 70–5, 94–8.

evolution of Britain's external trade. They set in train an evolutionary process that led to the modern prominence of London in the provision of financial services. Accumulating surpluses on current account transactions through the first half of the nineteenth century gave rise to further evolution of the foreign trade of Britain through substantial overseas investment.

Foreign investment and the evolution of global trade

It also gave rise to marked acceleration in the evolution of global trade. The second phase of accelerated evolution involved a global economy linked, in physical terms, increasingly by steamships but linked also by new companies formatted to provide telegraphic and later wireless transmission of commercial information. The telegraphic communications that facilitated the growth of railways in Britain facilitated also the growth of international trade. The first successful transatlantic cable was laid by the Anglo-American Telegraph Company, using Isambard Kingdom Brunel's ship *Great Eastern*, in 1866. Communications that previously could be made only as fast as a ship became almost instantaneous. A message could be sent and a reply received on the same day. Bargaining sets and bargaining positions depend on what is known, and consequently money-bargaining was substantially extended by the improvement in communications.

In the peak years of 1886–90 and 1906–14 British investment overseas exceeded fixed investment in Britain. Investment in railways constituted over 40 per cent of British overseas lending. Two-thirds of British portfolio investment overseas went into railways. In addition, a large part of the loans made to foreign governments were probably also spent on railways. The USA and India took substantial funds for investment in railways. The earlier surge in foreign investment ended in 1890 with the bail-out of Barings bank. Over-confidence had caused the bank to lend on projects which had not been adequately investigated.[20]

Much of the foreign investment came back to Britain in the form of payments for rails, locomotives and other machinery and equipment related to infrastructural and industrial investment. Up to the 1870s capital raised in London tended to be accompanied as a 'package deal' with orders for the material requirements of the investment. Railway finance could be provided along with a complete railway system – you bought the train set. Britain was, up to that date, the predominant supplier of metal goods and engineering products, so that investment in railways and other infrastructure almost inevitably meant orders for British companies. Later in the century the options open to buyers were wider, especially as British lending was seldom contractually tied to the purchase of British equipment.[21]

The inflows of capital to foreign countries gave opportunities for the format of companies in those countries. When the investment went into railways, there was the same effect as had been experienced in Britain. The railways extended bargaining sets, stimulating the evolution of economies through new opportunities for company formatting. British exports of iron products benefited from the overseas investment that used them, just as the new iron products had given rise to new formats in Britain. One prominent consequence of the investment in railways was to make feasible the extraction of agricultural produce and other primary products from the interiors of countries such as the USA, Australia, Canada, South Africa and Argentina.[22] Britain provided the vendor sets necessary to successful format for production of these commodities. The fall in corn prices in Britain in the late nineteenth century was partly a consequence of the extension of railways inland in the USA. When the new production replaced domestically produced commodities it was substantially detrimental to domestic landowners and agricultural workers.[23]

Distinctive new company formats were evolved to take advantage of the new opportunities arising from the accelerated evolution of economies around the world. Jardine Matheson became, by the end of the nineteenth century, the largest foreign trading company in the Far East. Much of its business originated in the termination, in 1834, of the East India Company's monopoly of British trade with China. It carried on the profitable trade in tea, and wanted to extend its trade in opium more deeply into China. To do so, it revived the old tradition of armed force as a means of establishing trade by encouraging the British government to engage in war with China. In due course, the British government obliged. Jardine Matheson's understanding of regional and international trade enabled it to develop a wide range of business interests. Mathias gives an idea of the range of the company's trade:

> They organized the raising of loans to Chinese provincial governments (on which they took their margin). They supplied the railways at a profit, sometimes shipped the equipment on their own shipping lines, which brought in freight charges, and supplied equipment and arms to the contestants in the wars whose strategy was being shaped by the railways.[24]

The comment illustrates the sophistication of the format developed by the company and the evolutionary streams that derived from such trading companies. Their format depended on their capacities for setting in train numerous very different but very rewarding transactions. They built bargaining position by virtue of the value to others of the capacities they developed in the provision of goods and services in the widest sense. They also built bargaining position by making themselves indispensable sources of the sort of services they could provide.

Intellectual support-bargaining and free trade

As was seen in the opening section of this chapter, foreign trade is, by definition, based on nation states. In intellectual support-bargaining, theory formation is a means of assembling support for interests, so theories of foreign trade are likely to be theories concerned with the advancement of national interests. Mercantilist theory was unabashedly out to advance national interest. The Navigation Acts were an expression of that interest. Outwitting foreigners, or even the armed repulsion of foreigners, was part of the process. The measures that protected British companies against foreign competition were easily understood as walls of a fortress that protected the blessed insiders from the depredations of outsiders.

Nevertheless, the cotton format suggested interdependence, and a potentially more profitable experience. The military model might not be so readily applicable to foreign trade. A nation might benefit from a degree of interdependence. A simple 'beggar-thy-neighbour' policy might forfeit considerable advantages of trade with neighbours. Emulating the cotton format required foreign sales. In response to these sentiments, and in keeping with the rational Enlightenment of the time, various philosophers investigated the implications of a non-partisan theory of foreign trade, in which nations traded on an equal footing. The rational foundations of such ideas were reckoned to give them a more dependable basis than that of partisan national interest. They offered, moreover, the bonus of all nations being better off from the conduct of foreign trade. Most prominent among the investigators in Britain were Adam Smith and David Ricardo, who produced theories of long-lasting impact.

There were, nevertheless, those who saw the conversion of Britain to a non-partisan theory of free trade as no more than partisan cunning. Frederick List accused England of dissembling her true objectives by 'cosmopolite expressions and discussions' to prevent others following the protective strategy that had brought her success. He continues:

> It is a vulgar rule of prudence for him who has reached the pinnacle of power to cast down the ladder by which he mounted, that others may not follow ... A nation which by protective duties and maritime restrictions has built up a manufacturing industry and a merchant marine to such a point of strength and power as not to fear the competition of any other, can pursue no safer policy than to thrust aside the means of elevation, to preach to other nations the advantages of free trade, and to utter loud expressions of repentance for having walked hitherto in the way of error, and for having come so lately to the knowledge of truth.[25]

England is, in effect, still formulating theory to assemble support for national interest, but the pursuit of interest is more subtle than that of the mercantilists. England claims to pursue the good of all. List accuses England, in effect, of engaging in intellectual support-bargaining to assemble support for an 'impartial' theory of foreign trade that will have the effect of promoting the interests of English traders.

Adam Smith and free trade

Adam Smith condemns protection as the promotion of the interests of manufacturers against the interests of their countrymen. People are forced to pay higher prices for products that could be provided more cheaply by foreign manufacturers.

The high profits available in protected industries mean that capital, and with it labour, are drawn into those industries at the expense of other industries which, in the absence of protective duties, would offer a more advantageous course of development. The productive capacity of the nation is misappropriated, to the detriment of consumers.[26] In order to gain their monopoly of the domestic market manufacturers may 'intimidate the legislature'. Members of Parliament find that they can gain a reputation for wisdom and insight into the affairs of business by supporting the introduction of protective tariffs.[27]

Smith sees the imposition of duties as direction of private people in the employment of their capital, when left to themselves they will make the choices that best serve the public interest. He notes that the tailor does not make shoes, but buys them from the shoemaker. Specialisation promotes a general expansion of production. On their own, people will develop those specialisations for which they are best suited, at the international level as on the domestic level. No statesman can judge better than private people where their capital should best be invested. Smith uses the famous phrase 'invisible hand' in his account of the automatic and beneficial allocation of capital under free trade.[28]

Smith recognises that protective duties may permit an industry to become competitive with foreign products more quickly than would otherwise be possible – what is now called the 'infant industry' argument. But he argues that this does not mean that the nation is necessarily the better for such duties. Industry augments only as its capital augments, and the rate of augmentation of capital depends on savings. Protecting industries from foreign competition reduces savings, hence reduces the augmentation of capital and hence reduces the augmentation of industry.[29] Smith also rejects the suggestion that duties are always justified in retaliation for the duties imposed by others. If retaliation is likely to bring about reversal of the decision of the foreign government to impose duties, then it is justified. But otherwise, retaliation merely adds to the injury already caused by the initial duties. It inflicts a general injury on top of a specific injury.[30]

In his critique of the mercantile system Smith argues the pre-eminence of consumption over production, while the mercantile system promotes the interests of producers:

> Consumption is the sole end and purpose of all production; and the interest of the producer ought to be attended to, only so far as it may be necessary for promoting that of the consumer. The maxim is so perfectly self-evident, that it would be absurd to attempt to prove it. But in the mercantile system, the interest of the consumer is almost constantly sacrificed to that of the producer; and it seems to consider production, and not consumption, as the ultimate end and object of all industry and commerce.[31]

The maxim, as Smith asserts, is perfectly self-evident, but a question arises as to how far it is necessary to attend to the interests of the producer in order to advance the interests of the consumer. Money-bargaining theory suggests that the evolution of companies has to be a primary objective if consumption is to rise. If consumers are to spend, they first need budgets, and the revenues for those budgets have, for the most part, to be derived from employment. People have to earn wages before they can be consumers. Companies are the main providers of employment and wages. For this reason alone, companies would be an appropriate focus of attention for the ultimate advancement of consumption. But the operations of companies are also more complex than consumption, not least because companies operate in a competitive environment. Companies have to be regulated in the public interest, but they have also to be regulated in such a way as to maintain their competitiveness in relation to the companies governed by the regulations of other support-bargaining jurisdictions. They also require physical infrastructure, in the form of roads, railways, etc. Consumption is the end, but companies are the essential means, and attention to the interests of companies must, therefore, necessarily be a major concern of governments. Governments must seek to open up opportunities for the format of viable companies and the payment of good wages. Consumption derives from the format of viable companies and their provision of wages. It was noted above that export of British capital in the nineteenth century generated opportunities for format of companies in the recipient countries, and generated budget revenues for employees, which allowed them to consume goods made by British and other companies. The idea of 'consumer sovereignty' has been adopted into neoclassical economics, with the understanding that consumers have only to exercise preferences over an array of products offered by 'firms' equating 'marginal cost' to 'market price'. The concept makes decisions over 'consumption' supreme, while companies react automatically to expressed preferences. But in terms of bargaining theory, the establishment of viable company formats is the demanding part of the process.

Smith, of course, wrote in an era in which very large sums of money were expended on military forces to acquire colonies and secure trading advantages for British companies. His objection to the attention given to the interests of companies arises partly from the cost of this aspect of the support accorded them. In this case, the favouring of companies may certainly have been inimical to the interests of consumers. Smith recognises the contributions of settler colonies to national wealth, but regards the empire more generally as a costly imposition on domestic consumers.[32] The importance of empire to the industrial revolution is still debated.[33]

More generally, Smith misses the importance of companies as the prime movers of economic activity. They format to meet the situation-related requirements of people, other companies and governments. If they find a viable format, they generate a range of payments to other companies and employees. Smith was concerned with a small-scale, pre-industrial economy in which 'companies' were represented by 'masters' or 'master-manufacturers'. It was a very personalised and individualistic system. In spite of his faith in the capacity of his system to allocate capital efficiently, he is distinctly uncomplimentary to the 'master-manufacturers'. They have, he asserts, an interest in deceiving and even oppressing the public.[34] Smith the moralist disapproves of unethical behaviour. But he seems also to disapprove of behaviour incompatible with the ethical economic system he wants to describe. His preconception – that the pursuit of private interest brings public benefit – demands that master-manufacturers behave in a way that results in 'natural prices'. To find them behaving otherwise is awkward. They are condemned and required to change their ways in accordance with the requirements of theory. Smith is ostensibly describing the workings of an economy, but he is, at the same time, assembling support for the sort of economy he favours, with the ethical behaviour required to bring about the ethical effects he envisages. But the master-manufacturers are not working in an ideal economy. They are building viable businesses. They seek profit rather than maximisation of production. Technology, rather than the division of labour, gives them bargaining position. The conditions for viable format are different from the conditions associated with the idea of 'natural prices'. In the years in which Smith worked, companies were increasingly evolving the formats that accelerated the evolution of the British economy and led to transformation of the global economy. Just as Smith wrote, the world about which he wrote was being transformed in ways that he did not fully recognise.[35] One of the principal changes related to the format of companies and the primary role they could play in the evolution of an economy.

Because of this failure of Smith to understand the way business operated, due to his inclination to impose an idealised system of exchange on the reality, Smith reached false conclusions regarding the benefits of free trade. The international economy was going to be no nearer the ethical ideal than the domestic economy. A theory of foreign trade has to be anchored in the actual observed behaviour of those who trade and those who regulate the economies from which the traders operate. Trade strategy has to be developed by reference to actual situations and capacities.

Ricardo and comparative advantage

Ricardo's theory of comparative advantage, set out in his work *On the Principles of Political Economy and Taxation*, published in 1817, has been adopted, with modifications, into neoclassical theory and become established as the basic demonstration of the universal benefits of free trade. Comparative advantage purports to show that all countries can benefit from free trade because no absolute advantage is required, only a comparative advantage, and if one country has a comparative advantage over another country in, say, the production of product A relative to the production of product B, then the other country must, by mathematical necessity, have a comparative advantage in the production of product B relative to product A. Specialisation by reference to comparative advantage means maximisation of output, to the potential benefit of both. By extension, all countries should specialise in the product or products in which they have comparative advantage, and all can benefit.

Ricardo made a fortune as a financier in the City of London before taking to political economy. He was a co-founder of the Political Economy Club, formed to promote free trade. Thomas Tooke, a member of the Club, wrote the petition for the advancement of free trade presented to parliament in 1820 by London merchants. Tooke hawked the petition round the city to get signatures, with little success at first. The city was, at best, lukewarm on free trade.[36] Ricardo became a Member of Parliament for an Irish constituency in 1819 and took his fight for free trade, and in particular repeal of the Corn Laws, to parliament.

His theory of comparative advantage admirably complemented his interest in the repeal of the Corn Laws and the introduction of free trade. Repeal of the Corn Laws would have, as Ricardo saw it, the beneficial consequence not only of reducing the price of corn, but also of reducing also the rents accruing to landlords, whom he saw as an 'unproductive' class of humanity. Ricardo takes issue with Malthus's idea of rent as the creation of value and, according to Andrea Maneschi, 'By showing it instead to be a transfer payment from consumers to landlords, Ricardo buttresses his contention that only the landlords stand to lose from the free import of corn.'[37] Leonard Gomes describes Ricardo's general concept of international trade as one of exchange between manufacturers, on the one hand, and, on the other, producers of food and raw materials: 'When he thought of free trade it was always in terms of a manufacturing country being able to obtain cheap food and raw materials from other countries better endowed with natural resources.'[38]

Ricardo's theory of comparative advantage has the unadorned universality of mathematics. Yet to make it stand up as a theory of international trade Ricardo is obliged to adopt assumptions that discredit it for that role. The dynamics of foreign trade are far removed from the assumptions of comparative advantage.

One assumption is that capital is internationally immobile. He writes:

> The labour of 100 Englishmen cannot be given for that of 80 Englishmen, but the produce of the labour of 100 Englishmen may be given for the produce of the labour of 80 Portuguese, 60 Russians or 120 East Indians. The difference in this respect, between a single country and many, is easily accounted for, by considering the difficulty with which capital moves from one country to another, to seek a more profitable employment.[39]

Because capital is assumed to be immobile between countries, substantial differences in output per head can occur between different countries, and form the basis of trade between them. Without a prohibition, capital would go to where it could most profitably be used. On the basis of his example of Portugal having absolute advantage over England in both wine and cloth production, Ricardo remarks:

> It would undoubtedly be advantageous to the capitalists of England, and to the consumers in both countries, that under such circumstances, the wine and the cloth should both be made in Portugal, and therefore that the capital and labour of England employed in making cloth, should be removed to Portugal for that purpose ... Experience, however, shews, that the fancied or real insecurity of capital, when not under the immediate control of its owner, together with the natural disinclination which every man has to quit the country of his birth and connexions, and intrust himself with all his habits fixed, to a strange government and new laws, check the emigration of capital.[40]

Risk and attachment to home make capital internationally immobile, so the labour of 100 Englishmen might be exchanged for that of 80 Portuguese. The export of textile machinery and some other devices from Britain was prohibited until 1833 to prevent textile manufacture abroad reaching British levels of productivity, suggesting that machinery was readily exportable if there were no regulations against it. In the normal course of trade, capital equipment could be exported, bringing convergence of productivities in the different countries. The build-up of British export of capital that continued through the nineteenth century had already begun when Ricardo was writing the *Principles*. It became of central importance to the global phase of the acceleration in economic evolution in the second half of the nineteenth century. Today, capital is highly mobile internationally.

Ricardo himself recognises in a later chapter that capital is internationally mobile, and that it is desirable it should be. Maneschi writes:

> These final paragraphs of chapter 31 are of interest because Ricardo implies that capital, in contradiction to what he had said in chapter 7 regarding 'the difficulty with which capital moves from one country to another, to seek a more profitable employment', is likely to move from a nation which discourages the adoption of machinery to one that does not.[41]

In Chapter 31 Ricardo opposes restrictions on the use of machinery with the comment:

> In making your exchanges with those countries, you might give a commodity which cost two days labour, here, for a commodity which cost one, abroad, and this disadvantageous exchange would be the consequence of your own act, for the commodity which you export, and which cost you two days labour, would have cost you only one if you had not rejected the use of machinery, the services of which your neighbours had more wisely appropriated to themselves.[42]

If capital were mobile, the Portuguese might shift their capital to England to improve the productivity of English workers. Eighty days labour in England might then produce the same as 80 days labour in Portugal. While, in Chapter 7, 'On Foreign Trade', capital is internationally immobile, in Chapter 31 the international mobility of capital becomes a reason for not restricting investment in machinery at home. Ricardo is suggesting that countries which restrict the use of machinery to protect labour will suffer from the export of their capital abroad. When the argument requires it, he treats capital as internationally mobile.

The adoption of Ricardo's theory into neoclassical economic theory and its consequent prominence in support of free trade owes much to its rationality and mathematical precision. It depends, however, on appeal to a decidedly partisan and irrational interest in keeping capital at home. Yet, in accordance with his rational approach, he is later obliged to recognise the rationality of free movement of capital, and the loss of the principal foundation of his theory of comparative advantage. Chapter 31 affirms the rational case for free movement of capital, at the expense of the factional pleas of Chapter 7.

A second assumption of Ricardo is that economic exchange is barter exchange. His theory of comparative advantage is stated in terms of physical productivities in wine and textiles for Portugal and England, and the exchange of these two commodities between the two countries in accordance with relative productivities. He holds that the use of money does not affect the rates of barter exchange, but provides a simple overlay to barter exchange. Money merely facilitates exchange by barter, without significantly affecting it. Currency moves into and out of countries to make up the surpluses and deficits that arise in accordance with the 'natural traffic' of barter. This affects the general level of prices. Prices in deficit countries fall and prices in surplus countries rise, so that comparative advantage takes effect through absolute advantage. Ricardo writes:

> Gold and silver having been chosen for the general medium of circulation, they are, by the competition of commerce, distributed in such proportions amongst the different countries of the world, as to accommodate themselves to the natural traffic which would take place if no such metals existed, and the trade between countries were purely a trade of barter.[43]

He reaffirms his position later: 'It is thus that the money of each country is apportioned to it in such quantities only as may be necessary to regulate a profitable trade of barter.'[44]

Samuel Hollander sees this concern with barter as basic to Ricardo's work on foreign trade: 'The primary task which Ricardo set himself was to demonstrate that the introduction of an international medium of exchange does not necessarily distort the pattern of resource allocation which characterizes barter systems.'[45] Subsequent writers on comparative advantage have mostly found it convenient to follow Ricardo's example. Textbook expositions of comparative advantage concentrate on the differences in physical productivity. Maneschi himself limits his discussion to the barter context: 'The traditional interpretations of Ricardo's trade theory have, however, limited themselves to that based on barter, and in order to evaluate and compare these contributions it seems appropriate to restrict consideration to this case.'[46] Ricardo's assumption of barter is not necessarily outmoded or 'historic'. The 1980 edition of Paul Samuelson's standard economics textbook describes money in terms of overlay to what is fundamentally a matter of barter:

> Even in the most advanced industrial economies, if we strip exchange down to its barest essentials and peel off the obscuring layer of money, we find that trade between individuals or nations largely boils down to barter.[47]

For neoclassical theory, money is an 'optional extra', not fundamental to the whole process of exchange, as it is under the idea of money-bargaining.

The assimilation of money into a barter system in the neoclassical context is not straightforward – another reason for confining discussion to barter. The arguments by which it is assimilated are likely to be intelligible and acceptable only within the neoclassical theory group.[48] But as with neoclassical economics in general, the assumptions are the chief stumbling block to conversion of the barter theory of international trade to a monetary context. Neoclassical assumptions are, if it is possible, even more anomalous in the international context than they are in a national context, and the assumptions specific to the international context are no more credible. For example, the neoclassical formulation of comparative advantage depends significantly on the notion of 'opportunity costs', but opportunity costs are not experienced when there are unemployed resources. There has to be an assumption of full employment. As in Ricardo's theory, labour and capital are assumed to be internationally immobile. Economies of scale, accepted as an adjunct to neoclassical theory in a domestic context, even though they involve sacrifice of claims to optimal allocation of resources, cannot be accommodated in the neoclassical account of comparative advantage. It was seen in Chapter 3 that large companies are particularly prominent in international trade. And the advantages apparently to be gained from free trade under neoclassical comparative advantage will not necessarily accrue to all. Specialisation expands production, but everyone will not necessarily share in the increased income. Neoclassical theorists of comparative advantage take refuge in the theoretical fact that 'winners' could potentially compensate 'losers'.

In classical and neoclassical economic theory issues regarding the maximisation of production are paramount. With standard products, there is nothing to improve but quantities. Money is not essential to the models devised. As was seen in the discussion of the Arrow–Debreu theory in Chapter 3, money is largely incidental to the model. In a money-bargaining system, however, money is of central importance. All the agents of the system operate money budgets. Companies seek viability and profitability in monetary terms – how much they produce is subordinate to these considerations. The function of the merchant trading with inland and coastal people, described in Chapter 2, is dependent on the use of money. The viability or profitability of a company will normally depend, in large measure, on its unit costs, since they put a lower limit on the price that must be charged and, hence, are likely substantially to determine the competitiveness of the company's output. 'Money-bargaining' is monetary exchange. It displaces barter, introducing new incentives for the agents of money-bargaining and new prospects for them.

So with Ricardo's barter theory of exchange, the introduction of money and the dynamic of money-bargaining introduce new considerations that override the concern for productivity in the theory of comparative advantage. The labour of 100 Englishmen cannot be given for the labour of 80 Englishmen because they are likely to use the same machinery and have the same productivity. They are also likely to be paid at the same wage rates. But the produce of the labour of 100 Englishmen may be given for the produce of the labour of 80 Portuguese, 60 Russians or 120 East Indians, whatever their productivity, if the prices are right, which means if they are paid at rates that make exchange advantageous.

Thus, if the 100 Englishmen produce 100 units of product at wages of £1.00 per head the total cost of their output is £100. If the 80 Portuguese produce 100 units of the same product then at any wage rate up to £1.25 the cost of their output will be below that of the Englishmen. Similarly if the 120 East Indians produce 100 units of the same product then at any wage rate below £0.83 the cost of their output will be below that of the Englishmen. If the productivity of the Portuguese in the one industry reflects the general level of Portuguese productivity, then the Portuguese will be able to export to England with wages up to £1.25 per head. Similarly East Indians will be able to trade with Englishmen if they keep their wages below £0.83 per head.

Table 8.3 illustrates two cases involving different levels of wage payment. The English, Portuguese, Russians and East Indians all produce 100 units of a product, recorded in column 2, but their differing levels of productivity mean that they take different numbers of days to do so, recorded in column 1.

In the first case, all workers are paid the same daily rate of £1.00. Those with higher productivity than the English (Portuguese and Russians) have lower unit costs; those with the lower productivity (East Indians) have higher unit costs. The former can undercut British prices, while the latter cannot. In the second case workers are paid precisely in accord with their productivity. The effects of productivity differences are then precisely offset, and the unit costs of all are the same. Below these wage levels, Portuguese, Russians and East Indians will all have lower unit costs than the English. They will be able to sell in England. Companies will try to negotiate wage rates that give them competitive unit costs. English companies will try to negotiate wage rates that allow them to compete, at their levels of productivity, with the foreign companies.

In the classical understanding disparities between wages and productivity levels cannot be sustained. Money would flow to the low-cost economies and, since there would be no unemployment, wages would rise to a level commensurate with the relative productivity of the workers. In a system of different national currencies,

Table 8.3 Comparative advantage and unit cost advantage

	Days	Output	Productivity (output per day) (2/1)	Wage rate (£ per day)	Cost of output (£) (1×4)	Unit cost (£) (5/2)
	1	2	3	4	5	6
CASE 1						
English	100	100	1.00	1.00	100	1
Portuguese	80	100	1.25	1.00	80	0.8
Russians	60	100	1.67	1.00	60	0.6
East Indians	120	100	0.83	1.00	120	1.2
CASE 2						
English	100	100	1.00	1.00	100	1
Portuguese	80	100	1.25	1.25	100	1
Russians	60	100	1.67	1.67	100	1
East Indians	120	100	0.83	0.83	100	1

the parity of currencies would adjust to bring wages into line with relative levels of productivity.

Confined by assumptions of mathematical formulation, which include the assumption that nothing else is relevant, the model carries some conviction – has carried some conviction for the past 200 years. But what is missing is crucial to the understanding of international trade. It is not productivity alone that determines wage rates; nor does productivity have the static quality attributed to it in the theory of comparative advantage. Economies evolve, so the productivities of one period are not necessarily those of the next. Economies will not move to equilibrium on the basis of comparative productivities because the productivities change.

The main agents of evolution in a money-bargaining system are, as has been seen, companies – the specialist money-bargaining agencies. Companies format to meet a viability condition. Their concern is not with the maximisation of production levels, but with attainment of profit. With the focus moved from resource allocation by productivity advantage to the competitive format of companies for profit, the entire character of international trade is changed. Productivity is only a means to an end – productivity improvements tend to bring about reductions in unit costs. With a focus on companies, furthermore, the importance of productivity is overshadowed by the importance of technology. Companies employ technology in their formats as a vital element in meeting the viability condition. It introduces new products and new production processes involving lower unit costs. It also commonly introduces economies of scale, where unit cost depends on the level of production. Companies engaged in international trade, in particular, have employed technology that gives them economies of scale. The cotton format is the early exemplar. Adam Smith's division of labour and Ricardo's specialisation on the basis of comparative advantage both give rise to productivity improvements, but both are eclipsed by the importance of technology.

International trade also, by its nature, potentially involves transportation of goods over long distances. Freight charges are, then, potentially prominent elements in overall unit costs. Freight costs may of themselves dictate what is traded and which nations become trading partners. Proximity is a major determinant of trade flows between nations. The theory of comparative advantage takes no account of distance and the costs incurred in overcoming distance, although such concerns seem inseparable from a type of trade characterised as 'international.'

The evolutionary impulse of money-bargaining is generated most fundamentally by the situation-related understanding of interests. Comparative advantage does not accommodate the constant changing of consumer demand, and the changing requirements of other buyers. Increments to production through specialisation have no value unless the products concerned have the features that give them places in the money-bargaining sets of potential buyers. Companies are necessary to ensure the match is made. The innovations of companies, technological and organisational, are predicated on the need to ensure their products gain places in the changing consumer bargaining sets that they must serve.

The concern of companies with unit costs implies a major concern with wage rates. As has been seen, classical theory has wage rates adjusting to relative productivities in conditions of full employment. In a money-bargaining system, however, there is no guarantee of full employment. Availability of labour will be an important factor in the negotiations of companies to obtain labour. It is apparent that companies most successful in international trade have often taken advantage of low wage rates in countries with labour of relatively high productivity to keep down unit costs and generate high profits.[49] Mobility of capital, which is availability of technology, means that companies can produce in different countries at similar levels of productivity, while adopting wage rates prevailing more generally in a country. Companies that are islands of advanced technology in countries of generally low technology can pay wages that, though commonly higher than those of less technologically advanced companies around them, are nevertheless substantially lower than would be paid with the same technology in another country. In many countries the operations of companies paying wages constitute islands of relative prosperity in seas of unemployment or informal and casual employment. These disparities arise and persist because the bargaining sets of money-bargaining may be sharply constricted, while the markets of neoclassical theory are seamlessly extensive. The former are dictated by the specific situations of different agents.

Comparative advantage has fitted neatly into the concepts of economics and international trade developed through the Western institutions of intellectual support-bargaining. It has been sustained because it has been convenient to dominant trading nations to have a theory that promotes the liberalisation of international trade. Ricardo would surely not have succumbed to such misconception had it not been convenient to his purpose. The theory of comparative advantage was constructed to attract support for abolition of the Corn Laws and the detriment of landlords. Its uptake owed much to its association, first, with the evolution of British manufacturers at the time towards a dominant position in global manufacturing and, second, with evolution from an ascendancy of landed interests to an ascendancy of companies.[50] Ricardo's misconception has been adopted into mainstream economics and accepted as the cornerstone of international trade theory. But economies must be understood as evolving money-bargaining systems rather than as anything to do with neoclassical equilibrium. International trade is a matter of companies and governments manoeuvring for money-bargaining position, aided and abetted by theory-makers, and constrained by national and international support-bargaining. The acceptance of comparative advantage in intellectual support-bargaining was possible only because the theory groups concerned allowed themselves to become detached from the realities they claimed to address.

Frederick List and productive power

List's arguments on Britain's conversion to 'free trade', introduced above, have a hint in them of support-bargaining, money-bargaining, the format of companies and, above all, an evolutionary process. List advocates the development of 'productive power' in a nation. He explains Britain's use of protection as a means of developing productive power.[51] 'Productive power' is a capacious concept attempting to capture the many factors that establish national pre-eminence. The whole activity of a society, from the training of its people to its legal system, beliefs and political structure, is involved in the realisation of productive power.[52] Productive power is a result of historical development: 'The actual condition of nations is the result of an accumulation of discoveries, inventions, improvements; the efforts of all previous generations.'[53] Industrial power is part of productive power. It involves not only the power of a single industry, but also the power brought about by the association of different industries – in particular, the interplay of manufacturing and agricultural industry. List argues that 'the School', meaning the school of Adam Smith, treats manufacturing as being on a par with agriculture in terms of economic implications, whereas for List the more extensive interconnections of manufacturing with other economic and social endeavour, including its requirements for infrastructure, and the accumulation of capital to which it gives rise, set it apart from and above agriculture as a generator of productive power.[54] List argues that an 'infant industry' cannot sustain competition from long-established and protected industry without being itself protected.

List recognises the importance of the division of labour in the generation of productive power, but maintains that Smith failed to recognise that productive power depends also on association. Cooperation is as important as division: 'The productive power of these operations belongs not merely to *division*, it essentially depends upon *association*.'[55] List also challenges the confinement of Smith's system to individual exchange and the resulting exchangeable value. The aim is not merely to increase exchangeable value, but to increase the productive power of a nation.[56] Smith's account of capital investment and the returns on capital is deficient because it is confined to exchangeable values, ignoring the intellectual, corporeal, social and political returns. Free trade allocates capital in accordance with material returns, but takes no account of these other returns.[57]

List argues from the point of view of a nation that has fallen behind and needs to catch up with a dominant power. Newcomers cannot compete with established manufacturing nations.[58] Manufacturing develops slowly and reaches its full productive power only after a long time.[59] Nevertheless, he sees free trade as the best policy once nations have reached parity in manufacturing:

> The protective system is the only means by which nations less advanced can be raised to the level of that nation which enjoys a supremacy in manufacturing industry – a monopoly not conferred by nature, but seized by being first on the ground; the protective system, regarded from this point of view, will be the most effective promoter of universal association among nations, and consequently free trade.[60]

List puts sharp limits on the application of his protectionist strategy. He is concerned with 'complete, great, independent nations' with extensive territory and potential for the foremost rank in agriculture, manufacturing and commerce and in maritime and continental power. It is not for colonies and small countries, which are expected, of necessity, to remain in agricultural production.[61] It is only the countries of the temperate zones that are deemed suitable for manufacturing; those of the torrid zones are regarded as suited to production of agricultural products and raw materials for manufacturers.[62] Protection is not appropriate for production of food and raw materials, since it will injure both producers and buyers.[63] List conceives trade in terms of export of manufactured goods from the first-rank countries of temperate zones and imports by them of agricultural products and raw materials from the torrid zones.

According to List, England's success in becoming the leading world power rested on her development of all aspects of productive power, by which 'she added power to power and productive force to productive force'.[64] This included the development of military power. The independence of nations depends on their productive power. List notes that a 'well-shaped territory' is necessary to productive power, and the desire to form such a territory is legitimate, even to the possible extent of war.[65] Holland, Belgium, Denmark and Switzerland might usefully be associated with Germany in pursuit of productive power. Germany is seen as potentially the centre of a durable continental alliance.[66] Colonisation plays a part in List's plans for German parity with England.[67] The importance of manufacturing lies partly in its connections with military capacity. Agricultural nations do not build navies or acquire colonies.[68] It is not possible to build a mercantile marine on the basis of an agricultural industry. An outright and belligerent call to arms would probably be widely condemned, rather than attract support, which perhaps accounts for its absence. But List seems to believe that to rival England it will probably be necessary to act like England in military and colonial matters.

List's focus on productive power clearly reflects awareness that companies are the driving force behind economic performance. Production, not consumption, is the key to economic strength. Association is as important as the division of labour. It reflects also a sense of a bargaining network in which the initiatives of some give rise to opportunities for others. Manufacturing industry, in particular, gives rise to formats that join up the bargaining network into interdependence and strength through diverse and dependable provision. Each part of the network adjusts to the requirements of others, both with regard to product and service innovation and with regard to pricing. Agriculturists, as was seen in Chapter 5, are probably less inclined to understand their work in terms of a format and, consequently, may not have, to the same degree, the innovative and progressive impulses of manufacturers.

The interconnections of money-bargaining with support-bargaining are also apparent. The nation state is recognised as the essential unit: 'between the individual and the whole human race there is the nation'.[69] In terms of bargaining theory, the nation state takes that primary position because formal support-bargaining systems are defined by national territories and national citizenship. Governments of nations are regulators and facilitators of money-bargaining systems within their national jurisdictions. In the spirit of the time, this meant not only regulating the money-bargaining system in favour of the companies falling within their jurisdictions, but promoting the viability of their formats by carving out overseas markets by diplomatic and sometimes violent methods.

List's account clearly involves also an evolutionary system, moving from situation to situation, with accumulation of historic effort. The basic situation he addresses is that of German backwardness in relation to the dominance of England. England's industrial innovation, companies, government, navy and colonies all combine to give England global supremacy. A concerted German effort, on all these fronts, is necessary to bring Germany to parity with England. With parity achieved, List sees the advantages of free trade, at least between the countries that will have similar status to England. 'Productive power' is an evolved outcome.

List's understanding of situation as the basis of interest extends to his account of the theories generated in society. List links the 'cosmopolite' theory of the physiocrats to the suppression of the peasantry in France at the time they wrote.[70] To List, it was obvious that the theory was conceived 'in reference to the situation of France at the time when it appeared, and that it was calculated only for that state of things'.[71] Smith's account of an economy and the virtues of free trade which it implies are linked by List to the interests of England in opening up opportunities for overseas sales, which are most likely to be sales of English companies. It is, according to List, as is apparent from the quotation at note 25 ('It is a vulgar rule ... knowledge of truth'), a theory designed to deter others from developing the strength in money-bargaining attained by Britain. Modern writers deploy the same argument in favour of protection in developing countries, though there is some irony in their adoption of List as theoretical mentor, since he regards protection in countries of the torrid zones as damaging.[72] It might be said that List's interest in the rise of Germany through the protectionist ladder led him to deny use of the ladder to those countries that had even more climbing to do.

List's account deals with the appearances of a bargaining system without identifying it as such. He identifies the centrality of interest, in this case national interest, and the situations that define interest. It is evolutionary, stressing the interrelations that develop and give strength over time. His assessments of the significance of the Navigation Acts and Britain's conversion to free trade seem shrewd. These connections with support-bargaining and money-bargaining are, however, woven into a strategy of national advance strong enough to alarm many, especially if they understood more than List was prepared to write. List's theories were highly influential in Germany, assembling support for the policies of Otto Von Bismarck and subsequent German leaders. With hindsight, they appear too much like signposts to the disasters of the twentieth century to be happily appreciated for their insight.

Rational equilibrium versus partisan evolution

Adam Smith's analysis of the functioning of an economy and international trade, applies the Enlightenment tool of reason. Unfettered competition, in which each individual seeks his own greatest return, leads to the establishment of 'natural prices' and the maximisation of output from the given resources of land, labour and stock. Ricardo refines the rational approach of Smith to confirm the political and social wisdom of the independent economy. If governments impose tariffs on imports, choice is skewed towards investment that is not the most productive.

Neoclassical theorists in the later nineteenth century selected the rational elements of classical theory and refined them into a mathematically conditioned system tending to equilibrium. Any traits that were inimical to this type of theory – which means much of human nature – were assumed away. Ricardo's theory of comparative advantage lent itself very readily to this kind of treatment, being itself based on mathematical relationships. It became, in the hands of neoclassical theorists, the pillar of orthodox economic trade theory.

The refinement of classical into neoclassical theory meant that the evolutionary element that is present in Smith's *Wealth of Nations* was lost. Smith recognised that human society evolves. Long sections of the *Wealth of Nations* comprise accounts of the historical emergence of different societies. It is possible to identify a 'stadial' theory in it of historical evolution, beginning with societies of hunters, becoming societies of shepherds, then on to farmers and arriving, finally, at a commercial age.[73] An evolutionary process is recognised, even if it is not systematically described. With the transition to neoclassical theory the evolutionary element cannot be accommodated. The rational dynamic requires no initial understanding of situation, only a few axioms regarding human behaviour. Without a concept of situation, there is no evolution of situation and no evolutionary dynamic.

This lack of a concept of situation in rational theory means also that there is no understanding of partisan or national interest. In money-bargaining interests are identified by reference to situation. Where situations differ, interests also will be different. People will pursue partisan interests when their situations differ from those of other groups. This is particularly important in foreign trade since it is, by definition – as has been seen – trade between nations of partisan interest. Rational theorists cannot comprehend that nations with different initial money-bargaining positions will experience different consequences from the establishment of a rational system that presupposes all nations start from nothing and nowhere. In fact, rather than starting from nothing and nowhere, rational theorists have supposed that rational theory applies to any situation anywhere – it is assumed to apply universally. In Germany's situation in the 1840s, List sees that different strategies are needed to enable Germany to catch up with Britain.

Nation states are built on partisan interest to the extent that if there were no partisan interest, there would be no nation states and consequently no 'foreign' trade. All trade would be the domestic trade between people functioning as a single society under the jurisdiction of a single support-bargaining system. If being 'rational' means being non-partisan or impartial, the concept of 'foreign' is irrational and 'a rational theory of foreign trade' is a contradiction in terms. Ricardo finds himself caught in precisely this bind when he calls to the support of his rational model the irrational assumption that capital is internationally immobile.

Ricardo takes logical and empirical liberties in moulding his theory to the purpose he is pursuing.

The impartial theory presupposes engagement of individuals with just those few axiomatic characteristics that make them all the same. In money-bargaining, companies are conceived as bargaining agencies in money-bargaining systems. They aim to develop bargaining strength. They use technology to format for viability and profit. Trade evolves through the creation and evolution of companies and bargaining sets, subject to regulations imposed by a support-bargaining system. The strongest companies will dominate international trade, as they have. The partisan interests of nations imply that they should develop the strongest companies if they wish to succeed in international trade, as they have done. The initial situation of differentiated bargaining positions crucially determines which nations are best placed to take advantage of any reductions in barriers to international trade.

The situations of nation states impose locational formats on their companies. The companies of one country find themselves next door to large vendor sets and can establish viable formats with reasonable ease. The companies of another country are separated by great expanses of sea from vendor sets. The costs imposed by distance and the costs of transport make it difficult to format viable companies. While mainstream economic theory is committed to the idea that comparative advantage is the basic determinant of trade, the empirical evidence indicates that geographical factors are of paramount importance. The 'gravity theory' of international trade gives a fairly accurate prediction of the level of trade between two nations. Under the gravity theory, the level of trade between two countries varies in accordance with the product of their GDPs and inversely with the distance between them.[74] Nations trade most intensively with their neighbours. The theory of comparative advantage, like neoclassical theory in general, cannot accommodate distance.

British businessmen in the mid-nineteenth century saw that an expansion of international trade was likely to open up opportunities for their dominant companies, especially since their dominant companies included some engaged in shipbuilding and the provision of shipping services. Many of the high-tech formats evolved in Britain needed a high level of production to realise low unit costs and, hence, needed large vendor sets, such as could be provided by overseas nations. Theories such as those of Adam Smith and Ricardo helped their cause by assembling support for free trade on a more elevated basis than that of pure self-interest. Businessmen could be self-interested and generous at the same time; narrow minded in pursuit of their own interests yet virtuous in pursuit of benefits to society. The non-partisan theory advanced the interests of the dominant partisan. Foreign trade in the nineteenth century evolved through the pursuit of partisan advantage – in particular, the partisan advantage of Britain.

The understanding of theory-making is crucial. Rational theorists assumed they were providing absolute theory about human society, with universal application. Rational theory could not be a matter of opinion. But, understood in the context of intellectual support-bargaining, it is immediately apparent that rational theory is no more than a means of assembling support for certain measures to the advantage of the theory-makers. Free-trade theory potentially gave the dominant producer access to the overseas markets it needed.

It was then the lack of understanding of the theory-makers about what they were doing rather than deceit that permitted them to present free trade as the answer to questions about the role of foreign trade. They undoubtedly believed that free trade was genuinely the best means of advancing the interests of the people of all nations. We instinctively formulate, support and believe theories that are conducive to our interests. It has been suggested that the capacity to recognise our situation and act to realise the implied interests has been essential to human survival.[75]

This contrast between the rational approach and the partisan nature of money-bargaining can be linked to their origins. The rational approach, as has been seen, derives from a recent period of change in human thought, involving transition from spiritual, superstitious and supernatural modes of thought to modes of thought characterised by observation, experiment and scepticism. It is a transition also from modes of thought that set communal interest much above individual interest to a mode of thought that recognises, to a much greater degree, the rights of individuals. Money-bargaining, by contrast, as was remarked in Chapter 1, derives from support-bargaining, which is seen as an essential mechanism of human survival, and part of a modified understanding of natural selection. Money-bargaining enhances, by its nature, the bargaining positions of individuals. When modes of thought became generally more sympathetic to individual expression, money-bargaining was given looser rein. Some demanded not just a looser rein, but 'freedom'.

The Enlightenment ideal included aspirations to eliminate the incessant warfare that had blighted Europe for centuries, replacing it with the reasonable deliberation of educated and temperate people. The proponents of Enlightenment thinking allowed this ideal to affect their perceptions of the functioning of human societies. The partisan and combative instincts of humans, violent or otherwise, cannot be overlooked without the risk of repercussions. Whatever benefits the rational approach may offer, there is always the risk that they will be overtaken by the partisan ambitions of intemperate people. The twentieth century was as much blighted by war as previous centuries. While there will be overwhelming support for the idea that temperate and reasonable people must seek to create societies of peace, harmony and prosperity, it will also be recognised that their prescriptions have to be based on understanding of society as it is, with a predominance of partisan ambition and assertion. The theory of support-bargaining and money-bargaining may help to assemble the support of reasonable and temperate people for a society of the peaceable type.[76]

Post-war expansion of world trade

Towards the end of the nineteenth century Britain lost the political and economic primacy it had achieved in the earlier years. The USA and Germany drew ahead of Britain in industrial output and in export volumes. In the twentieth century the costs of two world wars reduced Britain's accumulated wealth. Initiative in the evolution of world trade passed increasingly to other nations.

After both world wars efforts were made to moderate the nationalistic elements in world trade through the establishment of international forums. The heavy human and material costs of violence disposed all nations to seek reductions in the scope for warfare through settlement of conflicts of interest through support-bargaining. Trade, at least, might be conducted under an international support convention. Trade between nations might become more like trade within nations if it was regulated by institutions of international support-bargaining.

The rational theories of trade seemed tailor-made as the basis for such a process. They promised advantages to all from foreign trade. Ricardo's theory of comparative advantage came to be accepted as the basis for cooperation. The conversion of the USA to Ricardo and free trade after the Second World War, along with the consolidation of its position as the dominant trading nation and the 'superpower' of the free world, made the idea something like an official faith of developed Western nations. Those who questioned the doctrine of free trade were regarded as incapable of grasping the logic of comparative advantage. As noted above, the GATT, subsequently incorporated in the framework of the World Trade Organization (WTO), was based on the ideal of free trade. The partisan conflation of economic, political and military considerations in List's theory of 'productive power', and its consequent association with extreme forms of nationalism, made it easy to ignore. Under the auspices of the GATT and WTO successive rounds of negotiations brought significant reductions in tariffs on manufactured goods. These reductions and the elimination of other barriers to trade contributed to rapid growth in world trade in the decades following the war.

While the object of international cooperation has ostensibly been realisation of the universal benefits promised by the theory of comparative advantage, the reality is more easily understood in terms of partisan bargaining. Nations have found free trade intolerable in the context of actual negotiations on trade liberalisation. The main mechanism for the propagation of free trade in GATT was the most favoured nation (MFN) principle, by which nations undertook to extend to all nations the treatment they accorded to the nation they favoured most in trade in products.[77] In negotiations, however, the principle was quickly condemned as encouragement to 'free riding'. Nations would be accorded access to the markets of other nations without being obliged to concede any access to their own. Rather than pursue the liberalisation of trade under the MFN principle, nations might be inclined to concede next to nothing to anyone. A principle of 'reciprocity' was established as 'of great importance to the expansion of international trade'.[78] While not binding like the MFN commitment, 'in practice a balanced exchange of concessions is necessary for agreement to be possible'.[79] 'Free riding' was, of course, the intention of the formulators of the MFN principle as the means of propagating free trade. 'Reciprocity' is, of course, a necessary part of any bargaining process.

One consequence of the acceptance of an obligation to reciprocity was that trade negotiations became divided between industrial nations, with the capacity to deal with each other on a roughly equal basis, and developing nations, which lacked the capacity to reciprocate on a scale that was of interest to the industrial nations. The latter demanded and received special treatment in the form of preferential access to the markets of the industrial nations, though without the full freedom of access that the MFN commitment would have required. The industrial nations negotiated among themselves for access to each other's markets.

A further consequence of this division was that few reductions were made in agricultural tariffs. The industrialised nations, including the USA, the nations of the European Union and Japan, found it impossible to concede anything like comparative advantage in agriculture to the developing nations. Rather, they found it necessary to cultivate internal support through heavy subsidies to their farmers. The industrialised nations also found it difficult to reduce tariffs on textiles. These are, as has been seen, industries that require relatively simple technology and substantial unskilled labour, suggesting that anything like comparative advantage in textiles lay with countries seeking to introduce a manufacturing component into economies that were predominantly agricultural. The 'cotton format' initiated the acceleration in Britain's economic evolution. The governments of industrial nations found, however, that in their situation, with large numbers of their citizens engaged in textile production, they could not concede textile manufacturing to developing nations. The Multi-fibre Arrangement sustained the protection of textile industries in industrial countries while other tariffs on manufactured goods were being reduced.

The GATT also provided a way out of the MFN commitment through the formation of customs unions, free-trade areas or regional integration agreements. Under GATT Article 24, so long as substantially all restrictions on trade within a regional bloc were removed in a reasonable time, countries could establish trade arrangements among themselves without according the same terms to countries outside the bloc. The most important regional agreement was the formation of the EEC in 1957 through the Treaty of Rome. In this case, there were indications that the six nations forming the EEC might leave the GATT if their trade arrangements were condemned as inconsistent with the GATT. The trade arrangements of the EEC probably did not conform to the GATT requirements, but the issue was not pressed. The establishment of the EEC provided a precedent for the formation of other regional trade agreements that might not have conformed strictly to GATT requirements.[80]

The formation of regional trade blocs has become one of the main streams of evolution in international trade.[81] It is, as has been seen, generally easier to format viable companies on the basis of sales to neighbours rather than to distant countries. A sense of regional identity, implying readiness to support measures benefiting a neighbour, must also play a part. In the case of the EEC and the subsequent European Union, the creation of the single market was feasible partly because it was recognised that the nation states of the Union were at similar stages of industrial evolution, with companies of similar bargaining strength, and with similar domestic regulations governing trade and the treatment of workers. The risk of dramatic disruption to the economies of the constituent states was small.

Any discrepancies between what was conceded and what was gained by nations could be tolerated as the support of neighbours for one another and the promotion of peace on the continent.[82]

A bargaining process, based on partisan interest, rather than a rational ideal, governed the evolution of international trade in the twentieth century, just as it did in the previous century. The rational theory of comparative advantage has had ample support, and has been highly influential, but the outcomes indicate it has not been the prime factor in the liberalisation of trade. The breakdown in multi-lateral negotiations experienced in recent years reflects the difficulties of maintaining support for and, hence, maintaining the influence of a rational ideal in a world of partisan interest. The rational ideal has come to be seen as a means by which one group hoodwinks others into doing what it wants.

The rapid expansion of international trade in the post-war period is often attributed to the reductions in tariffs and other measures of trade liberalisation introduced under the auspices of GATT and the WTO. But the expansion can also be attributed in part to the technological innovations introduced by companies providing the freight services required for international trade. In the nineteenth century the expansion of trade was facilitated by the introduction of steamships. In the 1960s freight services companies began to format with intermodal containers. These lowered the unit costs of freight movement in ships, on trucks and by rail and, at the same time, lowered the unit costs of transferring freight between these modes. Because ships were obliged to spend less time in port, it was feasible to operate much larger vessels. Alongside the introduction of containers, specialist bulk carriers were built to carry oil, gas, cement, mineral ores and other bulk cargoes. The increasing size of such vessels brought lower unit costs. These innovations extended bargaining sets and influenced the volume, direction and content of international trade.

Company formats for trade in Japan and South Korea

The failure of rational theory is further apparent in the experience of those countries that have succeeded in the post-war period in making the transition from an agricultural economy to an industrial economy. Here, in particular, the importance of developing strong company formats is apparent. To compete with established multi-national conglomerate companies, countries such as Japan and South Korea recognised they would have to build their own companies of comparable bargaining strength. Of necessity, they evolved such companies from the military, political and economic situations in which they found themselves at the end of the Second World War.

The Japanese economy before the war was dominated by family-owned conglomerate organisations known as 'zaibatsu'. They were of major importance to the wartime strength of Japan. After the war, with Japan under American occupation, this wartime role, together with perceptions of monopolistic advantage and anti-competitive inclinations, led to the development of plans for the dissolution of the zaibatsu and the reconstruction of their functions in smaller units. In the evolving political circumstances of the time, however, it came to be seen that a strong Japan, with a strong economy, was needed as a bulwark against potential communist incursion. 'Keiretsu' were established as conglomerates, each controlled by a bank holding shares in the constituent companies, with the companies also bound together by interlocking shareholdings. The Mitsubishi, Mitsui (Sony, Fuji), Sumitomo (Mazda) and Toyota groups were all established on this format. The Japanese government, acting mainly through the Ministry of International Trade and Industry, provided extensive support to the keiretsu and other elements of the Japanese economy, particularly with regard to the development of export industries. The arrangements made Japan one of the most successful exporting countries in the world from the 1950s through to the 1980s, with corresponding rapid growth in the Japanese economy as a whole. The keiretsu formed the spearhead of the export drive. Employees of a keiretsu had more or less guaranteed employment for life and formed a privileged elite of citizens. James Fallows notes that Japan largely rejected the free-trade theory propagated by Britain and America, giving preference to a model of economic development that had more in common with that of List.[83] In terms of bargaining theory, Japan used the internal regulatory and promotional powers of the support-bargaining system to promote companies with strong bargaining positions in overseas vendor sets. The keiretsu were able to become established across international sets, displacing what were, in many cases, hitherto dominant Western conglomerate companies, even in their domestic markets.

In South Korea the conglomerates known as 'chaebol' played a similar role to that of the keiretsu. In this case, their origins lay in the takeover by Korean businessmen of Japanese companies in South Korea forfeited on the departure of the Japanese from the Korean peninsula after the war. The government identified the chaebol as the means by which the economy of South Korea could be transformed. It arranged for the provision of finance to them for specified projects and protected them in domestic markets with tariffs on imported goods. This government–business partnership successfully established South Korea as a major manufacturing nation and a major exporter of both consumer goods and heavy industrial goods. Samsung, LG Group and Hyundai became internationally prominent.

Alice Amsden draws out the contrast between the theory of free markets and free trade and the policies of the South Korean government:

> So deep is the belief in the explanatory power of these laws, so firmly held the conviction that if, and only if, they are free to operate will industrial expansion succeed, that any departure from them, whether in theory or practice, tends to be discredited, dismissed, disregarded, or disbelieved … In [South] Korea, instead of the market mechanism allocating resources and guiding private entrepreneurship, the government made most of the pivotal investment decisions. Instead of firms operating in a competitive market structure, they each operated with an extraordinary degree of market control, protected from foreign competition.[84]

Again, the parallel with List's theory is apparent. But the theory of money-bargaining, particularly the idea of companies formatting for viability and profit as money-bargaining agencies, provides the more comprehensive explanation of the success of the chaebol and keiretsu. To break in to international bargaining sets dominated by established conglomerate business organisations it was necessary to evolve organisations of comparable bargaining strength through concerted action of governments and business organisations. The method has drawbacks, principally in the abuse of strong domestic bargaining positions and the fostering of entitlements to continuous protection. But it created revenues for the budgets of the employees of the companies, the smaller companies that depended on them and the companies in which the employees spent their revenues. Beyond that, it created healthy budgets across Japan and South Korea. Living standards were dramatically raised in those countries by concentration on the establishment of companies with strong formats predicated on sales in international bargaining sets.

Amsden notes that technology played a major role in the establishment of the chaebol. It was, however, a different role from that played by technology in the industrialisation processes of Britain, Germany and the USA. In the earlier industrialisations, technological advance was a consequence of innovation. In the later industrialisation, it was a matter of learning about technology that already existed. She comments, 'The nature and role played by technical knowledge, therefore, separates the industrial revolutions in England, Germany, and the United States, on the one hand, from the industrialization that occurred in twentieth-century agrarian societies.'[85] The keiretsu also developed through the adoption of Western technology. In both cases, however, the companies evolved into significant technological innovators.

Notes

1 See Spread, Patrick, 2008, *Support-Bargaining: The Mechanics of Democracy Revealed*, Sussex: Book Guild, pp. 223–5.
2 Mathias, Peter, 2001, *The First Industrial Nation: The Economic History of Britain 1700–1914*, Abingdon and New York: Routledge, p. 79.
3 Mathias, 2001, p. 428. See also Table 6.1.
4 Mossner, E. C. and Ross, I. S. (eds), 1977, *The Correspondence of Adam Smith*, in Campbell, R. H. and Skinner, A. S., 1976–83, *The Glasgow Edition of the Works and Correspondence of Adam Smith*, Oxford: Clarendon Press, pp. 245–6. Quoted by Sutherland, Kathryn, 1998, Note to p. 303 of Smith, Adam, 1998, *Wealth of Nations*, Oxford: Oxford University Press, p. 550.
5 Mathias, 2001, pp. 266–7.
6 Mathias, 2001, pp. 270–3.
7 Deane, Phyllis and Cole, W. A., 1962, *British Economic Growth, 1688–1959*, Cambridge: Cambridge University Press, p. 235. For data on tonnage of sailing and steam ship construction and registration, see Mathias, 2001, p. 457.
8 Mathias, 2001, p. 286.
9 Deane and Cole, 1962, p. 236.
10 Smith, Adam, 2009, *An Enquiry into the Nature and Causes of the Wealth of Nations*, Adobe Digital Editions, pp. 330–2.
11 List, Frederick, 1856, *National System of Political Economy*, translated by G. A. Matile, Philadelphia: J. B. Lippincott, p. 118.

12 Mathias, 2001, pp. 272–5.
13 Robbins, Keith, 1979, *John Bright*, London, Boston and Henley: Routledge & Kegan Paul, p. 62.
14 Mokyr, Joel, 2011, *The Enlightened Economy: Britain and the Industrial Revolution 1700–1850*, London: Penguin, p. 154.
15 Mathias, 2001, pp. 276–7.
16 Mathias, 2001, p. 280.
17 Mathias, 2001, pp. 275–6.
18 Mathias, 2001, p. 278.
19 Mathias, 2001, pp. 282, 284, 287.
20 Mathias, 2001, pp. 297–8.
21 Mathias, 2001, pp. 298–9.
22 Mathias, 2001, p. 301.
23 Mathias, 2001, pp. 312–14.
24 Mathias, 2001, p. 301.
25 List, 1856, p. 440.
26 Smith, Adam, 1998, *Wealth of Nations*, Oxford: Oxford University Press, pp. 288–9, 291–3. First published as *An Enquiry into the Nature and Causes of the Wealth of Nations*, 1776.
27 Smith, 1998, p. 300.
28 Smith, 1998, p. 292.
29 Smith, 1998, pp. 293–4.
30 Smith, 1998, p. 296.
31 Smith, 1998, pp. 376–7.
32 Smith, 1998, pp. 344, 377–8.
33 See Mokyr, 2011, pp. 156–65.
34 Smith, 1998, pp. 156–7.
35 See also Spread, 2008, pp. 424–6.
36 Mathias, 2001, p. 269.
37 Maneschi, A., 1992, 'Ricardo's International Trade Theory: Beyond the Comparative Cost Example', *Cambridge Journal of Economics*, Vol. 16, No. 4, pp. 421–37, p. 433.
38 Gomes, Leonard, 1987, *Foreign Trade and the National Economy: Mercantilist and Classical Perspectives*, New York: St Martin's Press, p. 189. Quoted by Maneschi, 1992, p. 429, footnote 1.
39 Ricardo, David, 1951, *On the Principles of Political Economy and Taxation*, in Sraffa, Piero (ed.), 1951, *The Works and Correspondence of David Ricardo*, Vol. 1, Cambridge: Cambridge University Press, pp. 135–6.
40 Ricardo, 1951, p. 136.
41 Maneschi, 1992, pp. 432–3.
42 Ricardo, 1951, p. 397.
43 Ricardo, 1951, p. 137.
44 Ricardo, 1951, p. 140.
45 Hollander, Samuel, 1979, *The Economics of David Ricardo*, Toronto: University of Toronto Press, p. 465.
46 Maneschi, 1992, p. 426.
47 Samuelson, Paul, 1980, *Economics*, 11th edition, New York: McGraw–Hill, p. 49.
48 For a summary account of the neoclassical formulation of comparative advantage, see Schumacher, Reinhard, 2013, 'Deconstructing the Theory of Comparative Advantage', *World Economics Journal*, No. 2, pp. 83–105, ref. pp. 86–8. For full treatment, see Södersten, Bo and Reed, Geoffrey, 1994, *International Economics*, 3rd edition, Basingstoke and London: Macmillan, pp. 7–22, etc.
49 See Spread, Patrick, 2015a, 'Companies and Markets: Economic Theories of the Firm and a Concept of Companies as Bargaining Agencies', *Cambridge Journal of Economics*, Advance Access published 2 June 2015, doi:10.1093/cje/bev029. Reprinted

282 *The Evolution of Economies*

in Spread, 2015b, *Aspects of Support-Bargaining and Money-Bargaining*, E-Book, World Economics Association.

50 For further comment on international trade and the theory of comparative advantage, see Spread, 2008, Chapter 8, Corporate Format and Foreign Trade, and Chapter 9, Economic Theories of Foreign Trade.
51 List, 1856, pp. 117–18.
52 List, 1856, pp. 216–17.
53 List, 1856, pp. 217–18.
54 List, 1856, pp. 218–19.
55 List, 1856, p. 230. Original emphasis.
56 List, 1856, pp. 252–3.
57 List, 1856, pp. 308–9.
58 List, 1856, pp. 201, 411–12.
59 List, 1856, pp. 373–4.
60 List, 1856, p. 201.
61 List, 1856, pp. 366–7, 386.
62 List, 1856, pp. 278, 280.
63 List, 1856, pp. 275, 300.
64 List, 1856, p. 120.
65 List, 1856, p. 477.
66 List, 1856, pp. 265, 474, 480, 491.
67 List, 1856, pp. 494–7.
68 List, 1856, pp. 350–1.
69 List, 1856, p. 263.
70 List, 1856, pp. 417–20.
71 List, 1856, p. 417.
72 For example, Chang, Ha-Joon, 2008, *Bad Samaritans: The Guilty Secrets of Rich Nations & the Threat to Global Prosperity*, London: Random House Business Books; Chang, Ha–Joon, 2002, *Kicking Away the Ladder: Development Strategy in Historical Perspective*, London: Anthem.
73 See Sutherland, 1998, pp. xiii–xiv.
74 See, for example, Krugman, P. R. and Obstfeld, M., 2006, *International Economics: Theory and Policy*, 7th edition, Boston: Pearson Addison Wesley, pp. 11–14.
75 Spread, Patrick, 2011, 'Situation as Determinant of Selection and Valuation', *Cambridge Journal of Economics*, Vol. 35, No. 2, pp. 335–56, p. 354. Reprinted in Spread, Patrick, 2015b, *Aspects of Support–Bargaining and Money–Bargaining*, E-Book, World Economics Association.
76 On the ideological implications of support-bargaining and money-bargaining, see Spread, Patrick, 2004, *Getting It Right: Economics and the Security of Support*, Sussex: Book Guild, pp. 187–90.
77 GATT, Article 1, para. 1.
78 GATT, Article 28 bis, para. 1.
79 Hoekman, Bernard and Kostecki, Michel, 1995, *The Political Economy of the World Trading System*, Oxford: Oxford University Press, p. 27.
80 Hoekman and Kostecki, 1995, pp. 218–21.
81 Tussie, Diana and Woods, Ngaire, 2000, 'Trade, Regionalism and the Threat to Multilateralism', in Woods, Ngaire (ed.), 2000, *The Political Economy of Globalization*, London: Palgrave, pp. 54–76, pp. 54, 67.
82 For further analysis of international trade arrangements, see Spread, 2008, pp. 230–7.
83 Fallows, James, 1994, *Looking at the Sun: The Rise of the New East Asian Economies*, New York: Pantheon, pp. 179–207.
84 Amsden, A. H., 1989, *Asia's Next Giant: South Korea and Late Industrialisation*, New York: Oxford University Press, p. 139.
85 Amsden, 1989, pp. 3–4.

9 Information and the evolution of communications

The evolution of economies described in previous chapters was accompanied by a major expansion in the provision and use of information. This chapter is concerned with the way information is disseminated and used in bargaining societies and, hence, with the role it plays in the evolution of economies.

One major difference between neoclassical economic theory and the theory of support-bargaining and money-bargaining is that while the former has sought to evade information issues with an assumption of perfect information, in the latter the dynamics of information are a major part of the dynamics of the theory. In recent decades neoclassical theorists have developed an idea of 'asymmetric information' to escape the obvious weakness of an assumption of perfect information. But an assumption of perfect information is essential to the mathematics of the model, so that the introduction of asymmetric information to 'save' the model from its defects effectively invalidates it. The neoclassical approach to information is considered in later sections of this chapter.

Support-bargaining and money-bargaining systems run on information. Some part of the information is derived from direct observation of products and providers, but much the greater part is reported information in written or spoken form. Some services, such as financial services, are provided almost entirely on the basis of written information. In support-bargaining the dependence on reported information in written or spoken form is even greater than in money-bargaining. A capacious 'information interface' lies between bargaining agents and the realities that are their fundamental concern. It functions, in large measure, as an accessible and, hence, usable substitute for the realities. Our minds receive and process information, so that we necessarily make decisions and act on the basis of information. Its vital characteristic colours the whole bargaining system: it can be manipulated to advance the interests of bargaining agents.

The information interface is itself a creation of the bargaining process. Agents can only deal in what they know about, so information is basic to any transaction. But the terms under which transactions are made depend also on the information available about them, so every agent has an interest in ensuring that those he or she, or some organised agency, is dealing with have information conducive to favourable terms for himself or herself, or the organised agency. A selling agent wants a potential buyer to see that the object or service for sale is well fitted to the buyers' situation. This interest of the selling agent will not be altogether compatible with the interests of potential buyers, who want information that will enable then to assess whether their interests will be properly fulfilled. A potential buyer wants to know that what is being bought will fit his or her situation. Both sellers and buyers will want to impress the other that they have strong bargaining positions. Sellers, on the one hand, want to be 'exclusive' suppliers. They want bargaining sets constrained so that the buyer sees it as necessary to buy from them – 'Buy now while stocks last!' conveys the information that a stock situation imposes a time constraint on a bargaining set. Buyers, on the other hand, want it known that they have options.

There is further information relevant to both sides, relating to situations. As was seen in Chapter 1, the situations of buyers are not merely physical situations, but concepts of situation, derived from their social circumstances. Sellers will want potential buyers to have information implying that their situation is just such as will be accommodated by the product or service to be sold. In money-bargaining, the physical circumstances that are a considerable part of consumer situations give some stable grounding to a consumer situation, so that the fashions and fads developed through social support-bargaining have limited application in the definition of situation. In support-bargaining, situation concepts are ideas and ideologies, and potentially much more changeable. Ideologists and those who generate these abstract concepts of situation for the assembly of support tend to focus attention on 'iconic' events that play the role of physical things in the stabilisation of situation concepts. Democrats in England identify Magna Carta and the Glorious Revolution as vital to the understanding of their cause, though the details of these declarations are not entirely consistent with democratic ideals. The French Revolution is iconic to French nationalists, particularly French socialists, though the historical reality seems to have been extensively adapted to the requirements of later interest. British socialists see the 'Peterloo massacre' as critical exemplar of the struggle against elite authority. For proponents of Scottish independence, the Battle of Bannockburn encapsulates the ambition and prowess of the nation. These events give a degree of stability to the abstract notions they are held to exemplify, but the records of them are subject to adjustment through group support-bargaining to ensure they do the job required of them. What happened in the past is manipulated and supplemented to serve current purposes.[1]

As well as seeking to ensure that information conducive to their interests is in wide circulation, all agents will want to ensure that information detrimental to their interests is excluded from the information interface. Sellers of cars, computers, vegetables and all other products will not want any information in circulation that suggests the products are of poor quality, or not durable, or prone to breakdown. In the support-bargaining sphere, a government will not want information purveyed that indicates that its policies or actions are misconceived and unlikely to produce the results it has promised. Authoritarian regimes commonly depend heavily on the suppression of adverse information to maintain the support necessary to their continued ascendance.

For all these reasons, the information interface is shot through with the manipulation that agents apply to ensure that the interface is conducive to their bargaining advantage. The strength of motivation to gain bargaining advantage is such that fact is blurred easily into invention. Even the most egregious fiction gains support as fact if it advances important interests. Societies and their economies evolve from situation to situation, so that the information established and accepted regarding situations dictates the evolutionary course. Bargaining societies evolve through the information interface that their own bargaining systems create. Changes in the information interface transformed attitudes in Britain in the run-up to the industrial revolution. The disparities between the information interface prevalent at a certain time and the actual situation may become apparent later when the people of the later time, with different interests, review from their new perspective the situation of the former time and create an alternative information interface.

The relationship between the information interface and the reality it purportedly portrays is clearly of great importance to the evolutionary process. In some cases, the partisan interests of the agents concerned so dominate the creation of the interface that it becomes substantially detached from reality. The 'dodgy dossier' released by the British government prior to the invasion of Iraq gave a false impression of the armaments of Iraq. It played a part in what many now regard as an unwise decision by the British government to participate in the invasion of Iraq in 2003.[2] After 96 people were killed when a crush barrier collapsed at the Hillsborough football stadium in Sheffield in 1989, the police provided information indicating that Liverpool football fans had caused the accident by their unruly behaviour. An independent inquiry in 2012 found that police accounts of the incident had been primarily concerned to cover failings of the police. The police established an information interface that did not accurately portray the actual event. When societies evolve on the basis of an information interface that is far removed from the realities, they can become seriously unstable. The Soviet Union built an information interface in accordance with communist ideology, which proved to be so far detached from reality that the Union collapsed.

The information interface regarding immediate transactions of money-bargaining is largely created by companies engaged in selling goods and services. They disseminate information about their products designed to give them presence in the bargaining sets of potential buyers. In money-bargaining the physical nature of the goods that are bought and sold makes information about them generally less ambiguous than that which relates to abstract ideas about society. As has been seen, physical objects stabilise and harmonise perceptions, bringing greater confidence in the information that is shared about them. But it is still quite common for misinformation to cause people to buy products that turn out to be ill-fitted to their situation. With trade in services the potential for misinformation is greater than with physical goods.

In the provision of financial services information is of particular importance. It was seen in Chapter 7 that confidence is a critical factor in financial valuations.

Confidence is generated by group support, and group support is generated by assent to information. It is characteristic of financial securities that they exist at some remove from the realities on which their value depends. They are 'derivatives', with their underlying value depending on trading performances. In many cases, the underlying value depends on the trading performances of many organisations, so that it becomes a complex task to identify the underlying value. The 'market' value, the price investors will pay for them, depends on what investors believe they are worth. There is an information interface connecting the value of the securities with the value of the trading to which they are linked. Fed certain information, an investor group will escalate its valuation of a security. The information easily becomes detached from the realities it purportedly conveys, as happened with the sub-prime mortgage securities described in Chapter 7. The information is shaped primarily for the assembly of support and the generation of confidence in the securities at issue, not so much for the revelation of the truth about the transactions on which the value of the securities is dependent. Financial instruments offer particular scope for the divorce of information from the realities that determine their underlying value. In the case of the mortgage-backed securities traded in the early 2000s, the revelation of the divergence precipitated a major global financial crisis. Where the information interface diverges far from reality, whether a political, economic or financial reality, a sharp correction is likely to occur at some point, to be variously described as a 'revolution', 'insurrection', 'collapse', 'recession', 'depression', 'slump', 'crisis' or 'emergency'. In the economic and financial sphere, these corrections are invariably 'downwards', confirming that their origin lies in the 'talking up' of the interface for bargaining advantage.

The media and the information interface

Companies want information about themselves and their products purveyed in terms favourable to their sales. Businessmen then see opportunities to format companies to provide this service. They format companies that purvey the appropriate information in return for payments from the companies whose products they are promoting. Advertising agencies are employed by both money-bargaining and support-bargaining agencies to get across information that they want people to have about goods, services and policies.

Since all bargaining agents need certain information, there is scope also for the format of companies to provide information that will be paid for by its recipients. This has given rise to the emergence of a major industry whose activities have profoundly affected the evolution of bargaining systems, both political and economic. Media companies are formatted for provision of a great range of news, advertising, entertainment and business information. The size of media industries at any stage of economic evolution is not commonly as great in monetary terms as that of other leading industries, but their impact has probably been as great, or greater, than any of them. To a large extent, they make bargaining systems operable by disseminating the information necessary to their function. The information interface, at least with regard to quotidian events, is largely woven by and through the media.

Media formats commonly derive revenues both from those who want information, who buy newspapers, or internet, radio or TV services, and from those who want information disseminated, who buy advertising space, either directly or through advertising agencies. While neoclassical theory has the greatest difficulty in accommodating information as a 'product' and, hence, in the idea of buying and selling information, the buying and selling of information has been a major factor in the evolution of both money-bargaining and support-bargaining systems. Transport systems underpin essential physical aspects of money-bargaining, while the media underpin essential information requirements.

Much of the output of the media is concerned with support-bargaining rather than money-bargaining. It is in support-bargaining that information is most distinctively and copiously required. It goes into the construction of ideologies and the evolution of ideologies in response to current events. The media engage in a kind of intellectual support-bargaining akin to that of institutions of higher education. They assemble support for different interests by assembling support for ideas relating to those interests. But media organisations are primarily money-bargaining agencies, and their role in intellectual support-bargaining is heavily influenced by this primary function. The funding arrangements for institutions of higher education mean that their requirements for revenue are a less immediate influence on the dissemination of information and the formation of ideas.

Since the evolution of money-bargaining is heavily dependent on support-bargaining, the focus of media interest on support-bargaining does not mean that it has a minor role in the dissemination of information related to money-bargaining. An economy evolves on the basis of ideas established through support-bargaining. The freedoms accorded to companies or trade unions depend on support-bargaining. Economic policies are of central interest in support-bargaining, and a focus of media debate. Government budgets are shaped by support-bargaining and affect the conduct of the rest of the money-bargaining system. Through support-bargaining and the intellectual support-bargaining conducted in and around the media the ground rules for money-bargaining are established. The role of the state, as described in Chapter 6, derives very largely from intellectual support-bargaining carried on through the media.

While this intellectual support-bargaining largely determines the actions of the state in regulation of money-bargaining, it is apparent that the outcomes of debate in the media are conditioned by the function of media organisations as money-bargaining agencies. Only such information as people are prepared to pay for, or that they will pay to have propagated, goes into the making of the information interface by the media. The interlinking of support-bargaining and money-bargaining is critically close in the creation of the information interface which is the immediate object of support-bargaining.

The importance of the media in the intellectual support-bargaining involved in government means that its leading organisations and agents become effectively part of an 'insider group' that governs a country. In principle, 'democracies' are governed by the people and those who have some claim to 'represent' the people. Democratic societies establish formal support-bargaining structures that ensure that, in the last resort, the people's 'representatives' make the final decisions. But for practical purposes the groundwork on policy formation has to be done through wide-ranging discussions conducted, at least as far as public discussion is concerned, through the media. Editors, proprietors and leading journalists in the media have a major role in determining the information that reaches people and the way it is interpreted. They consequently have a big influence on movements in support in their societies. Their role in the provision of information means that they constitute part of the political process, whether or not the accepted ideology recognises or endorses their role. As the title of Lance Price's study of *Where Power Lies: Prime Ministers v The Media* indicates, the relationship between governments and the media in Britain is fractious. But he recognises that the media form part of the process of government:

> The media, or at least those in the media who help cover what goes on at Westminster, don't merely observe the political system; they are part of it. They don't just scrutinise the exercise of power ... they are elements of the machinery through which it is exercised.[3]

The revelations in 2010–13 regarding relationships between politicians and Rupert Murdoch's News International group made clear the extent to which media organisations participate in government. Leading politicians were negotiating for support from News International and dissemination of information favourable to their policies. There was public concern at the extent to which practice diverged from democratic principle, but those seeking to assemble support in a support-bargaining system must necessarily seek the support of those who shape the information that reaches their electorate.

The evolutionary expansion of the role of the media constituted a major change in the provision for government in Britain. It has profoundly affected the evolution of the British economy. Without the media, insider groups are small. In the later seventeenth century and in the eighteenth century grand Whig and Tory families engaged in insider support-bargaining in Mayfair salons, gentlemen's clubs in Pall Mall and country houses. Up to the end of the nineteenth century, and even into the twentieth century, insider groups in Britain remained 'upper crust', if not entirely aristocratic. The media increasingly enlarged and diversified the insider group. They have purveyed information beyond the insider group, permitting much more extensive and effective participation in the support-bargaining structures that determine government. Without the media and the intellectual support-bargaining they lead, assembly of support from beyond the immediate small circle of committed insiders becomes a crude matter of treating the tribe. Even in the nineteenth century in Britain elections were won and lost on the financial capacity of candidates to fête their electors.

Organisation of information

The dissemination of information around a bargaining society is a consequence of all agents trying to establish their bargaining positions in the money-bargaining system or the support-bargaining system, or, given their close interlock, in both. One of the keys to doing this is the establishment of basic concepts of situation that make people receptive to certain types of information. In a money-bargaining system, this basic reference point is well understood in terms of 'situation', implying certain physical surroundings and social circumstances. In support-bargaining the 'situation' is to be understood in more abstract terms as ideas, ideologies, faiths, theories or frames of reference. Democracy, fascism, socialism, communism, nationalism, business, humanitarian principles, freedom, etc. all provide means of selecting, excluding and organising information. They constitute organising frames for dealing with information. With such organising frames the information interface is created. It means that the interface is irregular, with concentrations of information around the organising frames adopted by a society and its subgroups. Like knots in a plank, the organising frames concentrate swirls of information around themselves.

These distinct frames that govern organisation of information are generally regarded by the groups using them as permanent and proper understanding of the social realities in which they find themselves. Other organising frames are looked on as deceptive, mistaken or prejudiced, and consequently to be opposed in pursuit of the social justice, rights or some more fundamental truth that is conceived as characteristic of their own organising frame. Their holders are rivals and, in some cases, enemies. The idea of support-bargaining distinctively accommodates a variety of organising frames. It provides a 'frame of frames' through which a great range of information, relating to different frames, can be assimilated and understood.[4]

It was suggested in *Support-Bargaining, Economics and Society* that there is a 'common theory' acquired by all, partly by biological inheritance and partly through social support-bargaining, that enables humans to make sense of the world and their societies.[5] As a 'default', information will be organised by reference to this common theory. People have in their common theory a more or less complete idea of their local situation – the houses, streets, people, shops, etc. which comprise their immediate physical surroundings. The common theory also incorporates understanding of the nature and status of the commonplace things that are bought and sold, so that much money-bargaining is conducted on the basis of common theory. The idea of ownership can be regarded as part of common theory. But common theory also incorporates ideas relating to personal and social identity or 'belonging', such as religious faith and national affiliation.

The more sophisticated frames of reference, the theories and ideologies formulated mainly in institutions of higher education, may be seen as derived from aspects of common theory by subgroups to assemble support for advance of their particular interests. They constitute composite ideas that give immediate grasp of highly complex situations, or at least the feeling of grasp. In effect, they enable us to orient ourselves amid a confusion of information. It was suggested in *Support-Bargaining, Economics and Society* that our brains act, in some respects, as symmetry computers and through a sense of symmetry we can assemble complex information into forms that give us a sense of comprehension.[6] We use the sense of symmetry also in the ordinary course of money-bargaining, to determine what furniture will fit into a room, or what new clothes will complement those we already have. The sense of symmetry is the essential cognitive faculty of money-bargaining and support-bargaining and, hence, also an essential factor in the selection, evasion, organisation and manipulation of information.

The function of frames of reference or organising frames is readily understood in the relatively uncontentious context of sporting competition. Common theory includes the sense of nationality, acquired early in life through social support-bargaining. Virtually everyone has a sense of nationality and will use it as a means of organising information. The Olympic Games are presented as a celebration of human sporting prowess, but without the sense of competition between nations it would lose much of its interest. People approach the Games through the understanding of nationality. Information consistent with an idea of national excellence is selected for propagation among people who share the commitment to a particular nation. The selected information is manipulated so that it confirms the preconceptions embodied in the nationalist ideal. Gold medallists of one nation get headlines in the media of their nation, but they are ignored in the media of another nation, who concentrate on their own successes. A British newspaper that concentrated its reports on the achievements of Frenchmen, Turks and Prussians would not achieve the sales necessary to maintain the viability of its format. Frenchmen, Turks and Prussians will not read much about the exploits of British athletes in their newspapers. Media treat the Games in this way because people take pleasure in information that confirms and sustains the nationalistic ideal, and will pay for newspapers and television channels that propagate information in this form. Their payments constitute an expression of support for nationalistic ideals. Information that does not accord with the nationalistic ideal is likely to be evaded altogether or conveyed in abbreviated form. The Games are serious enough to excite passion, but generally not so serious as to excite the fear and animosity that arises in other nationalistic conflicts. But they are not always fun. There have been occasions when the nationalistic understanding of the Games has involved extreme confrontation. The Olympic Games of 1936 in Berlin were used by Adolf Hitler to propagate Nazi ideology and claims of Aryan supremacy. The USA and other countries boycotted the 1980 Olympic Games in Moscow in protest at the invasion of Afghanistan by the Soviet Union.

The selection and evasion is not entirely attributable to the effects of preconceived organising principles. Information is necessarily circulated with varying degrees of compression, ranging from the 'sound bite' to several volumes, or many megabytes. Media reports are compressed in accordance with space available in the adopted format, so that selection and evasion are imposed even beyond the inclination to select and evade. The capacity of the human brain to deal with information constitutes a further factor augmenting the propensity of bargaining agents to select and evade. People are obliged to select and evade to cope with the increasing volumes of information available. If there were no use of organising frames, it would still be necessary to abbreviate.

In society in general there are many subgroups, each with its own organising frame for handling information. Within each subgroup the ability to agree on the organisation and significance of information received maintains mutual support within the group and maintains the cohesion of the group. The great number of subgroups means that there is extensive disagreement and dispute. People commonly belong to several subgroups and may find it difficult to decide exactly where their sympathies lie. The friction between different subgroups and their interlock and overlap of membership means that all frames are adjusted as support moves between the subgroups. People born in one country but adopting another may find they belong to more than one nationalistic group, and may experience a degree of confusion over who they want to win at the Olympic Games. Some potential for movement in support is essential to the operation of a 'democratic' order of government. Rigidity of groups is characteristic of authoritarian or autocratic societies.

On this understanding, information is both selected on the basis of a given frame of reference and, being selected, used to confirm that the frame of reference is of sound construction. A sense of national superiority focuses attention on the performance of certain nationals, and people exposed only to reports of the excellence of those nationals will find confirmation of their national superiority. Support is assembled more tightly around the nationalist principle. With such solidarity, the interests of the national group can potentially be advanced.

These organising principles or frames of reference provide the filters by which people select and evade, so that, as noted above, the most important step in ensuring dissemination of information favourable to a particular interest is implanting the appropriate frame of reference in the minds of as many people as possible. In former times people battled intellectually and physically to establish a particular faith, or a particular interpretation of a particular faith, as the supreme truth. Through the twentieth century battles raged over democracy, fascism, socialism, communism and other secular ideologies. The outcomes determined the structure of information interfaces around the world and the conduct of support-bargaining and money-bargaining.

Manipulation of information

While the manipulation of information depends most fundamentally on establishing the organising frames which will ensure the desired filtering of information, the extensive availability of information in modern society, consequent on the existence of multiple organising frames in multiple subgroups, means that it is difficult to evade entirely information that is in some degree inimical to the favoured frame. A degree of manipulation may be required to give at least a superficial fit to the chosen frame. In the context of intellectual support-bargaining, the process of reconciling theories with observed reality has been referred to as 'welding', deriving from a comment of Robert Louis Stevenson.[7] In the political sphere this manipulation of information to reconcile events or observations to a political ideology has come to be referred to in the English-speaking world as 'spin'. Whatever the matter, its communication can always bounce it to the credit of right or left. Agents manipulate information to sustain support for their group and its ideas or ideology and direct support away from rival groups.

The manipulation of information is, in large part, a matter of word selection. Language provides the words for elevation, denigration, exaggeration, encouragement and threat. What is favourable to the group is presented in terms that exaggerate its significance; what is unfavourable is described in nugatory terms. Emollient words can make extreme behaviour seem acceptable. As was seen in *Support-Bargaining, Economics and Society*, language is remarkably well-adapted to the requirements of bargaining, to the extent that it appears to have evolved in large part for the purpose of bargaining.[8]

But beyond language there are ways of manipulating information to a purpose. Human character and motivation are always open to imputation by interested agents and, since different human characteristics instantly evoke approval or disapproval, imputed motivations readily evoke support or rejection. Much of the effectiveness of word selection derives from the use of approving or pejorative words to describe imputed motivations. Information that reflects badly on a particular group can be attributed by members of the group to the malice of their opponents. Fox hunting is banned in Britain because it is cruel to animals, but fox hunters hold that its opponents were motivated more by animosities related to social class rather than concern for animal welfare. Allegations of misbehaviour by a group can be explained as no more than justified reaction to offences committed by their enemies. A group may act offensively because it is 'provoked' by another. Supporters of one team may claim a foul committed by one of their players was no more than reaction to a more heinous offence committed by a player from the opposing team. A group whose favoured athlete falls in a race may insist that their man was tripped by a malicious opponent. Taken further, the malice is part of a conspiracy to thwart the ambitions of a nation. The manipulations are readily accepted by those whose frames of reference make them harmonious. Chains of psychological causation may be used to transfer offensive motivation from one group to another. The evolutionary nature of societies and economies means that the essential factor in unfolding events is often uncertain, leaving scope for interested parties to identify the critical agents in accordance with their interests.

Ascription of motivation is significant beyond the relatively minor instances of the previous paragraph. It is used to justify wars and constitutes the basis of major ideologies. A nation may justify a declaration of war on another nation by insisting that its motivation is the reversal of previous humiliations imposed on it by that other nation. Doubts about the justice of the Versailles Treaty after the First World War gave Hitler a justification for later territorial incursions that might otherwise have been resisted. A nation may even engineer an offence to itself or its people by another nation so that it can justify a declaration of war by reference to an acceptable motivation. In the ideological sphere, businessmen are understood as motivated by desire to earn a living and become rich, or at least become prosperous. Such motivations are regarded as tolerable, even if not particularly virtuous. They are the more tolerated when they are seen as giving rise to employment and prosperity for others. But those opposed to capitalism impute to businessmen the motivation of greed and, in doing so, erode their support. 'Greed' is a word indicating disapproval of motivation in common theory. Socialists claim to be motivated by compassion for the poor and oppressed, and gain support for what is perhaps the most virtuous of motivations in common theory. But their opponents suggest that the motive is the desire to have what others possess without working for it, and to gain the political power that will enable them to realise their desire. In a democracy, 'the people' must be wooed, and displays of compassion attract support. The ascription of motivation plays an important part in the manipulation of information, since it is seldom possible to know with any assurance the motives of other people, while there are ideas in common theory regarding what are desirable and acceptable motivations and what are not.

Ascription of motivation plays a vital role even in the more recondite forms of theory formation. As was seen in Chapter 7, neoclassical economists in the 1930s were unable to overlook the very high levels of unemployment that could not be explained in their frame of reference. Manipulation of information was necessary to achieve conformity with the frame, or rather to modify the frame in such a way as to accommodate the observed phenomenon. 'Welding' was required to reconcile the observed phenomenon to the frame of reference. It depends heavily on the ascription of motivation to the agents of the system. In Keynes's account of savings and investment the relevant motivation is taken to be 'not consuming' rather than 'saving', so that saving is necessarily equal to investment and Keynes's theoretical construction is harmonious. Similarly, interest is regarded as the reward for 'not hoarding' rather than the return for providing funds that are wanted on loan by someone else. Again, the imputed motivation and reward makes for harmony with the theoretical construction. Keynes argues that unemployment can be 'involuntary', implying that the common motivation to avoid unemployment is not strong, not effective or not relevant. On the basis of these diverse motivations Keynes constructed an 'information interface' that was reasonably harmonious in itself, but was not close to reality. He could do so because a large and influential theory group shared his commitment to the neoclassical frame and its naive assumptions about information.

The uncertainties and ambiguities of the social sciences that distinguish them from natural science are largely attributable to uncertainties and ambiguities of motivation, which are, at the same time, uncertainties and ambiguities of interests. Given certain motivations, people will do almost anything and, by imputing motivations to people, behaviour can be explained in accordance with the motives of the explainer. Natural science has only to contend with the motives of the explainer.

The evolution of communications

The volume of information in circulation today presents as great a contrast with the paucity of information 200 years ago as modern business does to the landowners and agriculturalists of 200 years ago. The media that circulate information have been one of the major impelling streams of economic evolution. The evolution of communication of information and the media formats that drive it have impacted both support-bargaining systems and money-bargaining systems, and the connections between the two. As in other industries, the evolutionary process has involved the incorporation of innovations in technology into media company formats.

The format opportunities lie, first, in the demand for information for the understanding of situation and the means by which it can be improved and, second, in the requirement for dissemination of information to advance the interests of the disseminators. The more important effects of developments in communications have generally been understood as political. This is no doubt partly because the stakes are higher in support-bargaining, where matters of security are at issue. Failure to get a message through may cost a battle, or even a war. But it may also be partly because money-bargaining is seen as less sensitive to ambiguities of information. A sack of potatoes is evidently a sack of potatoes, and its weight and whereabouts is not likely to be much contested. The information interface is not as potentially distorting as that involved in political transactions. It was, as was seen in Chapter 1, partly because of the characteristics of physical objects that money emerged as an appropriate bargaining counter.

Nevertheless, communications have been of vital importance to the evolution of money-bargaining. As has been seen, people can only buy what they know about. For a product to feature in the bargaining set of a potential buyer, the potential buyer must know about it. He or she will want to know also the features of the product or its provider that will fit it to his or her situation, or that may preclude it from the bargaining set. As with transport and transport infrastructure, information extends bargaining sets. The laying of the transatlantic telegraph cables facilitated business between Europe and America by making it possible for vendors on each continent to make known rapidly what they had available for sale and the terms on which it could be provided. In the modern age the internet makes possible transactions on a global basis, even if the goods themselves have to move at a slower pace.

Communication involves codification of information and transmission of information. Codification has taken many forms. Pre-eminently information has been codified in spoken and written languages, but other forms of codification have been used, including pictures, sculpture and sound. The type of codification can dictate the form of transmission, and vice versa. Information written on paper required, until very recently, physical transportation. Telegraphic communication required the Morse code. In recent time the availability of digital forms of transmission has brought about digital codification. The codification of information in language through handwriting has been speeded up by typing, printing and digital processing. Pamphlets, newspapers and books have been produced. Transmission has evolved over centuries from simple face-to-face conversation to transfer of writing and pictures on stone, wax, papyrus, paper, canvas, film and by digital means.

Codification: the printing press

One of the major changes in the codification of information came with the invention of the printing press in Europe, probably by Johannes Gutenberg around 1450. Its impact is sometimes taken as being simply a consequence of its facilitating the distribution of information in larger volume. This may be partly because it is difficult to understand the commercial impact of the printing press in terms of a marginal cost of production and marginal revenues derived from a universal market in a commodity called 'information'. In neoclassical theory, 'perfect information' is an assumption, so the invention of a printing press would be incomprehensible to a devout neoclassical economist. Even if that assumption is dropped, it is still difficult to incorporate 'information' into a quasi-neoclassical framework. 'Information' is valuable only in so far it is relevant to a situation. Each 'piece' of information is unique, so there is none of the homogeneity necessary to a neoclassical commodity. But it is easy to see that the impact of the printing press arose from the scope it gave for the format of viable printing and publishing companies. Just as with the technology of cotton production or iron production, it became possible to format viable businesses in printing, since the technology offered major reductions in the unit cost of producing pamphlets and books. Instead of scribes laboriously copying out documents by hand, a sixteenth-century press could produce about 3,600 pages per day. People who wanted to disseminate information could have their material printed at much cheaper rates. People who wanted information found pamphlets and books available at much cheaper prices.

Perhaps most importantly, the printing press opened the way to the format of newspaper companies. It was found that sufficient numbers of people would pay a price for a newspaper that covered the unit cost of its production on a printing press to make provision of newspapers a viable company format. News modified to the interests of potential readers could be sold profitably. Proprietors of newspapers could even disseminate their own views profitably, provided their views coincided sufficiently well with what people were prepared to pay for – which meant broadly that they were members of the same political, ideological or interest groups as their potential readers. Independent wealth might not be essential to the dissemination of information conducive to the advancement of opinion. The successful format of a media business required moulding the product to a vendor set, and achieving unit costs that made feasible a price at which the volume of sales would produce viable revenues. The moulding process quickly established that scandal and sensation attracted coins from pockets. Murder, fornication, adultery and brutality all sold well. People would also pay for entertainment, in the form of comic strips and crosswords. Sober political news that might seem the citizens' most urgent requirement had limited reception. Successful newspapers were packages of information and entertainment.

The acceleration in the evolution of the British economy described in Chapter 5 increased the requirements for a great range of information, related not just to economic transactions, but also to political and social support-bargaining, as they evolved in response to economic change. New technology for the codification of information strengthened the formats of media companies. The new low-cost iron was used to replace the wood of printing presses. Charles Stanhope introduced an iron hand press in 1804 which doubled the rate of production on printing presses, with corresponding reductions in unit costs. Then Friedrich Koenig introduced the essential technology of the industrial revolution to the codification of information with a patented steam press. In 1814 a steam-powered printing press was installed in Printing House Square to print *The Times*. This press offered four times the productivity of the Stanhope press. It made it possible to start printing later and include more up-to-date news in the paper. The product was improved and its unit cost of production was reduced.[9] A steam-powered rotary press, invented by Richard Hoe in 1843 in the USA, further increased the rate of output of printed material and lowered the unit cost.

The output of printing and publishing companies may not have been high in monetary terms, but it probably had as much influence on the evolution of support-bargaining and money-bargaining as the cotton, iron, railway or shipping industries. It opened many bargaining sets by disseminating essential information. It created much of the information interface on which support-bargaining and money-bargaining were focused. It constitutes one of the central necessities of a bargaining system, without which little else can function effectively.

The spread of printing presses brought about a corresponding increase in requirements for paper. Paper was made by hand in Europe from rags for many years until advances in mechanised production reduced handmade paper to a small high-quality segment of the market in the mid-nineteenth century. The Foudrinier paper-making machine used in Britain from the early nineteenth century originated in a patent of Nicolas-Louis Robert in France, granted in 1799. The process produced broad widths and long lengths of paper, rather than the single sheets of those who produced by hand. The Foudrinier brothers commissioned Bryan Donkin, an engineer, to develop the machine. Steam power was first used for paper-making in Britain in 1786. Wood pulp began to be used for paper-making around the middle of the nineteenth century, stimulated by technical developments and a growing shortage of rags. In the last decade of the nineteenth century and into the twentieth century improvements in the technology for production of paper from wood pulp and the increasing scale of production significantly reduced the unit cost of paper production, thereby expanding the opportunities for format of printing and publishing companies.

It was suggested in Chapter 5 that the industrial revolution in the West was sustained because of the freedom to incorporate new technology in company formats that brought monetary returns and sustained incomes. In other countries, such as China, where technological advances comparable to those in the West had been made, often at earlier dates, the repression of commercial initiatives meant there was less scope to maintain advances in technology. This may be true with regard to the printing press. Presses with movable type were invented in China and Korea before their invention in Europe,[10] but they did not have the same impact, possibly because, as with other technological innovation, their commercial potential could not be so readily exploited. But printing presses posed further difficulties for authorities that could not tolerate the free format of companies. The dissemination of information by companies constituted a threat to the control of the authorities on the thinking of their people, and consequently a threat to their continued rule. The printing press was potentially an instrument for the assembly of support for rebellion.

In Europe it was used for that purpose. The Reformation of the sixteenth century made full use of printing presses to spread the new word in pamphlets and books. Many presses were established across Europe. Martin Luther and Erasmus were best-selling authors. Fox's *Book of Martyrs*, first published in 1563, was required reading for Protestants for centuries. But the increased capacity for dissemination of information aroused predictable alarm in those who, with the old technologies, controlled the dissemination of information and did not want information other than such information as they favoured made available to those who might threaten their positions. The Roman Catholic Church introduced the 'Index of Prohibited Books' to counteract the printed propaganda of the Protestants.[11] Churchmen in general were worried that the lower orders would be able to study the scriptures for themselves and draw conclusions. They would no longer be dependent on what they were told.[12] The fears of the conservatives were not entirely misplaced. Bloody religious wars raged across Europe in the seventeenth century.

The importance of information, and hence the importance of the printing press, in the evolution of societies is apparent in the different experience of countries that permitted format of companies with printing presses and those that did not. In Western Europe printing presses came to be accepted, and the socio-economic evolution of the countries of Western Europe proceeded at an accelerating pace. In countries where printing presses were forbidden, or where their introduction was highly restricted, the evolutionary process was retarded. In Russia, printing presses were only introduced when the Tsar himself saw advantages in them. Peter the Great established a printing press in St Petersburg in 1711 and further presses in subsequent years. Their locations suggest the Tsar was mainly concerned with the dissemination of knowledge about modern science and technology, especially military technology.[13] The suspicion of printing presses remained. One of the charges against Fyodor Dostoevsky when he was arrested in 1849, along with other members of the Petrashevsky Circle, was that he knew of the intention to set up a printing press. The constraints on the establishment of printing presses meant that the evolutionary process was deprived of its fuel. People did not know where they were and consequently could not tell where they should go. They were left vulnerable to extremist fantasies that took hold in the nineteenth century and became bitter reality in the twentieth century.

The authorities in the Islamic world were similarly reluctant to countenance the introduction of printing presses. The ruler of the Ottoman Empire, Sultan Selim I, issued a decree in 1515 prescribing death as the penalty for printing. Permission to establish the first printing press in Turkey was given only in 1726. Opposition from scribes and religious leaders meant that it printed few books and did not last long. The first official Turkish gazette was published in 1831 and the first unofficial Turkish newspaper in 1840.[14] The rulers of the Ottoman Empire protected their autocratic position by suppressing the communication of information that might permit the formation of situation concepts other than that which was already established in their people and cultivated in the mosques. The evolution of Islamic societies, and of Turkey in particular, was impeded by lack of information. The Islamic scholarly tradition of earlier centuries was not revived. The Ottoman Empire entered a long period of decline. In the early twentieth century Kemal Ataturk tried to compress the thwarted social evolution of centuries into a period of radical reform based on what European societies had become. In the twenty-first century, Islamic societies, arguably disoriented by centuries of stunted evolution, remain vulnerable to advocates of extreme reorientation.

Transmission of information

Even with printing presses there remained the question of how the books and pamphlets were to be transmitted to potential readers. Throughout most of human history written messages could be conveyed no faster than people could travel from place to place. Messages were conveyed by walking or running, by boat, on horseback or in horse-drawn carts and carriages. Horses formed the basis of early attempts to format companies for the transmission of information. In the sixteenth century the Tassis family formatted a business that dominated the provision of postal services in Europe with a courier system centred on Brussels.[15] In Britain Charles I opened his royal postal service to public use in 1635, with the costs of transmission of letters payable by the recipient. Technology, in the form of railways, displaced horses in the nineteenth century, increasing the carrying capacity, the speed and the geographical coverage of the postal service. Technology also improved the convenience of postal communication in 1840 with the introduction of the adhesive and perforated stamp, making it possible to pay in advance for transmission. Letters and parcels were delivered conveniently to the doors of those to whom they were addressed. The improved speed and convenience of the postal service was of particular value to businesses, though political pressure groups also found them useful. The Anti-Corn Law League used the post to great effect in its campaigns.[16] The advent of air services in the twentieth century speeded the transmission of information in written form to all parts of the world.

The evolution of the railways facilitated evolution of the telegraph as a form of information transmission, since the early wires could be strung along the routes used by the railways, where rights of way had already been established. Electric telegraphic communications started in Britain in 1837. While the wires of the early telegraph system in Britain followed the railway lines, electronic communications soon established their own evolutionary stream independent of modes of human travel. Intercontinental cables, wireless transmission and satellite transmission made communications virtually instantaneous over long distances. Messages were conveyed into homes and businesses, available at the touch of a button or the lift of a receiver. Telegraphic communications were of particular importance to the evolution of transport systems. Railway companies could keep their people down the line informed of changes to their schedules. Perhaps more importantly, the evolution of shipping services that was so important to global trade development, and to Britain's role in it, owed much to telegraphic communications. By means of the telegraph it was possible to keep shipping occupied and keep down its unit costs.

The effects of the modern evolution of mobile phones has had a particular impact in extending bargaining sets of farmers in remoter parts of the world where channels of communication have been historically very limited. They can obtain information about requirements and prices for their produce in distant and different bargaining sets. The scope for format of viable businesses has been significantly enhanced. The electronic media have also greatly enhanced the transmission of pictures, including moving pictures. Much information about goods can be conveyed by pictures of them. Potential buyers can be reassured with a picture that goods on offer will fit their situation.

Viability of transmitting companies

The speed, volume, range and convenience with which information can be delivered help to determine its unit cost and the viability of a business providing communications services. Because, as noted above, there are people who want information distributed to others and people who want information for themselves, providers of information have always had two potential categories of revenue to make their formats viable. Companies are ready to pay for the publication of information that promotes sales of their products. The more copies a newspaper sells, and the more affluent its readers, the more it can gain in advertising revenues. In the USA there were few qualms about newspaper advertising. The press was dependent on advertising from the eighteenth century on.[17] In Europe newspaper proprietors were generally more dependent on revenues from those who bought their product for the information in it that was valuable to them, and the entertainment provided along with it. The technology of communication evolved with the viability of the business formats it made possible.

The internet now approaches close to an ideal in speed, volume, range and convenience for the provision of information. Large volumes of information are available to hand almost instantaneously at minimal cost. The introduction of internet access through mobile phones and tablet computers has made access highly convenient. The contrast with earlier modes of transmission is particularly apparent in the use of the internet for sale of goods, where it has substantially superseded the mail order catalogues which, as was seen in Chapter 5, were pioneered as a method of sales by Sears, Roebuck in the late nineteenth century. While the internet plays much the same role as the catalogues, its evolution derives more from an evolutionary stream concerned with digital codification and transmission of information, involving a range of governmental, government-funded and business organisations. One of the end products made possible by the technological evolution is a fast, comprehensive, global, convenient and low-cost super-catalogue available to all for posting of their products. In its wake it has provided opportunities for the format of companies providing courier services to deliver goods bought from the super-catalogue. In this and other ways, the internet, like previous technological innovation in communications, is providing new impetus to the evolution of economies.

Information and neoclassical economics

The foregoing account of the role of information in the evolution of a money-bargaining system contrasts sharply with the treatment of information in neoclassical economic theory. Problems of information have been largely discounted in neoclassical theory by the assumption of perfect information. Consumers, labour and investors in a neoclassical system are assumed to be in possession of all relevant information about products, wages and prices. The assumption makes possible the application of reason and mathematics, and is consequently essential to neoclassical modelling. Without information, people, objects and abstractions cannot be defined in a way that permits their use in mathematical exposition. Any uncertainty opens the way to introduction of other human faculties that may be reasonable but are not strictly rational. The adoption of a frame of reference that assumes perfect information predisposes its users to ignore or skirt problems related to acquisition and use of information.

The model itself is so confined that the information required to make it work is very limited. Products are standardised so there are no issues of product differentiation or quality. Quantities can be measured and prices are public. Resources are standardised and everything about their productivity is known. To those enveloped in the model the assumption of perfect information may not appear as absurd as it does to those outside the theory group because the model requires only limited information.

The assumption of perfect information seems to have been justified also within the theory group by an idea that it keeps economics within the realms of 'common sense'. As noted above, in comparison with support-bargaining, the problems of information in money-bargaining may not seem acute. A sack of corn or a shirt is just what it seems to be, without any need for the complications of perception or projection of preconceptions. They can be counted, and prices can easily be attached to them. We see things wholly as they are, and that is enough for purposes of economic analysis. On this basis, economics is the down-to-earth subject that deals with 'things' as they obviously exist, without psychological complications or metaphysical abstraction. Such an understanding at least serves the purpose of those who merely require certain variables as starting points for mathematical analysis.

The idea that the assumption of perfect information was not too serious a drawback was sustained also by work suggesting that the market would function in much the same way with imperfect information as it did with perfect information, leading to much the same allocation of resources. Joseph Stiglitz argues that his work discounts this idea:

> These, and related, results of information economics show forcefully that the long-standing hypothesis that economies with imperfect information would be similar to economies with perfect information – at least so long as the degree of information imperfection was not too large – has no theoretical basis.[18]

The idea that moderate divergence from the state of perfect information was of little consequence with regard to the essential functioning and implications of the model made it possible for the theory group to maintain its commitment to the neoclassical model. It is, however, apparent that in the real world the availability of information is not only well short of perfect, but also that information is actively manipulated to advance interests. Imperfection of information implies a dynamic relating to the acquisition of information; imperfect information is systemically different to a state of perfect information.

Neoclassical theorists have also sought to deal with information simply as a 'product' much like any other. Stiglitz notes that:

> In the approach of many Chicago School economists, information economics was like any other branch of applied economics; one simply analyzed the special factors determining the demand for and supply of information, just as one might analyze the factors affecting the market for wheat.[19]

'Information', however, is the antithesis of the neoclassical product. A neoclassical 'product' is standardised. A potato is just a potato, with each indistinguishable from all others. Information is highly varied and, as was noted above, valuable only in so far as it fits particular situations. To fit any particular situation it may need shaping and refining to a particular form. Relevance is all. It is just that idea of shaping and refining products to situations that is an essential feature of products in a bargaining system, but entirely lacking in neoclassical theory. Information enables people to understand their situations, ranging from the highly abstract and ideological to the very precise and physical, and thereby judge their interests. It then enables them to identify what will advance their interests. Because of its value in these functions, information can itself be bought and sold. But because of its relation to situation, people will only value relevant information. Information can be traded in support-bargaining and money-bargaining systems, but it is beyond the understanding of neoclassical theory.

Even in bargaining systems, however, there is the problem of establishing what information is relevant before it is actually acquired. This dilemma is commonly resolved, to the extent possible, by buying information from sources that are regarded, on the evidence of experience or by report, as likely to provide information relevant to the extant situation. Achieving viability for a media organisation normally involves establishing a reputation as provider of relevant information with a requisite number of buyers.

Agents of bargaining systems will also receive copious information that others think is relevant to them. As was seen above, information is so important to the formation of ideas of situation and interests that agents of bargaining systems positively want certain information in circulation. Some information, far from being for sale, is forced upon people. Public relations operatives, ideologists, propagandists and advertisers distribute information free of charge as a means of advancing their interests.

Adaptation of neoclassical theory to information issues

It is apparent from the quotations from Stiglitz above that the peculiarity of the neoclassical assumption of perfect competition has not gone unremarked within the neoclassical theory group. In recent years it has come to be recognised that issues surrounding information are severely damaging to the neoclassical model. Stiglitz, in particular, argues that the differences in the information held by different agents are sufficient not only to expose the neoclassical paradigm as false, but also to constitute a new paradigm.[20]

The problem of information in neoclassical economic theory was first brought to the forefront of attention among orthodox economists by George Stigler. In his 1961 article on 'The Economics of Information' he suggests that price dispersion, the observable differences in price for the same product or service, is a consequence of imperfect information. Stigler introduces the idea of searching as a means of overcoming deficiencies of information and, hence, reducing price dispersion. Buyers are required to identify the best price, on the calculation that, 'If the cost of search is equated to its expected marginal return, the optimum amount of search will be found.'[21] The process conforms to the basic dynamic of the neoclassical model in requiring that the marginal cost be equated to the marginal return, even if it is only an 'expected' marginal return. Price dispersion as an anomaly of neoclassical theory is reconciled with neoclassical theory through a mechanism that is distinctly neoclassical.

Some years later, in a study of the market for automobiles, George Akerlof produced a mathematical model showing that where there are deficiencies of information such that it is not possible for buyers to distinguish the quality of different cars for sale, and with a single market price fixed on the basis of an 'average quality', cars of good quality may be withdrawn from sale because the owners cannot get what they think their car to be worth. The only cars that come onto the market are the bad cars because only they get a price acceptable to their owners. 'Lemons', bad cars, are sold more readily than good cars. In some circumstances it is possible to have, 'the bad driving out the not-so-bad driving out the medium driving out the not-so-good driving out the good in such a sequence of events that no market exists at all'.[22] Towards the end of his article Akerlof notes that 'counteracting institutions' have been established to overcome the difficulties involved with uncertainties over quality. These include the provision of guarantees by vendors and the use of brand names. But while these will reassure buyers who are deterred from markets by doubts over quality, they will not induce the sellers of good-quality cars to sell when they can only get the price that applies to all cars, based on average quality, as in Akerlof's mathematical model.

With a theory of situation-related interests it is apparent that the more likely origin of market extinction is the concerns of buyers as to whether they are going to get a product that will fit their situation. Car buyers opt for large cars, small cars, estate cars, hatchbacks, four-wheel drive vehicles or sports cars according to their lifestyle or situation. All, of course, want a car that is reliable. Most particularly, none will want a car that is going to break down irreparably within a month. If the experience of car buying is such that these last requirements relating to quality cannot be relied upon, then the car market might contract very sharply, and might even, in special circumstances, be extinguished altogether. The provision of guarantees seems designed to foster trade in cars and forestall any possibility of such contraction of the market.

Akerlof argues that the provision of health insurance is analogous to the 'lemons' problem in the car market.[23] The suppliers of health insurance withhold insurance from the over-65s because the premiums they would have to charge are so high as to attract only the health 'lemons'. The good risks are driven out of the market because they cannot get a premium that reflects the true risk of insuring them.

But the market for health insurance is different to that of cars. While in Akerlof's model of the car market it is the supplier who knows the quality of his or her car and opts to withhold it from sale at the price available, in the health insurance market it is the buyer who knows the state of his or her health and opts to forego insurance when the price is unreasonably high. With any applicant for health insurance, whatever age, the seller needs to know the health situation of the buyer, since he or she is taking on risk that is contingent on the health of the buyer. Health insurance is problematic because the seller is acquiring risk, and potentially heavy expense, that he or she cannot assess without the cooperation of the buyer.

The assumption of different qualities in products by both Stigler and Akerlof breaks with the neoclassical assumption, essential to the model and its optimal allocation of resources, that products are homogeneous. It also introduces notions of expectations, uncertainty, time and risk that mean the model is no longer a rational account of resource allocation. The proposed remedies are at best patches for a model that might be regarded as wholly discredited by such introductions. In their efforts to take consumer choice closer to reality, both writers invalidate the basic model. In *A Theory of Support and Money Bargaining* information is identified as one of the pivotal anomalies of neoclassical theory which can only be accommodated by the new paradigm of support-bargaining and money-bargaining.[24]

Michael Spence suggests that information deficiencies are overcome by 'signalling'. His model describes the emergence of equilibrium in an employment market, based on assumptions regarding educational level, productivity, costs of education and the relationships between them, including a feedback loop on observed productivity.[25] 'Signalling' is implicitly defined through the model as a means of imparting information relevant to investment decisions under uncertainty.[26] 'Signalling' has latterly been understood as the rather more simple circumstance in which information is passed, either intentionally or unintentionally, from one agent to another concerning a transaction. For example, a candidate for a job might signal his or her capacity to do the job by reference to education. An executive might unwittingly signal to another agent that the shares in his or her company are overvalued by selling his or her shareholding at the market price.[27] People buy cars and houses that signal their social and financial status, or are read as signalling their social and financial status.

Information is also acquired by 'screening'.[28] A person with deficient information may screen aspects of the behaviour of a potential counterpart in a transaction and draw conclusions. For a provider of health insurance, the fact that a potential client is ready to climb stairs to a fifth-floor office will suggest a healthy person and a good insurance risk.[29]

Asymmetric information

Akerlof identifies the 'lemon' in markets for automobiles as a matter of 'asymmetric information'. He contrasts the situation which potentially leads to the extinction of the market for cars with a situation of 'symmetric information', in which there is an advantage in utility, expressed in mathematical terms, over the case of asymmetric information. 'Asymmetric information' has been adopted as the central economic response to the problem of information. It has, however, come to be understood more in terms of differences in information between agents, and difference from 'perfect information', rather than as a specific contrast between circumstances of symmetric and asymmetric information. A situation of symmetric information, in the sense of complete equality of information, is little less absurd in the real world than the assumption of perfect information.

Stiglitz discusses asymmetric information mainly by reference to insurance, employment and credit markets, and Akerlof's used car market. Thus:

> Much of the research I describe here focuses on *asymmetries* of information, the fact that different people know different things. Workers know more about their own abilities than the firm does; the person buying insurance knows more about his health ... than the insurance firm. Similarly, the owner of a car knows more about the car than potential buyers; the owner of a firm

knows more about the firm than a potential investor; the borrower knows more about the riskiness of his project than the lender does; and so on.[30]

The common factor is that, in these transactions, one agent is better informed than the other. The differentials arise because each agent necessarily knows more about his or her own situation than the counterpart agent. Since interests relate to situation, each agent knows the interests arising from his or her situation.

Analysis on the basis simply of one agent being better informed than the counterpart misses some important differences, already alluded to in the context of Akerlof's study. In the case of employment and the sale of cars the relevant information is controlled by the sellers. A seller of work, the applicant for a job, knows his or her capacities and can assess their fit to the job on offer, as described by the potential employer. Similarly, the seller of a car knows the state of the car. In both cases the buyers have the job of assessing whether their acquisition will fit their situation. Relevant information is controlled by the counterpart agent.

The position in the case of employment is readily associated, or even confused, with the provision of health insurance and credit, since it is easy to look on the employer as the provider of employment – that is, something like a supplier – and, hence, an agent like the provider of health insurance or credit who is faced with the problem of eliciting vital information from a potentially reluctant counterpart agent. But while the provider of health insurance or credit is looking to receive payments, either as insurance premiums or interest, the provider of employment is expecting to pay for provision of work. There is further scope for association, or confusion, in that the providers of health insurance or credit are acquiring risk – and, hence, behaving something like buyers. They need to know the risk they are taking on, or 'buying into'. Applicants for health insurance or credit are buyers of health insurance or credit, but an applicant for employment is a seller of services. A provider of health insurance or credit is acquiring risk; but the provider of employment is a buyer of services. These three markets differ from ordinary markets in that there are distinct ambiguities about what is being supplied or provided and what is being bought or acquired. Agents are both providing and taking on, and information about what they are taking on is controlled by the counterpart agent.

These ambiguities have their origins in the nature of the 'product' being traded. The provision of health insurance, credit and employment is undertaken on the basis of information alone. There is no physical object involved. No physical identity changes hands. Even if the applicant for health insurance undergoes a medical examination, the results will reach the provider in the form of reported information. Similarly, assessment for employment is a matter of information. Whether a person has the capacities that will fit the requirements of the potential employer is largely a matter of written information. An interview may establish that an applicant has the muscles for ditch-digging or the personality for a receptionist, but that is information of a different type and dependability from that which arises from observation of the direct object of a transaction, such as a car, a blanket, or a sack of wheat. It is characteristic of markets for health insurance, credit and employment, and testament to the primacy of information regarding situations, that applicants will commonly be required to fill in application forms which reveal, in written form, the circumstances that qualify them for engagement in the transactions in prospect. The transactions depend on the fit of information to the situations or capacities of the agents concerned. With this achieved, monetary settlements can go ahead. In the car market, by contrast, the focus is on a physical object which is the direct object of exchange. Visual information confirms whether it is an estate car, a hatchback, a large car or a small car. Much information is conveyed as sense data, with the particular confidence people commonly have in what they see and touch. Close physical inspection can reveal important defects of quality. The contrast is between 'products' that are almost entirely defined by reported information and a product that is physical and subject to perceptual checks. If 'what you see is what you get', people are more confident in their choices. People are aware that reported information, the predominant content of the information interface, is provided in pursuit of interest and are inclined to be wary of its validity.

Doubts about the validity of reported information have to be overcome. Stiglitz notes that the problem of asymmetric information is overcome if people tell the truth, though he acknowledges immediately that they are unlikely to do so all the time.[31] To get round the problem, Stiglitz identifies the use of exams, with the objection that it gives potential for multiple equilibria, and so does not resolve his neoclassical problem of identifying a unique Pareto-optimal equilibrium. More important is the 'screening' process, whereby agents derive information from behaviour.[32] The 'screening' process can be understood as an aspect of situation-related interest and actions. Because interests and actions are situation-related, it is possible to deduce something about situations from observations of actions. At its simplest, it can be deduced that a person buying a pot of jam has a deficiency of jam in their cupboard. Or a person climbing stairs to a fifth floor is probably in good health. At a more sophisticated level, it can be deduced that a person who accepts a high excess on an insurance contract conceives himself or herself to be in a fairly secure situation, implying low risk for an insurer, whereas a person who will only take a low excess conceives himself or herself to be in an insecure situation, implying a high risk for an insurer.[33] 'Screening' provides relevant information because actions are situation-related. The idea of 'screening' substitutes for an understanding of situation-related selection and action. In markets for the common run of products, sellers and buyers know their own situations or capacities and can judge their interests, for the most part, sufficiently well to proceed with transactions. But in markets for health insurance, credit and employment relevant information relates to the situations of counterpart agents who are potentially reluctant to divulge it.

Beyond asymmetries

Asymmetric information is concerned with positions in which one agent in a transaction is better informed than another. Its importance is, naturally, most apparent in those markets where information is of paramount importance – broadly those markets where the product is entirely or very largely defined in terms of reported information. Because of this, Stiglitz concludes that asymmetric information is not universally important. He remarks in his 1985 article:

> Let me emphasise, in concluding this section, that I do not want to over-state my case: there may be situations, particular markets, in which information costs are low, and in which the traditional theory does apply ... Our contention is only that there are many situations where information costs are significant, and where the nature of the market equilibrium is, as a result, significantly altered.[34]

The idea of asymmetric information is, then, a means of accommodating within the neoclassical framework, as best can be done, certain transactions where information costs are high. Correspondingly, in some markets – for example, markets for wheat or corn – Stiglitz regards the incidence of asymmetric information as unimportant.[35]

In markets for wheat and corn buyers and sellers do not need such intimate knowledge of the situations of their counterpart agents to proceed with a transaction. Buyers know their own situations, and can assess the implied interests. They have sufficient information about the products on offer to be able to judge whether they will meet their interests. For the most part, they do not need to know the situation of the vendor. At the same time, vendors will know their own capacities and costs, and their interests will be satisfactorily accommodated by sales at the stipulated prices, without any need to know the particular situations of buyers. Most purchases of ordinary physical products do not require that a buyer or seller has intimate knowledge of the situation of the other. These are transactions in which 'what you see is what you get' and the risk of not getting what you want is reduced. They involve the common 'things' that are the essential conception of the neoclassical model.

Nevertheless, even here, knowledge of the counterpart's situation is potentially advantageous. If a buyer of grain could get the vendor to fill in a form about his level of stocks and their condition (assuming the vendor filled in the form honestly), the buyer might learn that the vendor had large stocks of grain in a deteriorating condition which had to be disposed of rapidly. He would know that, with a bit of haggling, he would be likely to get better terms than those immediately on offer. The buyer's bargaining position depends partly on the situation of the vendor. While the buyer is unlikely to get the seller to fill in such a revelatory form, he may still be able to establish certain features of the vendor's situation that affect his bargaining position. Similarly, if the vendor knows that the buyer urgently needs several tons of grain to meet a prior commitment, he may be able to exact a higher price. Information is important to bargaining position. In small routine transactions rooting out background information on situations in order to establish bargaining positions will seldom be worthwhile. But for large one-off transactions, or transactions involving long-term commitments, such research may bring important returns. If a transaction involves a large weight and high value of grain, for delivery over a long period, buyers and sellers are likely to be investigating the levels and condition of stocks, and watching the weather forecasts for the growing regions.

In this case, the concern is not so much with one agent knowing more than another, as in the case of asymmetric information, but of an agent having information relevant to the transaction. It is a circumstance that is not immediately apparent under the concept of asymmetric information. The idea of asymmetric information limits the scope of information issues, so that it is not conducive to full understanding of the role of information in a money-bargaining system. Even in transactions involving physical objects, reported information has a major role. In a money-bargaining system, and still more in a support-bargaining system, the central importance of information and the information interface become apparent. Information is an integral part of the dynamic of bargaining systems.

Relevant information and critical information

The idea of asymmetric information directs attention to the different holdings of information by individuals. This is, however, commonplace in the real world. Everyone is aware that different people have different information, especially with regard to their own situation. Only the contrast with 'perfect information' makes asymmetric information important. Accounting for the use of information in the real world means going beyond asymmetric information. In most cases agents are very ready to impart information to others. It was seen above that all agents are keen to put into circulation whatever information is conducive to their interests. Agents involved in particular transactions will be similarly ready to impart to their counterpart agent information that is conducive to their interests. Applicants for employment, for example, will be ready to divulge to the full extent the capacities they have which meet the requirements of a potential employer.

The difficulties arise when information relevant to a transaction is withheld, or even when it is suspected that relevant information is being withheld. Such behaviour may cause individual transactions to be abandoned and, if widespread in an economy, may bring about the contraction of an economy. Relevant information may be understood as information that might or will affect the terms of a transaction.

Vital information can be understood as relevant information that will certainly affect the terms of a transaction. People will provide all information that they anticipate will move the terms of a transaction in their favour, but they may withhold information that is likely to move the terms against them. An applicant for health insurance may choose to withhold information to the effect that close relatives have suffered from diabetes, on the grounds that it is not relevant to their own health insurance. But a provider of health insurance may regard it as not just relevant, but also vital information.

The contraction of markets is particularly likely if agents fear the withholding of critical information by those with whom they expect to transact business. Information is critical if it can determine of itself whether a transaction goes ahead or not. For the most part, critical information is freely available because it is advantageous to agents to provide it. If someone has a silk dress that needs washing, they will only buy soap powder that can be used with silk, and soap powders will commonly be labelled to indicate whether they are suitable for that material. The vendor wants to sell the soap powder, and must ensure that potential buyers are adequately informed with regard to the fit of the product to their situation. Without the labelling, the potential buyer is likely to decide 'not to risk it'. This critical information will have positive implications for some buyers, though negative for others. Someone seeking employment will also reveal critical information about themselves pertaining to an application for employment. An applicant for a job that requires the ability to speak French will readily inform a potential employer of their prowess in speaking French. Those who do not speak French are wasting their time if they apply.

But in some cases critical information may be withheld. If, for example, an applicant for employment has a criminal record and knows that such a record will, if known to the potential employer, disqualify them from employment, the applicant may choose to withhold that information. An applicant for health insurance may recognise that stating on his or her application form that he or she has had a stroke in the past six months will rule out acceptance for insurance. The applicant may choose to exclude that information from the form. If the seller of a car knows that the chassis is rusted to the point of collapse, the information may be withheld from potential buyers in order to complete a sale. Such information will have negative implications for all buyers.

The potential impact of the withholding of information is naturally greatest in those markets where the 'product' is defined largely or entirely in terms of information. Where sellers are taking on risk, as with health insurance and credit provision, the potential for disguising the degree of risk and the temptation to do so are high. In the case of health insurance, the market is itself dependent on the existence of risk, but dependent also on the availability of sufficient information to make possible assessment of the degree of risk being transferred. Insurance fraud is common because insurance is dependent on provision of information by applicants about their situation. Money-bargaining in insurance continues because insurers have found it possible to give themselves sufficient protection against fraud as to sustain viable formats. This protection has, however, only been possible through legislation established by formal support-bargaining processes.

Such legislation protects the money-bargaining system in general and ensures its continued evolution. Transactions that have been concluded only because relevant information has been withheld are likely to be held invalid if challenged. Since a great range of information may be relevant, and even critical, to one or other agent involved with a potential transaction, the legislation imposes extensive requirements for divulgence of information. The regulations regarding provision of information constitute an important way in which support-bargaining systems make possible the expansion and evolution of money-bargaining systems.

Changing the paradigm

Like Keynes's analysis of savings and investment in *The General Theory*, Stiglitz's analysis of asymmetric information is addressed mainly to his fellow economists. Only economists will regard the idea of 'asymmetric information' as in any way revelatory because only economists are trained to assume perfect information.

Stiglitz makes no mention in his three articles cited here of the buying and selling of information, except with reference to the analysis of the Chicago School, as quoted above. Yet the foregoing account of the evolution of communications suggests that the trade in information led by companies formatted for the provision of information was one of the major factors in the acceleration of the evolution of economies. Information is essential to support-bargaining and money-bargaining, and this value is reflected in the extensive buying of information, and the extensive payments made for the dissemination of information. The whole process of money-bargaining with information and its immense consequences for social and economic evolution remain inaccessible to neoclassical theory, even when supplemented by the idea of asymmetric information.

Stiglitz recognises the fundamental damage to the neoclassical paradigm arising from information issues. He, nevertheless, retains the neoclassical paradigm on the grounds that:

> It is not easy to change views of the world, and it seemed to me the most effective way of attacking the paradigm was to keep within the standard framework as much as possible. I only varied one assumption – the assumption concerning perfect information.[36]

Asymmetric information addresses a 'market failure' of the neoclassical paradigm, though a particularly pervasive failure.[37] Stiglitz retains the neoclassical concepts of market efficiency, rent, Pareto optimality and equilibrium to evaluate outcomes. The intellectual 'jump' from one paradigm to another is not made. From within, the paradigm can be modified, as Keynes modified the neoclassical paradigm to accommodate unemployment, but it cannot be displaced.

Stiglitz can see where a 'jump' might land. In a section headed 'Beyond Information Economics' he recognises that:

> Dynamics [of change] may be better described by evolutionary processes and models, than by equilibrium processes. And while it may be difficult to describe fully these evolutionary processes, this much is already clear: there is no reason to believe that they are, in any general sense, 'optimal'.[38]

In effect, Stiglitz is concluding that the neoclassical model is wholly misconceived. The theory itself is a 'lemon'. Yet Stiglitz cannot bring himself to abandon the unseaworthy ship, even when a rescue vessel, in the form of evolutionary explanations, is in sight. If Keynes, Douglass North and a host of other mainstream economists are there to plug the holes, man the pumps and look after the crew it is better to stay on board. Stiglitz, Akerlof and Spence shared a Nobel Memorial Prize in 2000 for their work on asymmetric information. George Stigler was awarded a Nobel Memorial Prize in 1982.[39]

Notes

1. This theme is pursued by Paul Cohen with case studies of the Battle of Kosovo, the fall of Masada, Chiang Kai-shek, Joan of Arc and the Second World War: Cohen, Paul A., 2014, *History and Popular Memory: The Power of Story in Moments of Crisis*, New York: Columbia University Press.
2. Price, Lance, 2010, *Where Power Lies: Prime Ministers v The Media*, London: Simon and Schuster UK, pp. 366–7.
3. Price, 2010, p. 7.
4. Spread, Patrick, 2008, *Support-Bargaining: The Mechanics of Democracy Revealed*, Sussex: Book Guild, pp. 341–3.
5. Spread, Patrick, 2013, *Support-Bargaining, Economics and Society: A Social Species*, Abingdon and New York: Routledge, Chapter 8, Common Theory and Personification. See also Spread, Patrick, 2004, *Getting It Right: Economics and the Security of Support*, Sussex: Book Guild, pp. 177–81.
6. Spread, 2013, Chapter 10, Social Symmetries.
7. See Spread, 2004, p. 16.
8. Spread, 2013, pp. 171–4.
9. Briggs, Asa and Burke, Peter, 2009, *A Social History of the Media: From Gutenberg to the Internet*, 3rd edition, Cambridge and Malden, MA: Polity Press, pp. 19, 106.
10. Briggs and Burke, 2009, p. 13.
11. Briggs and Burke, 2009, p. 41.
12. Briggs and Burke, 2009, p. 15.
13. Briggs and Burke, 2009, p. 14.
14. Briggs and Burke, 2009, pp. 14–15.
15. Briggs and Burke, 2009, p. 21.
16. Briggs and Burke, 2009, p. 131.
17. Briggs and Burke, 2009, p. 190.
18. Stiglitz, Joseph E., 2000, 'The Contributions of the Economics of Information to Twentieth Century Economics', *The Quarterly Journal of Economics*, Vol. 115, No. 4, pp. 1441–78, p. 1470.
19. Stiglitz, Joseph E., 2002. 'Information and the Change in the Paradigm in Economics', *American Economic Review*, Vol. 92, No. 3, pp. 460–501, p. 462. See also Stiglitz, 2000, pp. 1448–9.
20. Stiglitz, 2002, passim.
21. Stigler, G. J., 1961, 'The Economics of Information', in Lamberton, D. M. (ed.), 1971, *Economics of Information and Knowledge*, London: Penguin.
22. Akerlof, George A., 1970, 'The Market for "Lemons": Quality, Uncertainty and the Market Mechanism', *Quarterly Journal of Economics*, Vol. 84, No. 3, pp. 488–500, p. 490.
23. Akerlof, 1970, pp. 492–4.
24. Spread, Patrick, 1984, *A Theory of Support and Money Bargaining*, London: Macmillan, paras. 3.7–93; on Stigler, 1961, and Akerlof, 1970, see, in particular, paras. 3.19–32.
25. Spence, Michael, 1973, 'Job Market Signalling', *Quarterly Journal of Economics*, Vol. 87, No. 3, pp. 355–74.

26 Spence, 1973, p. 355.
27 Stiglitz, 2002, pp. 472–3.
28 Stiglitz, 2000, pp. 1452; 2002, pp. 471, 475, etc.
29 Stiglitz, 2002, p. 472.
30 Stiglitz, 2002, pp. 469–70. Original emphasis.
31 Stiglitz, 2002, p. 471.
32 Stiglitz, 2002, pp. 471–2.
33 Cf. Stiglitz, 2002, pp. 473, 475.
34 Stiglitz, 1985, p. 30.
35 Stiglitz, 2002, p. 488.
36 Stiglitz, 2002, p. 486.
37 Stiglitz, 2002, p.478.
38 Stiglitz, 2002, pp. 486–7.
39 For further comment on information issues, see Spread, Patrick, 2015c, 'Asymmetric Information, Critical Information and the Information Interface', *Real-World Economics Review*, Issue 70, February 2015. Reprinted in Spread, Patrick, 2015b, *Aspects of Support-Bargaining and Money-Bargaining*, E-Book, World Economics Association.

Conclusion

It was remarked in the Introduction that societies plainly evolve over time from one state to another and, over long periods of time, they can be transformed. The following chapters attempted to show that the evolution takes place through a process of support-bargaining and money-bargaining, centred on the pursuit of situation-related interests. Societies evolve from situation to situation.

While support-bargaining and money-bargaining are so interlinked as to be easily conceived as a single process, there is still a sharp distinction between them, implicit in their designation. Support-bargaining is exchange based on human requirements for and sensitivity to support. Money commonly has physical form, and is highly divisible, which suits it particularly to the exchange of physical goods between independent bargaining agents. The psychological nature of the use of support contrasts with the precise and physical nature of money, so that the two systems are observably distinct. Both support-bargaining and money-bargaining involve specialist bargaining agencies – the political parties and pressure groups of politics and companies as specialist money-bargaining agencies.

As was seen in Chapter 1, support-bargaining and money-bargaining are systemically linked through their concept of situation-related interest and the pursuit of bargaining position. Both are driven by the pursuit of interest by individuals and groups. People will act in a certain situation to gain support and will perform similar acts in another situation to obtain money. Through support-bargaining individuals with similar interests assemble the support necessary to define and attain their interests. But it is often the case that support alone is insufficient to attain interests. Money is often an essential complement to support for the advance of interests. In addition to its use in the common transactions of individual agents, monetary provision is often a tangible expression of support for some individual or organisation. People give to their favoured causes, whether political parties or charities. Well-supported groups tend to attract finance, so that their interests are advanced both through weight of support and by monetary expenditures.

The dynamic of money-bargaining is similar to that of support-bargaining. We have an instinct for money-bargaining because we have the instinct for support-bargaining and hone it early in our lives as a condition of social engagement. The violent implications of support, which give it implications for personal security, mean that support-bargaining is, for the most part, the dominant consideration. 'Power' in a society usually means having extensive support. But power deriving from support is rarely durable unless it is complemented with money.

Money permeates the support-bargaining system, but support-bargaining permeates the money-bargaining system. Control of the money supply is essential to stability of the value of money and, hence, to its efficacy as a bargaining counter. This control is normally exercised through a support-bargaining system. Further, left to itself, money-bargaining is inclined to degenerate into fraudulence, misrepresentation, exploitation of those who are not so good at it by those that are and a general un-readiness to fulfil commitments. The risks associated with money-bargaining in the absence of regulation and the means of enforcing regulations tend to reduce the scope for money-bargaining. People engage only with those they trust. Regulation is essential to wide-ranging money-bargaining and essential to the confidence that generates evolution and growth.

Support-bargaining and money-bargaining are thus functionally interdependent. A money-bargaining system cannot operate effectively except under the auspices of a support-bargaining system. A support-bargaining system, beyond its most basic forms, cannot function without money-bargaining. For these reasons, it is not appropriate to make any sharp distinction between the evolution of economies and the evolution of societies in general. While the evolution of economies is, in the broadest terms, the evolution of money-bargaining and the evolution of societies is more the evolution of support-bargaining, the two are so much interlinked that no satisfactory account can be given of the evolution of either without reference to the other.

Money-bargaining impinges on the balance of advantage between individuals and the group in determining the evolution of a society. Support-bargaining tends to establish the group as strongly dominant over the behaviour of individuals. In societies where money-bargaining has limited scope it can be difficult for individuals to step out of line with the expectations of their society. Money-bargaining enhances the opportunities for individuals to diverge from the group, to follow their own inclinations even in defiance of the group. Support-bargaining then becomes the essential means by which a workable balance of interest between individual and group is brought about. Support-bargaining determines the range of transactions in which money can be used. It also determines the monetary contributions that individuals must make to the group to maintain their place in the group.

Support-bargaining is also necessary to the functioning of the major bargaining agencies of money-bargaining systems. Companies, the specialist and strongest money-bargaining agencies, go to great lengths to promote cooperation among their staff. Formal hierarchical structures are only fully effective when supplemented by informal support-bargaining that draws people into a sense of common and valued purpose. Companies organise social events for their staff, sometimes specifically designed to generate a sense of communal purpose, which is also company purpose.

As the specialist money-bargaining agencies, companies necessarily play a major role in the evolution of money-bargaining systems. Changing situations generate interests, and interests generate opportunities for the format of companies. One of the major drivers of the evolution of money-bargaining systems is the formatting of companies, taking up opportunities presented by changing situations. The formats incorporate technology, both in their processes and in their products. They drive and are driven by a parallel evolution of technology. Locational factors are invariably important to viable format, and can be critical. Those nations which have established through support-bargaining the conditions in which companies can format freely are those whose money-bargaining systems have evolved most rapidly and achieved high levels of prosperity, both individual and communal.

The permeation of support-bargaining into money-bargaining is evident also in trade unions. These organisations depend for their money-bargaining strength on group cohesion. Workers must act in consort if they are to maintain their bargaining positions as suppliers of labour and exact high returns from employers. Trade unions need legislation whereby they can secure their money-bargaining positions through elimination of alternative sources of labour. The evolution of the British economy in the twentieth century was profoundly affected by the success of trade unions in developing bargaining positions in both political support-bargaining and in money-bargaining.

While the greater part of the interlinking of support-bargaining and money-bargaining is constructive with regard to the accommodation of interests, some is highly detrimental. Societies recognise that certain transactions should lie in the sphere of support-bargaining. Formal support-bargaining systems populate legislative assemblies whose members have obligations to their electors. Similarly, certain transactions are recognised as being matters of money-bargaining. The distinctions are maintained by communal assent and, in many cases, by legislation. Yet money is used to divert politicians from their obligations to their electorate. And political authority is used to interrupt, modify or impose monetary transactions. Bribery, corruption and the use of political power outside designated channels constitute the illegitimate linkage of support-bargaining and money-bargaining.

The interrelation of the two systems is apparent also in the way information is made available. Information defines situations and, hence, interests. It makes known what is available and what is wanted, and on what terms. In support-bargaining the benefits proffered for the assembly of support are often defined almost entirely in terms of information organised in accordance with ideological frames of reference. But the provision of such information to the society potentially affected by it rests extensively with companies formatted for the provision of information. The financial interests of media organisations permeate the conduct of government. The facility with which information can now be made available, due to advances in communications technology, provides a substantial contrast between present and past societies. Information disseminated to advance the bargaining position of the disseminators and information provided in response to user requirements, relating both to support-bargaining and money-bargaining positions, is copiously available. Evolution in the provision of information has had a major impact on the evolution of societies and their economies.

This being so, it is remarkable how little theory-makers have concerned themselves with information and its significance. The study of knowledge in society, or social epistemology, is pursued as a rather arcane speciality, without developing sufficient strength as a frame of reference to gain recognition of the dynamics of information and knowledge as an essential factor influencing behaviour across societies and without establishing such dynamics as fundamental to theoretical accounts of the functioning of societies. Rather, social scientific groups tend to develop 'absolutist' understanding of their theories and associated information. Theories calculated to advance factional interest are presented as theories of universal validity, with the implication that everyone should commit to them, as they must accept the facts of nature. It implies that support for a theory is non-negotiable. Rigid groups emerge among theory-makers and are as difficult to accommodate as rigid groups in the political sphere. They remove that flexibility in theory formation that is necessary to take account of new information and changes in situation.

The idea of democracy, essentially a partisan ideal of popular rule designed to help bring down autocrats, has been promoted around the world as a blueprint for government. Because it has been seen as a 'universal good' it has been promoted without regard to the circumstances of its potential users. The consequences have often been unforeseen and sometimes disastrous. Understood in terms of support-bargaining, democracy is far from the 'popular rule' that is idealised. It may not be feasible in people habituated to tribal and other authoritarian cultures. In such societies, just that flexibility of commitment needed for the movement of support and the operation of a formal support-bargaining system is lacking. Flexibility is, for the most part, provided by the formation of social groups on the basis of ideas, and the development of ideas implies a degree of educational attainment in a populace. Societies have to evolve, often over long periods, before they come to a point at which 'democracy', in the form of a support-bargaining society, can be sustained. In effect, the information interface, the way people understand their society, has to be reshaped so that the transactions of support-bargaining can be accomplished and the inclinations that are incompatible with support-bargaining systems are reduced to a manageable level.

Failures of theory

And then there is economic theory. Friedrich Hayek affirmed the weakness noted above in theories about knowledge and information, as well as the weakness in the economic approach to knowledge, when he wrote in his 1945 article on 'The Use of Knowledge in Society':

> It [Schumpeter's treatment of consumer choice] suggests rather that there is something fundamentally wrong with an approach which habitually

disregards an essential part of the phenomena with which we have to deal: the unavoidable imperfection of man's knowledge and the consequent need for a process by which knowledge is constantly communicated and acquired. Any approach ... which in effect starts from the assumption that people's *knowledge* corresponds with the objective *facts* of the situation, systematically leaves out what is our main task to explain.[1]

As was noted in Chapter 1, neoclassical economic theory has an 'absolute' understanding of knowledge and information. It constitutes a spectacular example of the divergence of the information interface from reality. Of course, it does not rival the divergence that gave rise to such disasters as that of the Soviet Union. But it is spectacular in its own context. It has been sustained in support-bargaining societies that pride themselves on their freedom to think; societies whose people believe such freedom will produce the right answers, in the sense of answers that take proper account of actual circumstances. It is faith in scientific method and evidence and, where these cannot be applied, it is faith that the observations of multiple observers will rise sufficiently above interest as to reveal the true state of society. Ironically, the institutional arrangements designed to minimise the impact of interest on theory formation gave scope for the indulgence of a new set of interests, resulting in the divorce of theory from reality.

The core marginal theory of the neoclassical model was developed from around 1870. In 1932 Lionel Robbins, fighting his corner in the intellectual support-bargaining of the time, defined economics as the study of the relationship between ends and scarce means. Robbins assembled enough support to emerge triumphant from the disputes and neoclassical theory became enshrined as 'economics'. Roger Backhouse wonders at the achievement:

> It is important to note that the relationship between theory and real-world problems may change over time. Up to the 1870s it is easy to tell the story of the development of economic theory in terms of factors external to the discipline ... With the advent of marginalist economics, however, this changed. Although economists continued to be concerned with practical issues, economic theory began to develop a momentum of its own. The calculus of maximizing behaviour provided a wealth of opportunities for abstract speculation, with theoretical puzzles playing an increasing role in setting the agenda for research. After the Second World War, as economists became better trained in mathematics, and hence in formal economic theory, this dominance of theory increased still further.[2]

The theory group generated ideas that could be pursued in academic isolation, and opted to pursue them at the expense of the older, outward-oriented approach. As noted in the Introduction, Backhouse designates the main theme of his study of the development of economic theory as, 'how a body of thought that was so closely concerned with practical, real-world problems developed into something akin to a branch of mathematics'.[3] Having set out on that course, anything that could not be accommodated within a mathematical framework was designated by the theory group as 'wrong' or 'irrelevant'. Thus Andersen comments:

> In all cases the evolutionary attempts could be seen by main-stream economists as representing sources of confusion, as misfit parts of economic analysis; in the language of fairy tales they were the ugly ducklings in the yard of economics. The marginalist revolution, the Keynesian revolution and the post-war formalist revolution each have made their contribution to the crowding out of evolutionary-economic offspring.[4]

Having gained ascendancy in institutional intellectual support-bargaining, mainstream economists drove alternative opinion out. In particular, for the institutional advantage of its adherents, it suppressed attempts to develop economic theory that took into account one of the primary features of economies – their evolutionary nature. They created their own fairy tale and mustered enough support where it mattered to see off those who favoured theory based on the observed characteristics of the real world.

Driving out the idea of evolution meant driving out history. The divorce of mainstream economics from the real world is nowhere more apparent than in its complete disregard for history. What happened in the past cannot be understood through static equilibrium theory, so the past is ignored. As Geoffrey Hodgson remarks, neoclassical economics has 'forgotten history'.[5] Economic historians struggle to reconcile historical economic changes with the neoclassical frame which most of them seem to acknowledge as 'proper' economics. The attempt has caused them to underestimate the importance of companies in the evolutionary process. Companies and their technological innovations now plainly dominate money-bargaining systems, but they are largely written out of economic theory on the specious argument that they do no more than minimise transaction costs.

The major part of this book has been concerned to show that the British economy evolved over several centuries from a situation in which economic and political power lay with landowners to a situation in which companies were the dominant agencies. There were few landowners, and each enjoyed substantial power. There are many companies and their strength lies predominantly in money-bargaining, but, collectively, they are vital institutions in the lives of their many employees and, hence, in the life of a nation. They are criticised for exercising undemocratic influence over governments and vilified by some for exercising undemocratic control over governments. Without doubt, their importance to all means that those engaged in support-bargaining have to take account of their interests. At the same time, the strength of the money-bargaining systems they have built makes it possible to conduct support-bargaining on a far more extensive and opulent scale than was conceivable while landowners predominated. Much of this essential change has been missed by commentators because the mainstream economic theory cannot accommodate such phenomena.

The contrast between evolutionary theory and mainstream economic theory is, in part, a contrast between evolution and equilibrium. In spite of the efforts at reconciliation, the two are irreconcilable. One of the main disruptors of equilibrium, and one of the main drivers of evolutionary economic change, is technology. Mainstream theory cannot accommodate the changes in technology that are so much a part of historic change. The concept of companies modelled mathematically in neoclassical theory is a far cry from the reality. Technology adapted to company formats made it possible to accelerate the evolution of the British economy during the eighteenth century and maintain the higher rate of evolution in subsequent decades. The particular evolutionary course taken by Britain meant that it could play a major role in spreading the evolution of technology and companies around the world.

The concept of economics as the study of the relationship between ends and scarce means, or the optimal allocation of resources, implied a separation of economics from other social sciences, which are more concerned with human relationships, social ascendancy and forms of governance. A closed system was required, in which given resources could be allocated through the choices of rational people. The separation of economics from the earlier 'political economy' dates from the inception of marginal theory in the later nineteenth century. The relationship between politics and economic processes has been poorly understood because of this division in academic disciplines. The special, exclusive status claimed by and largely accorded to the neoclassical economic theory group has inhibited other social scientists from investigating the links. It will be clear from all the foregoing that the evolution of economies involves social, political and intellectual support-bargaining, as well as money-bargaining.

Notes

1 Hayek, F. A., 1945, 'The Use of Knowledge in Society', *The American Economic Review*, Vol. 35, No. 4, pp. 519–30, p. 530. Original emphasis.
2 Backhouse, Roger E., 1994, *Economists and the Economy: The Evolution of Economic Ideas*, 2nd edition, New Brunswick, NJ, and London: Transaction, pp. 221–2. Partly quoted in Chapter 1, at note 19.
3 Backhouse, 1994, p. 196. Quoted in the Introduction, at note 1.
4 Andersen, Esben Sloth, 1996, *Evolutionary Economics: Post-Schumpeterian Contributions*, London and New York: Pinter, p. 17.
5 Hodgson, Geoffrey M., 2001, *How Economics Forgot History: The Problem of Historical Specificity in Social Science*, London and New York: Routledge.

Bibliography

Akerlof, George A., 1970, 'The Market for "Lemons": Quality, Uncertainty and the Market Mechanism', *Quarterly Journal of Economics*, Vol. 84, No. 3, pp. 488–500.
Ali-Yrkkö, Jyrki (ed.), 2010, 'Nokia and Finland in a Sea of Change', ETLA – Research Institute of the Finnish Economy, Helsinki: Taloustiete Oy.
Amsden, A. H., 1989, *Asia's Next Giant: South Korea and Late Industrialisation*, New York: Oxford University Press.
Andersen, Esben Sloth, 1996, *Evolutionary Economics: Post-Schumpeterian Contributions*, London and New York: Pinter.
Arrow, Kenneth J., 1950, 'A Difficulty in the Concept of Social Welfare', *Journal of Political Economy*, Vol. 58, No. 4, pp. 328–46.
Arrow, Kenneth J., 1967, 'Samuelson Collected', *Journal of Political Economy*, Vol. 75, pp. 730–7.
Arrow, Kenneth J., 1970, *Social Choice and Individual Values*, 2nd edition, New Haven, CT, and London: Yale University Press. First published 1951.
Arrow, Kenneth and Debreu, Gérard, 1954, 'Existence of an Equilibrium in a Competitive Economy', *Econometrica*, Vol. 22, pp. 265–90.
Arthur, Brian W., 1989, 'Competing Technologies, Increasing Returns, and Lock-In by Historical Events', *Economic Journal*, Vol. 99, No. 394, pp. 116–31.
Ashton, T. S., 1968/1948, *The Industrial Revolution 1760–1830*, Oxford: Oxford University Press.
Backhouse, Roger E., 1993, *Economists and the Economy: The Evolution of Economic Ideas*, 2nd edition, New Brunswick, NJ, and London: Transaction. 1st edition 1988, Oxford: Basil Blackwell.
Backhouse, Roger E., 2002, *The Penguin History of Economics*, London: Penguin.
Barry, Norman, 2000, *An Introduction to Modern Political Theory*, 4th edition, London: Palgrave.
Begg, David, Fischer, Stanley and Dornbusch, Rudiger, 1984, *Economics*, British edition, Maidenhead: McGraw-Hill (UK).
Blaug, Mark, 1985, *Economic Theory in Retrospect*, Cambridge: Cambridge University Press.
Boschma, Ron and Martin, Ron, 2010, 'The Aims and Scope of Evolutionary Economic Geography', in Boschma, Ron and Martin, Ron (eds), 2010, *The Handbook of Evolutionary Economic Geography*, Cheltenham and Northampton, MA: Edward Elgar.
Bowles, Samuel and Gintis, Herbert, 2011, *A Cooperative Species: Human Reciprocity and its Evolution*, Princeton, NJ: Princeton University Press.

Brandon, Robert N., 1990, *Adaptation and Environment*, Princeton, NJ: Princeton University Press.
Briggs, Asa and Burke, Peter, 2009, *A Social History of the Media: From Gutenberg to the Internet*, 3rd edition, Cambridge and Malden, MA: Polity Press.
Canals, Claudia, Gabaix, Xavier, Vilarrubia, Josep M. and Weinstein, David, 2007, 'Trade Patterns, Trade Balances and Idiosyncratic Shocks', Banco de España, Documentos de Trabajo.
Chandler, Alfred, 1977, *The Visible Hand: The Managerial Revolution in American Business*, Cambridge, MA, and London: Belknap Press.
Chandler, Alfred, 1990, *Scale and Scope: The Dynamics of Industrial Capitalism*, Cambridge, MA, and London: Belknap Press.
Chandler, Alfred, 2005, *Inventing the Electronic Century: The Epic Story of the Consumer Electronics and Computer Science Industries*, Cambridge, MA: Harvard University Press.
Chang, Ha-Joon, 2002, *Kicking Away the Ladder: Development Strategy in Historical Perspective*, London: Anthem.
Chang, Ha-Joon, 2008, *Bad Samaritans: The Guilty Secrets of Rich Nations & the Threat to Global Prosperity*, London: Random House Business Books.
Chapman, S. D., 1979, 'Financial Restraints on the Growth of Firms in the Cotton Industry, 1790–1850', *Economic History Review*, Vol. 32, No. 1, pp. 50–69.
Clower, R. W., 1965, 'The Keynesian Counterrevolution: A Theoretical Appraisal', in Hahn, F. H. and Brechling, F. (eds), *The Theory of Interest Rates*, London: Macmillan.
Coase, R. H., 1937, 'The Nature of the Firm', *Economica*, Vol. 4, No. 16, pp. 386–405.
Coase, R. H., 1960, 'The Problem of Social Cost', *Journal of Law and Economics*, Vol. 3, pp. 1–44.
Coats, A. W., 1958, 'Changing Attitudes to Labour in the Mid-Eighteenth Century', *Economic History Review*, 2nd series, Vol. 11, pp. 35–51.
Cohen, Paul A., 2014, *History and Popular Memory: The Power of Story in Moments of Crisis*, New York: Columbia University Press.
Coleman, D. C., 1977, *The Economy of England 1450–1750*, Oxford: Oxford University Press.
Commons, J. R. 1934, *Institutional Economics: Its Place in Political Economy*, New York: Macmillan.
Crafts, N. F. R., 1977, 'Industrial Revolution in Britain and France: Some Thoughts on the Question "Why Was England First?"', *Economic History Review*, Vol. 30, pp. 429–41.
Crafts, N. F. R., 1986, *British Economic Growth During the Industrial Revolution*, Oxford: Oxford University Press.
Crook, Paul, 1994, *Darwinism, War and History*, Cambridge: Cambridge University Press.
David, Paul A., 1985, 'Clio and the Economics of QWERTY', *American Economic Review*, Vol. 75, No. 5, pp. 332–7.
David, Paul A., 2005, 'Path Dependence in Economic Processes: Implications for Policy Analysis in Dynamical System Contexts', in Dopfer, 2005, pp. 151–94.
Davies, Glyn, 1994, *A History of Money from Ancient Times to the Present Day*, Cardiff: University of Wales Press, p. 27.
Dawkins, Richard, 1976, *The Selfish Gene*, Oxford: Oxford University Press.
Deane, P., 1979, *The First Industrial Revolution*, Cambridge: Cambridge University Press.
Deane, Phyllis and Cole, W. A., 1962, *British Economic Growth, 1688–1959*, Cambridge: Cambridge University Press.

Debreu, Gérard, 1959, *Theory of Value: An Axiomatic Analysis of Economic Equilibrium*, New York: Wiley.

Dewey, John, 1922, *Human Nature and Conduct: An Introduction to Social Psychology*, 1st edition, New York: Holt.

Dobb, Maurice, 1928, *Russian Economic Development since the Revolution*, London: Routledge.

Dopfer, Kurt, 2005, *The Evolutionary Foundations of Economics*, Cambridge: Cambridge University Press.

Drazen, A., 1980, 'Recent Developments in Macreoeconomic Disequilibrium Theory', *Econometrica*, Vol. 48, No. 2.

Ellison, T., *The Cotton Trade of Great Britain*, London, 1886.

Fallows, James, 1994, *Looking at the Sun: The Rise of the New East Asian Economies*, New York: Pantheon.

Ferguson, Niall, 2002, *The Cash Nexus: Money and Power in the Modern World 1700-2000*, London: Penguin.

Fransman, Martin, 1994, 'Information, Knowledge, Vision and Theories of the Firm', *Industrial and Corporate Change*, Vol. 3, No. 3, pp. 713–57.

Freeman, Alan, Chick, Victoria and Kayatekin, Serap, 2014, 'Samuelson's Ghosts: Whig History and the Reinterpretation of Economic Theory', *Cambridge Journal of Economics*, Vol. 38, No. 3, pp. 519–29.

Gairdner, James (ed.), 1983, *The Paston Letters*, Gloucester: Sutton.

Geanakoplos, John, 2004, 'The Arrow–Debreu Model of General Equilibrium', *Cowles Foundation Paper No. 1090*, Cowles Foundation for Research in Economics at Yale University.

General Agreement on Tariffs and Trade (GATT), 1947; World Trade Organisation, 1994.

Gillingham, John, 2001, 'The Early Middle Ages (1066–1290)', in Morgan, 2001.

Gomes, Leonard, 1987, *Foreign Trade and the National Economy: Mercantilist and Classical Perspectives*, New York: St Martin's Press.

Great Exhibition: Official Catalogue. Available at http://www.gracesguide.co.uk/1851_Great_Exhibition:_Official_Catalogue. Accessed 8 October 2012.

Griffiths, Ralph A., 2001, 'The Later Middle Ages (1290–1485)', in Morgan, 2001.

Guy, John, 2001, 'The Tudor Age (1485–1603)', in Morgan, 2001, p. 258.

Hayek, F. A., 1945, 'The Use of Knowledge in Society', *The American Economic Review*, Vol. 35, No. 4, pp. 519–30.

Hicks, J. R., 1939, *Value and Capital: An Inquiry into some Fundamental Principles of Economic Theory*, Oxford: Clarendon Press.

Hodgson, Geoffrey M., 1988, *Economics and Institutions*, Cambridge: Polity Press.

Hodgson, Geoffrey M., 1996, *Economics and Evolution: Bringing Life Back into Economics*, Ann Arbor: University of Michigan Press.

Hodgson, Geoffrey M., 1997, 'The Ubiquity of Habits and Rules', *Cambridge Journal of Economics*, Vol. 21, No. 6, pp. 663–84.

Hodgson, Geoffrey M., 1998, 'The Approach of Institutional Economics', *Journal of Economic Literature*, Vol. 3, No. 1, pp. 166–92.

Hodgson, Geoffrey M., 2000, *Evolution and Institutions*, Cheltenham and Northampton, MA: Edward Elgar.

Hodgson, Geoffrey M., 2001, *How Economics Forgot History: The Problem of Historical Specificity in Social Science*, London and New York: Routledge.

Hodgson, Geoffrey M., (ed.), 2002, *A Modern Reader in Institutional and Evolutionary Economics*, Cheltenham and Northampton, MA: Edward Elgar.

Hodgson, Geoffrey M., 2004, *The Evolution of Institutional Economics: Agency, Structure and Darwinism in American Institutionalism*, London and New York: Routledge.

Hodgson, Geoffrey M., 2006, 'What are Institutions?', *Journal of Economic Issues*, Vol. 40, No. 1, pp. 1–25.

Hodgson, Geoffrey and Knudsen, Thorbjørn, 2010, *Darwin's Conjecture: The Search for General Principles of Social and Economic Evolution*, Chicago and London: Chicago University Press.

Hoekman, Bernard and Kostecki, Michel, 1995, *The Political Economy of the World Trading System*, Oxford: Oxford University Press.

Hofstadter, Richard, 1983, *Social Darwinism in American Thought*, Boston, MA: Beacon Books. First published 1944.

Hollander, Samuel, 1979, *The Economics of David Ricardo*, Toronto: University of Toronto Press, p. 465.

Howitt, P., 1987, 'Macroeconomics: Relations with Microeconomics', in Eatwell, J., Milgate, M. and Newman, P. (eds), *The New Palgrave*, Vol. 3, New York: Stockton, pp. 273–6.

Hull, Charles Henry (ed.), 1899, *The Economic Writings of Sir William Petty, together with The Observations upon Bills of Mortality, more probably by Captain John Graunt*, 2 Vols, Cambridge, Cambridge University Press. Petty's papers originally produced 1662–87. Available online at The Online Library of Liberty: http://oll.libertyfund.org/index.php?option=com_staticxt&staticfile=show.php%3Ftitle=1677&Itemid=27

Keynes, John Maynard, 1961, *The General Theory of Employment, Interest and Money*, London: Macmillan, New York: St Martin's Press. First published 1936.

King, Willford, 1915, *The Wealth and Income of the People of the United States*, New York.

Knight, Frank, 1921, *Risk, Uncertainty and Profit*, Boston: Houghton Mifflin.

Kropotkin, Peter, 2008/1902, *Mutual Aid: A Factor of Evolution*, Hong Kong: Forgotten Books. First published 1902.

Krugman, P. R. and Obstfeld, M., 2006, *International Economics: Theory and Policy*, 7th edition, Boston: Pearson Addison Wesley.

Lamberton, D. M. (ed.), 1971, *Economics of Information and Knowledge*, London: Penguin.

Lewontin, Richard, 1974, *The Genetic Basis of Evolutionary Change*, New York: Columbia University Press.

Liebowitz, Stan J. and Margolis, Stephen E., 2000, 'Path Dependence', in Bouckaert, B. and De Geest, G. (eds), *Encyclopaedia of Law and Economics*, Cheltenham: Edward Elgar and Ghent: University of Ghent.

Lindert, P. H. and Williamson, J. G., 1982, 'Revising England's Social Tables 1688–1812', *Explorations in Economic History*, Vol.19, pp. 385–408.

List, Frederick, 1856, *National System of Political Economy*, translated by G. A. Matile, Philadelphia: J. B. Lippincott. First published in German in 1841.

Lucas, R. E. and Sargent, T. J., 1979, 'After Keynesian Macroeconomics', *Federal Reserve Bank of Minneapolis Quarterly Review*, Vol. 3, No. 1.

MacCulloch, Diarmaid, 2010, *A History of Christianity*, London: Penguin.

Maneschi, A., 1992, 'Ricardo's International Trade Theory: Beyond the Comparative Cost Example', *Cambridge Journal of Economics*, Vol. 16, No. 4, pp. 421–37.

Marshall, A. and Marshall, M. P., 1994, *The Economics of Industry*, Bristol: Thoemmes Press. First published 1879.

Marshall, Alfred, 1920, *Principles of Economics*, 8th edition, London: Macmillan. First published 1890.

Martin, Ron and Sunley, Peter, 2010, 'The Place of Path Dependence in an Evolutionary Perspective on the Economic Landscape', in Boschma and Martin, 2010, p. 68.

Mathias, Peter, 2001, *The First Industrial Nation: The Economic History of Britain 1700–1914*, Abingdon and New York: Routledge.

McKenzie, L. W. 1954, 'On Equilibrium in Graham's Model of World Trade and other Competitive Systems', *Econometrica*, Vol. 27, pp. 54–71.

McKenzie, L. W., 1959, 'On the Existence of General Equilibrium for a Competitive Market', *Econometrica*, Vol. 27, pp. 147–61.

McLeay, Michael, Radia, Amar and Thomas, Ryland, 2014a, 'Money in the Modern Economy: An Introduction', *Bank of England Quarterly Review, March 2014*, pp. 4–13.

McLeay, Michael, Radia, Amar and Thomas, Ryland, 2014b, 'Money Creation in the Modern Economy', *Bank of England Quarterly Review, March 2014*, pp. 14–27.

Meade, James, Stone, Richard and Stone, Giovanna, 1944–72, various editions of *National Income and Expenditure*, varying authorship and contributors, published variously by Oxford: Oxford University Press; Cambridge: Bowes and Bowes; London: Bowes.

Menger, Karl, 1892, 'On the Origin of Money', *The Economic Journal*, Vol. 2, No. 6, pp. 239–55.

Metcalfe, Stanley J., 2005, 'Evolutionary Concepts in Relation to Evolutionary Economics', in Dopfer, 2005, pp. 391–430.

Micklethwait, John and Wooldridge, Adrian, 2005, *The Company: A Short History of a Revolutionary Idea*, London: Phoenix.

Mitchell, B. R., 1988, *British Historical Statistics*, London: Cambridge University Press.

Mokyr, Joel, 2005, 'Is there a Theory of Economic History?', in Dopfer, 2005, pp. 195–218.

Mokyr, Joel, 2011, *The Enlightened Economy: Britain and the Industrial Revolution 1700–1850*, London: Penguin.

Morgan, Kenneth O., 2001, *The Oxford History of Britain*, Oxford: Oxford University Press.

Morgenson, Gretchen and Rosner, Joshua, 2012, *Reckless Endangerment*, New York: St Martin's Griffin.

Mossner, E. C. and Ross, I. S. (eds), 1977, *The Correspondence of Adam Smith*, in Campbell, R. H. and Skinner, A. S., 1976–83, *The Glasgow Edition of the Works and Correspondence of Adam Smith*, Oxford: Clarendon Press.

Nelson, Richard R. and Winter, Stanley G., 1982, *An Evolutionary Theory of Economic Change*, Cambridge, MA: Belknap Press.

Nordhaus, William D. and Tobin, James, 1973, 'Is Growth Obsolete?', in *The Measurement of Economic and Social Performance*, National Bureau of Economic Research. Available at: http://www.nber.org/chapters/c7620.pdf. Accessed 3 February 2014.

North, Douglass, 1994, 'Economic Performance through Time', *American Economic Review*, Vol. 84, No. 3, pp. 359–67.

North, Douglass C., 1981, *Structure and Change in Economic History*, New York: Norton.

North, Douglass C., 1990, *Institutions, Institutional Change and Economic Performance*, Cambridge and New York: Cambridge University Press.

North, Douglass C., 2005, *Understanding the Process of Economic Change*, Princeton, NJ, and Oxford: Princeton University Press.

Peirce, C. S., 1934, 'Pragmatism and Pragmaticism', Vol. V, in Hartshorne, C. and Weiss, P. (eds), *Collected Papers of Charles Sanders Peirce*, Cambridge, MA: Harvard University Press.

Pigou, A. C., 1932, *The Economics of Welfare*, London: Macmillan.

Pigou, A. C., 1933, *The Theory of Unemployment*, London: Macmillan.

Pimbley, Joseph M. and McDevitt, Laurel, 2014, *Banking on Failure: Fixing the Fiasco of Junk Banks, Government Bailouts and Fiat Money*, New York: Maxwell Consulting.

Porter, Roy, 2000, *The Creation of the Modern World: The Untold Story of the British Enlightenment*, New York: W. W. Norton.

Price, Lance, 2010, *Where Power Lies: Prime Ministers v The Media*, London: Simon and Schuster UK.

Ricardo, David, 1951, *On the Principles of Political Economy and Taxation*, in Sraffa, 1951, pp. 135–6. Ricardo's *Principles* first published 1817; Sraffa, 1951, based on 1821 (3rd) edition.

Rizvi, S. Abu Turab, 1994, 'The Microfoundations Project in General Equilibrium Theory', *Cambridge Journal of Economics*, Vol. 18, No. 4, pp. 357–77.

Robbins, Keith, 1979, *John Bright*, London, Boston and Henley: Routledge & Kegan Paul.

Robbins, Lionel, 1932, *An Essay on the Nature and Significance of Economic Science*, London: Macmillan.

Rose, Jonathan, 2002, *The Intellectual Life of the British Working Classes*, New Haven and London: Yale Nota Bene.

Rutherford, Malcolm, 2001, 'Institutional Economics: Then and Now', *Journal of Economic Perspectives*, Vol. 15, No. 3, pp. 173–94.

Samuelson, Paul, 1980, *Economics*, 11th edition, New York: McGraw–Hill.

Sanderson, S. K., 1990, *Social Evolutionism: A Critical History*, Cambridge, MA, and Oxford: Basil Blackwell.

Schumacher, Reinhard, 2013, 'Deconstructing the Theory of Comparative Advantage', *World Economics Journal*, No. 2, pp. 83–105.

Schumpeter, J. A., 1954, *History of Economic Analysis*, New York: Oxford University Press.

Schumpeter, Joseph A., 1934/1911, *The Theory of Economic Development: An Enquiry into Profits, Capital, Credit, Interest and the Business Cycle*, London: Oxford University Press.

Smith, Adam, 1998, *Wealth of Nations*, Oxford: Oxford University Press. First published as *An Enquiry into the Nature and Causes of the Wealth of Nations*, 1776.

Smith, Adam, 2009, *An Enquiry into the Nature and Causes of the Wealth of Nations*, Adobe Digital Editions.

Södersten, Bo and Reed, Geoffrey, 1994, *International Economics*, 3rd edition, Basingstoke and London: Macmillan.

Spence, Michael, 1973, 'Job Market Signalling', *Quarterly Journal of Economics*, Vol. 87, No. 3, pp. 355–74.

Spiegel, Henry William, 1991, *The Growth of Economic Thought*, Durham, NC, and London: Duke University Press.

Spread, Patrick, 1984, *A Theory of Support and Money Bargaining*, London: Macmillan.

Spread, Patrick, 2004, *Getting It Right: Economics and the Security of Support*, Sussex: Book Guild.

Spread, Patrick, 2008, *Support-Bargaining: The Mechanics of Democracy Revealed*, Sussex: Book Guild.

Spread, Patrick, 2011, 'Situation as Determinant of Selection and Valuation', *Cambridge Journal of Economics*, Vol. 35, No. 2, pp. 335–56. Reprinted in Spread, 2015b.

Spread, Patrick, 2012, 'The Evolution of Economic Theory: And some Implications for Financial Risk Management', *Real-World Economics Review*, No. 61, 26 September, pp. 125–35.

Spread, Patrick, 2013, *Support-Bargaining, Economics and Society: A Social Species*, Abingdon and New York: Routledge.
Spread, Patrick, 2015a, 'Companies and Markets: Economic Theories of the Firm and a Concept of Companies as Bargaining Agencies', *Cambridge Journal of Economics*, Advance Access published 2 June 2015, doi:10.1093/cje/bev029. Reprinted in Spread, 2015b.
Spread, Patrick, 2015b, *Aspects of Support-Bargaining and Money-Bargaining*, E-Book, World Economics Association.
Spread, Patrick, 2015c, 'Asymmetric Information, Critical Information and the Information Interface', *Real-World Economics Review*, Issue 70, February 2015. Reprinted in Spread, 2015b.
Spread, Patrick, 2015d, 'The Political Significance of Certain Types of Group', in Spread, 2015b.
Sraffa, Piero (ed.), 1951, *The Works and Correspondence of David Ricardo*, Cambridge: Cambridge University Press. Sraffa (ed.), 1951, based on 1821 (3rd) edition of Ricardo's *Principles*.
Stigler, G. J., 1961, 'The Economics of Information', in Lamberton, 1971. First published 1961 in *The Journal of Political Economy*, Vol. 69, pp. 213–25.
Stiglitz, Joseph E., 2000, 'The Contributions of the Economics of Information to Twentieth Century Economics', *The Quarterly Journal of Economics*, Vol. 115, No. 4, pp. 1441–78.
Stiglitz, Joseph E., 2002. 'Information and the Change in the Paradigm in Economics', *American Economic Review*, Vol. 92, No. 3, pp. 460–501.
Stiglitz, Joseph E., Sen, Amartya and Fitoussi, Jean-Paul, 2009, Report by the Commission on the Measurement of Economic Performance and Social Progress. Available at http://www.stiglitz-sen-fitoussi.fr/documents/rapport_anglais.pdf. Accessed 3 February 2014.
Stone, Richard and Brown, Alan, 1962, *A Computable Model for Economic Growth*, London: Chapman and Hall.
Sutherland, Kathryn, 1998, Notes, in Smith, 1998.
The Economist, 22 June 2013.
Thompson, E. P., 1991, *The Making of the English Working Class*, London: Penguin.
Thornton, Henry, 1802, *An Enquiry into the Nature and Effects of the Paper Credit of Great Britain*, London: J. Hatchard.
Tool, Marc R., 2002, 'Contributions to an Institutionalist Theory of Price Formation', in Hodgson, 2002.
Tussie, Diana and Woods, Ngaire, 2000, 'Trade, Regionalism and the Threat to Multilateralism', in Woods, 2000, pp. 54–76.
Veblen, Thorstein B., 1899, *The Theory of the Leisure Class: An Economic Study in the Evolution of Institutions*, New York: Macmillan.
Veblen, Thorstein B., 1919, *The Place of Science in Modern Civilisation and Other Essays*, New York: Huebsch. Reprinted, 1990, New Brunswick, NJ: Transaction.
Veblen, Thorstein, 1998/1898, 'Why is Economics not an Evolutionary Science?', *Cambridge Journal of Economics*, Vol. 22, No. 4, pp. 403–14. Originally published in the *Quarterly Journal of Economics*, July 1898, pp. 373–97.
Voth, H.-J., 1998, 'Time and Work in Eighteenth Century London', *Journal of Economic History*, Vol. 45, pp. 29–58.
Wilson, Edward O., 2000/1975, *Sociobiology: The New Synthesis*, Cambridge MA: Belknap Press. First published 1975.

Wilson, Edward O., 2004/1978, *On Human Nature*, Cambridge, MA: Harvard University Press. First published 1978.
Witt, Ulrich, 2004, 'On the Proper Interpretation of "Evolution" in Economics and its Implications for Production Theory', *Journal of Economic Methodology*, Vol. 11, No. 2, pp. 125–46.
Woods, Ngaire (ed.), 2000, *The Political Economy of Globalization*, London: Palgrave.
Wrigley, E. A. and Schofield, R. S., 1981, *The Population History of England, 1541–1871: A Reconstruction*, Cambridge: Cambridge University Press.
Wrigley, E. A., 2010, *Energy and the English Industrial Revolution*, Cambridge: Cambridge University Press.
www.ukpublicspending.co.uk. Accessed 27 March 2014.

Index

Afghanistan 290
aggression xi, 2, 5, 205
Akerlof, George 302–5, 311, 320
Alchian, Armen 97
Ali-Yrkkö, Jyrki 64, 320
American Civil War 136, 163
Amsden, Alice 279–80, 282, 320
Andersen, Esben 94, 96–7, 103–4, 106, 318–20
Anti-Corn Law League 254–5, 298
Apple 30, 157–8
Argentina 258
Arkwright, Robert 133, 149
Arrow, Kenneth 20, 33, 45, 49–55, 65, 82, 174, 203, 227, 266, 320, 322
Arrow-Debreu model 49–55, 65
Arthur, Brian 86, 92, 97, 99–100, 106, 320
Ashton, T. S. 147, 166, 168, 172–4, 206, 245–6, 320
Asia 25–6, 39, 127, 131, 282, 320, 322; export of silver to 25–6
Ataturk, Kemal 298
Athens 16
attitudes 8, 73–4, 118–25, 140, 156, 168–9, 171, 173, 177, 195, 285, 321
Australia 258
Ayres, Clarence 70

Backhouse, Roger ix, xi, 9–10, 12, 26–7, 33–4, 36, 47–8, 54–5, 64–6, 171, 242, 245–7, 317, 319–20
balance of payments 27–8, 240, 256
balance of trade 24–5, 240
Bank Charter Act 204, 206
Bank of England 27–9, 129–30, 202–6, 210, 213–14, 236–7, 247, 324
Bank of Spain 39, 64
bankers and banking 25, 27, 29, 57, 202, 204–5, 208–16, 229, 235–7, 243–4, 256

Banque Royale 130
bargaining counters 1, 14–15, 18–19, 203, 233, 294, 314
bargaining position x, 6, 9, 12, 19, 29, 31, 40, 54, 56, 59, 61–2, 78, 94, 100–1, 108–14, 117–18, 120–1, 124–5, 130–1, 148, 153, 155, 157, 160–4, 168, 181–2, 187, 189, 194–5, 197, 207, 231, 234, 238, 240, 242, 249–50, 253–4, 257–8, 262, 269, 273–5, 279–80, 284, 289, 307, 313, 315–16
bargaining sets x, 38, 51–2, 57, 143, 155, 158, 194, 199, 209, 229, 238, 251, 257, 268–9, 274, 278, 280, 284–5, 294, 296, 299
Barry, Norman 33, 320
barter economy 14–16, 22, 53, 265–7
Begg, David 245, 247, 320
Belgium 271
Bessemer, Henry 139–40
Bismarck, Otto Von 272
Black Death 109–12
Blaug, Mark 9, 12, 320
Booth, Henry 160
Boschma, Ron 97, 106–7, 320, 324
Bouckaert, B. 107, 323
Boulton, Matthew 149, 159–60
Bowles, Samuel 5, 12, 320
Bowley, A. L. 36
Brandon, Robert N. 69, 104, 321
Brechling, F. 65, 321
Briggs, Asa 311, 321
Bright, John 254
Brookings Institute (USA) 36
Brown, Alan 41, 64, 326
Brunel, Isambard Kingdom 160, 257
Bubble Act 129–30, 144
budgets 6, 16, 29–32, 42, 52–3, 56–9, 61, 63, 78, 85, 99–100, 122, 135, 142, 153,

158, 162, 165, 175, 179, 188–9, 190, 195–7, 199, 207, 209, 211, 214, 217, 219, 227–9, 231–4, 239–42, 244–5, 250, 255, 261, 266, 280, 287
Bullion Committee 27–8
Bureau of Economic Research (USA) 36, 64, 324
Burke, Peter 311, 321
business cycles 55, 62–3, 94, 106, 218–19, 227, 231, 240, 242, 325

calculus 10, 49, 317
Cambridge Journal of Economics x–xi, 11–12, 33–4, 65, 103–5, 174, 281–2, 322–3, 325–6
Campbell R. H. 280, 324
Canada 258
Canals, Claudia 64, 321
capacity xi, 5, 8, 19, 30, 63, 101, 150, 204, 262, 276–7, 288, 297–8; government 22, 223, 240, 245; of companies 30–1, 143, 146, 209, 239, 258, 260, 306–7; personal 1, 4–5, 17, 19, 99, 165, 186, 195, 229, 232, 275, 290, 304–6, 308; violent 1–3, 88, 109, 126–7, 198, 249, 271
capital 16, 28, 36, 38, 48, 56–7, 63, 106, 117, 121, 129, 133, 138–40, 142–4, 155, 163, 195, 201, 206, 208–9, 213, 222, 227, 238, 257, 260–1, 263–5, 269–70, 325; international mobility of 263–4, 266, 273; marginal efficiency of 221–3, 226–7, 230–1, 233
career 71, 82, 101
cartels 160–1
Cartwright, Edmund 137, 150
causation 2, 8, 148, 292
Central Economic Information Service (UK) 36
chaebol 279–80
Chandler, Alfred 39, 64, 157, 173, 239, 247, 321
Chang, Ha-Joon 282, 321
charity 116, 189, 212, 215, 313
Chicago School 301, 310
Chick, Victoria xi, 322
China 135, 156, 258, 296–7
church-state relationship 122–3, 125
Clark, Colin 36
Clinton, President William J. (Bill) 211
clipping money 25–6
Clive, Robert 128
Clower, R. W. 45, 65, 321
coal 67, 133, 138, 143, 149, 151–2, 168, 223

Coase, Robert 11, 31, 34, 70, 83–90, 95, 103, 105–6, 167–8, 321
Coats, A. W. 171, 321
Cobbett, William 186
Cobden, Richard 254
Cohen, Paul 311, 321
coinage 15–17, 23–8, 203–4, 235, 295; debasement of 23, 25, 28
Cole, W. A. 116–17, 120, 133–4, 136, 143, 170–2, 174, 251–2, 280, 321
Coleman D. C. 33, 112–14, 118, 120–1, 124, 126, 148, 167, 170–77, 182, 199, 249, 321
commodity money 14–15
common theory 8, 50, 93, 116, 118, 176–7, 197, 289, 293
Commons, John R. 27, 70, 76, 104, 321
communal approach 3, 29, 32, 56–7, 59, 62, 88, 130, 169, 179–82, 186, 188, 190, 193, 195–6, 198, 275, 314
communications 40, 79, 257, 283, 294, 299, 300, 310, 315; postal 298; telegraphic 257, 294, 298–9
Compagnie d'Occident 130
companies ix–x, 6, 11–12, 21, 29–32, 34, 39–41, 48, 55–62, 75–6, 78–80, 83–5, 88–9, 95–6, 98–9, 105, 107, 116–17, 123, 126–32, 135, 139–45, 147–8, 150–69, 173–4, 178, 180–1, 184, 187, 189, 194–7, 199, 201–2, 206, 219, 229–30, 238–41, 244, 248–9, 251, 253–4, 256–62, 266–9, 271–2, 274, 277–80, 282, 285–7, 295, 297–300, 313–15, 318–19, 326; chartered 126–32, 157, 161, 180–1, 187, 249; cotton format 133–8, 145, 168; financial services 211–14, 216, 229, 232–5, 237, 244; for distribution 163–4; format of x, 26, 31, 48, 55–6, 59, 61–3, 85, 99, 121, 127–8, 130–3, 135, 137–40, 142–3, 145–53, 155–69, 173, 190, 194–6, 199, 201, 204–6, 225–6, 229, 232–5, 238–40, 242, 244, 249, 251, 253–9, 261–2, 268–9, 271, 274, 277–80, 286, 290, 294–300, 315, 319; iron format 133, 138–40, 146, 168, 193; joint-stock 117, 126, 128–30, 203–5, 209; large 39–40, 56, 61–2, 78, 157, 160, 163, 238–9, 266; locational format x, 99, 107, 143, 150–3, 158, 165, 173, 224, 274, 315; media 286–8, 294–6, 302, 310, 315; partnerships 129, 135, 204–5; railway format 133, 141, 143–5; regulated 128, 130

Index 329

Companies Act 145
comparative advantage, theory of 167, 250, 262–9, 273–8, 281–2, 325
confidence 2, 10–11, 15–17, 22–3, 25, 27–8, 44, 47, 61–3, 199, 201–19, 223, 225–7, 231–3, 240, 244–5, 257, 285–6, 306, 314; and currencies 27–9
cooperation xi, 7, 12, 18, 42, 91, 100, 162, 182, 276, 303, 314, 320
Corn Laws 254–5, 263, 269
Cort, Henry 138, 141, 146, 150–1
Countrywide Financial 211
Crafts, N. F. R. 116–17, 136–7, 153–4, 167–8, 170–4, 321
creative destruction 95
credit 48, 52–3, 56–7, 106, 132, 199, 201–12, 214–18, 220, 230, 232, 235–7, 240, 243–5, 292–3, 304–6, 309, 325
Crompton, Samuel 135, 149
Cullen, William 148
cultural evolution xi, 1, 5, 7, 15, 19, 102, 176
Currie, Laughlin 47

d'Alembert, Jean 177
Darby, Abraham 150–1, 168
Darwin, Charles xi, 1–5, 7, 68–9, 71–2, 75, 95–7, 102, 104, 322
David, Paul 92, 97–8, 106–7, 321
Davies, Glyn 14, 33, 321
Dawkins, Richard 104, 321
De Geest, G. 107, 323
Deane, Phyllis 116–17, 120, 133–4, 136, 143, 153, 170–4, 251–2, 280, 321
Debreu, Gerard 45, 49–55, 65, 82, 174, 203, 227, 266, 320, 322
definition 4, 9, 50–3, 79–83, 96–7, 101, 103, 125, 153, 165–6, 179–81, 195–6, 224–5, 227–8, 230, 242–3, 247, 258, 273, 284
deity ix, 7, 15, 17, 122–3, 125; *see also* religion
democracy x–xi, 12, 20, 64–5, 105, 111, 158, 170, 183, 199, 210–11, 215, 247, 280–1, 288–9, 291, 293, 311, 316, 325
Denmark 271
Descartes, René 177
devaluation 23–4, 26
Dewey, John 75, 104, 322
Dickens, Charles 208
Diderot, Denis 177
distance 10, 35, 38, 40, 45, 52–3, 62, 97, 102, 142, 194, 268, 274, 299

division of labour 83, 117, 130–1, 167, 262, 268, 270–1
Dobb, Maurice 83, 85, 105, 324
Domar, Evsey 48
Domesday Book 108
Donkin, Bryan 296
Dopfer, Kurt 104, 107, 174, 321–2, 324
Dornbusch, Rudiger 245, 247, 320
Dostoevsky, Fyodor 297
Drazen, A. 45, 65, 322
Dutch East India Company 126–7
Dvorak keyboard 92, 99

East India Company 25–6, 39, 128, 131, 249, 258
Eatwell, J. 65, 323
economic geography 97–9, 101–2, 106, 155, 274, 320
economies of scale 51–2, 54, 82, 85, 92, 100, 139, 154, 161, 167, 238, 266, 268, 296, 320
Economist, The 39, 64, 326
education ix, 32, 37, 48, 55, 57, 59–60, 124–5, 147–8, 176–7, 192–3, 195–7, 223, 287, 289, 304; and British workforce 125, 196
Education Act 196
Ellison, T. 172, 326
employment 3, 11, 25, 32, 37–8, 45–8, 54–7, 59–62, 74, 101, 108, 114, 116–17, 120, 132, 152, 154–5, 159–60, 162, 165, 169, 182, 187, 188–9, 198, 217–20, 222–5, 228–31, 237, 239–41, 243, 248, 254, 261, 263–4, 266–7, 269, 279, 293, 304, 306, 310; in railway construction and operation 142; involuntary unemployment 220–1, 224–5, 243, 293; recruitment 304–5, 308–9
enclosure 111–12, 114, 118, 185–7
Enlightenment 123–4, 168, 171, 177–8, 259, 272, 275, 325
equilibrium ix, 9, 35, 40, 44–7, 49–54, 60, 63, 65, 67, 78, 82, 94–5, 97–8, 101–2, 156, 218, 220–1, 224, 227, 230, 236–9, 268–9, 272–3, 304, 306–7, 310, 318–20, 324–5
Erasmus 297
Evelyn, John 25
evolution of societies 1, 8–9, 37, 92, 94, 99, 102, 297, 314, 316
evolutionary economics x–xi, 1, 3, 11, 29, 31–2, 41, 56, 67–107, 133, 151, 153, 156–7, 162, 197, 225, 239, 257–8, 283, 300, 310, 314, 318–20, 322, 324, 327

fact-formation x
factories ix, 37, 64, 118, 120, 125, 131, 137–8, 152–4, 159–60, 189, 206
factors of production 36–8, 87, 238
Fallows, James 279, 282, 322
Fannie Mae 211–13, 215
Fastolf, Sir John 183
Federal Reserve Bank (US) 65, 212–13, 323
Ferguson, Niall 171, 322
financial services 47, 52–3, 56–7, 62, 132, 201–2, 205–7, 215–16, 225, 227, 230, 232–6, 240, 243–5, 257, 283, 285–6
Finland 39, 64, 320
Fischer, Stanley 245, 247, 320
Fisher, Irving 219
Fitoussi, Jean-Paul 64, 326
Ford, Henry 163, 165
foreign trade x, 22, 24, 127, 130, 155, 199, 248–51, 255, 257–9, 262–3, 265, 273, 275–6, 322; gravity theory 268, 274
formal support-bargaining x, 8, 20, 38, 57–8, 63, 88, 144, 162, 169, 183–6, 189–90, 193, 195, 198–9, 202, 208, 214, 248–9, 271, 273–4, 279, 288, 309, 315–16
Fothergill, Benjamin 160
Foudrinier paper machine 296
Fox's Book of Martyrs 297
frames of reference x, 81, 101, 177, 179, 242–3, 289–93, 300, 315–16; frame of frames 289
France 27–8, 41, 113, 124–6, 130, 132–3, 173, 204–6, 249–50, 272, 284, 296, 309, 321
Fransman, Martin 96, 106, 322
Freddie Mac 211–13, 215
free riding 276
free trade 190, 197, 237, 250, 253, 255, 259, 260, 262–4, 266, 269–70, 272, 274–7, 279
free will 5, 12
Freeman, Alan xi, 322
freight services 278

Gabaix, Xavier 64, 321
Geanakoplos, John 49–50, 52–4, 65–6, 322
General Agreement on Tariffs and Trade (GATT) 250, 276–8, 282, 322
General Equilibrium Theory (GET) 45, 47–8, 54–5
Germany 39, 125, 132–3, 163, 165, 254, 271–3, 275, 280–1, 323
gift economy 13, 15–18, 202, 209
Gillingham, John 169, 171, 322

Gintis, Herbert 5, 12, 320
Glorious Revolution 123, 130, 284
gold 14–17, 22–6, 28, 203, 205, 265, 290; gold standard 24–9, 219
Goldman Sachs 212
Gomes, Leonard 263, 281, 322
government, role of 35, 37, 43, 46–7, 57–9, 87–9, 124, 178–9, 181, 185, 189, 195, 197, 237–45; defence 13, 27, 42–4, 57, 112, 179–80, 190, 192–3, 196; financial services 202–4, 206, 208, 214; in Keynesian theory 222–3; merit goods 196, 200, 209; public goods 178–80, 200, 209; public works 47, 57, 59, 139, 195, 219, 241; regulation 44, 57, 74, 85–7, 89, 127, 157, 159, 175, 179–82, 195, 197, 208, 213, 215, 235, 239–40, 244, 248–9, 261, 264, 271, 274–5, 277, 279, 287, 309, 314; revenues and expenditures 179, 190–3, 195–6, 217, 219, 245, 250–1, 287; supply of money 17, 22–4, 26–8, 199, 203, 205–6, 211, 218, 221, 227, 236–7, 240, 314; taxation 56–8, 60, 111, 126, 162, 179, 186, 188–91, 206, 210, 214, 217, 222, 237, 244–5, 250, 255
government, role of government: financial 203
Great Debasement 23
Greenspan, Alan 212, 216
Griffiths, Ralph 110, 170, 322
Gross Domestic Product (GDP) 36–9, 41–4, 60, 136, 190–1, 217, 274
group formation 2, 5–6, 8, 14, 18, 20–1, 64, 95, 118–19, 169, 179, 182, 187–8, 226, 291
group purpose 7, 71, 276, 297
guilds 128–30, 157, 161, 171, 180–1, 187
Gutenberg, Johannes 295, 311, 321
Guy, John 111, 170, 322

habits of thought 67–9, 72, 74–5
Hackforth, Timothy 141
Hahn, F. H. 65, 321
Hargreaves, John 133, 149
Harley, Robert 129
Harrod, Roy 48–9
Harrod-Domar model 48–9
Hastings, Warren 128
Hayek, Friedrich 316, 319, 322
health insurance 303–6, 308–9
herd instinct 74, 214, 226, 234
Hicks, John 46, 65, 322
hierarchy 29, 34, 76, 93, 109, 112–13, 118–20, 140, 158–60, 165–7, 186, 314
Hitler, Adolf 290, 292

Hodgson, Geoffrey 7, 12, 69, 71–2, 75–82, 95, 102, 104–6, 170, 318–19, 322–3, 326
Hoe, Richard 296
Hoekman, Bernard 282, 323
Hollander, Samuel 265, 281, 323
Hoover, President Herbert 219
house purchase 210–14, 216, 228; sub-prime mortgage crisis 211–14, 215–17, 286
Hull, Charles Henry 64, 323
Hume, David 22, 127, 177

impossibility theorem 20
incorporation 116–17, 128, 143–5, 194
Index of Prohibited Books 297
India 127–8, 156, 257
industrial revolution 11, 31, 33, 37, 103, 124–5, 132, 138, 147, 152–5, 163, 166–8, 170–3, 177–8, 200, 206, 245, 261, 280–1, 285, 296, 320–1, 324, 327
inflation 22–3, 211, 214, 219
information ix–x, 8, 10–11, 17, 30, 38, 41, 58, 67, 77–8, 81, 83–5, 87, 90–1, 124–5, 185, 195, 216, 224, 257, 283–312, 315–17; and relevance 4, 81, 86, 225, 284, 295, 301–2, 304–9; and 'screening' 304, 306; and 'signalling' 304, 311, 325; as product 295, 301, 310; asymmetric 11, 51, 209, 283, 304–8, 310–12, 326; codification of 294–6, 300; critical 309, 312, 326; integral to bargaining systems 308; interface 283–7, 289, 293–4, 296, 306, 308, 312, 316–17, 326; manipulation of x, 181, 283–5, 290–4, 297, 301; perfect 209, 283, 295, 300–1, 304, 308, 310; transmission of 294, 298–9; vital 308
infrastructure 32, 47–8, 57, 59, 98–9, 133, 139–40, 194–5, 242, 257, 261, 270, 294
institutional economics 3, 67–72, 76–83, 90, 93–5, 145, 179, 183, 321, 323, 326
intellectual support-bargaining x–xi, 8–10, 47, 54, 70, 78, 101, 118, 124–5, 169, 175–7, 181, 199–200, 202, 242–3, 258–9, 269, 274, 287–8, 291, 317–19
interest rates 205, 207–8, 212, 217–23, 225–7, 232–7, 239
internet 158, 287, 294, 299, 300, 321
investment 16, 28, 37, 47–8, 56–7, 123, 126, 129, 139, 142, 144, 148, 153, 156, 163, 196, 202, 206, 210, 218–43, 251, 264, 270, 273, 279, 293, 304, 310; foreign 257–8, 261
Ireland 36, 215, 255

Ireton, General 119, 185
Islam 298
issue of notes 27–8, 204–5, 210
Italy 168

Japan 39, 278, 279
Jardine Matheson 258
Joint-Stock Companies Act 145

Kant, Immanuel 177
Kayatekin, Serap xi, 322
Keir, James 147
keiretsu 279–80
Keynes, John Maynard 11, 36, 47, 56, 64, 202, 219–43, 246–7, 293, 310–11, 323
King, Gregory 36, 114–17, 123, 136, 170
King, Willford 36, 64, 323
Knight, F. H. 83–5, 105, 323
Knudsen, Thorbjørn 69, 75, 104, 322
Kostecki, Michel 282, 323
Kropotkin, Peter 14, 18, 33, 323
Krugman, P. R. 282, 323
Kuznets, Simon 36

Labour Party 162, 165, 199
Lamarck, Jean-Baptiste 95–6
Lamberton, D. M. 311, 323, 326
land ix, 4, 7, 13–14, 36, 38, 63–4, 100, 108–14, 116–21, 123, 128, 140, 142, 144, 154–7, 160, 164, 182–6, 191, 194–5, 198, 210, 241, 254, 273
landowners 51, 108–14, 117, 119–21, 123, 128, 140, 142, 153, 160, 162, 169, 182–4, 187, 194, 198, 254–5, 258, 269, 294, 318
language 5, 71–2, 76, 292, 294
left wing 3, 42
Lehman Brothers 213
leisure 120
Lewontin, Richard 69, 104, 323
Liebowitz, Stan 107, 323
limited liability 128–9, 144–5, 158, 205, 235
Limited Liability Act 145
Lindert P. H. 170, 323
linkage of support-bargaining and money-bargaining 6, 110, 169, 183, 188, 190, 197, 199, 287, 313–15, 319
liquidity preference 221–2, 227, 232–5
List, Frederick 254, 259, 269–73, 276, 279–82, 323
Liverpool-Manchester line 141, 147, 194–5
Lloyds Bank 39
Lloyds TSB 214
Locke John 25–6, 177, 208

Index

Lombe, Thomas 138, 149, 168
London School of Economics (LSE) 81
Lucas, R. E. 45, 65, 323
Luther, Martin 297
Lydia 16

MacCulloch, Diarmaid 171, 323
macroeconomics 35, 39–40, 44–9, 53, 55–6, 63, 65, 82, 114, 179, 220, 237, 239, 242, 323
Magna Carta 109, 284
Malthus, Thomas 2–3, 263
Malynes, Gerard de 23–6, 219
Maneschi, A. 263–5, 281, 323
marginal efficiency of capital 221–3, 226–7, 230–1, 233, 238
Margolis, Stephen E. 107, 323
mark-up price 31, 78, 235
Marshall, Alfred 81, 105, 218, 220, 222, 224, 227, 246, 323
Marshall, M. P. 218, 227, 246, 323
Martin, Ron 97–8, 101–2, 106–7, 320, 324
Marx, Karl 74–5
mathematics ix, 9–11, 30, 38, 47–52, 54–5, 82, 84–5, 94–6, 102–3, 147, 168, 178, 224, 230, 242, 262–4, 268, 273, 283, 300–4, 317–19
Mathias, Peter 28, 34, 113, 115–17, 120, 138–40, 142, 144, 146–7, 149, 150–1, 158, 161, 165, 170–4, 200, 205, 245–6, 251, 256, 258, 280–1, 324
Matile, G. A. 280, 323
McDevitt, Laurel 247, 325
McKenzie, L. W. 45, 49, 65, 324
McLeay, Michael 247, 324
Meade, James 36, 64, 324
media 9, 36, 177, 185, 190, 286–7, 288, 290, 294, 299, 311, 315, 321, 325
Menger, Karl 14, 33, 324
mercantilism 24, 127
Merchant Adventurers 25, 128
metallic standard for coinage 23–5, 27; *see also* gold: gold standard
metal-working 149, 160, 168
Metcalfe, Stanley J. 69, 104, 324
Micklethwait, John 129, 143, 164–5, 167, 171–4, 324
microeconomics 35, 38, 45–9, 55, 237
Microsoft 30, 39, 100–1, 157
Milgate, M. 65, 323
Mill, John Stuart 46, 220
Misselden, Edward 23–6, 219
Mitchell, Wesley 70, 172, 191–2, 324

Mokyr, Joel 124, 147, 150, 152, 154, 156, 159, 167–8, 171–4, 177–8, 181, 185, 200, 208–9, 245–6, 281, 324
monopoly, 109, 125–7, 130–1, 141, 143, 150, 161, 195, 258, 270
Morgan, J. P. 164, 169, 170
Morgan, Kenneth O. 322
Morgenson: Gretchen 211–12, 246, 324
Mossner, E. C. 280, 324
Most Favoured Nation (MFN) principle 276–7
motivation 26, 58–9, 82, 154, 156, 187, 189, 196, 203, 228–34, 236, 241, 285, 292–3
Multi-fibre Arrangement 277
Mun, Thomas 23–6, 202, 219
Murdoch, Rupert 288

Napoleonic wars 26–8, 139, 193, 205
national accounts 35–9, 41, 47, 49, 55–6, 59–60, 63, 170, 224, 230, 243
National Income 36, 38, 41, 47, 55, 64, 136–7, 139, 230, 253, 255, 324
natural science 5, 9, 68, 70, 146–8, 158, 177, 293
natural selection xi, 1–7, 67–9, 71–2, 95–6, 102, 275
Navigation Acts 162, 249, 253–4, 256, 258, 272
Nelson, Richard 45, 65, 95–7, 102, 106, 324
neoclassical economic theory ix–x, 3, 9–12, 19–21, 30–2, 35, 38–42, 44–9, 52–5, 58, 60, 62–3, 67–8, 70–1, 74, 76–8, 81–91, 94–8, 101–3, 153–4, 156, 160, 166–8, 178–81, 196–7, 202–3, 209, 213, 215–16, 218, 224, 227, 234, 236, 242, 261–2, 264–6, 269, 273–4, 281, 283, 287, 293, 295, 300–4, 306–7, 310, 317–19; as stumbling block 91, 94–5, 98, 102, 266
Netherlands 126–7, 249, 253–4, 271
New Deal 219
Newcomen, Thomas 138, 146, 149, 152, 168
Newman, P. 65, 323
newspapers 287, 290, 295–6, 298–9
Nielson, James 139
Nokia 39, 64, 320
Nordhaus, William 40, 43–4, 55, 64–5, 324
North, Douglass 70–1, 79–82, 90–4, 97–8, 102, 104–6, 168, 170, 185, 200, 311, 324
Northern Rock 214

Obstfeld, M. 282, 323
Olympic Games 290–1
organisations x, 6, 8–9, 12, 29, 32, 34, 77, 79–82, 116–17, 128, 130–1, 144, 156, 158, 173, 199, 202, 206, 212, 214, 216, 225, 244–5, 250, 278, 280, 286–8, 300, 315
Ottoman Empire 298

Panasonic 30, 157
paper 23–4, 26–7, 45, 96, 149, 153–4, 202–3, 208, 235, 294–6
Pareto optimal allocation 9, 35, 49–50, 52, 54, 58, 63, 74–5, 83–5, 88, 91, 154, 167, 179–81, 196–7, 232, 236, 266, 303, 306, 310, 319
Paston family 183, 185, 200, 322
patents 144, 148–50, 181, 296
path dependence 71, 92–3, 97–102, 107, 151, 166, 321, 324
Peel, Robert 255
Peirce, C. S. 76, 104, 324
Peter the Great 297
Petty, William 36, 64, 114, 178, 323
physics 10, 49
pigeon theory 68, 71, 95
Pigou, Arthur 86, 90, 105, 220, 246, 324
Pimbley, Joseph M. 247, 325
political parties 8, 199, 313
Poor Laws 120, 132, 189
population 37–8, 41, 64, 69, 72, 99, 109–12, 114, 116, 120, 126, 132–3, 137, 142, 152–3, 160, 163, 169–70, 187, 189, 327
Porter, Roy 171, 325
Portugal 126–7, 263–7
poverty ix, 121, 156, 162, 183, 189
price stability 17, 22–6
Price, Lance 288, 311, 325
prices, relative, of industry output 137–8
printing press 295–8
private sector 59–60, 62, 194, 223
productive power 254, 270–1, 276
productivity 32, 38, 48, 58, 60–2, 99, 120–1, 130–1, 167–8, 264–9, 296, 300, 304
public choice theory 19–20, 33
public sector 42–4, 58, 60, 194
Putin, Vladimir 18

Quantitative Easing 237
QWERTY keyboard 92, 99–100, 106, 321

Radia, Amar 247, 324
railways 99, 133, 138–45, 147, 152, 155–6, 158, 160, 163–4, 189, 194–5, 251, 257–8, 261, 296, 298–9

Railways Act 195
Rainhill trial 141
rationality ix, 9–10, 20, 82–3, 90–1, 177, 179–80, 197, 209, 236, 259, 264–5, 272–6, 278, 300, 303, 319
Reed, Geoffrey 281, 325
Reformation 123, 297
regional trade blocs 277, 326
rejection of money 18
religion 82, 103, 121, 123–5, 129, 176–7, 189, 208, 289, 297–8
rent: economic 40, 167, 179–81, 310; of land, property 37, 56, 100, 110–14, 116, 120, 182, 194, 228, 263
Representation of the People Act 111, 184, 198
resources 9–11, 21, 30, 32, 35, 38–9, 41–2, 44–5, 49–50, 53–4, 58, 62–4, 75, 82–6, 88, 91, 93, 99, 153–4, 165, 167, 179–81, 193, 232, 236–7, 241, 244, 263, 265–6, 268, 273, 279, 301, 303, 319
Reynolds, William 147
Ricardo, David 220, 250, 259, 262–6, 268–9, 273–4, 276, 281, 323, 325–6
right wing 3, 10
rights 86–90, 111, 120, 126–7, 162, 175, 179, 185, 275, 289, 298; common 111–14, 186; monopoly 40, 126, 128–30, 148, 161, 179–80, 187, 195, 204, 253, 260, 278; property 119–20, 178, 183–5
rigid groups 7–8, 12, 118, 170, 198, 316
Rizvi, Abu Turab 45–6, 49, 65, 325
Robbins, Keith 255
Robbins, Lionel 81–2, 91, 102–3, 105, 179, 281, 317, 325
Robert, Nicolas-Louis 296
Roberts, Richard 159
Rockefeller, John D. 164, 167
Roman Catholic Church 297
Roosevelt, President Franklin D. 219
Rose, Jonathan 125, 171, 325
Rosner, Joshua 211–12, 246, 324
Ross, I. S. 280, 324
Rousseau, Jean-Jacques 177
Royal Bank of Scotland 214
rules, routines and habits 40, 52, 67–9, 71–80, 82, 87, 91–6, 101, 104, 145, 169, 178, 185–6, 226, 323
Russia 18, 263, 266–7, 297
Rutherford, Malcolm 70, 104, 325

Samsung 30, 39, 157, 279
Samuelson, Paul xi, 65, 265, 281, 320, 322
Sanderson, Stephen 70, 104, 325

Sargent, T. J. 45, 65, 323
Sarkozy, President Nicholas 41
savings 17, 47–8, 51–3, 56, 167, 202, 207, 214, 218, 220–1, 225, 227–37, 239, 260, 293, 310; as residual after consumption 225, 228–33, 235, 243; compulsory 231–2
Say, Jean-Baptiste 220
Schofield, R. S. 116, 137, 170, 327
Schumacher, Reinhard 281, 325
Schumpeter J. A., 9, 12, 41, 94–8, 102–3, 106, 316, 325
Sears, Roebuck 163, 300
self-preservation xi, 2, 4–6
Selim I, Sultan 298
Sen, Amartya 41, 64, 326
Sharpe, Thomas 160
Sherman Anti-Trust Act 164
ships and shipping 98, 132–3, 138, 144, 158, 161, 175, 193, 249, 251–4, 256, 258, 274, 296, 299
Siemens-Martin production method 140
silver 14–17, 22–3, 25–6, 39, 127, 203, 265
Simon, H. A. 36, 97, 311
situation x, 1, 3–8, 11–12, 15, 17–18, 21, 25, 29–30, 33, 37, 43–4, 51–3, 55–7, 59–63, 65, 75, 78, 85–7, 96–102, 110, 112–14, 117–18, 121, 123–5, 130, 132, 143, 145–9, 152–4, 156, 162, 165–6, 169, 177, 187–9, 195, 197, 201, 205–7, 214, 216, 218–19, 224–5, 227–31, 233–5, 237–40, 255, 261–2, 268, 272–5, 277–8, 282, 284–5, 289, 294–5, 298–9, 301–9, 313, 315–18, 325
Skinner A. S. 280, 324
slavery 129, 132, 135–6, 138
smartphones 157, 299
Smith, Adam 10, 24, 28, 40, 130–1, 177–8, 250, 253–4, 259–62, 268, 270, 272–4, 280–1, 324–6
smuggling 250–1
Social Accounting Matrix (SAM) 41, 56, 58
Social Darwinism 2, 11–12
social evolution xi, 1, 4–7, 64, 67–9, 97, 99, 104, 132, 146, 176, 298, 322, 325
social welfare 20, 32–3, 36, 42, 57, 89, 90, 189–90, 193, 217
social welfare function 20
Södersten Bo 281, 325
Sony 30, 279
South Africa 258
South America 23, 127, 129
South Korea 39, 135, 278–80, 282, 320
South Sea Company 129, 204, 213

Soviet Union 75, 238, 285, 290, 317
Spain 24, 127, 129, 215, 321
spatial issues: see distance
Spence, Michael 304, 311–12, 325
Spencer, Herbert 3, 7
Spiegel, Henry William 33, 325
Spread, Patrick xi, 11–12, 33–4, 64–5, 103, 105–7, 170–1, 173–4, 199–200, 245–7, 280–2, 311–12, 325–6
Sraffa, Piero 281, 325–6
Stanhope, Charles 296
steam power 117, 133, 137–8, 141, 146, 148–54, 156–7, 159–60, 163, 168, 193, 253, 280, 296
steel 133–4, 139–40, 143, 160, 164, 168, 249
Stephenson, George 141, 147, 160
Stephenson, Robert 141, 147
Stigler, George 302–3, 311, 326
Stiglitz, Joseph 11, 41, 44, 60, 64–6, 301–2, 304, 306–7, 310–12, 326
Stockton and Darlington line 141
Stone, Giovanna 64, 324
Stone, Richard 36, 41, 64, 324, 326
sub-prime mortgage crisis: see house purchase
Sunley, Peter 97–8, 101–2, 107, 324
support convention x, 3, 8, 20, 88, 111, 119, 121, 169, 176–8, 183–5, 198–200, 248; international 276
Sutherland, Kathryn 280, 282, 326
Switzerland 271
symmetry xi, 15, 33, 243, 290

Tassis family 298
technology 30–1, 40, 45, 59, 67, 85, 92, 94, 102, 106, 117, 121, 125, 130–2, 135, 138, 140, 145–7, 148–50, 153–60, 162–3, 165, 167–9, 193–4, 224–5, 233, 235, 238–9, 242, 262, 268–9, 274, 277, 280, 294–9, 315, 319, 320
territory 2, 35, 38, 108, 119, 126–8, 186–7, 198, 249, 270–1, 292
theory formation x, 8–9, 11, 55, 70, 73–4, 82, 105, 176–7, 200, 242, 258, 269, 274, 293, 316–17
theory groups 9–11, 30, 38, 47, 49, 53–5, 70–1, 74, 80–2, 85, 91, 101–3, 179, 181, 186, 196, 209, 239, 242–3, 266, 293, 300–1, 317–19
theory making: see theory formation
Thomas, Ryland 247
Thompson, E. P. 170, 186–7, 189, 198, 200, 326
Thornton, Henry 27, 33, 202, 205, 245, 326

time dimension 6, 10, 38, 52, 56, 67, 91–2, 101, 105, 127, 150, 153, 163, 166, 169, 195, 201, 203, 207, 210, 214, 224, 227–8, 231–2, 235, 237, 270, 272, 284, 303, 313, 317, 324; in Arrow-Debreu model 50–4; in Keynesian analysis 227–8
time disparities 53, 56, 201–3, 206–7, 210, 214, 216, 227, 229, 232, 237
Tobin, James 40, 43–4, 55, 64–5, 324
Tooke, Thomas 262
Tool, Marc 77–8, 105, 326
Tories 123, 199, 204, 288
trade reference for exchange rate 24–5, 27–8
trade unions 64, 129, 162, 173, 181, 197, 199, 287, 315
transaction costs 11, 31, 83–7, 90–1, 167–8, 185, 318
transitive preferences 20–1
Trevithick, Richard 141, 160
Turkey 298
Tussie Diana 282, 326

unit cost of output 30–2, 52, 56, 59–62, 76, 85, 92, 96, 99, 131, 135, 137–40, 143, 146, 148, 151–2, 154–61, 163–4, 168, 190, 219, 230, 235, 238–40, 248, 251, 253, 256, 266–9, 274, 278, 295–6, 299
United States 36, 39, 47, 64, 125, 129, 135, 142, 162–5, 202, 210–11, 215–16, 219, 254, 257–8, 275–7, 280, 290, 296, 299, 323
urbanisation 37, 97, 133, 139, 150–3, 160, 169, 188–9

Vanderbilt, Cornelius 164, 167
variation, selection and inheritance 68–9, 102
Veblen, Thorstein 67–72, 74–6, 95, 103, 326

viability condition 31–2, 52, 56, 61, 76, 78, 83, 85, 99, 117, 121, 135, 137–9, 143, 148, 156–7, 160, 182, 189, 226, 268
Vilarrubia, Josep M. 64, 321
violence 2–3, 8, 13, 20, 71, 86, 88, 108–9, 111, 119, 126–8, 169, 176, 182–6, 189, 193, 197–8, 208, 248–50, 272, 275–6, 313
Vodaphone 30
Voltaire, François-Marie 177
votes 8, 19–20, 38, 58
Voth, H.-J. 171, 326

Wales 33, 115, 117, 131, 151–2, 321
Wallace, Alfred Russell 5
Walras, Leon 9, 94–5, 102
Warburton, Clark 36
watch-making 117, 146
Watt, James 138, 141, 146–9, 159–60
Wedgwood, Josiah 147
Weinstein, David 64, 321
West Indies 129, 132, 135
Wicksell Knut 218
William of Normandy 108
Williamson, J. G. 170, 323
Williamson, Oliver 70
Wilson, Edward 5, 12, 327
Winter, Stanley 45, 65, 95–7, 102, 106, 324
Witt, Ulrich xi 327
Woods, Ngaire 282, 326–7
Wooldridge, Adrian 129, 143, 164–5, 167, 171–4, 324
World Trade Organisation (WTO) 276, 278
Wrigley, E. A. 116, 136–7, 170–2, 327

Young Arthur 120, 125

zaibatsu 278